Trial of Willi

(Editor: George H. Knott)

Alpha Editions

This edition published in 2024

ISBN : 9789362091185

Design and Setting By
Alpha Editions
www.alphaedis.com
Email - info@alphaedis.com

PREFACE.

IN preparing this report of a trial more than half a century ago, the chief difficulty one might expect would be to obtain an accurate contemporary account. A State trial one knows where to find; but how could newspaper reports of a trial lasting twelve days, and involving the most technical evidence on anatomy, physiology, and toxicology, be relied upon for anything like accuracy? Fortunately, if this trial was not a State trial in the ordinary sense, it so seized the minds of the country at the time that a complete record is to be found in the "Verbatim Report of the Trial of William Palmer, Transcribed from the Shorthand Notes of Mr. Angelo Bennett, of Rolls Chambers, Chancery Lane," and published in 1856. A copy is not easily met with now-a-days. Official verbatim reports of criminal trials, that is made by an officer of the Court itself, were not then known. I suppose, though it is not so stated, that Mr. Bennett's notes were taken by him on the instructions of the Treasury for reference each day by the Court and Counsel. They are the basis of the following report. Medical and medico-chemical evidence constitutes the greater part of this trial; it is also far the most important part; and in dealing with it I have had the benefit of the professional skill of Dr. William Robertson, of Leith, who has read the proofs. Some of the evidence, as it stood, showed that it had been a little too much for the erudition of the shorthand writer, and needed editing. I hope that, with the aid of Dr. Robertson, this appears now as it was intended to be by the experts who gave it.

The question of portraits has caused some difficulty. Photographs were not common, to say the least, in 1856. Most woodcuts met with seemed not worth reproduction. This accounts for the few portraits which appear; though the number of Judges and Counsel was exceptionally large. Palmer alone is shown more satisfactorily than any of the others in the well-known figure at Madame Tussaud's. Their modeller was present in Court and I have seen his casts of Palmer's head and face taken after execution. The striking sketch of Palmer by Mr. Joseph Simpson, the well-known artist, has been made from a photograph of this figure, and from a contemporary print.

Palmer has the distinction of an article in the Dictionary of National Biography. Many of the contemporary accounts cannot be relied on; they are too evidently sensational and designed for excited and morbid imaginations. By the kindness of Dr. George Fleming, J.P., of Highgate, London, who is a treasury of Palmeriana and of Rugeley tradition, I have been able to use his collection of "Jane" letters. The substance of these letters appears in the Introduction. They reveal a sinister episode in Palmer's career not to be found related elsewhere. Moreover, it was a real link in the chain of circumstances that led to Palmer's crime and his trial. The letter from Palmer to his wife was kindly lent for reproduction by Dr. Kurt Loewenfeld, of Bramhall, Cheshire.

G. H. K.

INTRODUCTION.

SIR JAMES STEPHEN, in his "History of the Criminal Law," observes that he was present at the trial of William Palmer, and that it made an impression on him which the subsequent experience of thirty-four years had only confirmed and strengthened. He considers that the trial, as a whole, was one of the greatest trials in the history of English law, and eminently deserving the attention of students of the law, and we may add of students of human nature.

Palmer was convicted, but there has always been a certain amount of doubt and mystery about the trial. We can hardly imagine a reader not being satisfied morally as to the guilt of Palmer, but were he to take the medical and chemical evidence alone, which forms so large a part of the following report, we could at least imagine him holding his judgment in suspense. He might well believe that Palmer administered poison to Cook, whom he was charged with murdering, without admitting that the poison was strychnia. And there remains the ambiguous language of Palmer himself, who neither positively admitted nor denied his guilt, but declared, "I am innocent of poisoning Cook by strychnia." Sir James Stephen, who will not allow that the defence was impressive, is yet struck with this defect in the evidence, and suggests that Palmer may have discovered a method of administering strychnia so as to disguise its normal effects. If this is so, his secret has never been disclosed. Perhaps it is equally probable that he selected some poison allied to strychnia—bruchsia, for example—and that the medical and chemical experts of sixty years ago were not sufficiently acquainted with the strychnoid poisons to trace all their differences. The evidence of the chemical witnesses suggests something of this kind, so inconsistent were their opinions; and this remark applies even more strongly to the evidence of the doctors as to the difference between the disease of tetanus and the effects of strychnia. This is one of the great subjects of interest in the report of the trial. A constant and alert attention is needed in reading it, and it is a professional discipline for either lawyer or doctor.

Our personal opinion is that, had it not been for one or two definitely known cases of strychnia poisoning in the human subject, the prosecution would have failed, in spite of all the experiments on animals from which analogies as to Cook's symptoms were attempted to be drawn. There had been no trial for poisoning by strychnia before Palmer's. But it happened that while the Palmer case was pending Dr. Dove, of Leeds, was accused of poisoning his wife by strychnia, and the symptoms of poison were more certainly ascertained. Yet Dr. Nunneley, of Leeds, who made a report on this case, was called for the defence, not for the prosecution.

In this preliminary sketch I shall not attempt to convey any idea of the chemical and medical evidence by a formal summary. It would be impossible, as Sir James Stephen remarks, to treat satisfactorily such an extensive, so technical, and so contradictory a body of testimony, and only such a general statement will be made of the circumstances as will enable the reader the easier to follow the case of the prosecution.

In the English procedure counsel's speech for the prosecution begins the proceedings. In the Scottish the evidence is led at once. The trial is treated in this respect as if it were a Scottish trial on account of its extreme bulk, as it extended over twelve days. Neither in the Scottish series, which are already published, nor in the English series, now beginning, is there a trial of equal length; nor do I know any other murder trial so long, with the exception of that conducted by Browning in "The Ring and the Book." In this trial, as in every English trial, the opening speech was intended to inform the jury merely of the facts and prepare their minds for the evidence, and lucidity of statement, at the most, is the only forensic effect aimed at. I accordingly omit the Attorney-General's speech *qua* speech, and found this preliminary statement on it. The point of interest as regards forensic oratory is reached with the speech of Serjeant Shee, the leading counsel for the defence. He analyses the evidence led for the prosecution, challenges its cogency, outlines the case in reply which will be an answer to every point made, appeals eloquently and pathetically for the prisoner, and, we may add incidentally, asserts his absolute belief in his client's innocence, thus bringing on himself the presiding judge's reproof for transgression of the rules of advocacy. The culmination is attained in the reply of the Attorney-General. Nothing, unless it is of the most temporary interest, is omitted in these two speeches, and every reference and argument in them will be intelligible in the light of the examinations and cross-examinations as given, which, not less than the speeches, are classic examples of the forensic art.

There is a tradition that Palmer, a racing man, expressed his sense of the deadly effect of Sir Alexander Cockburn's examination, cross-examination, and speech in racecourse language, "It was the riding that did it."

With the Lord Chief-Justice's summing up I have dealt freely. It occupied two days, and the form of it, to a great extent, was this. Lord Campbell would say to the jury, "Now, gentlemen, I will take the witness So-and-So and read you his evidence. It is for you to say what the effect of this evidence is." Then would follow comments directing the jury's attention to this or that feature. What the jury thought is not important now, but what the reader thinks with the evidence before him. Where Lord Campbell made special comment on any particular evidence the passages are given. Nothing material is omitted, and the general effect of his address is preserved.

The events occurred in November, 1855, at Rugeley, in Staffordshire, where Palmer, who was about thirty-one years of age, had been a medical practitioner until two or three years previously, when he transferred his business to the Mr. Thirlby mentioned in the report. He had abandoned medicine for the turf, kept racehorses, attended race meetings, and betted. By the year 1853 he was in pecuniary difficulties, and was raising money on bills with moneylenders.

Mr. John Parsons Cook, whom Palmer was charged with poisoning, was a young man of about twenty-eight who had been articled as a solicitor, but he inherited some £12,000, and did not follow his profession. He also went on the turf, kept racehorses, and betted, and it was in this common pursuit that Palmer and Cook became acquainted.

Palmer's pecuniary circumstances in 1854 are important. He had raised money on a bill for £2000, and discounted it with Padwick, a notorious moneylender and racing man of the day. He had forged his mother's name as acceptor, and, as she was wealthy, the bill had been discounted on the security of her name. It was this bill and others similarly forged which, according to the prosecution, led to the murder of Cook.

Previously to this Palmer had only been able to pay off debts to the amount of £13,000 on bills which were in the hands of another moneylender, Mr. Pratt, who figures so conspicuously in the trial, out of money received on the death of his wife, whom he had insured for £13,000.

At the close of 1854 he took out another policy for £13,000 on the life of his brother Walter. This policy was deposited as security with Pratt to cover a series of bills which began then to be discounted. These, by November, 1855, amounted to £11,500. His mother's name as acceptor had also been forged on these bills by Palmer.

In the month of August, 1855, Walter Palmer died, but the office refused to pay on the policy, and the question was still in dispute in November when the death of Mr. Cook occurred. If the policy were not paid Pratt would sue Mrs. Palmer, as Palmer himself had no means, so that Palmer was in the same peril of being shown to be a forger both by Pratt and Padwick.

This policy was never paid, and we may add that when Palmer was tried for the murder of Cook there were two other indictments against him for the murders of his wife and brother, but they were not proceeded with as he was convicted on the Cook charge.

What happened about the bills was this. On the 6th of November Pratt issued two writs for £4000 against Palmer and his mother, but withheld them from service pending arrangements that Palmer might make. Pratt wrote to him on the 13th of November, a memorable day in the history of the case, when "Polestar," Cook's mare, won the Shrewsbury Handicap, that steps would be taken to enforce the policy on Walter Palmer's life; so that Palmer's problem was to keep paying portions of the bills until the question of the policy was settled, and thus keep Pratt quiet.

The pecuniary position of Cook is quickly explained. He had practically nothing but what came to him through the winning of "Polestar" at Shrewsbury on the 13th of November. His betting book showed winnings which amounted, with the stakes, to £2050. It was proved that he had £700 or £800 in his pocket at Shrewsbury from the bets he actually drew there, and £1020 remained to be settled at Tattersall's on the following Monday, the 19th November.

The evidence will show how Palmer obtained payment of the bets with the exception of £120, and applied them to paying instalments on Pratt's bills.

We now come to the circumstances of the illness and death of Cook. Palmer and Cook went together from Rugeley to Shrewsbury races, and stayed at the Raven Hotel. On the night of the 14th of November, and the day after "Polestar" had won the race, Cook was taken ill at the Raven with severe retchings and vomitings in consequence of having taken a glass of brandy and water into which the prosecution alleged Palmer had put antimony in the form of tartar emetic. The only direct testimony as to this was that of a Mrs. Brooks, who attended races. She knew Palmer, and called on him at the Raven on some business connected with racing. She swore that, as she turned into the lobby, she saw Palmer holding up a tumbler to the light of the gas, looking at it "with the caution of a man who was watching to see what was the condition of the liquid," according to the Attorney-General's statement. Having looked at it so he withdrew to his own room, and presently returned with the glass in his hand, and then went into the room where Cook was, and where he drank the brandy and water. There was much evidence from other witnesses as to what happened in connection with the brandy and water incident.

The state of Cook's health previous to the incident at Shrewsbury was of the utmost importance. It was admitted by the prosecution that Cook was delicate of chest, but otherwise he was asserted to be hale and hearty. In May of 1855 he had consulted Dr. Savage for supposed syphilitic symptoms. He suffered from his throat, and had some eruptions about his mouth, and he had been taking mercury. Dr. Savage stopped this treatment, and advised that the symptoms were not those of syphilis. The post-mortem showed the cicatrised wound of an old chancre, but not of anything recent. The defence sought to show that Cook's death was connected with his history of ill-health.

When the races were over Palmer and Cook returned together to Rugeley—a curious fact, seeing that Cook had accused Palmer of putting something into his glass. Cook stayed at the Talbot Arms, which was opposite to Palmer's house, and it was at this inn that Cook's death occurred. Their arrival was on the night of Thursday, the 15th of November. When asked how he was Cook said that he was better than he had been at Shrewsbury. Cook dined next day with Palmer, and nothing happened that night. Early on Saturday morning Palmer saw Cook in his bedroom, and ordered him some coffee, which was brought there by Elizabeth Mills, the chambermaid, who gave most important evidence as to the various episodes of the illness until the death on the night of Tuesday, the 20th November. The coffee was given to Palmer, and he gave it to Cook, Mills having left. "Immediately after that the same symptoms set in which had taken place at Shrewsbury, and throughout the whole of that day and the next day" (Saturday and Sunday) "the prisoner constantly administered everything to Cook." One incident was a bowl of broth being obtained by Palmer through a woman named Rowley. She was sent for it to the Albion, an inn in Rugeley. She took it to Palmer's house and put it in a saucepan on the kitchen fire to warm. Palmer, whilst she was absent in the back kitchen, poured the broth into a basin, brought it to her, and told her to take it up to Cook, and say Smith had sent it. This was Jeremiah Smith, an attorney in Rugeley, a common friend of Palmer and Cook. A spoonful of the broth made Cook sick. But the full significance of this intended inference is not seen until we take the evidence of Mills that she drank a spoonful and became sick in about half an hour, and had to go to bed.

And here we may refer to the evidence of this Jeremiah Smith, who was called as a witness on behalf of Palmer. His cross-examination was the most dramatic scene of the trial. He was shown to have been concerned with Palmer in the insurance schemes, and not a rag of his credit remained. But Sir James Stephen remarks, "No abbreviation can give the effect of this cross-examination. The witness's efforts to gain time, and his distress as the various answers were extorted from him by degrees, may be faintly traced in the report. The witness's face was covered with sweat, and the papers put into his hands shook and rustled."

During Saturday and Sunday Cook was attended by Mr. Bamford, a medical man in Rugeley. As Mr. Bamford's age gave rise to some observation, I may mention that he was eighty. He was told by Palmer on the Saturday that Cook had had a bilious attack owing to having taken too much wine at the dinner the day before, but when Mr. Bamford mentioned this Cook replied that he had only two glasses of champagne, and Mr. Bamford, in fact, found that the symptoms were not bilious.

On Sunday, as the sickness continued, Mr. Bamford prepared two opiate pills containing half a grain of morphia, half a grain of calomel, and four grains of rhubarb. The ingredients are important. The following Monday is a crucial day. Palmer went to London and saw Herring, a betting man, gave him a list of Cook's winnings, and instructed him to attend Tattersall's and settle. Herring was not Cook's regular agent, but Fisher, the man to whom Cook had entrusted his money at Shrewsbury whilst he was ill. Fisher declared that he had, in fact, advanced £200 on the strength of the money which Fisher expected to draw at Tattersall's. This £200, at the request of Cook, in a letter written by him from Rugeley on the 16th of November (Friday), was applied by Fisher to one of Pratt's acceptances. This letter was used by the defence to show that, as Palmer alleged, the bills were for the joint transactions of himself and Cook, and by parity of reasoning that Palmer had probably Cook's authority to draw his bets. Herring drew £900 of the £1020 at Tattersall's, and, as Palmer had instructed him, he paid £450 to Pratt. He was also instructed to pay Padwick £350 for a bet which Padwick had won, partly from Palmer and partly from Cook, but for which Palmer was liable: again a suggestion of joint transactions between Palmer and Cook. This payment was to be made, according to the prosecution, to keep Padwick quiet over his £2000 forged acceptance, half of which remained unpaid. Herring, however, did not pay Padwick. If he had done so he would have been out of pocket, as it had been agreed between him and Palmer that part of the money he was to draw should be applied to debts of his own due from Palmer.

Palmer finished his business in town by going to Pratt. He paid him £50, so that this, the £450, and Fisher's £200, with £600 Palmer had previously paid, wiped off £1300. He then returned to Rugeley, arriving there at an hour which was certainly mistaken by the prosecution, and which derived its chief importance from the story told by Jeremiah Smith of his meeting Palmer returning much later, and the account he gave of their movements together. If his story were true, that of the witness Newton, who spoke to the purchase by Palmer from him of strychnia that night, would be suspect. As it was, doubt was cast upon it by Newton never mentioning it until the day of the trial. Cook during Palmer's absence had no sickness, though in the morning Palmer, who had gone early to the hotel, had given him coffee, and Cook had vomited. But after Palmer left for London Mr. Bamford had come, and given him a new medicine. It was arguable, therefore, that the irritation of the stomach was soothed by the new medicine. Cook dressed, got up, recovered his spirits, and saw and talked with several people, and so he continued till night. This has the most important bearing, as will be seen by the medical evidence, on the vital point whether Cook's symptoms were either those of strychnia poisoning, or idiopathic or traumatic tetanus, or of some other form of nervous disease with tetanic convulsions.

On Palmer's return to Rugeley he went to see Cook, and he remained, going in and out of his room, until about eleven o'clock. He then left, and about twelve the house was alarmed by violent screams from Cook's rooms. I shall refer the reader for the details of this illness to the evidence.

According to the prosecution Palmer had gone previously on that night to Newton, who was the assistant of a surgeon at Rugeley named Salt, and had purchased three grains of strychnia. This was Newton's statement. Whilst Palmer was away in London Mr. Bamford had sent to the Talbot Arms the same sort of pills, in which were morphia, calomel, and rhubarb. They were taken by the maid upstairs, and put in the usual place for Palmer to administer, as he had done before.

The Attorney-General put his case thus to the jury, "It will be for you to say whether Cook took the pills prepared by Mr. Bamford, and which he had taken on the Saturday and Sunday night, or whether, as this accusation suggests, the prisoner substituted for the pills of Mr. Bamford some of his own concoction in which strychnia was mixed."

On Tuesday morning, the 20th, the day of his death, Cook was comparatively comfortable after his violent attack.

That same morning Palmer went to the shop of a druggist at Rugeley, Mr. Hawkins. He asked for six grains of strychnia, with some prussic acid and some liquor of opium. While Hawkins' assistant Roberts was putting up the prussic acid Newton came into the shop. Palmer took him by the arm, and saying, "I have something I want to say to you," led him outside, and began to talk to him about an unimportant matter. While they were talking a man Bassington came up, and when he and Newton were fully engaged in talk Palmer went back into the shop, and stood in the doorway. Palmer went away with what he had bought, and then Newton went into the shop and inquired what Palmer had bought, and was told.

At the preliminary inquiry before the coroner Newton only told of this incident at the shop. He did not tell of Palmer having purchased strychnia from him on the Monday night until the day before the Attorney-General was making his speech for the prosecution. An explanation will be found in Newton's evidence.

Before coming to the actual circumstances of Cook's death on Tuesday night two other facts must be mentioned. On the previous Sunday Palmer wrote to Mr. Jones, a medical man living at Lutterworth, with whom Cook lived when he was at home. He said Cook had a bilious attack with diarrhœa, and asked Jones to come and see him as soon as possible. On Monday he wrote to him again desiring him to come.

The Attorney-General said, "I should not be discharging my duty if I did not suggest this as being part of a deep design, and that the administration of the irritant poison, of which abundant traces were found after death, was for the purpose of producing the appearance of natural disease, which could account afterwards for the death to which the victim was doomed."

The irritant poison referred to is antimony, but one of the main facts, if not altogether the most important one, on which the defence relied, was that no strychnia was found in the body of Cook.

Mr. Jones came on the Tuesday about three o'clock, and was with Cook throughout till his death.

The other fact referred to is that during the same day (Tuesday) Palmer sent for Cheshire, the postmaster at Rugeley. Palmer produced a paper and asked him to fill in a cheque on Messrs. Wetherby (of Tattersall's) in Palmer's favour for £350 (the amount of the Shrewsbury Handicap stakes), saying "Poor Cook is too ill to draw the cheque himself, and Messrs. Wetherby might know my handwriting." Palmer was a defaulter at Tattersall's. Cheshire did what he was asked to do. Palmer took the cheque away. It was sent that night, and returned to Palmer by Messrs. Wetherby. Notice to produce the cheque was given to the defence. This was not done, and the prosecution in these circumstances insisted that Cook's signature was forged by Palmer. If the cheque had been produced, and Cook's signature proved genuine, the defence would have had a strong case that Palmer drew the bets by Cook's instruction for their joint transactions.

Cheshire was brought from prison to give evidence. Palmer had induced him to intercept letters addressed to Palmer's mother to prevent her becoming aware of the forged bills. Besides this, Cheshire informed Palmer of the contents of a letter from Dr. Taylor, the analyst, who tested the remains for poison after the post mortem on the coroner's inquiry. This letter informed Mr. Stevens, Cook's stepfather, that no strychnia had been found, and Palmer was sufficiently audacious and foolish to write to the coroner, a Mr. Ward, a lawyer, emphasising this fact. More foolishly still he sent the coroner gifts of game. The prosecution asserted that much of the evidence given by some of the witnesses, Mills, for instance, at the trial, but not found in the depositions at the inquest, had not been given there because the coroner had conducted the inquiry so laxly. The defence, of course, disputed this.

We come to the actual scene of Cook's death on the Tuesday night. There was a consultation of the three doctors in Cook's presence at seven o'clock. Cook suddenly said to Palmer, "Palmer, I will have no more medicine to-night; no more pills." It was arranged that the pills should be made up as before without Cook knowing what they contained. Palmer went with Mr. Bamford to the latter's surgery for the pills, and Mr. Bamford was surprised at Palmer's asking him to write the directions on the box, as Palmer himself was to give the pills, but he did so. Palmer took the pills, and they were in his possession three-quarters of an hour before he returned to the Talbot. On opening the box he called the attention of Mr. Jones to the directions, saying "How wonderful it was that a man of eighty should write so good and strong a hand." Cook at first refused to take the pills, but Palmer insisted, and Cook took them. They were taken about half-past ten. A little before twelve o'clock Jones, who was to sleep in Cook's room, came in and undressed, and went to bed. In fifteen or twenty minutes he was roused by a scream from Cook, who called out, "For God's sake, fetch the doctor, I am going to be ill as I was last night."

I shall not set out the symptoms of Cook throughout this attack which ended in his death. They were the battle-ground of the case, and the scientific evidence must be referred to the reader's consideration. But the length of time from the administration of the pills to the first outcry of Cook must be particularly noted. The defence urged that strychnia could not possibly be so long in taking effect. This and the non-detection of strychnia in the body were the two chief difficulties of the prosecution.

On Thursday or Friday, the 22nd or 23rd, after Cook's death Palmer sent again for Cheshire, and, producing a paper with Cook's signature, purporting to be an acknowledgment by Cook that £4000 worth of bills had been negotiated for Cook's benefit, asked him to sign it as witness. Cheshire refused, exclaiming, "Good God! the man is dead!" The prosecution asserted Cook's signature to be a forgery; they gave notice to produce the document, and this was not done.

We come to the appearance in Rugeley of Mr. Stevens, Cook's stepfather. His conversations with Palmer on money matters, his suspicions aroused by the appearance of the body, Palmer's ordering a coffin without his orders, and especially the fact that Cook's betting book and other papers had disappeared, with Palmer's evasions about them, all put him on the alert. Besides, at the time, the inquiries by the insurance office were going on in the neighbourhood about Walter Palmer's death. On Saturday, the 24th, both Stevens and Palmer had left Rugeley to go to London, Stevens to consult his London solicitor, Palmer to pay Pratt another £100, he, as the prosecution pointed out, not having had any money at Shrewsbury, and having lost on the races there. Stevens and Palmer met in the train on the return journey, and Stevens told Palmer that he was determined to have a post-mortem and to employ a solicitor to investigate.

The post-mortem, the chemical analysis, the coroner's inquest, and the trial followed. In the meantime Padwick had arrested Palmer for the debt on his bills, the story of his mother's forged acceptances became known, and the Palmer case of 1855-6 became as intense a source of popular curiosity and excitement as the Crippen case of 1910. To the circumstances of the Cook case were also added the exhumations of Palmer's wife and brother, and the public inquiries relating to them, and the rumours that Palmer had poisoned many others.

I shall not attempt to give the facts as to the post-mortem and the analysis. It would be a futile effort. Not a fact was undisputed either by one side or the other, and the value of the evidence, for the reader, consists in the exercise of the patience and memory and judgment required to master their complicated details, and to see the relations of one fact to another. In the speech for the defence by Mr. Serjeant Shee, and the final speech by Sir Alexander Cockburn, he will further see how the same facts may be rendered for opposite purposes by advocates of the first rank.

The trial marked an important step in English criminal procedure. In the ordinary course Palmer would have been tried by an Assize Court in Staffordshire, but the prejudice against him there was so strong that it was felt he would not have a fair trial. An Act was therefore passed, the 19 Vict. cap. 16, for enabling the trial to take place at the Central Criminal Court in London. Since then that Act has been available in any similar circumstances. To the magnitude and difficulty of the Palmer case must be assigned the reason for three judges, Lord Chief Justice Campbell, Mr. Justice Cresswell, and Mr. Baron Alderson being appointed to try it: a very rare occurrence in England. The bar on each side was remarkably strong. Sir Alexander Cockburn became the successor of Lord Campbell; Mr. Edward James, Q.C., was one of the most brilliant advocates of his day, and was only prevented from rising to the highest professional honours by certain private incidents in his career which happened subsequently; Mr. Huddleston became Baron Huddleston; Mr. Bodkin and Mr. Welsby were the leading men of their time in the special practice of the Old Bailey. Mr. Serjeant Shee, the leader for the defence, became Mr. Justice Shee, and Mr. Grove, Q.C., who was one of the most distinguished physicists of his day, and wrote a famous book on "The Conservation of Energy," became Mr. Justice Grove. Mr. Kenealey was subsequently the famous Dr. Kenealey, the counsel for the Tichborne claimant, a man of great learning and natural genius, inferior to none of his professional contemporaries.

In an English criminal trial an inquiry into the family history of the accused, or into his personal character and previous career, has no place unless insanity is in issue. Such matters were rigidly excluded from the trial of Palmer. This trial as it stands is simply a great forensic contest famous in the records of the criminal law. The criminal himself is, as it were, an abstraction or automaton, his acts are only taken into account as part of certain outward events which enter into the general body of circumstances connected with the particular case. The motive is investigated, but strictly in relation to the particular crime; and in atrocious crimes the pecuniary motive always seems inadequate. Deadly hate or fierce passion, or an access of unreasoning fear in some circumstances, may be more intelligible. Yet such crimes seem always inexplicable, unless we can refer them to some abnormality in the character of the criminal himself, and either ascribe it to his ancestry or deduce it from his own doings outside the culminating crime which he commits. The normal man, we say, does not become base at a stroke.

In Palmer's case there is available evidence of both kinds bearing on abnormality. It may not amount to insanity. It may be only the "wickedness" of which Sir James Stephen speaks in a quotation given below. Whatever it may be called, it is traceable in Palmer throughout his life.

Palmer's father was a wealthy man who died worth £70,000, at Rugeley, in Staffordshire, Palmer's birthplace. The origin of this fortune began with his maternal grandfather, who had been associated with a woman in Derby whom he deserted, taking with him some hundreds of pounds said to belong to her. In Lichfield he became prosperous and respectable. His daughter married the elder Palmer, who was at the time a sawyer, a rude, uneducated man. A previous suitor of Mrs. Palmer had been the steward of the Marquis of Anglesea. The two men were intimate after the marriage, and associated in dealings with the Anglesea timber; and to these dealings, and similar ones with stewards of other estates, the elder Palmer's wealth was attributed by the country tradition. After her husband's death Mrs. Palmer used her freedom in several love affairs that caused scandal. One of these was with Jeremiah Smith, the attorney, Palmer's associate in many nefarious transactions, who was called for the defence, and was cross-examined mercilessly by the Attorney-General on his relations with Mrs. Palmer.

William, the Palmer of this trial, was the second son in a family of five sons and two daughters. Of these, William, his brother Walter, and a sister lived badly and died miserably. Walter would have died from drink if his brother William had not hurried him away by poison for his insurance money. Other members of the family were reputable citizens.

William Palmer was first apprenticed to a firm of wholesale druggists in Liverpool. After a time considerable amounts of money sent through the post by customers to the firm were lost, and, after much inquiry, Palmer confessed he had stolen them, and his indentures were cancelled. His mother then for the first time began to cover up her son's misdeeds by advances of money. This story runs throughout the trial, and Palmer fleeced his mother without compunction.

At the age of eighteen he was next apprenticed to Mr. Tylecote, a surgeon, near Rugeley. In consequence of discreditable conduct with women, and in money matters, Palmer left, and Mr. Tylecote refused to take him back. He was then admitted into the Stafford Infirmary as "a walking pupil." Four years after, in 1846, he was back at Rugeley, and there, at an inquest held on a man named Abley, it was proved that Palmer had incited the man to drink large quantities of brandy. There was talk of Palmer's connection with Abley's wife, and a suspicion that the affair was something more than a "lark."

In this year Palmer went to London and joined Bartholomew's Hospital. He obtained his diploma of surgeon in August, and returned to Rugeley as a medical practitioner. A year after he married Annie Brookes, a ward in Chancery, the illegitimate daughter of a Colonel Brookes, of the Indian Army, who had settled in Stafford, and had as housekeeper Mary Thornton, Annie Brookes's mother. By his will Colonel Brookes left Annie Brookes (or Thornton) considerable property in money and houses, but his estate was administered in Chancery. The guardians were opposed to the marriage, but it took place in 1847 by order of the Court. One of the love-letters written by Palmer and read by Serjeant Shee during the trial appears elsewhere.

Whether Palmer intended or not at first to settle down to his profession, he was almost without practice in two or three years after his marriage. Horses and racing occupied him in place of medicine. He had means without practice, and, as Rugeley is a great horse-dealing centre, he was always familiar with men connected with horses and racing, and they were his chosen company. In 1853 he was in pecuniary difficulties due to his racing transactions, and was raising money on bills with moneylenders.

Withal he kept up an appearance of great outward respectability. Church-going sixty years ago was more than now one of its marks. In the diary, some extracts from which will be found in the Appendices, there are references in the year when he poisoned Cook to attendances at the Sacrament. It is not necessary to read into this church-going anything more specific than the radical falsity of Palmer's character. Great formalism and profession of rigid theological dogma were the usual mental furniture of the middle classes of Palmer's day. After all the disclosures of the trial Palmer used the customary pietistic phrases, and it was characteristic of the times that, after his conviction, his counsel, Serjeant Shee, sent him a beautifully bound copy of the Bible. The profession of religion, indeed, as a cloak to evil seems to have been purposeless, as he was notorious for seductions, as well as of bad odour in other details of his life.

One intrigue of illicit gallantry, which began probably in the lifetime of Mrs. Palmer, and was certainly going on at the time of Walter Palmer's death, has a sinister connection with the death of Cook. It is not mentioned in any account published of Palmer. Jane Burgess, a young woman of respectable position living in Stafford in 1855, left, at the house where she resided, a bundle of thirty-four letters written to her by Palmer. They show that a practitioner in Stafford, chosen by Palmer, and described by him as one "who would be silent as death," had performed an illegal operation. On the 13th of November the day notable in the trial, when "Polestar," Cook's racehorse, won at Shrewsbury, there is a letter to her from Palmer, which shows that she had made a demand for money as a condition of returning his letters. He was surprised, he wrote, to learn that she had never burned one of his letters. He says, "I cannot do what you ask; *I should not mind giving £30 for the whole of them*, though I am hard up at present." Another letter is dated the 19th November, the day on which Palmer was accused of administering strychnia for the first time to Cook. He offers £40 "to split the difference." On the 21st, the day on which, in the early morning, Cook had died, he sends the halves of eight £5 notes, and on the 24th the remainder. The letters were probably never returned, because the trouble threatened about Cook's death became common talk in Rugeley and Stafford.

Shortly after his marriage began a series of suspicious deaths which were attributed to Palmer after investigation started into the circumstances attending the death of Cook. An illegitimate child he had by a Rugeley woman died after it had visited him. Mrs. Thornton, his mother-in-law, was persuaded to live at his house, and she died within a fortnight. Palmer acquired property from her by her death. In 1850 a Mr. Bladon, a racing man, stayed for several days with Palmer, who owed him £800 for bets. Bladon died in circumstances very like those attending Cook's death, and Palmer buried him with the haste he attempted in the case of Cook, and he narrowly escaped a similar accusation.

In 1854 Palmer effected insurances to the amount of £13,000 on his wife's life. Within six months she died much as Bladon had died, and as Cook was to die. Dr. Bamford, a medical man of eighty-two, whom Palmer seems to have hoodwinked into serving his purposes, certified the death of Mrs. Palmer, as he had done the death of Bladon, and as he was to certify a year later that of Cook. Palmer drew the insurance money from the offices concerned. They were influenced by the popular suspicions and rumours in Rugeley and in the sporting circles Palmer frequented, but they paid after some hesitation and suggestion of inquiry, and Palmer was freed from the most pressing of his liabilities. His diary contains this entry—"Sept. 29th (1854), Friday—My poor, dear Annie expired at 10 past 1." Nine days after this—"Oct. 8th, Sunday—At church, Sacrament." Nine months after his maidservant, Eliza Tharm, bore an illegitimate child to him. Within three months of his wife's death Palmer, with the assistance of Pratt, the moneylender, whose claims had been met by the insurance on Mrs. Palmer's life, was making proposals to various offices, amounting to £82,000, on the life of his brother Walter. Ultimately an insurance for £13,000 was effected, and the policy was lodged with Pratt to secure advances. After this the rest of Palmer's life-history is directly connected with the story of the trial. The account we have given will suggest the, perhaps unprecedented, interest with which the trial was anticipated throughout the Midlands, and afterwards with what absorbed attention it was followed by all England as well as on the Continent.

I conclude this sketch by quoting a characteristic description by Sir James Stephen, who knew Palmer, had studied the criminal type, and himself presided at one of the most famous trials for poisoning. He says of Palmer— "His career supplied one of the proofs of a fact which many kind-hearted people seem to doubt, namely, the fact that such a thing as atrocious wickedness is consistent with good education, perfect sanity, and everything, in a word, which deprives men of all excuse for crime. Palmer was respectably brought up; apart from his extravagance and vice, he might have lived comfortably enough. He was a model of physical health and strength, and was courageous, determined, and energetic. No one ever suggested that there was even a disposition towards madness in him; yet he was as cruel, as treacherous, as greedy of money and pleasure, as brutally hard-hearted and sensual a wretch as it is possible even to imagine. If he had been the lowest and most ignorant ruffian that ever sprang from a long line of criminal ancestors, he could not have been worse than he was. He was by no means unlike Rush, Thurtell, and many other persons whom I have known. The fact that the world contains an appreciable number of wretches, who ought to be exterminated without mercy when an opportunity occurs, is not quite so generally understood as it ought to be—many common ways of thinking and feeling virtually deny it."

LEADING DATES IN THE PALMER TRIAL.

1855

August.   Walter Palmer, William Palmer's brother, dies. Payment of policy on his life for £13,000 assigned to William Palmer, and held by Pratt, moneylender, as security, refused by insurance office. Negotiations about it continue up to Cook's death.

Nov.   6. Writs issued by Pratt against Palmer and his mother for £4000, Mrs. Palmer's acceptance being forged. Writs not served, for Palmer to have opportunity of raising instalments.

"   13. (Tuesday) Palmer and Cook go together from Rugeley to Shrewsbury Races. Cook's mare, "Polestar," wins Shrewsbury Handicap, and he has in his possession, in consequence, £700 or £800, and is entitled to stakes of £350 and bets, to be paid at Tattersall's the Monday following, of over £1000.

"   14. (Wednesday night) Cook ill at the Raven, Shrewsbury, where he and Palmer stayed. Palmer is alleged to have dosed his drink.

"   15. Palmer's horse, "Chicken," beaten in his race, and Palmer loses heavily.

Cook and Palmer return to Rugeley, and Cook puts up at the Talbot.

"   16. Cook dines with Palmer and Jeremiah Smith. Cook apparently in usual health.

"   17. (Saturday) Cook ill in bed, with the same symptoms as at Shrewsbury.

"   18. (Sunday) His illness continues, and during the two days Palmer is in constant attendance, and orders and administers food, drink, and medicine. Dr. Bamford called in.

19. (Monday) Palmer goes to London and arranges with Herring to draw Cook's bets at Tattersalls and make payments to Pratt and Padwick, the moneylenders.

Cook is better all the Monday while Palmer is away.

Nov. 19. Palmer returns in the evening. Goes to Newton, the assistant of Mr. Salt, surgeon at Rugeley, and purchases 3 grains of strychnia. Is in and out of Cook's room up to eleven o'clock. Gives Cook pills, and leaves about eleven o'clock. These pills were professedly those sent by Dr. Bamford, but were alleged by the prosecution to have been substituted by Palmer with others containing strychnia. Jeremiah Smith gave evidence that Cook had taken Dr. Bamford's pills before Palmer's arrival.

About twelve o'clock Cook is taken ill with violent spasms, and awakens household with violent screaming. Palmer is sent for.

20. (Tuesday) Cook "comparatively comfortable" in the morning.

Palmer during the day purchases from Roberts, the assistant at the shop of Mr. Hawkins, druggist at Rugeley, prussic acid, 6 grains of strychnia, and liquor of opium.

Palmer requests Cheshire, the Rugeley postmaster, to fill up cheque on Wetherby for Cook's stakes won at Shrewsbury.

Mr. Jones, surgeon, of Lutterworth, Cook's most intimate friend, comes, at Palmer's request, to stay with Cook.

Pills again made up by Dr. Bamford at his house and taken away by Palmer. Pills administered by Palmer at 10.30. Jones sleeps in Cook's room. Cook taken ill again as on Monday, about twelve o'clock, and in a few minutes dies. Palmer had been sent for, and was present at the death.

21. (Wednesday) Wetherby declines to pay £350 cheque, as the stakes were not received from Shrewsbury.

Palmer writes to Pratt that he must have "Polestar."

THE TRIAL.

Within the Central Criminal Court,
Old Bailey, London.
WEDNESDAY, 14TH MAY, 1856.
The Court met at Ten o'clock.

Judges—

LORD CHIEF JUSTICE CAMPBELL.

MR. JUSTICE CRESSWELL.

MR. BARON ALDERSON.

Counsel for the Crown—

THE ATTORNEY-GENERAL (*Sir Alexander Cockburn*).

Mr. EDWARD JAMES, Q.C.

Mr. BODKIN.

Mr. WELSBY.

Mr. HUDDLESTON.

Counsel for the Prisoner—

Mr. SERJEANT SHEE.

Mr. GROVE, Q.C.

Mr. GRAY.

Mr. KENEALEY.

The prisoner, William Palmer, surgeon, of Rugeley, aged thirty-one was indicted for having at Rugeley, county of Stafford, on 21st November, 1855, feloniously, wilfully, and with malice aforethought, committed murder on the person of John Parsons Cook.

On being called upon the prisoner pleaded not guilty.

The jury having been duly empanelled and sworn, the Attorney-General opened the case for the Crown.[A]

Evidence for the Prosecution.

Ishmael Fisher

ISHMAEL FISHER, examined by Mr. JAMES—I am a wine merchant. I attend races occasionally, and knew the deceased, John Parsons Cook, for about two years. I was at Shrewsbury Races in November, 1855, and I remember the race for the Shrewsbury Handicap won with a mare called "Polestar," the property of Mr. Cook. That was on Tuesday, the 13th of November. I saw Mr. Cook, the deceased, that day upon the course. He appeared in his usual health and spirits. At Shrewsbury I stopped at the Raven Hotel. I know Palmer, the prisoner, very well. I have known him a little longer than I have known Mr. Cook. Mr. Cook and Mr. Palmer were also stopping at the Raven Hotel, and were occupying a room near me. There was only a wooden partition between my room and theirs. Between eleven and twelve on the night of Wednesday I went into the sitting room, in which Mr. Cook and Mr. Palmer and Mr. Myatt were. Myatt is a saddler at Rugeley, and is a friend of Palmer. They each appeared to have some grog before them. In my presence Mr. Cook asked Mr. Palmer to have some more brandy and water. Mr. Palmer said, "I shall not have any more till you have drunk yours." Mr. Cook said then, "I will drink mine," and he took up his glass and drank it at a drop, or he might have made two drops of it. After he had drunk it he said, "There is something in it." He also said, "It burns my throat dreadfully." Mr. Palmer then got up and took up the glass. He sipped up what was left of the glass, and said, "There is nothing in it." There appeared to be certainly not more than a teaspoonful left by Mr. Cook. At that time a Mr. Reid, whom I knew, came in. He is a wine merchant, and attends races. After Palmer had put his glass to his mouth and said, "There is nothing in it," he handed the glass to Reid, and asked him if he thought there was anything in it. The glass was also handed to me. We each said the glass being so empty we could not recognise anything. I said I thought there was rather a strong scent upon it, only I could not detect anything besides brandy. About ten minutes after this Cook retired from the room. Cook then came back and called me out of the room, and I went with him into my sitting room. Cook at that time was very ill. He had been sick. He said he had been very sick, and he thought that Palmer had dosed him. On that occasion he handed me over a sum of money, between £700 and £800 in bank notes. It was given to me to be taken care of. He did not say till when. Mr. Palmer and Mr. Cook jointly occupied a sitting room. They occupied different bedrooms. After Cook had given me this money he was immediately seized with sickness. I saw him in the same room and in his own bedroom. He again complained of suffering during the time he was absent, and said he had been again very sick. He asked me to go with him to his bedroom, which I did. A Mr. Jones, a stationer, went with me to his bedroom. While we were there he was violently vomiting again, so much so that we thought it right to send for the doctor, Mr. Gibson. We left him that morning in his room about two o'clock or a little after. Mr. Gibson came about half-past twelve or a quarter to one. I again sent for Mr. Gibson, as Cook was so ill. The second time I sent was about one, as near as I can remember. After taking some medicine Cook became more composed. The medicine was sent by Mr. Gibson, but he did not administer it himself. Mr. Jones and myself gave him the medicine. The next morning about ten o'clock I saw Palmer in my own sitting room. He was in the sitting room when I got downstairs. He said that Cook had been stating he had given him something last night, that he had been putting something in his brandy, or something to that effect. Palmer said he never played such tricks with people. He said, "I can tell you what he was; he was very drunk." Cook certainly was not drunk. I did not see him at dinner, but I saw him some time after, and from what I observed of him he was certainly sober. On the same morning Mr. Cook came up to my bedroom after he had got up. He was looking very ill. I gave him back his money. On that day (Thursday) I saw Mr. Cook on the racecourse at Shrewsbury. It would be about three o'clock. He looked very ill. I frequently had been in the habit of settling his bets for him when he did not settle them himself. I was in the habit of paying and receiving for him at Tattersall's and other places. At Shrewsbury I saw Cook's betting book in his possession. It was a little more than half the size of this (a small memorandum book). As nearly as I can remember, it was very nearly this colour (a dark colour). On the 17th, which was Saturday, I paid to Mr. Pratt, by direction of Mr. Cook, £200 in a cheque. As his agent I expected to settle his Shrewsbury account at Tattersall's on the following Monday, and I should have been entitled to deduct the £200. That was the course of dealing between us, but I did not settle that account, as it turned out.

[A] See Introduction, p. 2.

Cross-examined by Mr. SERJEANT SHEE—I have known Mr. Palmer a little longer than Mr. Cook. I knew that they were a good deal connected with racing transactions. They appeared to be very intimate, and were a great deal together. They generally stayed at the same hotels. I knew that Cook won considerably at Shrewsbury. I knew that "Polestar" was his mare. I do not know whether Palmer also won. I saw Mr. Cook after the race on the course. He appeared very much elated and gratified. "Polestar" won easily. In the room to which I went in the evening, in which Mr. Cook, Mr. Palmer, and Mr. Myatt were, I remember seeing a glass before Mr. Palmer and before Mr. Cook. I could not answer for Myatt's glass. I believe there was one decanter on the table. I did not observe sufficiently the glasses to see whether both had been drinking. Mr. Cook asked me to take some brandy. I do not recollect drinking any, but I cannot positively remember. I was not tipsy. I do not think I drank anything. I believe I am a good judge of brandy by the smell. I smelt this glass, and said that it had a strong smell about it, but I thought there was nothing in it unlike brandy. The glass was perfectly empty, and had been completely drained. I had been in the Unicorn in the evening before this occurred. I saw both Cook and Palmer at the Unicorn on Wednesday night about nine o'clock, or between nine and ten. I cannot say if he was drinking then. I do not know that a good number of people happened to be ill at Shrewsbury on that Wednesday or Tuesday. I had a friend who was rather poorly there from a different kind of illness to Mr. Cook. Wednesday was rather dull. I do not know that it rained, but it was damp under foot I remember. I saw Mr. Cook about the racecourse several times on Wednesday. On Thursday I remember the weather was rather cold and damp, but I cannot say whether it rained or not. On the 16th or 17th of November I received a letter from Mr. Cook, dated Rugeley, 16th November, 1855—

Dear Fisher,—It is of very great importance to both Mr. Palmer and myself that the sum of £500 should be paid to Mr. Pratt, of Queen Street, Mayfair, to-morrow, without fail. £300 has been sent up to-night, and if you will be kind enough to pay the other £200 to-morrow on receipt of this, you will greatly oblige me. I will settle it on Monday at Tattersall's. I am much better.

I received this on the 17th at No. 4 Victoria Street, London. I considered that Palmer and Cook were for some time jointly connected with racing transactions, but there is no proof of it. Cook was not more elated after winning than people usually are.

Thomas Jones

THOMAS JONES, examined by Mr. WELSBY—I am a law stationer, and was at Shrewsbury Races last November. I stayed at the Raven. On the Monday night Cook supped with me and some other friends. He appeared well on that occasion, as he also did on the Tuesday and Wednesday. On Wednesday night, between eleven and twelve, Mr. Cook came into my room at the Raven and invited me into his. I went there, and found, amongst other people in the room, Palmer. After the party broke up Mr. Fisher said something to me about Cook, in consequence of which I went up to Cook's bedroom. I found him there, and he complained of a burning in his throat. He was vomiting. Some pills and a draught were brought. Mr. Cook refused to take the pills, in consequence of which I went to the doctor, Mr. Gibson, and got some liquid medicine from him, which I brought back and gave to Mr. Cook. He drank about a wineglassful of the medicine, and after that he also took some of the pills. Next morning, between six and seven, I again saw him. He looked pale, and appeared to be unwell.

George Reid

GEORGE REID, examined by Mr. BODKIN—I was acquainted with the deceased Mr. Cook and the prisoner Palmer. I saw them at Shrewsbury Races in November. On the Tuesday and Wednesday Cook appeared to be in his usual health. On Wednesday night I went into the room at the Raven where Palmer and Cook were. There was another gentleman present. We had a glass of brandy and water before the time to rest. Almost immediately after I arrived there I noticed that Cook was in pain. I heard him say to Mr. Palmer there was something in the brandy and water. Mr. Palmer handed me the glass to taste from it. I said, "What is the use of handing me the glass when it is empty?" The next time I saw Cook was about eleven o'clock the next morning. He said he was very ill.

Cross-examined by SERJEANT SHEE—I should consider that Cook's general state of health was delicate. He always had a pallid complexion, and did not look like a strong man.

W. S. Gibson

WILLIAM SCAFE GIBSON, examined by Mr. HUDDLESTON—I am assistant to Mr. Heathcote, surgeon, at Shrewsbury. On 14th November last, between twelve and one at night, I was sent for to the Raven Hotel, and saw there Mr. Cook in his bedroom. He was not in bed. He complained of pain in his stomach and heat in his throat, and said he thought he had been poisoned. His pulse was about 90; his tongue was perfectly clean. I advised him to take an emetic, which he did, and he was then very sick. Nothing came away but water. I sent him two pills and a draught. The pills consisted of rhubarb and 3 grains of calomel. The draught consisted of mistura sennacum. Later on in the same night I gave Mr. Jones some medicine for Cook. I never saw Cook after that occasion.

Cross-examined by Mr. SERJEANT SHEE—I treated Cook as if he had taken poison. I took him at his word, that he had taken poison, not from his symptoms. He seemed a little excited by drink.

E. Mills

ELIZABETH MILLS, examined by Mr. JAMES—I was chambermaid at the Talbot Arms at Rugeley in November last. I had been there about two years. I knew the prisoner. He was in the habit of coming to the Talbot Arms. I remember on Thursday, the 15th, between nine and ten at night, Mr. Cook, along with Mr. Palmer, came to the Talbot Arms. He retired to rest between ten and eleven. He said he had been poorly, and was feeling poorly then. The next morning he got up about twelve o'clock, and said he felt no worse, but still he was not well. That night he retired to bed about half-past ten. He said he had been to Mr. Palmer's and had dined there. On Saturday morning about eight, Palmer, who lived opposite to the Talbot Arms, came over. He ordered a cup of coffee for Mr. Cook, which I believe I gave to Mr. Cook in his bedroom. Mr. Palmer was in the room at the time. I did not see Cook drink it, but about half an hour afterwards I returned into the room and found that the coffee had been vomited. On that occasion I observed a jug in the room which did not belong to the Talbot Arms. It was sent down to me by Lavinia Barnes to make some more toast and water. During that Saturday I saw Palmer perhaps four or five times in Cook's room. I heard him say to Mr. Cook that he would send over some broth. I did not see it brought over, but I saw the broth in the kitchen. The cook told me that it had come over from Mrs. Rowley. The broth had not been made at the Talbot Arms. Later in the day I took up the broth to Mr. Cook. About a quarter of an hour after the broth came over I met Palmer coming up the stairs to Cook's room. He asked if Cook had had his broth. I told him I did not know that any was come for him. During this conversation Lavinia Barnes came forward and said she had taken up the broth to Mr. Cook as soon as it had come, and he had refused to take it, saying that it would not stay in his stomach. Palmer said that I must go and fetch the broth, which I did, and took it into the room. Mr. Palmer was there, and I left the broth in the room. About an hour and a half afterwards I went up to the room again and found that the broth had been vomited. About six o'clock that evening some barley water was made for Cook. I took that up to him, but I cannot remember whether that stayed in his stomach or not. At eight o'clock that evening I took up some arrowroot to Cook. The first time I saw Mr. Bamford [the doctor at Rugeley] was about three o'clock on the Saturday afternoon. Between seven and eight on the Sunday morning I went into Mr. Cook's room. During the night Mr. Smith, a friend of Mr. Cook, had slept in the same room. I asked Mr. Cook if he felt worse. He said he felt pretty comfortable, and had slept well since twelve o'clock. Upon the Sunday a large breakfast cup of broth was brought to the Talbot Arms by Charles Hawley. I took some of it up to Mr. Cook's room in the same cup in which it was brought. I tasted about two tablespoonfuls of the broth before I took it up. It was between twelve and one, before my dinner, that I tasted this broth. About half an hour afterwards it made me very sick, and I vomited violently all the afternoon till about five o'clock. I was obliged to go to bed. Up to that time I had been quite well. I had taken nothing that I am aware of that had disagreed with me. In the evening and on the morning of the Sunday I saw Mr. Cook several times. He appeared to be better during that evening, and to be in good spirits. The last time I saw him on the Sunday night might be about ten or a little after that. I saw him between seven and eight on the Monday morning. I took him up a cup of coffee. He did not vomit that. Palmer was there that morning about a quarter or half-past seven. I saw him coming downstairs as though he had been to see Mr. Cook. Mr. Cook got up at one o'clock on that Monday. He appeared a great deal better, and he washed and dressed and shaved himself. He said he felt exceedingly weak. On the Monday Ashmall, the jockey, and Mr. Saunders, Cook's trainer, visited him. As soon as Cook got up at one o'clock I gave him some arrowroot, which he retained in his stomach. I believe he had a cup of coffee about four or five. About eight o'clock that night Miss Bond, the housekeeper, gave me a pillbox to take upstairs to Mr. Cook's room, which I did, and placed it on the dressing-table. It was wrapped up in white paper. I do not know whether the box contained pills or not. After I had placed the pillbox on Cook's dressing-table Palmer came, and went into Cook's room. I saw him sitting down by the fire between nine and ten. I retired to rest between ten and eleven. About a quarter or ten minutes before twelve Lavinia Barnes, the waitress, called me up. I heard a noise of violent screaming whilst I was dressing. The screams came from Cook's room. My room is on the floor above Cook's room. I heard the screams twice, and went down to Cook's room. As soon as I entered the room I found him sitting up in bed. He desired me to fetch Mr. Palmer directly. I walked to his bedside, and I found the pillow upon the floor. There was one mould candle burning. I picked up the pillow and asked him would he lay down his head. At that time he was sitting up and was beating the bed-clothes, with both his arms and hands stretched out. He said, "I cannot lie down. I shall suffocate if I do. Oh, fetch Mr. Palmer." His body, his hands, and neck were moving then—a sort of jumping or jerking. His head was back. Sometimes he would throw back his head upon the pillow, and then he would raise himself up again. This jumping and jerking was all over his body. He appeared to have great difficulty in breathing. The balls of both the eyes were much projected. It was difficult for him to speak, he was so short of breath. He screamed three or four times while I was in the room. He called aloud "Murder" twice. He asked me to rub one hand. I found the left hand stiff. It appeared to be stretched out as though the fingers were something like paralysed. It did not move. It appeared to me to be stiff all the way up his arm. I did not rub him very long. The stiffness did not appear to be gone after I had rubbed him. During the time I was rubbing his hands Palmer was in the room. Cook was conscious while this jerking of the body was going on. He recognised Palmer when he came in, and said, "Oh, Palmer, I shall die," or "Oh, doctor, I shall die." Palmer replied, "Oh, my lad, you won't." Palmer then left to fetch something, and asked me to stay by the bedside with him. He returned in a few minutes, during which time I merely stood by the bedside. He brought back with him some pills. He gave him something else, but whether he brought it with him or not I do not know. He gave him a drop from a wineglass after giving him the pills. Cook, when he took the pills, said he could not swallow them. At Palmer's request I gave Cook a teaspoonful of toast and water, which he took. When I gave it him from the spoon his body was then jerking and jumping. He snapped at the spoon like that [describing it] with his head and neck, and the spoon was fast between his teeth. It was difficult to get it away. He seemed to bite it very hard. While this was going on the water went down his throat and washed the pills down. Mr. Palmer then handed him the draught from the wineglass. It was something liquid, and the wineglass was three parts full with a liquid of a dark, heavy-looking nature. Cook drank it. He snapped at the glass just the same as he did at the spoon. He swallowed the liquid, which was vomited up immediately. I supported his forehead with my hand while he vomited. The stuff he vomited smelt, I should think, like opium. Palmer said that he hoped the pills were not returned, and he searched for the pills with a quill. He said, "I cannot find the pills." After this Cook seemed to be more easy. This second attack lasted about half an hour, or it might be more. He appeared to be conscious during the whole of that time. He asked Palmer to feel his heart after he had got more composed. I do not know whether he did so or not. Palmer made some slight remark as to its being all right, or something of that kind. I left Cook and Palmer about three o'clock in the morning. Cook was dozing when I left him, and Palmer was asleep in the easy-chair.

E. Mills

I next saw Cook again about six o'clock on the Tuesday morning. I said, "Has Mr. Palmer gone?" and he said, "Yes; he left a quarter before five." I asked him how he felt, and he said he had been no worse since I left him in the morning. He asked me if I had ever seen any one suffer such agony as he was in last night, and I said no, I never had. I asked "What do you think was the cause of all that, Mr. Cook?" and he said the pills that Palmer gave him at half-past ten. When I saw Cook on the Tuesday morning I did not observe any of those jerkings or convulsions about him. About twelve o'clock he rang his bell and desired me to send the boots over to ask Palmer whether he might have a cup of coffee. The boots returned and said he might have a cup of coffee, and that Mr. Palmer would be over immediately. I took the coffee up a little after twelve. Palmer was in Mr. Cook's room at that time. I gave the coffee to Mr. Palmer, who tasted the coffee in my presence. I then left the room. Mr. Jones arrived by the three o'clock train that afternoon. He went and saw Mr. Cook upon his arrival. About four, or it might be between four and five, I took up to Mr. Cook's room another cup of coffee. At that time I saw Palmer in the room. I left the room, and afterwards I saw Palmer, who told me that Mr. Cook had vomited the coffee. He spoke from the door of Cook's room, but did not call me in. I saw Cook several times that evening before I retired to rest. He appeared to be in very good spirits, and talked about getting up the next morning. I believe I gave him some arrowroot that evening about half-past ten. Palmer was with him in his bedroom when I left him. I gave Palmer a jug of toast and water for Cook. Mr. Palmer asked Cook if I could do anything more for him that night, and Mr. Cook said he would want nothing more. That was about half-past ten. I did not go to bed that night, but I remained in the kitchen, as I was anxious to see how Mr. Cook went on. While I was in the kitchen the bell of Mr. Cook's room rang violently a little before twelve [Tuesday night]. Mr. Jones was sleeping in Cook's bedroom, which was a double-bedded room, and where a bed had been made up for him. I went upstairs to Mr. Cook's room on hearing the bell. He was sitting up in bed, and Mr. Jones appeared to be supporting him. Mr. Cook said, "Oh, Mary, fetch Mr. Palmer directly." He was conscious at the time. I went over for Mr. Palmer. I rang the surgery bell at the surgery door. I expected him to come to the window and as soon as I stepped off the step into the road he was at the bedroom window. He did not put up the sash. At that time I could not see whether he was dressed or not. I asked him to come over to Mr. Cook directly, as he was much the same as he was the night before. I then went back to the hotel. Palmer came two or three minutes afterwards. I was in the bedroom when Palmer came, and he remarked that he had never dressed so quickly in his life. That was the first thing he said when he came into Cook's room. Mr. Cook was sitting up in bed, supported by Mr. Jones. After Mr. Palmer came I remained on the landing, just outside the door. After I had been waiting a short time Palmer came out. I said to him that Mr. Cook was much about the same as last night, and he replied that he was not so ill by the fiftieth part. He then went downstairs as though he was going into his own house, and after a very short time he came back to Cook's room. After Palmer had returned I heard Cook ask to be turned over on his right side. I was at the door at the time, which was open. I did not go in. I was not in the room when Cook died. I went in, I believe, just before he died, but I came out again. I saw Mr. Jones supporting Cook. Mr. Palmer was then feeling Mr. Cook's pulse, and he said to Mr. Jones, "His pulse is gone." Mr. Jones pressed the side of his face to Cook's heart. Mr. Palmer asked me to fetch Mr. Bamford, and I did so. From the time I was called up, about ten minutes before twelve, till Cook's death would be about three-quarters of an hour. Mr. Bamford came over, and I saw him when he came downstairs. He said, "He is dead. He was dead when I arrived." Mr. Jones came out of the room and told me that Mr. Palmer wanted me. I went into the room and saw Mr. Palmer. There was no one with him. I said, "It is not possible Mr. Cook is dead," and he said, "Oh, yes, he is dead." He asked me to arrange about laying out Cook. I had seen a book in Mr. Cook's room, a dark book with a gold band round the edge. It had a pencil going into it on one side. Cook stopped at the Talbot Arms perhaps two or three months before this time. I saw the book on the Monday night before Mr. Cook's death. He wrote something in it, and took from a pocket in the book a postage stamp. I placed the book back at the looking-glass on the dressing-table. I have never seen that book since Cook's death. I have searched everywhere for it. When I went into the room where Cook's body was lying Palmer was there. I noticed that Cook's clothes were placed on a chair. I saw Palmer searching the pocket. That was on the Tuesday night about ten minutes after Cook's death. He also searched under the pillow and bolster. After Cook's death I saw some letters on the mantelpiece which were not there before.

The Court then adjourned.

Second Day, Thursday, 15th May, 1856.

The Court met at ten o'clock.

E. Mills

ELIZABETH MILLS, cross-examined by Mr. SERJEANT SHEE—I had been at the Talbot Arms about three years at the date of Mr. Cook's death. He first came to the Talbot Arms about three months before he died, and up to the time of his death he was constantly coming back and forward. During the time he was there I never heard him complain of anything except a sore throat or something of that kind through cold. I never noticed that he had any soreness about his mouth or that he had difficulty at all in swallowing. I have seen him with a foul tongue about once or so. He never complained in my hearing of the tongue being sore so as to render it difficult to swallow. I do not know of caustic having been applied to it while he was there. Before he went to Shrewsbury he had not been ailing at all to my knowledge. When he came back he said he was poorly. After Cook's death I stayed at the Talbot Inn till the day after Christmas. I then went to my home in the Potteries, Shelton. Since then I have been in service in Dolly's Hotel, Paternoster Row, London. I stayed six weeks there as chambermaid. About a week after I came to London I saw Mr. Stevens (the stepfather of Cook) about six or seven times. Two or three times I saw him alone; at other times perhaps Mrs. Dewhurst, the landlady of the inn, or Miss Dewhurst was there. It was not always about Mr. Cook's death that he spoke to me. He would merely call to see how I liked London, and whether I was well in health, and all that.

E. Mills

Mr. Stevens is a man not in your station. He is a gentleman. Do you mean to say he called to see how you liked London?—Just to see whether I liked the place. I had some conversation with him at the Talbot Inn just before the funeral. I really cannot remember what he spoke about beyond Mr. Cook's death. During the time I was at Dolly's Hotel I never received a farthing from him, and he never made me any promise to get a place. The last time I saw him out of Court was on Tuesday last at Dolly's Hotel. He never spoke to me about Mr. Cook's death. When I saw him at that time there were other people present, including Lavinia Barnes, Mr. Gardner, and Mr. Hatton, the chief officer of police in Staffordshire. Mr. Gardner is an attorney at Rugeley. I cannot say what all the talk was about. Mr. Cook's death might be mentioned. I daresay it was. I will undertake to say that there were other subjects of conversation between us besides the subject of Cook's death. I do not wish to mention what they were. They did not, so far as I heard, talk about the evidence I was to give. They did not ask me what I could prove, nor did they read my depositions before the coroner to me. There was nothing read to me from a newspaper or anything else. Mr. Stevens never at any previous interview read anything from a newspaper to me. He never talked to me about the symptoms which Mr. Cook exhibited before his death. Before last Tuesday I had seen Mr. Hatton about twice. I saw him once at Dolly's, when he dined there. I did not wait upon him. I merely saw him there. He might have talked about Mr. Cook's death, but I cannot remember. I have seen Mr. Gardner there three or four times since Mr. Cook's death. I have seen him at Dolly's, and have met him in the street. I have merely said, "How do you do," or "Good morning." I have had no other talk with him. I do not remember to have read the case of a Mrs. Dove in the newspapers, but I may have done so. I have heard spoken of a case that lately occurred at Leeds of a lady who was said to have been poisoned by her husband, but I did not read it. It was not mentioned to me by Mr. Stevens, nor by Mr. Gardner, nor by Mr. Hatton.

Were you told when you heard of it what the symptoms of Mrs. Dove were?—I think not. I merely heard there had been strychnine used at Leeds, another strychnine case.

Were the symptoms of strychnine ever mentioned to you by any one?—No, never.

When, and to whom, did you first use the expression "twitching," which you mentioned so repeatedly yesterday?—To the coroner, I did. If I did not mention twitching, I mentioned something to the same effect. I will not swear I used that word at the coroner's. I cannot remember when I first used the word "twitching." I cannot remember when I first used the word "jerking" to anybody. I will undertake to swear it has never been used to me by anybody.

You stated yesterday that on the Sunday some broth was brought in a breakfastcup between twelve and one o'clock; that you took it up to Cook's bedroom; that you drank about two tablespoonfuls; that you were sick the whole afternoon, and vomited till five o'clock. Did you state one word about that in your deposition before the coroner?—It never occurred to me until three days afterwards.

Did you state before the coroner that there was nothing peculiar in the taste of the broth?—I believe I was examined three times before the coroner. My attention had been called to the fact of broth having been sent over on one occasion, but I do not remember whether it was the first. I was asked if I had tasted it, and I stated I had tasted it, and thought it was very good. It never occurred to me to mention that I was sick and vomited frequently in the course of the afternoon.

You went to bed in consequence of the vomiting?—Yes.

E. Mills

I suppose sickness of that kind repeated frequently in the course of an afternoon is not a very common occurrence with you?—No, I have a bilious attack sometimes, but not such violent vomiting as I had that afternoon. I could not at all account for it at the time. I only took two tablespoonfuls. The vomiting came on from half an hour to an hour after I took them.

On the Saturday morning did Cook express a wish to have coffee for breakfast, or was it from Palmer the first you heard that his breakfast was to be coffee?—I do not know whether Palmer told me to bring coffee or whether it was Cook. I never knew Mr. Cook to take coffee in bed before. He generally took tea.

I understood you to say yesterday Palmer came over at eight o'clock and ordered a cup of coffee for Cook. Do you adhere to that?—I cannot remember whether Palmer ordered it or not. If I said it yesterday it is correct, but I cannot remember whether Palmer ordered the coffee or not now. I will swear now that Palmer ordered the coffee, and I took it and gave it into Cook's hands, and Palmer was there.

You swear to it now?—Yes.

You doubted it a moment ago?—If that was stated yesterday I do not doubt it was correct.

Is that your only reason for stating it to be correct?—I believe it to be correct.

Will you swear that it is correct?—Yes; it is no doubt correct if I said so.

Why should that make it more correct if you cannot say it now from your own recollection?—I cannot remember as well to-day as I did yesterday. I cannot remember that I stated before the coroner that Cook had coffee for breakfast at eight o'clock, that he ate nothing, and that he vomited directly he had swallowed it, and that up to the time I had given him the coffee I had not seen Palmer. I cannot remember whether I stated before the coroner anything about the pillbox on Monday night. It was sent over wrapped up in paper. I will swear that Palmer was there between nine and ten o'clock. He brought a jar of jelly to the Talbot, and I opened it. I should say he was there nearer to ten than nine. I do not recollect whether he was there when I left Cook at half-past ten.

You stated yesterday that you asked Cook on the Tuesday afternoon what he thought the cause of his illness was, and he said, "The pills which Palmer gave me at half-past ten"?—Yes.

Did you say that before the coroner?—No.

E. Mills

Have you been questioned by any one since Mr. Cook's death respecting what you did say before the coroner as to when these pills might have been given or respecting anything you have said about these pills before the coroner?—Yes; I was questioned by Dr. Collier at Hitchingly. I did not tell him that the gentleman in London had altered my evidence on that point, and that my evidence was now to be that "Cook said the pills which Palmer gave him at half-past ten made him ill."

Did he state anything about your evidence being altered since?—Yes; he said he had not got that down in what I had given to the coroner in the coroner's papers. I said "No, I thought it was down in some of the papers. I had given it to a gentleman in London." The evidence has been altered by myself since. I do not remember who the gentleman was that I had given it to. I gave it to him at Dolly's. The gentleman came to me at Dolly's and asked if I would answer him a few questions. I said I would, and I saw him in a sitting-room. I was with him about half an hour. He asked me not very many questions, and during the time I was answering the questions he was writing. He did not tell me who he was or whom he came from, but he mentioned Mr. Stevens' name.

What did he say about Mr. Stevens?—Mr. Stevens was with him. He called Mr. Stevens by name.

Why did you not tell us that before?—You did not ask me.

Then, although you did not know who he was, you knew he was an acquaintance of Mr. Stevens because he came with him?—He did. All that I said then was taken down. I do not remember saying before the coroner that when Cook was ill on Monday night and sitting up in bed beating the bed-clothes he said, "I cannot lie down; I shall suffocate if I do." I do not remember whether I mentioned the word "jerking" before the coroner.

Did you say before the coroner, "He would throw his head back and raise himself up again"?—Yes.

You will say you said that?—Yes. I do not know whether I mentioned the word "jerking." I said the whole of the body was in a jumping, snatching way. I believe I mentioned it was difficult for him to speak, he was so short of breath. I did not mention about him calling "murder" twice. I do not remember whether I mentioned before the coroner that Mr. Cook said the pills stuck fast in his throat and he could not swallow them. I did not answer the coroner anything more than he asked me. If he had asked me I should have answered him as I am answering now.

The first time that you were examined before the coroner was Dr. Taylor present?—I believe he was.

E. Mills

Were you not recalled after you had been examined once for the purpose of describing the symptoms for Dr. Taylor to hear?—I was not. I was never examined as to the symptoms when I knew the medical gentlemen were there. I cannot remember how Mr. Palmer was dressed when he came over on the Tuesday night. He had a plaid dressing-gown on, but I cannot remember what sort of cap he had. When Mr. Jones asked me to go into the room after Mr. Cook's death I went in at once, and it was then that I saw Palmer searching the pockets of the coat. When I went in he did not seem at all confused.

Re-examined by Mr. JAMES—I was under examination before the coroner perhaps a couple of hours on different occasions. The coroner put the questions to me, and the coroner's clerk, I believe, wrote down my answers. The coroner asked me if the broth had any effect on me, and I said not that I was aware of.

By Mr. SERJEANT SHEE—What brought to your mind afterwards the vomiting after taking the broth?—I do not know. I believe it was some one else in the house that mentioned my sickness first. It did not occur to me until some one else mentioned it about a week after the coroner was there.

Re-examination resumed—I cannot remember who it was, but it was some of my fellow-servants in the house. A person of the name of Dr. Collier called upon me and represented that he was for the Crown. He asked me questions about the inquest and about the death of Mr. Cook. That would be about three weeks or a month ago, at Hitchingley.

J. Gardner

JAMES GARDNER, examined by the ATTORNEY-GENERAL—I am an attorney, and attended for Mr. Stevens at the inquest. The inquest lasted five days, and on each of these days I had several times occasion to expostulate with Mr. Ward, the coroner, as to questions which he put or omitted to put, and I observed that the clerk omitted to take down answers given to the questions which had been put.

Cross-examined by Mr. SERJEANT SHEE—A great many questions were put by the jury after the examination of the professional men.

By the ATTORNEY-GENERAL—The jury made very strong observations as to the necessity for further questions.

Objection to statement of these observations allowed.

Mrs. ANNE BROOKS, examined by the ATTORNEY-GENERAL—I live in Manchester, and am in the habit of attending race meetings. I was at Shrewsbury races in November, 1855. About eight o'clock in the evening of Wednesday, the 14th, I met Palmer in the street. I had some conversation with him as to horses that were running during that week at Shrewsbury. About half-past ten the same evening I went, along with some friends, to the Raven, where I knew Palmer was staying. I had been there frequently before. I left my friends downstairs and went upstairs to go to Palmer's room, which I knew. As I approached Palmer's room a servant called my attention to Palmer himself, who was standing at a small table in the passage. When I first saw him he had a glass tumbler in his hand, in which there appeared to be a small quantity of liquid like water. I did not see him put anything in the glass. I saw him shaking up the fluid that was in it. There was a light in the passage. It was nearer to me than to him. He held up the glass as if he were looking at the light through it. He then said to me, "I will be with you presently." He noticed me the moment I got to the top of the stairs. After he made that remark to me he stood for a minute or two holding the glass in his hand up to the light once or twice and shaking it now and then. The only observation he made was about the fine weather we had. After this he carried the glass into a sitting room adjoining his own. The room, I imagined, was empty, as I heard no one speaking. He remained there two or three minutes, and came out with the glass still in his hand, and carried it into his own sitting room, shutting the door after him. Three or four minutes afterwards he came out to me, bringing me a glass—it might be the same one, it was very like it—with some brandy and water in it. I took the brandy and water, and it produced no unpleasant consequences in me. We had some conversation regarding the next day's racing, and he said he should back his own horse "Chicken." "Chicken" lost. Palmer never told me afterwards whether he had won or lost on the race.

Cross-examined by Mr. SERJEANT SHEE—I am a married woman, and am in the habit of attending race meetings, but my husband does not sanction my going when he knows about it. Several people were taken ill in Shrewsbury on the Wednesday. One of my company was dreadfully ill, and there was a wonder what could cause it; we made an observation. We thought the water might have been poisoned. We were all affected the same way by sickness.

Can you tell me in what way it affected persons?

By the ATTORNEY-GENERAL—Any person you saw. Whom did you see yourself affected in that way?—There was a lady that came to meet me there;

she was one; and there was another party in my company who was so ill that he could not go to the races on Thursday.

By Mr. SERJEANT SHEE—They were affected by sickness and purging.

You saw Palmer with the glass in his hand?—I did.

Anne Brooks

Did he put it up to the light?—He held it just carelessly up. I did not see any substance in the glass. He was doing this in a passage that led to a great many rooms. I could not say if there was more than one light in the passage. I think it was a chandelier. He said, "I will be with you presently," when he carried the glass into the room which I supposed to have been unoccupied.

Did he also say that while he was holding it to the light?—Yes, just in this manner, quite carelessly.

And at that time you thought nothing of it?—I thought he was mixing up some cooling draught, and was waiting for some water. I was not examined before the coroner.

By the ATTORNEY-GENERAL—The brandy and water he gave me was cold, not hot. I have known Palmer for a great number of years as a racing man.

L. Barnes

LAVINIA BARNES, examined by Mr. JAMES—In November, 1855, I was in service as waitress at the Talbot Arms. I knew both Palmer and Mr. Cook. I saw Mr. Cook on 12th November on his way to the Shrewsbury Races. He seemed quite well then. I saw him on Thursday, the 15th, on his return from the races. On Friday I saw him between nine and ten, when he came back after having dined with Palmer. He was quite sober. I saw Mr. Cook twice on Saturday. On that day I remember some broth being sent over, which I took up to Mr. Cook. He could not take it, as he said he was too sick. I brought the broth down to the kitchen. I saw Palmer, and told him that Cook would not take the broth, as he was too sick. Palmer said he must take it, and it was taken up again to him by Elizabeth Mills. I did not see any broth being brought over on the Sunday. Between twelve and one on the Sunday Elizabeth Mills was taken ill, and had to leave her work and go to bed. I saw her; she was vomiting violently. Between four and five she returned to work, and complained to me of having been ill from the vomiting. I saw some broth in a basin in the kitchen on the Sunday. I do not know where it was made. It was in a sick cup with two handles. The cup did not belong to the Talbot Arms, and it went back to Palmer's. Between seven and eight on Sunday morning I heard Palmer say he was going to London on the Monday. On Monday I saw Cook after dinner. Mr. Saunders, the trainer, visited him, and I took up some brandy and water to them. On that night I slept in the room next Mr. Cook's. I saw Palmer between eight and nine that night going upstairs in the direction of Cook's room. I saw him in the room afterwards between twelve and one o'clock. About twelve o'clock I was in the kitchen, when Mr. Cook's bell rang violently. I went up to his room, and found he was very ill. He asked me to send for Mr. Palmer. He was screaming "murder," and was in violent pain. He said he was suffocating. His eyes looked very wild, and were standing a great way out of his head. He was beating the bed with his hands. I sent the boots for Palmer, and went and called Elizabeth Mills. After Palmer came I went up to the room again. Cook seemed to be more composed. Palmer told him not to be alarmed. I saw Cook drinking a darkish mixture in a glass. I cannot remember who gave it to him, but Palmer was in the room when it was given. When Cook put the glass to his mouth he snapped at it. I both saw and heard him do it. He vomited the black-looking draught. I left the room between twelve and one, and he seemed more composed then. I saw him again on the Tuesday, and he seemed to be much better. A few minutes before twelve o'clock on the Tuesday night Elizabeth Mills and I were in the kitchen. Mr. Cook's bell rang, and Elizabeth Mills went up to answer it. I followed her upstairs, but did not go into the room. I heard Cook scream. Elizabeth Mills went for Palmer, and he came. He was dressed in his usual way, with a black coat on. There was nothing peculiar about his dress. He wore a cap. After Palmer went into the room I remained on the landing. I did not hear what was going on inside. Palmer came out and went downstairs for something. When he came out Elizabeth Mills asked him how Mr. Cook was, and he replied, "Not so bad by a fiftieth part." She and I were both together when he said this. I went into the room before Mr. Cook died. Mr. Jones was there in attendance upon him. Before I went into the room, and when Palmer was there, I heard Cook ask to be turned over. After I went into the room I do not remember hearing anything. I came out again before Cook's death, and did not see him die. I returned to the room afterwards, and saw Palmer there with one of Cook's coats in his hands. He was feeling the pockets. I also saw him feel under the bolster I left him in the room with the dead body. On the Thursday following I met Palmer in the hall of the hotel. He asked me for the key of Cook's room, and I fetched it from the bar. He said he wanted some books and papers and a paper knife, which were to go back to the stationer's where he had them from, or he should have to pay for them. I went into the room with him. While there he asked me to go to Miss Bond, the housekeeper, for some books she had. I brought them back with me to the room, and found Palmer there searching on the chest of drawers among some books and clothes belonging to Mr. Cook. I thought it was the paper knife he was looking for, as he said, "I cannot find the knife anywhere." Miss Bond then came into the room, and I left. I saw Mr. Jones, who had visited Cook on the Tuesday, on the Friday with Palmer. I heard him ask Palmer if he knew where Cook's betting book was. I cannot remember what Palmer replied. He said it would be sure to be found, and asked me and the chambermaid to go and look for it. He also said, "It was not worth anything to anybody but Cook." This would be between three and four o'clock, and Mr. Stevens, who was at the Talbot Arms that day, left about half-past four. We went to look for the betting book. Palmer did not go with us. We searched under the bed and all round the room. We did not look in the chests of drawers, of which there were two in the room, both unlocked. We went downstairs and told Palmer we could not find the book. He said, "Oh, it will be found somewhere; I will go with you and look myself." He did not go, but went out of the house, and I did not see him afterwards. I cannot say how long Palmer was in the room on the Thursday. There was no reason why we did not search the drawers for the betting book. There were some people in the room with Mr. Cook's corpse, nailing the coffin, and they stood at the side of the drawers.

Cross-examined by Mr. SERJEANT SHEE—Shortly after Cook refused to take the broth, saying he was too sick, Palmer came over and said, "He must have it."

Did he say why he must have it?—No.

Did he say anything to the effect, "Why, he has eaten nothing for several days"?—I cannot remember that he did.

Did he ask whether anything had been eaten by him?—Not of me.

You know, in fact, that Mr. Cook had had no substantial food?—He had some coffee and cocoa, and something like that.

You say that on the Monday evening you saw Palmer between eight and nine o'clock going upstairs. Are you sure it was before nine o'clock?—I am not quite certain.

Are you sure it was before half-past nine o'clock?—No, I did not pay particular attention to what the time was.

Are you quite sure it was before ten o'clock?—Yes, I knew he had been to London.

Did you know what hour the train came back from London?—I did not. An omnibus goes from the hotel to the station, starting from the hotel about half-past seven. It is not one mile from the station. I can give no notion of what time the express train comes into Rugeley from London, nor do I know if it stops at Rugeley.

Do you persist that it must have been before ten o'clock that you saw Palmer come in?—I think it was.

May it not have been a quarter past ten o'clock? You can easily have been mistaken about an hour; are you quite certain it was before ten o'clock?—I cannot remember now.

You have stated that when Palmer left on the Monday evening he gave Cook something to drink in a glass; he snapped at the glass, and you said, "I cannot remember who gave it to him"; did you see the glass in Mr. Cook's hands?—I cannot remember whether I saw the glass in Cook's hands.

L. Barnes

Did you see his hand up to the glass?—I think I did. I think it was as if he was going to catch hold of it, but somebody else was holding it.

Did you see the hand touch the glass?—I cannot remember that. I remember some one was holding it for him.

Might he not be holding it too?—He might.

Anne Rowley

ANNE ROWLEY, examined by Mr. WELSBY—I live at Rugeley, and have been employed by Mr. Palmer as charwoman. On the Saturday before Mr. Cook died I remember being sent by Palmer to Mr. Robinson, of the Albion, for a little broth for Mr. Cook. The Albion is an inn in Rugeley, and a small distance from the Talbot Arms. I brought the broth, which was not warm, to Palmer's house and put it by the fire. I left it at the fire and went back to my work in the kitchen. When the broth was hot Mr. Palmer brought it to me in the back kitchen. He poured it into a cup, which I held while he did so. He told me to take it across to the Talbot Arms for Mr. Cook, and to say to whoever I gave it to to ask Mr. Cook if he would take a little bread or a little toast with it, and to say that Mr. Smith had sent it. I took it to the Talbot Arms. He did not say why I was to say Mr. Smith had sent it. Mr. Jeremiah Smith is an attorney in Rugeley. He goes under the name of Jerry Smith, and is a friend of Palmer. I gave the broth to Lavinia Barnes.

Cross-examined by Mr. SERJEANT SHEE—Mr. Smith was in the habit of putting up at the Albion, and took his meals there a good deal. He was intimate with Mr. Cook. I have not known them to dine together, but Mr. Cook was to have dined at Mr. Smith's that day, but was unable to do so. The time between the broth being brought in to me and the time it was taken to the Talbot Arms would be about five minutes.

C. Hawley

CHARLES HAWLEY, examined by Mr. BODKIN—I am a gardener in Rugeley, and was occasionally employed by the prisoner in that capacity. I was in his house on the Sunday before Mr. Cook died, between twelve and one, and Mr. Palmer asked me whether I would take some broth to Mr. Cook. He gave me some broth in a small cup with a cover, and told me to take it over to the Talbot Arms. I gave it to one of the servant girls, either Mills or Lavinia Barnes. I cannot tell whether the broth was hot or not.

Sarah Bond

SARAH BOND, examined by Mr. HUDDLESTON—I was housekeeper at the Talbot Arms in November last. I saw Mr. Cook on the Thursday after he returned from Shrewsbury Races. I heard him say he was very poorly. About eight o'clock on Sunday evening I saw him in bed. He said he had been very ill, but was better. Soon after I came into the room I saw the prisoner. I asked what he thought about Mr. Cook, and he told me he was better. On the Saturday night I spoke to him about the advisability of having some one to be with Mr. Cook during the night. He said that either he or Jerry Smith would be there. I also spoke to him about it on the Sunday night, but he said that Cook was so much better he would not require any one. He would be much better without it. I asked him if Daniel Jenkins, the boots, should not sleep in the room, but he said he would much rather not. On Monday morning, a little before seven, he came into the kitchen to me. He said Cook was better, and asked me to make a cup of coffee for him. I made the coffee. He remained in the kitchen while I was making it, and took it from me to give to Mr. Cook. He said he was going to London that day, and he had asked Mr. Jones to come to be with Cook while he was away. Between eleven and twelve on Monday night the waitress came and told me that Mr. Cook was very ill. I went up to his room. There was no one with him. He was sitting up a little on the bed, and seemed disappointed when I came in that it was not Palmer. He said it was Mr. Palmer he wanted. I did not remain in the room above two or three minutes. I did not go downstairs, but remained on the landing, and was still there when Mr. Palmer came. I could see into the room from where I was standing. Palmer went into the room, and I heard he was giving him some pills. He then came out to fetch some medicine, and was not many minutes away before he came back. After he returned, I heard Mr. Cook was very sick and very ill. He told Mr. Palmer he thought he should die, and he must not leave him. Mr. Palmer came out again, and I asked him if Cook had any relatives. He said he had only a stepfather. I saw Cook on Tuesday, between three and four, when Mr. Jones came. I took him a little jelly shortly after six. He seemed very anxious for it, and said if he did not have something he thought he should die. He seemed a little better. I did not see him again alive.

Sarah Bond

Cross-examined by Mr. GROVE—I did not see Palmer on the Monday evening until a little before twelve. The last train, which stops at Rugeley at eight o'clock, is not an express train. The express does not stop at Rugeley, and passengers coming by the express have to take some conveyance from Stafford. I cannot say when they would arrive in the ordinary course. On the Monday night when I went up to Cook's room he seemed disappointed that it was not Mr. Palmer. He seemed to be worse than he was. At that time Barnes had gone to fetch the doctor. Mr. Palmer came directly I left the room. I was led to ask what relatives the man had as he seemed so very ill, and I heard him telling Mr. Palmer he thought he should die.

W. H. Jones

Mr. WILLIAM HENRY JONES, examined by the ATTORNEY-GENERAL—I am a surgeon and medical practitioner at Lutterworth, and have been in practice for fifteen years. I have known the deceased, Cook, intimately for nearly five years. I have known of his acquaintance with William Palmer for over a year. He looked upon my house at Lutterworth as his home, and I attended him if there was anything the matter with him. His health was generally good, but he was not very robust. I think he hunted and played cricket. On the Tuesday of the Shrewsbury Races, the day on which his horse "Polestar" won, I spent the day with him at his invitation. We dined together in the evening at the Raven Hotel. He accompanied me when I left for the station. On our way there we called at the house of Mr. Fraill, the clerk of the course. I was present during a conversation they had along with Whitehouse, the jockey. Cook produced his betting book and calculated his winnings. He had seven to one. Cook was with me till I left the hotel at ten o'clock. He was not in the least the worse of liquor, and seemed to be in his usual health. On the Monday I received the following letter from Mr. Palmer:—

November 18, 1855.

My dear Sir,—Mr. Cook was taken ill at Shrewsbury, and obliged to call in a medical man; since then he has been confined to his bed here with a very severe bilious attack, combined with diarrhœa, and I think it advisable for you to come and see him as soon as possible.

W. H. Jones

I was ill on the Monday when I received the letter, and did not arrive at the Talbot Arms, Rugeley, till half-past three on Tuesday afternoon. I saw Cook there, and he expressed himself as very comfortable, but said he had been very ill at Shrewsbury. I examined Cook in Palmer's presence. His pulse was natural and his tongue was clean. When I remarked upon this to Palmer he said, "You should have seen it before." I prescribed nothing for Cook at that time. I visited him several times in the course of that afternoon, and he seemed improved in every way. I gave him a little toast and water, which was in the room, and which he vomited. There was no diarrhœa as far as I was aware. Mr. Bamford, who I learned from Palmer had been attending, came about seven o'clock. He expressed his satisfaction with Cook's improved state of health. Whilst Bamford, Palmer, and I were consulting what we should prescribe for him, Cook objected to the pills he had had the previous night. He said they made him ill. The three of us then withdrew, and Palmer proposed that Mr. Bamford should make up the morphine pills as before, but not to mention what they contained, as Cook objected so much to morphine. Mr. Bamford agreed to it, and went away. Palmer and I went into Cook's room. I was in and out of the room during the whole evening, and he seemed very comfortable. I observed no more vomiting nor any diarrhœa. There were no bilious symptoms whatever, nor were there any signs of his having recently suffered from a bilious attack. About eight o'clock I went with Palmer over to his house. I returned to Cook's room in about a quarter of an hour. Palmer came back about eleven o'clock with a box of pills. He opened them in my presence and showed me the directions on a slip of paper round the box. He remarked, "What an excellent hand for an old man upwards of eighty to write." It was very good writing indeed. Palmer proposed to Cook to take the pills, but he protested, as they had made him so ill the previous night. Ultimately he did take them, and he immediately vomited into the utensil. Both Palmer and I, at his request, searched the utensil for the pills, but we found nothing but the toast and water, so that the pills were retained. After he vomited he lay down very comfortably, and we left him. Before he had taken the pills he had expressed himself stronger, and had got up and sat in a chair. During the evening he had been very jocose, speaking of what he should do during the winter, and of his future plans and prospects. After he had taken those two pills, at eleven o'clock, I went downstairs and had some supper. I returned about twelve to his room, had some conversation with him, and then went to bed, it being arranged that I should sleep in his room, which was a double-bedded one, that night. At the time I last talked to him he seemed rather sleepy, but quite as well as usual, and there was nothing to excite any apprehension in my mind. I had been in bed ten minutes, and had not gone to sleep, when he suddenly started up in bed and called out, "Doctor, get up; I am going to be ill; ring the bell for Mr. Palmer." I rang the bell, and the chambermaid came to the door. He himself called out to her, "Fetch Mr. Palmer." He asked me to rub his neck. I rubbed the back part of his neck and supported him with my arm while doing so. There was a stiffening of the muscles; a sort of hardness about the neck. Palmer came very soon indeed; two or three minutes at the most. He made the remark, "I was never so quickly dressed in my life." I did not observe how he was dressed, as I was so engaged. He gave Cook two pills, which he said were ammonia pills. Directly he swallowed the pills he uttered loud screams, threw himself back in the bed, and was dreadfully convulsed. As the pills had immediately before been taken, it certainly could not have been from their action. He said to me, "Raise me up or I shall be suffocated." The convulsions lasted five or ten minutes. It was at the commencement of the convulsions that he called out to raise him up or he should be suffocated. All the muscular fibres were convulsed; there was a violent contraction of every muscle of the body, and a stiffening of the limbs. When he called out to me to raise him, I endeavoured to do so with the assistance of Mr. Palmer, but found it was quite impossible owing to the rigidity of the limbs. When he found I could not raise him up he asked me to turn him over, which I did. He was quite sensible. After I had turned him over I listened to the action of his heart. I found it gradually to weaken. I requested Palmer to fetch some spirits of ammonia in the hopes of reviving him. Palmer fetched a bottle from his house. He was not away above a minute. When he returned, Cook's heart was gradually sinking, and life was almost extinct. He died very quietly. He was not able to take the ammonia, and it was very soon after Palmer returned that he died. From the time when he raised himself in bed and called upon me to go for Palmer to the time when he died would be from ten minutes to a quarter of an hour. In my judgment, as a medical man, he died from tetanus, or, in ordinary English parlance, lockjaw.

Does it involve, ordinarily speaking, a mere locked jaw?—Yes, that is the common term. Locked jaw is one of the symptoms of tetanus. Every muscle in the body was affected in the same manner.

How would you express in ordinary English the general symptoms of what you call tetanus in one word?—Violent spasmodic affection of all the muscles of the body. That effects the immediate cause of death by stopping the action of the heart, and also the breath, from its effect on the diaphragm. It affects the respiratory muscles and stops respiration. It is that spasm of the respiratory muscles which causes the sense of suffocation. When death took place he was still upon his side. He remained in that position after death. I did not turn the body upon its back. The outward appearance of the body after death was very dark. As there was only one candle in the room, I could not make the observation I otherwise should have made. Both his hands, the left hand particularly, which I had in my hand, were clenched. I observed the clenching of the hands immediately the attack took place, when he threw himself back immediately after taking the pills Palmer brought over. When I was rubbing his neck I did not see the hands clenched.

Did you observe either before or at the time of death, or immediately afterwards, anything in the position of the head and neck?—Yes; the head was quite bent back.

When you say bent back, do you mean bent back into an unnatural position?—Yes; by spasmodic action. The body was twisted back like a bow; the backbone was twisted back.

W. H. Jones

By LORD CAMPBELL—When did you observe that appearance—immediately after death, or all the time?—Indeed, after throwing himself back, he was immediately drawn back.

Examination resumed—If I had placed the body at that time upon the back, on a level surface, it would have rested upon the head and heels. As his face was turned away from me, I did not observe anything immediately after or at the time of death about the jaw. After death I saw the jaw was not in its natural condition; it was all affected by spasmodic action. I spoke to Palmer about the laying out of the body, and left him alone in the room while I went downstairs to see Miss Bond. I returned in a few minutes and found Palmer with Mr. Cook's coat in his hand. He remarked that I, being Cook's nearest friend, should take possession of his effects. I did so, and took possession of his watch and his purse, containing five sovereigns and five shillings. That was all I could find. I did not find any betting book or any papers. After that, before Palmer left, he said something to me upon the subject of affairs as between Cook and himself. He said, as near as I can recollect, "It is a bad thing for me, as I was responsible for £3000 or £4000, and I hope Mr. Cook's friends will not let me lose it. If they do not assist me, all my horses will be seized." Nothing was said by him about securities or paper.

By LORD CAMPBELL—In the consultation which we three medical men had on Tuesday night nothing was said about the symptoms, the spasms, which had occurred the night before.

Cross-examined by Mr. SERJEANT SHEE—I know that Mr. Cook had been under treatment by Dr. Savage for some time.

You knew he had treated himself a good deal with mercurial treatment?— No, not a great deal. I know that he had had a sore throat for two or three months. In the summer it was bad. It was slightly ulcerated; not a very extreme case; the back part of the tongue. He could swallow, but it gave him a little pain occasionally. It depended upon what he did swallow. I knew he had found it necessary to apply caustic to his tongue. For two months before his death he had ceased to do it. After that he never complained of occasional pain in his throat or his tongue. I did not see much of him during these two months. He was attending most of the races.

W. H. Jones

Was he apprehensive about some spots which appeared upon his body?—I never heard him mention it. I had heard him express apprehensions of his being affected by secondary symptoms of venereal disease. His habits were, generally speaking, correct, though he may occasionally have gone astray, and perhaps was not very particular. I do not know that he had a chancre at the time he died, although I believe he had one twelve months ago. I was not present at either of the post-mortem examinations. I was at Shrewsbury Races with him on the Tuesday, and I knew he was very anxious, as the winning of the race was of great consequence to him. After the race was run he was so excited that for two or three minutes he could not speak to me. He was elated and happy the rest of the day, but he was not at all intoxicated. He was a very temperate man. That night when he was first attacked, and when Palmer came, Cook said, "Palmer, give me the remedy you gave me the night before." I was rubbing his neck for about five minutes, I should think. After I turned him over on his side to the time of his death three or four minutes would elapse. He died so very quietly that I could hardly tell when he did die. I have seen cases of tetanus before.

You said nothing about tetanus at the inquest?—Yes, I did; convulsions and tetanus.

Did you not say at the time it was from over-excitement that he died?—I could not tell the cause. I was so much taken by surprise. I said I had no idea of the cause of death.

Whatever you said about "violent convulsions," did you say, "I could not tell the cause; I imagined at the time it was from over-excitement"?—Yes.

[The deposition of the witness before the coroner was read.]

You say in your deposition you had been in your bed a quarter of an hour or twenty minutes. Was it not as much as twenty minutes?—I do not think it was. I had not begun to dose. I do not remember ever having stated I thought he died of epilepsy. Mr. Bamford said it was apoplexy; I said it was not. I could not make up my mind what sort of fit it was. I said it was more like an epileptic fit than apoplexy.

Re-examined—There was a partnership between Cook and Palmer about the mare "Pereine," but it was discontinued some months before Cook's death, and the mare became the property of Palmer. I have only seen one case of traumatic tetanus.

Was that from a wound?—From a wound in the thumb. It ended in death.

How long was the patient in dying from the time he received the wound?—Three days. The patient died of lockjaw. I have seen cases of epilepsy.

Are there any such symptoms in epileptic fits as those convulsive spasms of the muscles?—No; the consciousness is lost, and there is none of this rigidity of the muscles. In apoplexy consciousness is generally lost too. I am satisfied in my own mind that this case was not apoplexy.

W. H. Jones

By LORD CAMPBELL—Supposing he had any secondary symptoms of syphilis, do you think they could have produced the symptoms you saw on the Tuesday night?—No, I say not, decidedly, and for two months before death he was clear of them, and the throat was well.

E. Mills

ELIZABETH MILLS was recalled and said that on the Monday morning Cook told her that during the night he had been disturbed. He said, "I was just mad for two minutes." She asked him why he did not ring the bell, and he replied he thought we should all be fast asleep, and it passed over. He said he thought he was disturbed by hearing a quarrel in the street.

By LORD CAMPBELL—What did he say about the street?—He thought he was disturbed by hearing a quarrel in the street. He was not sure that it was that which had made him ill; that he might have been asleep, and the quarrel might have disturbed him. I cannot positively recollect whether he said so or not.

H. Savage

HENRY SAVAGE, examined—I am a physician. I have known the deceased man Cook for about four years. He was not a man of robust constitution, but his general health was good. In the spring of 1855 he consulted me about some spots on his skin—one on his arm and one on his forehead. He had two shallow ulcers on the tongue corresponding to bad teeth. He thought these spots and ulcerations were secondary syphilitic symptoms, and had been undergoing a mild mercurial course. I recommended its immediate discontinuance, and prescribed him quinine as a tonic, and an aperient containing cream of tartar, magnesia, and sulphur. I never at any time gave him antimony. He was quite well by the end of May. He still continued to see me, as he was not quite sure about the correctness of my notions of his not having syphilis. I examined him from time to time, and the only thing the matter with his throat was that one of his tonsils was slightly enlarged; it was red and tender. There was nothing of a syphilitic character in the appearance of his throat. I saw him about a fortnight before his death, when I recommended him to go abroad for two years, as I wished to get him away from his turf associations. I examined him thoroughly at that time, and beyond a very shallow scar of some former excoriation, to which he told me he was liable, there was nothing venereal about him. There was no chancre nor any sore on any other part of his body.

Cross-examined—He was a weak man, and apt to take the advice of any person he might be in company with. The last time I saw him he had a redness over one tonsil, showing there was tenderness. He had three or four superficial ulcers on his lips.

CHARLES NEWTON, examined—I am assistant to Mr. Salt, practising surgeon at Rugeley. On Monday, 19th November, about nine o'clock in the evening, Palmer came in to Mr. Salt's surgery. He asked me for three grains of strychnia, which I gave to him. I do not think he was in the shop above two minutes. Between eleven and twelve on the next day I saw him again in the shop of Mr. Hawkins, a druggist. He was in the shop when I went in. He put his hand between my shoulders and said he wished to speak to me. I went to the door with him and out into the street. He asked me when Mr. Edwin Salt, the son of Mr. Salt, was going up to his farm at Sudbury. Palmer had nothing to do with that at all. While we were talking, a Mr. Brassington came up and entered into conversation with me about some bills for money he had against my employer. Palmer left us and returned to the shop, and came out again while we were still talking. He went in the direction of his own house, which is between 200 and 300 yards away. I went into the shop after my conversation with Mr. Brassington and saw Roberts, who was serving. I know Mr. Thirlby, who deals in drugs. He was formerly an assistant to Palmer, and succeeded to his business. He dispenses all Palmer's medicines for him. About seven o'clock in the evening of Sunday, the 25th November, I went to Palmer's house in consequence of being sent for by him. There was no one else there. He asked me what dose of strychnia would kill a dog, and whether it would be found in the stomach. I told him a grain, and that there would be no inflammation, and I did not think it would be found. I think he said, "It is all right," as if speaking to himself, and snapped his fingers. I heard the next day that the post-mortem examination of Cook's body was to take place. On my way to the post-mortem, about ten o'clock in the forenoon, I saw Palmer at Bamford's, and I told him where I was going. He, Dr. Harland, and I went down together to the Talbot Arms for the examination. Palmer and I were left alone together in the entrance to the hall. He remarked it would be a stiff job, and asked me to go over to his house for some brandy. We did so. While we were taking the brandy he said, "You will find this fellow suffering from diseased throat; he has had syphilis." We then returned to the Talbot Arms. I was examined before the coroner, but I said nothing about giving Palmer the three grains of strychnia on Monday night.

Cross-examined—When I was first examined on behalf of the Crown I mentioned the circumstance of the conversation about poisoning the dog. Before that I mentioned it to Mr. Salt, but I cannot remember when. I gave a statement to Mr. Gardner some time after the inquest. I mentioned about the dog, but did not speak about the 3 grains of strychnia. I made no mention about these matters at the inquest. I gave evidence about my conversation with Palmer at the door of Hawkins' shop. I knew my evidence was with reference to the supposed purchase of strychnia by Palmer at the shop. The first time I informed the Crown with reference to the purchase of the 3 grains on the Monday was on Tuesday last. At the post-mortem examination I did not point out any chancre to the medical men there. It was not mentioned at all, and I did not see one nor the marks of one.

Re-examined—The reason why I did not mention about the purchase of the 3 grains of strychnia before last Tuesday to the Crown was because Mr. Salt was not on speaking terms with Mr. Palmer, and I thought Mr. Salt would be angry at my letting him have it. I communicated the fact of my own accord.

The Court then adjourned.

Third Day, Friday, 16th May, 1856.

The Court met at ten o'clock.

C. J. Roberts

CHARLES JOSEPH ROBERTS, examined by Mr. JAMES—In November last I was an apprentice to Mr. Hawkins, a chemist at Rugeley. I remember that between eleven and twelve o'clock on Tuesday, 20th November, Palmer came into the shop and asked me first for 2 drachms of prussic acid. Whilst I was putting it up for him Mr. Newton came in. Palmer said he wanted to speak to him, and the two of them went out of the shop together. I saw Brassington come up and speak to Newton when Palmer left them and came back into the shop. I was putting the prussic acid into the bottle, and he asked me for 6 grains of strychnine and 2 drachms of Batley's solution of opium. While I was making the things up Palmer stood at the shop door with his back to me, looking into the street. He then took them away and paid for them. After he left Newton came into the shop, and I had some conversation with him. It would be two years before this transaction that Palmer bought drugs in our shop. He always dealt with Thirlby, who previously was his assistant, and is now practising as an apothecary in Palmer's name.

Cross-examined—I did not make any entry of the transaction in our book. I am not in the habit of doing so when things are sold over the counter.

W. V. Stevens

WILLIAM VERNON STEVENS, examined by the ATTORNEY-GENERAL—I am a retired merchant living in the city. I am the step-father of John Parsons Cook, having married his father's widow eighteen years ago. He did not live with me, but we were always on friendly terms. He became entitled to property worth about £12,000. The last time I saw him alive was at Euston station at two o'clock on the afternoon of 5th November. He looked better than I had seen him for some time, and I said, "My boy, you look very well; you do not look anything of an invalid now." He struck himself firmly on the chest and said he was quite well. The next time I saw him was after his death, information of which I received from Mr. Jones, who came to my house on the Wednesday. I went to Lutterworth on the Thursday to search for a will and any papers he had left. I found a will. When I reached Rugeley the next day I went to the Talbot Arms, and met Palmer in the passage. I had only seen him once before. Mr. Jones introduced us in the inn, and we then went up and viewed the body. I was greatly struck by the appearance of the countenance, the tightness of the muscles across the face. We all then went down to one of the sitting rooms, and I said to the prisoner that I understood from Mr. Jones he knew something of my son's affairs. He replied, "Yes, there are £4000 worth of bills out of his, and I am sorry to say my name is to them; but I have got a paper drawn up by a lawyer, signed by Mr. Cook, to show that I have never had any benefit from them." I told him I feared there would be no money to pay them, and asked if he had no horses or property. He replied that he had horses, but they were mortgaged. He mentioned one debt of £300 that was owing to Cook. It had nothing to do with sporting matters, and was a personal debt from a relative of his. I then turned round to Palmer and said that, whether Cook had left anything or not, he must be buried. Palmer immediately said, "Oh! I will bury him myself if that is all." I replied I could not hear of that. Cook's brother-in-law was there at the time, and he also expressed a wish to bury him. I said it was my business, as executor, to bury him, and that I intended to bury him in London in his mother's grave, and that the body would have to be at the inn for a day or two. Palmer said that would be of no consequence so long as the body was fastened up at once. Some short time afterwards I asked Palmer for the name of some respectable undertaker in Rugeley, so that I might order a coffin at once. He replied, "I have been and chosen that. I have ordered a shell and a strong oak coffin." I expressed my surprise, and said he had no authority to do so. At my invitation, my son-in-law, Mr. Jones, and Palmer all dined with me at the inn. We dined about three, as I was going back to London by the quarter-past four train. Before I left I asked Mr. Jones to go upstairs and bring me Cook's betting book and any papers. He went along with Palmer, and in about ten minutes he returned, saying he could find no book or paper. I expressed my astonishment, and Palmer said, "It is of no manner of use if you find it." I said I was the best judge of that, and I understood my son won a great deal of money at Shrewsbury. Palmer replied that when a man dies his bets are done with, and that Mr. Cook had received the greater part of his money on the course at Shrewsbury. I said that the book must be found, and he replied in a much quieter tone, "Oh, it will be found, no doubt." The body was in the shell, and I noticed that both the hands were clenched. I then returned to town. The next morning I communicated with the uncle of the deceased and with my solicitor, who gave me a letter to Mr. Gardner, of Rugeley. I returned to Rugeley by the two o'clock train, arriving there about eight. Palmer travelled by the same train. I met him first at Euston station, when he told me he had been summoned to London by telegraph. I saw him again in the refreshment room at Wolverton. We had some conversation, and I remarked that it would be as well to know something of the complaint of which Cook died, and that I should like his body opened. Palmer replied, "That can be done very well," or "That can be easily done," or something of that sort. I saw him again in the refreshment room at Rugby, and mentioned to him my determination to see a solicitor in Rugeley about my son's affairs. From Rugby to Rugeley we travelled in the same carriage, but no further conversation took place. When we arrived at Rugeley he again spoke about me employing a solicitor, and offered to introduce me to one. I refused his offer, and said I would find one myself. I then immediately purposely changed the tone of my voice and manner, and said, "Mr. Palmer, if I should call in a solicitor to give me advice, I suppose you will have no objections to answer him any questions he might choose to put to you?" He replied, with a spasmodic affection of the throat, which was perfectly evident, "Oh, no, certainly not." I also expressed my desire of taking a solicitor to Hednesford, where Cook's horses were kept. I ought to say that, when I first mentioned the post-mortem, there was not the slightest change in Mr. Palmer's manner; he was perfectly calm and collected. We then parted, he to go home and I to go and look for Mr. Gardner. Later in the evening Palmer came to me again, and the first thing he spoke about was the bills. He said, "It is a very unpleasant affair for me about these bills." I remarked that I had heard a different account of Mr. Cook's affairs, and that his affairs could only be settled in the Court of Chancery. All he replied was, "Oh, indeed," in a lower tone. The next day, Sunday, I saw him again in the coffee room of my hotel. He advised me not to take a solicitor to Hednesford, but I told him I should use my own judgment upon that. Later in the evening, I think, I saw him again. I asked him who the Mr. Smith was who had sat up with my son, as I wished to make inquiries regarding the missing betting book. He replied he was a solicitor of that town. I asked him if he attended my son medically, and he said no. He then asked me if I knew who was to perform the examination, and I told him I did not. On the Friday, when I twice saw the body, I did not perceive any decomposition or anything which called for its being speedily put into a shell; on the contrary, the body did not quite look to me like a dead body.

W. V. Stevens

Cross-examined by Mr. SERJEANT SHEE—The last time my stepson stayed in my house was for about a month, in January and February of last year. He had a slight sore throat then, but I do not know that it was continuously sore. He did not complain of it. I never noticed any ulcers about his face. Between that time and the 5th November I saw him several times, and he did not appear to be more delicate than usual. The reason why I mentioned to him on 5th November that he was looking very well was because he had complained of being an invalid the winter before. His brother and sister were rather delicate, and his father died at the age of thirty or thirty-one.

J. T. Harland

Dr. JOHN THOMAS HARLAND, examined by Mr. BODKIN—I am a physician residing at Stafford. On 26th November I made a post-mortem examination of Mr. Cook. I called at the house of Mr. Bamford, and on my way there I was joined by Palmer, whom I had frequently seen and spoken to at Rugeley. He said, "I am glad you have come to make a post-mortem examination; some one might have been sent whom I did not know; I know you." I asked him what the case was; that I heard there was a suspicion of poisoning. He replied, "Oh, no! I think not; he had an epileptic fit on Monday and Tuesday night, and you will find an old disease in the heart and in the head." Palmer offered to lend me instruments, as I had brought none with me. He said a queer old man seemed to suspect him. He also said, "He seems to suspect that I have got the betting book, but Cook had no betting book that would be of use to any one." After we reached Bamford's house, Mr. Bamford and I went to Mr. Frere's, a surgeon in Rugeley, and from there to the Talbot Arms, where the post-mortem examination was proceeded with. Palmer and several others were in the room. Mr. Devonshire operated and Mr. Newton assisted him. The body seemed to me to be stiffer than bodies generally are six days after death. The muscles were strongly contracted and thrown out, which showed there was a strong spasmodic action in the body before death. The hands were clenched; firmly closed. The abdominal viscera were the first parts of the body examined internally. They were taken out of the body, and were in a perfectly healthy state. The liver was healthy. The lungs were healthy; there was blood in them, but not more than could be accounted for by gravitation. The brain was quite healthy. There was no extravasation of blood nor serum on the brain. There was nothing in its appearance that would cause unnatural pressure. The heart was contracted, and contained no blood. This did not appear to be the result of disease, but from spasmodic action. The stomach was taken out. At the larger end there were numerous small yellowish-white spots about the size of mustard seed. These would not at all account for death, nor would they have any effect on the health of any one. There may have been numerous follicles, nothing more. The kidneys were full of blood that had gravitated since death, and had no appearance of disease. The blood was in a fluid state, which is a rare occurrence even in cases of sudden death. About the whole body generally there was no appearance of disease that would account for death. The lower part of the spinal cord was not minutely examined on this occasion. The upper part presented a perfectly natural appearance.

J. T. Harland

On the 25th of January the body was again exhumed, so that we might examine the spinal cord with more attention. Dr. Monckton and I jointly made a report on the matter. I am still of the opinion that there was nothing in the appearance that I have described to account for the death of the deceased. When the stomach and intestines were removed from the body in the first examination they were separately emptied into a jar by Mr. Devonshire and Mr. Newton. Palmer was standing at the right of Mr. Newton. When the intestines and stomach were being placed in the jar, and while Mr. Devonshire was opening the stomach, I noticed Palmer pushed Mr. Newton on to Mr. Devonshire, and he shook a portion of the contents of the stomach into the body. I thought a joke was passing among them, and I said, "Do not do that," to the whole. Palmer was the only one close to them when Mr. Newton and Mr. Devonshire were pushed together. After this interruption the opening of the stomach proceeded. It contained about, I should think, 2 or 3 ounces of brownish liquid. It was stated that there was nothing particular found in the stomach, and Palmer remarked to Mr. Bamford, "They will not hang us yet." The stomach was then emptied into the jar along with the stomach itself. The intestines were then examined, and nothing particular found in them. They were contracted and very small. They were placed in the jar, with their contents, as they were taken from the body. I then tied the jar over with two bladders and sealed it, and placed it on the table beside the body. At that time Palmer was moving about the room. My attention had been called away by the examination, and I missed the jar for a few minutes. I called out, "Where is the jar?" and Palmer, from the other end of the room, said, "It is here; I thought it more convenient for you to take it away." Palmer was standing a yard or two from a door at that end of the room. I got the jar from him. I found there was a cut, hardly an inch long, through both bladders. The cut was quite clean, as if nothing had passed through. I asked who had done this, and Palmer, Mr. Devonshire, and Mr. Newton all seemed to say they had not done it. I told Palmer I should take the jar to Mr. Frere. He said, "I would rather you take it with you to Stafford, if you would take it there," but I took it to Mr. Frere's house, tied and sealed in the way I have told. When I noticed the slit in the bladders I immediately cut the strings and replaced the bladders, and tied them separately again, so that the slit was not at the top. When I returned to the Talbot Arms Palmer asked me what I had done with the jar. I said I had left it with Mr. Frere, and that it would go to either London or Birmingham that night for examination.

Cross-examined by SERJEANT SHEE—On the occasion of the first examination you say you observed follicles under the tongue; are those pustules?—Not under the tongue, on the tongue. They are not pustules; they are large mucous follicles, not containing matter.

Is it a sort of thickening, then, of the skin?—Of the mucous follicles at the base of the tongue. They appeared to be of long standing, and were very numerous.

Do they indicate that there had been much soreness there?—I have no doubt they would produce inconvenience. They must have given some slight degree of pain in eating and speaking.

Will you undertake to say they were not enlarged glands, enlarged by the irritation of disease?—I do not believe they were; I have seen them frequently.

Do you adhere to your opinion that the lungs were healthy?—Yes.

Did not Mr. Devonshire, in your presence, express a contrary opinion, and say they were unhealthy?—He said he thought there was emphysema, as well as congestion of the lungs.

Is that not a diseased state of the lungs?—Yes, it is an abnormal state. I examined the white spots on the wider part of the stomach.

How did you examine them?—By removing the mucous that was on the surface of the stomach by the finger or scalpel. I had no lens, no glass. I should have examined them with a lens if I had had one.

Was your examination of these appearances satisfactory to you without a lens?—Yes.

You said that the brain was healthy; what sort of examination did you make of the brain?—The brain was carefully taken out; the external part was first of all examined; the membranes were examined, and slices were taken off from the apex to the base of the brain. These slices were, I should think, a quarter of an inch thick.

Is that as thick as it should be to make a full examination?—I think that would show any disease if there was any. The spinal cord was examined down to the first vertebra, and we found no appearance of disease.

Supposing you had discovered a softness of the spinal cord on that occasion, after a full examination, might not that have been sufficient to account for the death of Mr. Cook?—No, certainly not; softening would not produce tetanus at all; it might produce paralysis.

J. T. Harland

Do not you think in the case of a man dying by convulsions, in order to ascertain with any degree of certainty what the cause of his death might be, it was necessary shortly after his death to make a careful examination of the spinal cord?—No, I do not. It was afterwards thought desirable. It was first suggested on 26th December.

It was in January the second examination took place; supposing there had been a softening, do not you think, in order to discover it, it was necessary to examine the spinal cord at an earlier period after death than two months?—If there had been a softening it would have been detected at the second examination; the body remaining unexamined for a long time would not produce hardening of the spine.

That is your opinion; might not any softening at that late period be the result of decomposition?—The spine was very little soft indeed. There were some appearances of decomposition upon it. I examined him to see if there was any disease on him of the venereal kind. I observed there was a loss of substance from past disease. It was cicatrised over, and on the cicatrix there was a small abrasion.

Then it must have been in a sore state?—The excoriation might be a little sore. It was very small. It was a mere excoriation; merely a little of the excoriation rubbed off.

Re-examined—There were no chancres, nothing beyond what I would term an excoriation, except the cicatrix from the old disease. There was no symptom of ulcerated throat, nor any appearance of anything syphilitic there. The follicles in the tongue are often produced by a disordered stomach, and are of no serious consequence to health. The congestion of the lungs, which Mr. Devonshire spoke about, was due, in my opinion, wholly to the gravitation of blood after death. There was nothing whatever in the brain to indicate the presence of any disease. Even if there had been, I have never heard or read of any diseased state of the brain occasioning death by tetanus. There is no disease of the spinal cord with which I am acquainted which produces tetanus and that form of death. Sometimes with inflammation of the membranes of the spinal cord there is tetanus; but there were no appearances of inflammation whatever.

C. J. Devonshire

CHARLES JOHN DEVONSHIRE, examined by Mr. HUDDLESTON—I am an undergraduate of London University. I performed the post-mortem on 25th November at the Talbot Hotel. The body was pale. The fingers were clenched firmly; the thumb of the left hand was thrown into the palm, and the fingers were clenched over. The mouth was a little contracted. The body was stiff, much beyond the usual stiffness of death. I took out the stomach and opened it with a pair of scissors. As I was opening the stomach there was a pressure or push from behind. I did not pay any attention to it, and I do not think any of the contents of the stomach escaped. I punctured the anterior surface of the stomach, and a spoonful of the contents fell out on the chair. I tied up where it was punctured, and it was put into a jar and sealed by Dr. Harland. On the same day I got the jar at Mr. Frere's, and gave it, on the 28th, to Mr. Boycott, Messrs. Lander & Gardner's clerk. The body was opened again on the 29th to get the liver and kidneys and spleen. They were taken from the body with some blood, placed in a stone jar, which I sealed and handed to Mr. Boycott on the 30th. In consequence of something Mr. Palmer had said, I examined the body to find if there were any indications of syphilis, but I found none. I also took out the throat, and found there were natural papillæ there; they were larger than usual at the base of the tongue.

John Myatt

JOHN MYATT—I am postboy at the Talbot Arms at Rugeley. On 28th of November last I was engaged to drive Mr. Stevens to Stafford station. Before I started Mr. Palmer asked me if I was going to drive them to Stafford. I told him I was. He asked if I was going to take the jars. I said I believed I was. He said there was a £10 note for me if I would upset them. I told him I should not. I saw him next morning, and he asked me who went with the fly. I said Mr. Stevens, and I believed one of Mr. Gardner's clerks.

Cross-examined—How did you know what he meant by "going to drive them to Stafford"?—I knew I was going to take some one to Stafford.

Did he use the name "Stevens" before he used these words to you?—He mentioned Mr. Stevens afterwards.

You understood the word "them" to mean Mr. Stevens and his party?—Yes.

Were the words used not to this effect, "I should not mind giving £10 to break Mr. Stevens' neck"?—I do not remember that.

The "£10 to upset him"?—These were the words to the best of my recollection.

When he said "to upset him" did he say anything about him at the time?— He did say something about it, that it was a humbugging concern, or something to that effect. I do not recollect him saying he was a suspicious, troublesome fellow.

S. Cheshire

SAMUEL CHESHIRE—I was for upwards of eight years postmaster at Rugeley. I am now from Newgate suffering punishment for having opened a letter as postmaster. I know the prisoner very well, he and I having been schoolfellows together. I was with him at Shrewsbury Races the day "Polestar" won. I saw Mr. Cook at the Talbot Arms on the Saturday, 17th November. He was in bed at the time. On the Tuesday following Palmer asked me to meet him at his house and bring a receipt stamp with me. I did so. He said he wanted me to write out a cheque, which, he said, was for money Mr. Cook owed him. He produced a copy from which I was to write, and I copied it. He gave me as a reason why he wanted me to write it that Mr. Cook was too ill, and he said Wetherby would know his writing. After I had written it I left it with him, and he said he was going to take it over for Mr. Cook to sign.

The ATTORNEY-GENERAL—We know that it went out of his possession afterwards, and therefore perhaps we ought to follow it.

[Evidence was then given to show that this cheque for £350 was sent to Mr. Wetherby, the secretary to the Jockey Club, that it was returned to Palmer, that notice to produce it was given by the prosecution, and that it was not produced.]

S. Cheshire

SAMUEL CHESHIRE, recalled—After Mr. Cook's death, on the Thursday or Friday, Palmer sent for me again. I went to his house and saw him there. He had a sheet of quarto paper in his hand, which he asked me to sign.

LORD CAMPBELL—Was there anything written upon this quarto sheet of paper?—There was.

Examination resumed—I asked him what it was, and he said, "You know that Cook and I have had some dealings together, and this is a document which he gave me some days ago, and I want you to witness it." I asked him what it was about, and he replied, "There is some business that I have joined him in, and which was all for Mr. Cook's benefit, and this is a document stating so," or something of that kind. The paper was a post quarto paper of a yellow description. I observed the writing on it, and thought it was Mr. Palmer's. I told him I could not sign it, as I might perhaps be called upon to give evidence in the matter at some future day. I said I had not seen Cook sign it, and that the post office authorities would not like me to be called on to give evidence as to a document which took place while I was absent. Palmer replied that it did not matter my signing it, and he dared say they would not object to Mr. Cook's signature. I gave the paper back to him and left.

(Notice to produce this paper was given, but it was not produced.)

S. Cheshire

Palmer was in the habit of calling for letters addressed to his mother, and which I gave to him. I cannot remember whether during October and November, 1855, I gave him letters addressed to his mother or addressed to Mr. Cook. I remember seeing Palmer while the inquest was going on. He came to me on the Sunday evening previous to 5th December, and asked me to let him know if I had seen or heard anything fresh. I understood that was a temptation for me to open a letter, and I told him I could not do that. He said he did not want me to do anything to injure myself. The letter which I read, and for which I am suffering, was a letter from Dr. Taylor to Mr. Gardner, the solicitor. I did not give nor send that letter to Palmer. I merely told him in few words of its contents. I only read part of the letter, and told Palmer the contents as much as I remembered. That was on the morning of the 5th of December. I told Palmer that I found in Dr. Taylor's letter that there were no traces of strychnia found. I cannot recollect what else I told him. He said he knew they would not, for he was perfectly innocent.

Captain JOHN HAINES HATTON—I am chief constable of the police of Staffordshire.

Did you obtain this letter, which I have just proved to be in Palmer's handwriting, and envelope from Mr. Ward, the coroner?—I did; I endorsed it.

My dear Sir,—I am sorry to tell you that I am still confined to my bed. I do not think it was mentioned at the inquest yesterday that Cook was taken ill on Sunday and Monday night in the same way as he was on the Tuesday night when he died. The chambermaid at the Crown Hotel, Masters, can prove this. I also believe that a man by the name of Fisher is coming down to prove he received some money at Shrewsbury. Now here he could only pay Smith £10 out of £41 he owed him. Had you better not call Smith to prove this? And again, whatever Professor Taylor may say to-morrow, he wrote from London last Tuesday night to Gardner to say "We have this day finished our analysis, and find no traces of either strychnia, prussic acid, or opium." What can beat this from a man like Taylor, if he says what he has already said, and Dr. Harland's evidence? Mind you, I know, and saw it in black and white, what Taylor said to Gardner, but this is strictly private and confidential, but it is true. As regards his betting book, I know nothing of it, and it is of no good to any one. I hope the verdict to-morrow will be that he died of natural causes, and thus end it.—Ever yours.

SAMUEL CHESHIRE, recalled, cross-examined—I knew Cook very well, but I could not speak to his handwriting. I am sure that when Palmer came to me he used the words, "seen or heard anything." He did not simply ask if I had "heard anything." On the Saturday before Cook's death I dined with Palmer and Mr. Smith. Cook was expected to dine also, but he was too ill. Palmer said he must call in Bamford.

GEORGE HERRING—I knew Mr. Cook. I was at Shrewsbury Races last November, staying at the Raven, and saw Cook each day. I saw him with money on the Wednesday. He was counting up a lot of Bank of England and other notes. I could not say how many there were, but there were a considerable number. He showed me his betting book, containing entries of bets made at the races. On Monday, 19th November, I received a letter from Palmer asking me to call upon him at 7 Beaufort Buildings at half-past two that day. I called, and he said he wished to see me about settling Cook's account, as the physician had advised Cook not to go out that day, it being damp. Palmer had a paper in his hand, and read out from it a number of items which he asked me to take down. I did so, and I have here the list I made. He said—"Receive of Ingham, £350; Barr, £300; Green, £140; Morris, £200; Nelson, £30; pay yourself £6 and Shelley £30." I said that made it £984, and he said—"That is what Cook makes it; if I give you £16 it will make £1000; out of that pay yourself for my bill." I said, "I know no difference between the two bills"; he said, "Pay Padwick £550 and Pratt £450, making £1000." He asked me to send cheque for the last two at once. I refused to do so, as I had not received the money. He wished me particularly to pay Pratt the £450, as he said it was for a bill or joint-bill of sale on the mare. I had an account of £45 against Palmer, while he had one of £40 against me. He settled this £5, along with the £16 to make up the £1000 previously spoken to, by a Bank of England £50 note. I do not know the number of the note. Before he left he pressed me to send the cheques to Pratt and Padwick immediately before the closing of the bank. He said, "When you have settled this account write down word to either me or Cook." I replied, "I shall certainly write to Mr. Cook," because I thought I was settling Mr. Cook's account. He said, "It does not matter which." I asked him if I addressed the letter, "Mr. Cook, Palmer, Rugeley, would that be correct," and he said "yes." I received all the money at Tattersall's on Cook's account, except £110 of Mr. Morris, who only paid £90 instead of £200. I sent a cheque for £450 to Pratt from Tattersall's. I wrote a letter to Cook from Tattersall's. The next day I received a telegraphic message, which I gave to Captain Hatton on the coroner's inquest. In consequence of this message I wrote a letter the same day to Cook.

(Evidence was given to show that Herring held three bills of exchange, each for £200, on which Cook and Palmer were jointly responsible to him. He received £200 from Cook on one bill; another £200 bill he deducted, as instructed by Palmer from the £1000. The third bill he paid himself for by not paying Padwick as Palmer instructed him. Besides these bills Herring held a fourth for £500 drawn by Palmer on his mother, and endorsed by him and Cook. It was proved that this acceptance was not in Mrs. Palmer's handwriting.)

The Court then adjourned.

Fourth Day, Saturday, 17th May, 1856.

The Court met at ten o'clock.

> George Bate

GEORGE BATE, examined by Mr. JAMES—I am a farmer, and was in the employment of the prisoner during September, October, and November of last year. I was engaged to look after his horses, and received no stated salary, sometimes two sovereigns and sometimes one sovereign a week. I remember in the month of September, 1856, being in the company of Mr. Cook and Mr. Palmer. Something was said by one of them to me about an insurance being proposed on my life.

Mr. SERJEANT SHEE objected to this evidence, and his objection was sustained.

> T. B. Curling

Mr. THOMAS BLIZZARD CURLING, examined by the ATTORNEY-GENERAL—I am a Fellow of the College of Surgeons, and surgeon to the London Hospital. I have published a work on the subject of tetanus. Tetanus signifies spasmodic affection of the voluntary muscles of the body. There are two sorts of tetanus, idiopathic and traumatic. Idiopathic tetanus is tetanus originating, as it were, as a primary disease, without any wound. Traumatic is from a wound. During twenty-two years I have been surgeon to the London Hospital. I have never seen a case of idiopathic tetanus. I have seen over fifty cases of traumatic tetanus. Traumatic tetanus first manifests itself by a stiffness about the jaws and the back of the neck; rigidity of the muscles of the abdomen usually sets in; a dragging pain at the pit of the stomach is almost a constant attendant of spasm of the diaphragm, and in many cases the muscles of the back are sensibly affected. Then the spasms, though continuous, are liable to aggravation in paroxysms. As the disease goes on these paroxysms become more frequent and more severe. When they occur, the body is drawn backwards; in some instances, though less frequently, it is bent forwards; then, in an acute case, a difficulty in swallowing is a very common thing; a difficulty in breathing also during the paroxysm, a choking sensation. The disease may end, supposing it be fatal, in two ways; the patient may die somewhat suddenly of suffocation, owing to closure of the opening of the windpipe, or the patient may be worn out by the severe and painful spasms, and the muscles may relax and the patient gradually sink and die.

Traumatic tetanus is generally fatal, and the locking of the jaw is an almost invariable symptom. A symptom very characteristic of the disease is a contracted condition of the eyelids, a raising of the angles of the mouth, and a contraction of the brow. The lower extremities are sometimes affected, and sometimes the upper; the muscles affected are chiefly those of the trunk. I have never heard of traumatic tetanus being produced from sore throat or from chancre. A case of traumatic tetanus which ends fatally takes from one day to four days, or longer, before death ensues. I never heard of a case in which a man would be attacked one day and then have twenty-four hours' respite, and be again attacked the next. The symptoms of the death of Mr. Cook, given by Mr. Jones, the surgeon, were not consistent with any form of traumatic tetanus I ever heard of. There was the sudden onset of the fatal symptoms; in all cases that have fallen under my notice the disease has been preceded by the milder symptoms of tetanus. The symptoms given by the woman Mills as to the Monday night were not those of tetanus. The sudden onset and rapid subsidence are not consistent with what I call the true form of tetanus. The poison, nux vomica, produces tetanic convulsions.

Cross-examined by Mr. SERJEANT SHEE—Any irritation of the nerves proceeding to the spinal cord might produce tetanus. I agree with Dr. Watson in his "Lectures on the Principles and Practice of Physic," that all the symptoms of tetanic convulsions may arise from such slight causes as the sticking of a fish bone, the mere stroke of a whip lash under the eye, from the cutting of a corn, from the bite on the finger by a tame sparrow, from the extraction of a tooth, from the operation of cupping, and simple things of that character. Idiopathic tetanus would not be so likely to bring the patient to the hospital as a sudden wound leading to traumatic tetanus. A syphilitic sore would not be likely to lead to tetanus.

Re-examined by the ATTORNEY-GENERAL—A medical practitioner who saw a case of convulsions would be able at once to know the difference between symptoms of general convulsions and of tetanus. One of the characteristic features of tetanus is that the consciousness is not affected.

Robert Todd

Dr. ROBERT TODD, examined by the ATTORNEY-GENERAL—I have been in practice as a doctor for twenty-five years, and have been a physician to King's College Hospital for many years. I have lectured on the disease called tetanus, and have published the lectures. I have seen two cases of what seemed to be idiopathic tetanus. It is a very rare thing. The term tetanus ought not to be applied to cases of poisoning, for the symptoms are so essentially distinct from the disease. I have had under my own observation cases of traumatic tetanus. When once the disease has begun there are remissions, but not complete; rather a diminution of the severity of the symptoms. There are two classes—an acute class and a chronic class. The acute cases will terminate in the course of three or four days, and the chronic cases will go on from nineteen to twenty-two or twenty-three days, perhaps longer. Sometimes epilepsy will produce convulsions, and sometimes the convulsions from epilepsy assume somewhat of a tetanic character, but they are essentially distinct from tetanus. When the epileptic convulsions assume somewhat of the tetanic form, it is quickly over, not continuous. In epilepsy there is an abolition of consciousness for the time. I have heard the symptoms described which accompanied this gentleman's seizure and death, and also the appearances after death and the post-mortem examination. I am of opinion there was neither apoplexy nor epilepsy. There are poisons which will produce tetanic convulsions. The chief of these poisons is nux vomica. I have seen animal life destroyed by strychnia, but never human life. The effects of a large dose, such as a grain of strychnia given in a liquid form to a cat or dog, would be apparent in the course of ten minutes. The symptoms would be spasmodic action of the muscles, chiefly of the trunk, the spine, the spinal muscles, producing a very marked opisthotonos, as it is called, where the spine is thrown back, the head thrown back, and the trunk bowed in a very marked manner. The extremities are generally stiffened, jerked out with violent jerks. The muscles are rendered stiff and rigid from the spasms. The stiffness remains, and does not perfectly relax. Fresh paroxysms come in always attended with the peculiar curving back of the head and neck and spine. The extremities of the animals are powerfully stiffened out, distended, every now and then powerfully bent, and jerked out again. Death ensues within half an hour, unless it is a small dose. There is a marked difference between cases where death ensues after taking strychnia and a case of tetanus such as I was describing just now from idiopathic or traumatic causes. The continuity of the symptoms in strychnia poisoning is very characteristic: as long as the poisonous influence lasts, the symptoms last, but the poisonous symptoms will subside after a time. The shortness of the duration of the symptoms is decidedly in favour of strychnine poisoning. There are no other poisons that I know of that produce convulsions of a tetanic character. The symptoms described which attended this gentleman's death are not referable to idiopathic or traumatic tetanus. I have never seen a person die from the administration of strychnia, but I have seen a person suffer from the consequences of an overdose. There was the opisthotonos and there was the consciousness perfectly retained. There was also dilation of the pupils, a peculiar convulsion of the muscles of the trunk, and the limbs were stiffened out. Difficulty of breathing is common to both tetanus and to tetanic convulsions from strychnia. In the case of Mr. Cook, I think it is an important distinction that he seems to have been able to swallow sufficiently easy, and there was no rigidity of the muscles of the jaw which is characteristic of tetanus, of disease, or of wound. I think the symptoms in his case, judging from my own experience, were those of tetanus from strychnia.

Cross-examined by Mr. GROVE—The proximate effect of tetanus, whether caused by idiopathic or traumatic tetanus, or strychnia, is probably the same on the nerves leading from the spine. The particular affection of the nerves is unknown. In the disorder of convulsions there are cases of very slight affection, others more serious, and so on. I adhere to the opinion given by me in my lectures on "Diseases of the Brain and Nervous System," that the results of the administration of strychnine exactly imitate the convulsions of tetanus. It does not produce the exact phenomena of the disease in a clinical sense. I have no doubt the peculiar irritation of the nerves in tetanus is identical with the peculiar irritation of the nerves in strychnine poisoning. In traumatic tetanus I do not recollect any instance of the limbs being affected before the jaw. An examination of the spinal cord in tetanic affections shortly after death is of importance. If it were deferred as late as two months, there would be, to a certain extent, a fallacy. There are morbid appearances produced by wounds after death which sometimes simulate diseased conditions before death.

Supposing the spine to be affected by decomposition, would not what may be called the diseased softening of the spine previous to death be confused or obliterated?—You would not be able to speak with certainty as to simple softening if the examination had been long after death. There is nothing in the post-mortem examination on which any one could positively say that the patient died from the ordinary disease of tetanus. I think granules on the spinal cord, such as I have heard of here, are not likely to cause tetanus. In the cases of the animals to whom strychnia was administered they went off into a second spasm immediately they were touched. They retained that tendency as long as the influence of the poison lasted. I examined the animals that were killed by strychnia anatomically. The right side of the heart was not generally full; it was empty, and the heart contracted. Death where strychnine was administered is partly due to the difficulty of action of the respiratory muscles, but chiefly to a general nervous exhaustion which the violence of the paroxysm produces.

Would not the difficulty of action of the respiratory muscles producing death tend to leave the heart full?—I do not think it was asphyxia.

Robert Todd

Then I think I may take you as differing from the great mass of authorities on strychnia poisoning?—I don't know; I think there are differences of opinion on that subject. Persons sometimes have convulsions after poison by morphia. The time in which convulsive symptoms come on after morphia would depend on the dose entirely. I cannot say whether it would be later than strychnia. It is not a question I have devoted attention to.

Re-examined by the ATTORNEY-GENERAL—In death resulting from tetanus I should not expect to find anything peculiar about the heart. I heard the evidence of the gentlemen who examined the spinal cord after Mr. Cook's death. From their description it appeared to me that those parts were in such a condition that any indication of disease might have been discovered.

Sir B. Brodie

Sir BENJAMIN BRODIE, examined by Mr. JAMES—I was surgeon at St. James's Hospital for a great number of years, and have had a considerable practice. I have had many cases of death from tetanus. Death from idiopathic tetanus is very rare in this country. I heard the description of the symptoms attending the death of Mr. Cook. As far as the spasmodic contraction of the muscles is concerned, the symptoms resemble those of traumatic tetanus; as to the course the symptoms took, that was entirely different. I heard about the attack on the Monday night and its ceasing, and the patient being comfortable and composed during the Tuesday, and then the attack again about ten minutes before twelve on the Tuesday night. The symptoms of traumatic tetanus always begin, so far as I have seen, very gradually; the stiffness of the lower jaw being, I believe, invariably the symptom first complained of; then the contraction of the muscles of the back is always a later symptom; the muscles of the extremities are affected in a much less degree than those of the neck and trunk, except in some cases where the injury has been in a limb, and an early symptom has been a spasmodic contraction of the muscles of that limb. I do not recollect a case in which in ordinary tetanus there was that contraction of the muscles of the hand which I understand was stated to have existed in this instance. Ordinary tetanus rarely runs its course in less than two or three days, and often is protracted to a much longer period; I know one case only in which the disease was said to have terminated in twelve hours.

LORD CAMPBELL—Probably in that case the early symptoms had been overlooked?—I never knew these symptoms of ordinary tetanus to last for a few minutes, then subside, then come on again after twenty-four hours.

Examination continued—I do not believe that death here arose from what we ordinarily call tetanus, either idiopathic or traumatic. I never knew a death from tetanus to result from a sore throat, or a chancre, or any other form of syphilitic disease. The symptoms of the death of Mr. Cook are not consistent with a fit of apoplexy. I never saw a case in which the symptoms that I heard described arose from any disease.

Cross-examined by Mr. SERJEANT SHEE—I remember one case of idiopathic tetanus in our hospital, but I doubted its deserving the name of tetanus.

Considering how rare tetanus is, would you think that the description of a chambermaid and of a provincial medical man, who had only seen one case of tetanus, could be relied upon by you as to what the disease observed was?—I must say I thought the description very clearly given. I have never seen the syphilitic poison produce convulsions except as a consequence of disease in the bones of the head.

Mr. HENRY DANIEL, examined by the ATTORNEY-GENERAL—I was for upwards of twenty-eight years surgeon to the Bristol Hospital. I have seen fully thirty cases of tetanus, of which two were idiopathic. One of these two ended fatally. Idiopathic tetanus is of very rare occurrence. The symptoms are not so severe as those in traumatic tetanus. The symptoms which accompanied the attack of Mr. Cook before his death were quite distinguishable from those cases of tetanus which have come within my experience. In pointing out the differences I would repeat very probably the words of Sir Benjamin Brodie. Tetanus, so far as my experience goes, begins with uneasiness in the lower jaw, followed by spasms of the muscles of the trunk, and most frequently extending to the muscles of the limbs. Lockjaw is almost invariably a symptom of traumatic in particular. It is one of the earliest symptoms. I have seen the clenching of the hands, but I do not think it is an ordinary symptom of common tetanus. I cannot recollect a case the duration of which has been less than from thirty to forty hours. I have never known a syphilitic sore producing tetanus. The symptoms I have heard described in Mr. Cook's case are not referable to either apoplexy or epilepsy. In both these there is a loss of consciousness, but in cases of tetanus that I have seen consciousness has been retained throughout all the period. In my experience of tetanus the symptoms have been invariably continuous without any interruption. In my judgment the symptoms of Mr. Cook could not be referred to idiopathic or traumatic tetanus.

Henry Daniel

Cross-examined by Mr. GROVE—I do not know that cases are mentioned in books where there is a long interval of some hours between the symptoms. I have not read Dr. Todd's book, nor Mr. Curling's book, nor Dr. Copland's book on the subject. I have been out of practice some seventeen or eighteen months, and have not looked into the reported cases of tetanus of late. In my opinion the symptoms of tetanic convulsions do not vary much in different cases. There may be an affection of a muscle in this man that there is not in the other, in a leg or an arm. In tetanic affections death is caused by exhaustion and suffocation.

Samuel Solly

Mr. SAMUEL SOLLY, examined by Mr. WELSBY—I have been connected with St. Thomas's Hospital as lecturer and surgeon for twenty-eight years. I have either seen or had under my care twenty cases of tetanus, all of which were traumatic, except one, in which I was doubtful whether it was traumatic or idiopathic. In the latter case the symptoms were slower in their progress and generally rather milder. The shortest period I can remember before the disease arrived at a point is thirty hours. The difference between Mr. Cook's attacks and the cases I have seen is that, in my experience, there has been a marked expression of the countenance—that is the first symptom; it is a sort of grin, and the symptoms have always been continuous. The symptoms in Mr. Cook's case are not referable to either epilepsy or apoplexy, or any disease that I ever witnessed.

Cross-examined by Mr. SERJEANT SHEE—A marked expression of the countenance, a sort of grin, frequently occurs in all violent convulsions, which assume, without being tetanus, a tetanic form and appearance. They are not a numerous class. It is difficult to distinguish between them and idiopathic tetanus in the onset, but not in the progress. I heard the account given by Mr. Jones of the last few moments before Mr. Cook died.

That he uttered a piercing shriek, fell back, and died, did he not?—Yes.

The ATTORNEY-GENERAL—I beg your pardon; there was an interval.

Mr. SERJEANT SHEE—No, no; five or six minutes.

LORD CAMPBELL—He died very quietly.

Cross-examination resumed—I heard the description of the shriek with the convulsion; but it was the shriek that called the medical man into the room. That was at the height of the attack. In some respects that last shriek and the paroxysm that occurred immediately afterwards bear a resemblance to epilepsy. Death from tetanus accompanied with convulsions seldom leaves any trace behind; but death from epilepsy leaves behind it some few effusions of blood on the brain or congestion of the vessels.

Samuel Solly

Re-examined by the ATTORNEY-GENERAL—Convulsions that take place in epilepsy are not at all of tetanic character. I say that Mr. Cook did not die from epilepsy, because there were none of the symptoms there. When a patient dies with epilepsy he dies perfectly unconscious. Ulceration of the brain from injury, a sudden injury to the spinal cord, irritation of the teeth in infants, all produce convulsions. But those convulsions in their progress are not similar to the convulsions of tetanus. There is no progressive movement and no appearance about the face or jaw of having tetanus.

R. Corbett

Dr. ROBERT CORBETT, examined by Mr. JAMES—I am a physician in Glasgow. I remember a patient of the name of Agnes Sennet who died in the Glasgow Royal Infirmary on 29th September, 1845, after taking some strychnia pills intended for another patient. I saw her while she was under the influence of the poison. The symptoms I noticed were a retraction of the mouth, face much suffused and red, the pupils dilated, the head bent back, the spine curved, and the muscles rigid and hard like a board. She died about an hour and a quarter after taking the pills. There would be a quarter of a grain in each of the three pills she took.

Cross-examined by Mr. SERJEANT SHEE—The retraction of the angles of the mouth was continuous, but it was worse at times. I did not observe it after death. The hands were not clenched, but semi-bent after death. That semi-bending of the hand is a very common thing in cases of death by violent convulsions. Twenty minutes after taking the medicine she was attacked by the symptoms.

Dr. Watson

Dr. WATSON, examined by the ATTORNEY-GENERAL—I am one of the physicians in the Glasgow Royal Infirmary, and attended the case of Agnes Sennet spoken to by the last witness. I saw her about a quarter of an hour after the symptoms first began. She was in violent convulsions; her arms were stretched out and rigid; her feet and legs were also rigid. Just at that moment she did not breathe. That paroxysm subsided almost immediately, and fresh ones came on after a very short interval. They occurred at intervals until they destroyed her. She was about half an hour in dying. She seemed perfectly conscious during the time. At the post-mortem examination the spinal cord was quite healthy. The heart was contracted.

Mary Kelly

MARY KELLY, examined by Mr. BODKIN—I was a patient in the Glasgow Royal Infirmary, and saw Agnes Sennet take the pills, which were intended for another patient. I saw her take two pills only. After taking the pills she went and sat down by the fire, and in about three-quarters of an hour she was taken ill. She fell back on the floor, and a nurse and I lifted her into bed. The nurse cut her clothes off, and she never moved after she was put upon the bed; she was just like a poker. She never spoke after she fell.

C. Hickson

CAROLINE HICKSON, examined by Mr. JAMES—In October, 1848, I was nurse and lady's maid in the family of Mrs. Serjeantson Smith, at Romsey, in Hampshire. On the 30th of that month Mrs. Smith was unwell, and some medicine was sent to her in the afternoon, about six o'clock, by a Mr. Jones, a druggist in Romsey. Shortly after seven o'clock next morning I saw her take about half a wineglass of the medicine. About five or ten minutes afterwards I was summoned to her bedroom, and on entering I saw her leaning upon a chair, and I thought she had fainted. She appeared to suffer from what I thought spasms. I went out and sent for Mr. Taylor, surgeon, and on returning to the bedroom I found some of the other servants assisting to support Mrs. Smith. She was then lying on the floor and screaming very much, very loudly, but did not open her teeth. She asked me to have her legs pulled straight, and I found them drawn up very much. She still screamed as if in great agony, and requested some water to be thrown over her, which I did. Her feet were turned inwards. I put a hot-water bottle to them, but this had no effect. Shortly before she died she said she felt easier, and her last words were, "Turn me over." I did so. A few minutes after this she died. She was conscious, and knew me during the whole time. From the time she took the medicine until she died would be about an hour and a quarter.

Cross-examined by Mr. GROVE—From the time I first saw her in the spasms she could not sit up at all. It was a continuous, recurring fit, and lasted about an hour. She only seemed easy for a very short time before her death. Her teeth were clenched during the whole time.

F. Taylor

Mr. FRANCIS TAYLOR, examined by Mr. WELSBY—I am a surgeon at Romsey. I was summoned one morning to the house of Mrs. Serjeantson Smith. I arrived between eight and nine o'clock, shortly after she died. I saw the body then. The hands were clenched; the feet were contracted, turned inwards; and the soles of the feet were hollowed up. This appeared to have been from recent spasmodic action. The limbs were remarkably stiff. The body was still warm. The eyelids were totally adherent, almost to the eyeballs. I made a post-mortem examination three days after death. The contraction of the feet continued, but it was gone off somewhat from the rest of the body. No trace of disease was found. The heart was contracted and perfectly empty, and the blood was fluid. I analysed the medicine Mrs. Smith had taken. It originally contained nine grains of strychnia, and Mrs. Smith had taken one-third. As the truth was so apparent, only a very general examination of the stomach and bowels was made, but still sufficient to find traces of strychnia.

Jane Witham

JANE WITHAM, examined by Mr. JAMES—In March last I was in attendance on a lady who died. I remember her taking some medicine, after which she became ill. She first complained of her back, and when I went to her I observed her head was drawn back, and I could not get at her back. She was in bed. I noticed she had twistings of the ankles, and her eyes were drawn aside and staring. She first complained of illness on the 25th of February, and she died on 1st March. She had several attacks, between each of which she got better. She generally complained of a pricking in her legs and twitching of the muscles in the hands, and she compared them to a galvanic shock. During the attacks she requested her husband to rub her legs and arms. The first attack was on the Monday, and she died on the Saturday about ten minutes to eleven at night.

(This case was that of Dr. Dove's wife.)

Cross-examined by Mr. SERJEANT SHEE—It was on the commencement of the spasms that she requested her legs to be rubbed. On the Saturday night she could not bear them to be touched. On that night the spasms were much stronger than on the other days. On the Saturday she did not speak but once or twice. During the interval of the spasms on the Saturday touching her brought the spasms on. She could swallow on each of the days except the Saturday, when her mouth was quite closed. After death her body was stiff.

G. Morley

Mr. GEORGE MORLEY, examined by Mr. WELSBY—I was the medical attendant on the lady referred to by the last witness. I had been attending her for about two months before her death for a functional derangement. I saw her on the Monday before her death lying in her bed. I observed several convulsive twitchings of her arms. I saw her on the Saturday about the middle of the day. She was much better, and in a composed state. She complained of an attack she had had in the night, and spoke of pains and spasms, affections of the back and neck. I and another medical gentleman made a post-mortem examination on the Monday. We found no disease which would account for death. There were no abrasions, nor any wound or sore. The hands were semi-bent, the fingers curved, and the feet were strongly arched. We applied several colour tests to the contents of the stomach for the purpose of detecting the presence of poison. On each occasion we produced the appearance characteristic of strychnia. After the separation of the strychnine by chemical analysis we inoculated two mice, two rabbits, and one guinea pig with the stuff taken from the stomach. We observed in each of the animals more or less the effects usually produced by the poison strychnia—general uneasiness, difficult breathing, convulsions of the tetanic kind, muscular rigidity, bending backwards, especially of the head and neck, a violent stretching of the legs. In the case of the animals where death resulted the muscular rigidity continued without any intermission. There was an interval of relaxation, but immediately after death the muscles became very rigid, more so than at rigor-mortis. We afterwards made a similar series of experiments on some animals with strychnia itself, both in solid and liquid forms. The symptoms and the results generally were exactly the same as those I have described in the case of the other animals.

Cross-examined by Mr. GROVE—I did not see the patient during any severe attack. I observed that when the animals were touched it brought on the symptoms. That is a very marked result. Directly they are touched they give a sudden start, and pass into a severe spasm. At the post-mortem examination the lungs were very much congested. The muscles generally were dark and stiff. There was a decided quantity of bloody serous effusion over the brain. There was a notable quantity, but not a large quantity, of serum slightly tinged with blood in the membranes of the spinal cord. The large spinal veins were very much congested, as were the membranes of the spinal marrow. We opened the head first, and that led to a great deal of blood flowing from the head. That would make it uncertain whether the heart was full or empty. The right sides of the hearts of animals that have been poisoned by strychnia are generally full. From one to two hours is the longest time in animals at which I have perceived the first effect of strychnia come on after it has been taken. I made experiments in conjunction with Mr. Nunneley, and my impression is that the interval has been as long as one hour. I discovered strychnia with all the tests I applied with more or less distinctness. I have detected strychnia in the stomach two months after death, and after decomposition had proceeded to a considerable extent.

G. Morley

Re-examined by the ATTORNEY-GENERAL—I have given to the animals which I have killed from half a grain to two grains. The animals experimented on were cats, rabbits, and dogs. The strychnia, I think, acts on the nerves, but a part may be taken into the blood also and act through the blood. The poison is absorbed. We searched the stomach to find the presence of the strychnia. The strychnia which we found in the stomach would be that which was there in excess beyond that which had been absorbed in the system. The strychnia that has been absorbed into the system is sufficient to destroy life. The excess that remains in the stomach is inactive. I should expect to fail sometimes to find strychnia in the stomach if the minimum quantity capable of operating to the destruction of life had been administered. If death resulted from a series of minute doses of this poison, administered for a space of several days, it is my opinion that the appearances would be likely to be different after death from what they would, supposing death was produced rapidly by one dose.

Re-cross-examined by Mr. SERJEANT SHEE—Is it your theory that in the act of poisoning the poison is absorbed and ceases to exist as poison, as strychnia?—I am inclined to think so. I have thought much upon that question. I am not decided in my own mind.

What chemical reason can you give for your opinion?—My opinion rests on the general fact that organic substances acting on the human body, such as food or medicine, are frequently changed in composition. It is possible that strychnia may have been discovered in the blood and liver after effecting the operation of poisoning, but I do not know that it has.

Do you know whether strychnia can be decomposed by any sort of putrefying or fermentative process?—I have no fact to show that it can, and I doubt if it is.

E. D. Moore

Mr. EDWARD DUKE MOORE, examined by Mr. HUDDLESTON—I was formerly in practice as a surgeon. About fifteen years ago I was attending a gentleman for paralysis, and had been giving him some very small doses of strychnia. Subsequently I made him up a stronger dose containing a quarter of a grain. In about three-quarters of an hour I was summoned to come back and see him. He was stiffened in every limb. His head was drawn back, and he was screaming, frequently requesting that we should turn him, move him, and rub him. His spine was arched. We tried to give him a mixture of ammonia with a spoon. He snapped at the spoon with a sort of convulsive grasp to take it. He was suffering about three hours altogether. He survived the attack, and was perfectly conscious the whole time.

Cross-examined by SERJEANT SHEE—He recovered from the spasms in about three hours, but the rigidity of the muscles remained for the rest of the day and part of the next day. He was completely recovered the next day after the attack, and the patient himself said he thought his paralysis was better.

The Court then adjourned.

Fifth Day, Monday, 19th May, 1856.

Alfred Taylor

Dr. ALFRED TAYLOR, examined by the ATTORNEY-GENERAL—I am a Fellow of the College of Physicians, a lecturer on medical jurisprudence at Guy's Hospital, and the author of a well-known treatise on poisons and on medical jurisprudence. Among other poisons, I have made strychnia the subject of my attention. It is the produce of the nux vomica. There is also in the nux vomica a poison of an analogous nature called bruchsia, which differs from it only in point of strength. The difference of the two poisons is relatively estimated from one-sixth to one-twelfth, bruchsia being one-sixth to one-twelfth the strength of strychnia. I have never witnessed an instance of the action of strychnia on the human subject. I have tried a variety of experiments, I think about ten or twelve, on animal life with strychnia. Rabbits have always been used for these experiments. The symptoms produced by the poison have been on the whole very uniform. I have given a quantity varying from one-half to two or three grains. I have found half a grain sufficient to destroy the life of a rabbit. I have given it in both solid and liquid form. When given in a fluid state it produced its operation in two or three minutes; when given in a solid state, in the form of pill or bolus, from about six to eleven minutes, I think. The time is influenced by the strength of the dose, and also by the strength of the animal. The poison is first absorbed into the blood; it is then circulated through the body, and the poison especially acts on the spinal cord. That is the part of the body from which the nerves affecting the voluntary muscles proceed. The entire circulation through the whole system is considered to take place about once in four minutes.

LORD CAMPBELL—Are you speaking of the human circulation?—Yes; the circulation in the rabbit is quicker.

Examination resumed—How is it the absorption would be quicker in a rabbit?—I think it is from the effects produced; that will also depend on the state of the stomach, as to whether there be much food in the stomach and whether the poison comes in immediate contact with the inner surface of the stomach. The poison must first, I believe, be absorbed before it acts on the nervous system.

Alfred Taylor

Will you describe the series of symptoms from the commencement to the close?—The animal for about five or six minutes does not appear to suffer; it moves about freely and actively. It then, when the poison begins to act, suddenly falls on its side. There is a trembling of the whole muscles of the body, a sort of quivering motion arising from the poison producing those violent and involuntary contractions. There is then a sudden paroxysm of it; the fore legs and the hind legs are stretched out, the head and the tail are drawn back so as to give it the form of a bow. The jaws are spasmodically closed, the eyes are prominent, protruding. After a short time there is a slight remission of the symptoms, and the animal appears to lie quiet, but the slightest noise or touch reproduces convulsive paroxysms. There is sometimes a scream or sort of shriek; the heart beats very violently during the fit, and after a succession of these fits the animal dies quietly.

There is not invariably, immediately prior to death, a remission of the symptoms?—I have only known an animal has died by having the hand over the heart. It has been in a state of spasms at that time. In one or two cases the animal has died quietly, as if there was a remission; sometimes it dies apparently during the spasms itself.

What appearance have you observed after death which would be different from the ordinary appearances—the outward appearances? Are the muscles more than usually rigid?—In some instances the animal has been rigid throughout; that is to say, it has died in a spasm, and the rigidity has continued, the muscles so strongly contracted that for a week afterwards it was possible to hold the animal horizontally extended by the hind legs without the body falling. In an animal killed the other day the body was flexible at the time of death, but it became rigid about five minutes after death. I have opened the bodies of animals that have been thus destroyed. I have found no appearances in the stomach or intestines which would indicate any injury there. I have found in one or two cases congestion of the vessels of the membranes. In other cases I have not found any departure from the ordinary state of blood. The membranes of the spinal cord and brain are a continuation one of the other, so that it is not easy to have congestion of one without congestion of the other. The congestion of those membranes has been due to fits which the animal has had before death. In three out of five cases I failed to discover any abnormal condition of the spinal cord or brain. As to the hearts of animals thus killed, from all that I have seen the heart has been congested with blood, the right side especially. The description given by Elizabeth Mills and Mr. Jones of the symptoms which accompanied the attack on Mr. Cook are similar to those I have seen in animals to which I have administered strychnia.

Alfred Taylor

How long does it take in the case of rabbits to which you have administered strychnia from the time the first symptoms manifest themselves to the time of the death?—They have died in various periods—one died in thirteen minutes, one in seventeen minutes; that, I should mention, would be the whole time. The symptoms appear more rapidly when the poison is administered in a fluid state, and death has taken place in five or six minutes after. The experiments which I have particularly noticed and performed lately, and which I am about to detail, have been in reference to solid strychnia. In the first the symptoms began in seven minutes, and the animal died in thirteen minutes from the time the poison was given; in the second the symptoms appeared in nine minutes, the animal died in seventeen minutes; in the third the symptoms appeared in ten minutes, the animal died in eighteen minutes; in the fourth the symptoms appeared in nine minutes, and the death took place in twenty-two minutes; in the fifth the symptoms appeared in twelve minutes, and the death took place in twenty-three minutes. In the human subject, supposing this poison to be administered in the shape of pills, I should expect it would take a longer period before the poison began to act, because it requires that the pill structure should be broken up in order to bring the poison in contact with the mucous membrane of the stomach.

Alfred Taylor

Given that the poison is administered in both cases, to the rabbit and the human subject, in the shape of pills, should you expect a longer period before it began to act on the human subject than the rabbit?—I do not think we can fairly draw any inference; the circulation and absorption are very different. It is very probable that there would also be a difference between one human subject and another in the power of taking the thing up with more or less rapidity. The strength of the dose would make a difference; a large dose would be more rapid than a small dose. I have experimented upon the intestines of animals to reproduce the strychnia or to discover it. (Dr. Taylor described the chemical tests.) These colour tests, as they are called, are, I think, very fallacious. There are other vegetable matters to which, if these colour tests are applied, similar results as to colour would be obtained. A mixture of sugar and bile will produce the purple and red tint, for instance. Vegetable poisons are more difficult of detection by chemical processes than the mineral ones, and the tests are more fallacious. In four cases of animals destroyed by strychnia Dr. Rees and I endeavoured to reproduce the strychnia, and then applied to it those colouring tests which I mentioned just now. We also tried the effect of taste. In one case by the colour test we satisfied ourselves of the presence of strychnia; in another there was a bitter taste in the liquid, but no indication of strychnia by the colour test. In other two cases there was no indication at all of the presence of strychnia. In the first case we had given a dose of two grains at intervals; in the second case one grain; in the other two cases one grain and half a grain.

How did you account physiologically for the absence of any indication of strychnia where you know strychnia to have been given and to have caused death?—By absorption into the blood so that it is no longer in the stomach; it is in a great part too changed in the blood. In the case of the larger dose there would be a retention of some not absorbed. That would be in cases beyond what was required for the destruction of life. If the minimum of the quantity required to destroy life was given, I do not think I would find any.

It would be removed by absorption, and no longer discoverable in the stomach.

Are there any chemical means you are acquainted with whereby the presence of this poison can be detected in the tissues?—There are not; there is no process I am acquainted with when it is in a small quantity; so far as I know it cannot be detected.

In addition to this distribution of the half grain, which you tell us is known to have destroyed human life, over the whole system, in your opinion does it undergo decomposition as it mixes itself with the animal tissues?—I believe it undergoes some change in the blood. That increases the difficulty in detecting it in the tissues. I have never heard of its being separated in a crystallised state from the tissues.

Alfred Taylor

After the post-mortem examination on the body of Mr. Cook some portion was sent up to me. I experimented to ascertain if there were any poison present. We sought for prussic acid, oxalic acid, morphia, strychnia, veratrea, a poison of white hellebore, the poison of tobacco, hemlock, arsenic, mercury, antimony, and other mineral poisons generally. We only found small traces of antimony. The part which we had to operate upon was in the most unfavourable condition for finding strychnia if it had been there. The stomach had been completely cut from end to end; all the contents were gone, and the fine mucous surface, on which any poison if present would be found, was lying in contact with the outside of the intestines, all thrown together. There was also succulent matter on the surface of the mucous membrane, derived from the intestines, the contents of which partly escaped. The inside of the stomach had been forced into this mass of intestinal succulent matter; at any rate, it was lying so. In journeying up to London it must have been shaken in every possible way. The contents of the intestines were there, but the contents of the stomach were gone. If there had been any of this poison present I should have expected to have found it in the contents of the stomach and on the mucous membrane. At my request other portions of the body were sent—the liver, the spleen, and the two kidneys; in addition, a small bottle of blood, unlabelled, giving us no idea whence it was taken. We analysed all those portions. We searched for mineral poison in the liver and kidneys, and discovered antimony in an eighth part of the liver; we analysed only the left kidney and the spleen, and there were traces of antimony in each. The quantity was less in proportion in the spleen than in the other parts. The blood contained antimony.

Would its being found in the blood enable you to form any opinion how shortly before death the antimony had been given?—It is impossible to say with any precision, but I should say shortly before death—within some days; the longest period known at which antimony has been found in the blood, after a person has ceased to take it, was eight days. I heard the account by the servant girls of the vomiting of Mr. Cook; I also heard the account given of his vomiting at Shrewsbury, and by the medical men, Gibson and Jones, and Dr. Bamford's deposition as to the concomitant symptoms. In my opinion, the vomiting would be such as might be produced by antimony. Tartar emetic is soluble in fluids, and if mixed with broth or toast and water would not affect the colour.

From these traces of the antimony can you form any judgment as to the time when the antimony was taken?—It is impossible to say with any precision, but I should say within two or three weeks at the outside. We did not find any perceptible quantity dissolved in the fluids of the body and the washings of the stomach; therefore I should infer there was no evidence of any given within some hours of death. I think that which I found in the liver might have been administered within eighteen hours of death or within two days. I know by experience it takes a shorter time to get to the liver. Antimony does not affect the taste of anything if it is given in quantities which would cause vomiting. If a large quantity was taken at once it might leave a choking or constricting sensation, as if the throat was contracted. There was no trace of mercury. I should have expected to find mercury according to the quantity taken. If a few grains had been taken recently before death I should expect to find some trace in the liver. Supposing a man had been taking mercury for any syphilitic affection within anything like a recent period before death I should expect to find it. I heard the evidence which was given as to the deaths of Mrs. Smith, Agnes French, and the lady referred to, and also the case of the gentleman of whom Mr. Moore spoke. Judging by the results of my own experiments and studies, I agree that those deaths were occasioned by strychnia. Mr. Cook's attacks appear to me to be of a similar character.

As a professor of medical science do you know any other cause in the nature of human diseases to which the symptoms of Mr. Cook's death can be referred except to strychnia?—I do not.

Alfred Taylor

Cross-examined by Mr. SERJEANT SHEE—In the course of your examination you have frequently used the words "traces of antimony." What was the meaning of "trace"?—A very small quantity.

In analytical chemistry does it mean an imponderable quantity?—I do not apply it in that shape. Some chemists mean that. I mean we obtained some quantity in that sense from many parts, and that the quantity thus calculated would make a ponderable quantity in the whole. We have about half a grain.

You did not actually ascertain it to amount to half a grain?—No. I do not think a quarter of a grain would have explained the quantity we obtained. I will undertake to say there was half a grain to the best of my judgment.

In all parts of the body you examined?—There was more in the parts of the body examined, but we extracted that quantity.

In your judgment would that be sufficient to cause death?—No. I was first asked to investigate this case on Tuesday, 27th November, by Mr. Stevens. Either on that day or subsequently he mentioned the name of Mr. Gardner to me. After Mr. Stevens spoke to me he and Mr. Boycott came together with these jars.

You wrote a letter, the whole of which I will read to you. It is in reply to a letter received from Mr. Gardner—

Dr. Rees and I have compared the analysis to-day. We have sketched a report, which will be ready to-morrow or next day. As I am going to Durham Assizes on the part of the Crown, in the case of *Reg.* v. *Wooler*, the report will be in the hands of Dr. Rees, No. 26 Albemarle Street. It will be most desirable that Mr. Stevens should call on Dr. Rees, read the report with him, and put such questions as may occur. In reply to your letter received here this morning, I beg to say that we wish a statement of all the medicines prescribed for deceased (until his death) to be drawn up and sent to Dr. Rees. We did not find strychnia nor prussic acid or any trace of opium. From the contents having been drained away, it is now impossible to say whether any strychnine had or had not been given just before death. But it is quite possible for tartar emetic to destroy life if given in repeated doses; and, as far as we can at present form an opinion, in the absence of any natural cause of death, the deceased must have died from the effects of antimony in this or some other form.

Was that your opinion at the time?—It was. That was all we could infer from the chemical analysis.

Alfred Taylor

Have you not told me to-day that the quantity of antimony that you found in Cook's body was not sufficient to account for death?—Perfectly so; but what was found in Cook's body was not all he took. We found antimony, and we could not account for its being there. I wrote to know whether antimony had been given as a medicine, and I considered, as people had died from antimony, it was necessary to have information of the symptoms connected with the man's death, which I knew nothing about at the time; finding antimony there and no explanation, I put it as the only hypothesis to me to account for death.

Had you any reason to think any undue quantity had been administered to him?—I could not speculate on that from the quantity there, for I did not know at all what quantity he had taken, and whether it had been prescribed medicinally.

May not the injudicious use of quack medicines containing antimony, such as James' powder or other mixtures, have accounted for as much antimony as you found in the body of Mr. Cook?—Any antimonial preparation would account for it. I knew strychnia was bought before we sent in the report. Mr. Gardner gave the information in a letter in reply to that which has been read that strychnia, prussic acid, Batley's sedative of opium, had been bought by the prisoner. After giving my evidence at the inquest I returned to town. Soon after I knew that the prisoner had been committed on the charge of wilful murder.

You knew, of course, that his life depended in a great degree on your opinion?—No; my opinion was in reference to the death by poison; I expressed no opinion of the prisoner's guilt. I knew I would be examined as a witness upon his trial. I wrote a letter to the *Lancet* on the subject, contradicting several misstatements which were made regarding my evidence. I have never had under my own observation the effects of strychnia on the human body; but I have written a book upon the subject.

Do you, from your reading, know of any fatal case in which the patient under strychnia poison has had, while the paroxysm lasted, as much command over the muscles and voluntary motion as Mr. Cook had on the Monday and Tuesday nights, according to the evidence of Mills and Jones?—I do not see that he had much command over the muscles of voluntary life. His symptoms are quite in accordance with the ordinary action of strychnia.

Can you tell me a single case of a patient seized with tetanic symptoms by strychnia poison sitting up in his bed talking?—He was seized with the tetanic symptoms after he sat up in his bed.

Do you know of a single case of the symptoms of poison by strychnia commencing or exhibiting themselves during any time of the paroxysm by the operation of beating the bed?—There have been only about fifteen cases altogether; I have not heard of a person taken ill in bed before.

Alfred Taylor

Is not the beating of the bed well known under the name of malasaux; is it not a very common symptom of ordinary convulsions?—No, I do not think it is the case, not to my knowledge. I have not a case of a person sitting up in bed and beating the bed.

Have you known any instances in which the patient has screamed before he was seized with the fit?—No. That is common in convulsions not occasioned by strychnia poisoning. In many cases they scream very soon after the spasm sets in; the pain felt is very severe.

This is before the convulsions begin?—No, I have never known that. I have known cases in which they speak freely, but not after the paroxysm has commenced; I do not remember a case at the present time.

Can you tell me or refer me to any one case in which the effect of the strychnia affection or paroxysm in a fatal case has been as long after the ingestion of the poison as in Cook's case on Tuesday night?—Yes. In a case communicated to the *Lancet* of 31st August, 1850, p. 259, by Mr. Bennett, one grain and a half of strychnia, taken by mistake, destroyed the life of a healthy young female in an hour and a half, which is remarkable, as no symptoms appeared for an hour.

May I take it that is the longest period which has elapsed between the ingestion of the poison and the commencement of the symptoms on record?—No, I think not.

Do you know a single case in which the symptoms have manifested themselves as long as an hour and a half after the ingestion of the poison?—No, I do not.

Do you know any case of strychnia poison in which the patient has recovered from a paroxysm in as short a time as Mr. Cook did, he being well before the morning?—I do not remember any, but I can conceive in medical practice such cases.

Do you know any case of strychnia poison in which there was so long an intermission of the paroxysm as between the two fits of Monday and Tuesday night?—No, I do not.

As you choose to go upon rabbits, do you not know that it constantly happens, even in rabbits, that the spasm and the contraction instantly cease immediately with death, or just before death, and that the body becomes perfectly pliant?—No, I do not. It does so in some instances, in one out of five cases.

Alfred Taylor

Do you agree in this opinion of Dr. Christison—"I have not altered the statement as to this point in the former edition, that is, that the rigidity supervenes at an early period after death; yet I strongly suspect the authors who describe the spasm which precedes death to continue as it were without the rigidity that occurs after death must have observed inaccurately, for, in the numerous experiments that I have made and witnessed upon animals, flaccidity of limb continued after death"?—Dr. Christison speaks from his own experience; I speak from my own.

Have you any reason to say that the clenching of the hand is a distinctive feature of strychnia poison?—It is the result of violent tetanic spasms. It occurs in other violent spasms.

In all forms of convulsion?—No; the great point is this, that in tetanus it remains so; in other convulsions it comes and goes.

Is it always so?—That is according to my knowledge.

Re-examined by the ATTORNEY-GENERAL—I have met with three cases in a human subject in which it has appeared that the heart was found empty after death, where the death had taken place from strychnia. I think the emptiness of the heart is owing to spasmodic affection, the effect upon the heart in the last moment of life. I know of no reason why that should be more likely to be the case in the human subject than in a small animal like a rabbit. The only thing I would observe is, that I think the heart is generally more affected by the paroxysm, so that the blood accumulates.

Suppose the paroxysms short and violent, and cause death in a few minutes?—That is the kind of case in which I should expect to find it empty. The rigidity after death in the cases where I found it always affected the same muscles, the muscles of the limbs, specially the muscles of the back. In the case of poisoning by strychnia, where the rigidity was relaxed in death, it returns while the body is warm.

Would the rigidity of the extremities as long as two months after death, the clenching of the hands, and the twisting of the feet, afford you any indication of whether the person died of tetanus?—I have never known such a case. That would indicate, in my opinion, great violence of the spasm with which the party died.

With regard to the duration of time in which the effects of the poison would begin to act, to show itself, would it be uniform, do you think, in all persons to whom the same quantity of poison might be given?—It would vary according to the constitution and the strength, according to the power of absorption.

Dr. GEORGE OWEN REES, examined by Mr. JAMES—I am a Fellow of the College of Physicians, and Lecturer on Materia Medica at Guy's Hospital. I believe strychnia is absorbed always before it produces the symptoms. If enough strychnia is given to destroy life, that might be done without our being able to discover it after death. I agree with Professor Taylor that it is the excess that is found. Where vitality is destroyed by the effects of the poison, and an excess remains, I would expect with care to discover that excess. The symptoms in the cases of death from strychnia that have been given are analogous, in my opinion, to those of Mr. Cook, and to those produced by strychnia in the experiments I have seen made on animals.

Professor ROBERT CHRISTISON, examined by the ATTORNEY-GENERAL—I am a Fellow of the Royal College of Physicians and Professor of Materia Medica to the University of Edinburgh. I published in 1845 a treatise on poisons in relation to medical jurisprudence. Among other poisons, I have turned my attention to strychnia. It acts upon the human frame by absorption into the blood, and then by acting on the nervous system. I have seen a case of strychnia poisoning, but not a fatal one, in a human subject. I have frequently seen experiments tried upon animals—frogs, rabbits, cats, dogs, and one wild boar. In most of my experiments I have given very small doses, a sixth part of a grain, but sometimes as much as a grain. The first symptom that I have observed has been a slight tremor and unwillingness to move, then frequently the animal jerks its head back slightly, and very soon after that all the symptoms of tetanus come on, which have been so often described in the evidence of previous witnesses. There is occasionally an intermission of the spasms for a short while. Where the poison has been introduced into the stomach, between five or six minutes and twenty-five minutes have elapsed from the commencement of the symptoms to the death of the animal. From the giving of the poison to the first symptoms coming on, the appearance of tremor, I have seen as long as twelve minutes elapse, and from the first commencement of the symptoms to their termination in death from five or six minutes to twenty or twenty-five minutes. The symptoms have always been very much the same. Where we can trace it very correctly, I think the jaws and the back of the neck are affected first, then the trunk and the extremities in such rapidity that it is very difficult to follow them in succession. I have sometimes observed differences in individuals of the same species; the intermission sometimes is wanting; some lie in one long continuous spasm, with scarcely any intermission, but that is uncommon. I have generally found that the animal is in a state of flaccidity about the period of the termination of life. I have always observed an interval before the rigidity that takes place after death. There is a cessation of the symptoms immediately before death; the rigidity is gone, the body is flaccid. The rigidity is renewed very soon after death. I have frequently opened the bodies of the animals that have thus been killed. I never could find that the poison had produced any apparent effect upon the stomach or intestines. I have never found any apparent effect on the spinal cord or brain which I could trace satisfactorily to the poison. I have always found that the heart of the animal after death contained blood. Others have found it devoid of blood, but I have not. In the one case of the human subject which I saw the symptoms were the fixing of the jaw, spasmodic retraction of the head, slight grinning expression of the mouth, and a slight stiffness of the arms and legs. There was no convulsion of the muscles of the trunk, nor any convulsive movement of the arms and legs in that case. I have collected all the cases that have occurred up to the time of the publication of my book as far as I am aware. The poison appears to require a longer time in producing its effect in the larger animals than the small. In the case of the wild boar, the poison was injected into the chest. The animal died in ten minutes, from the third of a grain. I think there are cases where strychnia, given to the human subject in the shape of nux vomica, has not operated for about an hour. Strychnia itself is generally given in the solid form, sometimes in the fluid form. When given in the fluid form the symptoms are not so long in appearing as when given in the solid form. When given in the shape of a pill the time it takes to act depends very much upon the material used for making the pill. To make the appearance of the symptoms as late as possible the poison might be mixed up with resinous materials, which are all difficult of digestion. Such materials would be within the knowledge and reach of a medical man, and some are often used for making ordinary pills. Absorption would not begin until the pill came to be broken up or digested; the less soluble the pill the longer would be the period required.

Now, independently of that, does the state of knowledge upon this subject enable you to predicate with anything like certainty or accuracy the period that would be required in the human subject before such poison would begin to operate after it has been taken into the stomach; does the state of science enable you to form an opinion as to the precise time, or near the precise time, that it would require for this poison to operate?—I do not think we can fix from our present knowledge the precise time for the poison beginning to operate. When we give poison to an animal for the purpose of watching the effect of the poison, we give it in a manner in which it would act most rapidly, whether in the fluid or the solid form. We take care that the animal is fasting, and have every circumstance favourable for the action of poison. We mix it up with materials that are readily soluble in the stomach. I have seen a good many cases of tetanus arising from wounds, but very few from natural diseases.

R. Christison

Is there, in your opinion, any marked difference between what I may call natural tetanus and the tetanus of strychnia?—I would not rest much upon the little difference of particular symptoms, but rather upon the course and the general circumstances attending them. First, that in all the natural forms of tetanus the symptoms begin and advance much more slowly; and, secondly, they prove fatal much more slowly. When once set up in natural forms of tetanus there is no intermission. Where the first paroxysm does not prove fatal there are short intermissions in tetanus from strychnia. I heard the evidence given by Elizabeth Mills of what took place on the Monday, and by Mr. Jones of what took place on the Tuesday night when Mr. Cook died.

Now, of the two classes of tetanus, to which should you refer the spasm and other symptoms spoken to by those two witnesses?—To strychnia, or one of the natural poisons containing it—nux vomica, St. Ignatius's bean, snakewood, and a poison called exhetwick. They belong to different plants of the same genus, from all of which strychnia may be obtained. There is no natural disease that I have ever seen or that I otherwise know to which I can refer these symptoms which I have heard described.

When death takes place from tetanus or tetanic convulsions, does consciousness continue?—As long as one can make an observation upon it, it remains. When the animal is in a state of strong universal spasm it is impossible to make any observation on its consciousness. The heart of a human subject killed by strychnia has sometimes blood in it and sometimes not. Whether the heart contains blood or not depends upon the particular mode of death, or the dose varying. Spasms of the heart would expel the blood.

Where death has taken place from strychnia I should not expect to find it where the quantity taken is small, but where there is a considerable excess over the quantity necessary to destroy life by absorption I should expect to find it. Colouring tests are, I think, uncertain in some respects. Vegetable poisons are generally more difficult to detect. There is one I know for which there is no test I know of. The stomach that was sent to Dr. Taylor to operate upon, from the description that he gave of it to-day, was in a very unsatisfactory condition. If I had been called upon to analyse such a stomach, I should not have entertained any reasonable expectation of doing any good with it if I had not been informed that there was a considerable quantity of strychnia present. I have no doubt, from the evidence I have heard as to the Leeds case, the Glasgow case, and the Romsey case, that they were deaths from strychnia. The symptoms in these cases appear to me very similar to those of Mr. Cook.

R. Christison

Cross-examined by Mr. GROVE—From my own observation, I should say that animals who die from strychnia die of suffocation—asphyxia; but in another part of my book which is referred to, I leave the question open. By asphyxia I mean stopping of the respiration.

Where is it in your book?—It is under the head of nux vomica, at the bottom of page 898.

I do not find that meets the case?—It leaves the question open; it takes place through an influence on the heart sometimes, and through an influence on the respiration; it is now more open, particularly from the cases which have occurred of death from strychnia.

In the animals poisoned by strychnia that you examined was there blood in the right cavity?—Yes, in both.

You state in your book, and you tell me that when death does not take place suddenly in a fit of spasms, the person continues to be affected for twelve or fourteen hours, with small or milder paroxysms. Is that a statement which, according to your subsequent knowledge, is correct?—I have known the effects cease in a shorter time.

You state on page 903, after mentioning a case where the body was rigid, "the state of rigidity, however, does not invariably occur; on the contrary, in animals the limbs become very flaccid immediately after death, but the usual rigidity supervenes at an early period." I presume the rigidity of which you speak is the rigidity of death, rigor-mortis?—Yes.

You have a note—"I have not altered the statement as to this point in a former edition, yet I strongly suspect that authors who describe the spasms which produce death, and continue the rigidity after death, must be inaccurate." Is that your present opinion?—I think it is very likely, the interval being very short, that the attention may not have been attracted to the fact of there having been an interval of flaccidity. There have been some cases mentioned, very strong indications certainly, of the spasm having continued from the spasm of life to what we call spasm of death; but I still think the differences which are indicated in different cases may be explained on the supposition that there has been a want of minute and accurate attention.

Now, you mention a case on page 906, where a boy, when he was touched, was immediately thrown into a fit. Is it your present impression that, in cases of poisoning by strychnia, there is a tendency to throw the patient into a fit when touched?—That is the only case. In animals it is very remarkable; it is not noticed in the generality of cases. I have been struck with the fact that it has not more often been noted. Dr. Watson's book mentions one. It is not that the absence of it is noted, but that it is not mentioned at all. I have invariably observed it in animals, unless you touch them very gently indeed.

R. Christison

You stated that care was taken in administering strychnia to animals to administer it to them fasting. Do you think it not likely it would supervene more quickly if administered to an empty stomach?—Certainly.

If resinous substances were used in a pill, would they not be found in the stomach on analysis afterwards?—No; if they were not acted upon they might pass into the intestines and be carried off.

Then the strychnia would be discharged with them, would it not?—Certainly, or gradually acted upon with the resinous substances.

I suppose if the resinous substances prevented the poison acting rapidly, it would prevent its absorption into the blood?—For a time.

If so, the more likely to leave portions of it in the stomach or intestines as the case may be?—The more likely.

Re-examined by the ATTORNEY-GENERAL—Would that materially depend on the quantity of the dose?—Both on the dose and on the time during which the pill was allowed to remain. It appears that colour tests are not to be relied upon in the case of strychnia in an impure condition. In the first place, you may not find indications of strychnia, and secondly, they are subject to fallacy, even if the strychnia is pure, from other substances not containing strychnia presenting similar appearances.

The Court then adjourned.

Sixth Day, Tuesday, 20th May, 1856.

The Court met at ten o'clock.

John Jackson

Dr. JOHN JACKSON, examined by Mr. JAMES—I am a member of the College of Physicians. I have been in practice for twenty-five years in India, and have seen cases of idiopathic and traumatic tetanus. Idiopathic is more common in India than in this country. I have seen not less than forty cases. It is common with children. In children there is a more marked symptom of lockjaw, but in adults there is no difference between the symptoms of idiopathic and traumatic. I have always seen idiopathic tetanus preceded by a peculiar expression of the countenance, stiffness in the muscles of the throat and of the jaw. In infants it will kill in forty-eight hours; in adults, arising from cold, it is of longer duration, and may continue many days, going through the same grades as the traumatic form.

Cross-examined by Mr. SERJEANT SHEE—The patient always appears uncomfortable for some time before the attack comes on. His appetite and desire for food are not much affected. He may take his food as usual within twelve hours of the preliminary symptoms.

During the twelve hours, supposing the attack to be the first one under which he suffers, does he seem not to relish his ordinary food?—His attention is more directed to the stiffness of his mouth and the stiffness of his neck.

You said to within twelve hours of the attack he relishes his food as if no attack was impending, but does he not appear less desirous of food and less inclined to eat it?—I have never heard that complaint.

Re-examined by the ATTORNEY-GENERAL—What interval has occurred in those cases that have come under your attention between the preliminary symptoms and the tetanic convulsions?—In an infant, not more than twelve hours, and in an adult, from twelve to twenty-four hours; sometimes more than that.

And from the commencement of the tetanic convulsions to death, what time?—That will vary; three days to ten days; it may take place early sometimes, perhaps in two days, but that is early.

Does that apply to traumatic as well as to idiopathic tetanus?—They are both alike, when the disease sets in, as regards the course of the symptoms.

Are the symptoms more or less severe in India than in this climate?—I do not see there is any difference; when once set up, the symptoms of tetanus are the same.

John Jackson

In all your experience, did you ever know a case in which the disease ran its course and ended in death in the space of twenty minutes or half an hour?—I have never seen it.

[The rest of this day, after Dr. Jackson's evidence, was occupied with taking evidence that there was nothing in Palmer's papers to show joint transactions between him and Cook; as to Pratt's and Padwick's accounts; as to Palmer's pecuniary position generally; as to the forgery of his mother's name, and the forgery of an endorsement on a cheque for £375 of Cook's name, by which he passed into his own account that sum which was intended for Cook.]

The Court then adjourned.

Mr. Serjeant Shee.

Seventh Day, Wednesday, 21st May, 1856.

The Court met at ten o'clock.

Speech for the Defence.

Serjeant Shee

Mr. SERJEANT SHEE—May it please your lordships, gentlemen of the jury— I should pity the man who could rise to perform the task which it is now my duty to attempt unoppressed by an overwhelming sense of diffidence and of apprehension. Once only before has it fallen to my lot to defend a fellow-creature upon trial for his life; it is a position, even if the effort should last but for a day, of a nature to disturb the coolest temperament and try the strongest nerves; how much more so when, during six long days, in the eye of my unhappy client, I have been standing between him and the scaffold; conscious that the least error of judgment on my part might consign him to a murderer's doom, and that through the whole time I have had to breast a storm of public prejudice such as has never before imperilled the calm administration of justice! Gentlemen, it is useless for me to conceal what you know perfectly well, what your utmost endeavours cannot wholly have effaced from your recollection, that for six long months, under the sanction and upon the authority of science, an opinion has universally prevailed that the voice of the blood of John Parsons Cook was crying up unto us from the ground, and that that cry was met by the whole population under an impression and conviction of the prisoner's guilt in a delirium of horror and indignation by another cry of "blood for blood"! You cannot have failed to have entered upon the discharge of the duties, which you have, as I have observed, most conscientiously endeavoured to perform, without having been to a great extent influenced by that cry; you could not know that it would be your duty to sit in that box to pass between the Crown and the prisoner; you may with perfect propriety, understanding that the facts had been ascertained before a coroner's jury, and reading such evidence as was there taken, have formed an opinion upon the question of the guilt or innocence of the prisoner; but you cannot but know that whatever that opinion may have been it is your duty to discard it, at least until you have heard the evidence on both sides.

Serjeant Shee

Gentlemen, the very circumstances under which we meet in this case are of a character to excite mingled feelings of encouragement and alarm. Those whose duty it is to watch over the safety of the Queen's subjects felt so much apprehension lest the course of justice should be disturbed by the popular prejudice which had been excited against the prisoner, so much alarmed that an unjust verdict might in the midst of that popular prejudice pass against him, that a resolution was taken, not only by the Queen's Government and the Legislature, upon the motion of the noble and learned judge, who presides here, in the House of Lords, that an Act of Parliament should be passed to prevent the possibility of the ordinary forms of law being, in the case of William Palmer, made the instrument of popular vengeance. The Crown, under the advice of its responsible Ministers, resolved also that this prosecution should not be left in private hands, but that its own law officer, my learned friend the Attorney-General, should take upon himself the responsibility of conducting it properly, at once sternly in his duty to the public and fairly to the prisoner at the bar; and my learned friend, when that duty was entrusted to him, did what I must say will, in my opinion, for ever redound to his honour—he insisted that in a case in which so much prejudice had been excited all the evidence which it was intended on the part of the Crown to press against the prisoner should, as soon as he received it, be communicated to the prisoner's counsel; everything, I must say and tell my unhappy client, everything which the constituted authorities of this land, everything which the Legislature and the law officers of the Crown could do to secure a fair and impartial trial in this case, has been done, and the whole responsibility, if unhappily injustice should on either side be done, now weighs with terrible pressure upon my lord and upon you.

Serjeant Shee

Gentlemen, one great misfortune has befallen the accused—a most able man who had been selected by him as his counsel many weeks ago has been, unfortunately, by illness prevented from discharging that duty to him. I have endeavoured, to the utmost of my ability, to supply his place; I cannot deny that I am awed—that I am moved—by the task I have undertaken; but the circumstances to which I have already adverted, the national effort, so to speak, through the Government of the country, to ensure a fair trial is a great cause of encouragement, and I am not dismayed. I have this further cause for not being altogether overcome by the duty which I have of defending the prisoner and of discussing the mass of evidence which has been laid before you, that though, of course, like everybody else, I knew generally and loosely, very loosely indeed, the history of these transactions at Rugeley, I had formed, when the papers came into my hands, no opinion upon them, no opinion upon the guilt or the innocence of the prisoner at the bar, and my mind was perfectly free to form what I trust will be declared by you a right judgment in this case. I commence his defence, I say it in all sincerity, with an entire conviction of his innocence. I believe that there never was a truer word pronounced than the words which he pronounced when he said "Not guilty" to this charge. If I fail in establishing that to your satisfaction I shall be under a great misgiving that my failure was more attributable to my own ability to do justice to this case than to any weakness in the case itself; and I will give you this proof of the sincerity with which I declare upon this evidence my conviction of his innocence, that I will meet the case of the prosecution foot to foot at every stage. I will grapple with every difficulty which has been suggested by my able friend the Attorney-General. You shall see that I avoid no point because I fail to approach it, and if you find that I do thus deal fairly with you from the beginning, and it is my duty to do so, I hope I may be sure, indeed I know I may be sure, of a willing and considerate attention to an address which must, I fear, be long, but in which there shall be no observations, no tone, and no topic of discussion which do not properly belong to the case.

Gentlemen, the case which the Crown undertakes to establish against the prisoner at the bar, and to support by entirely circumstantial evidence, is, or may be, shortly stated thus. They say that the prisoner having in the second week in November made up his mind that it was his interest to get rid of John Parsons Cook, deliberately prepared his body for deadly poison by the slower poison of antimony, and afterwards despatched him by the deadly poison of strychnia. No jury will convict a man of the crime thus imputed to the prisoner, unless in the first place it be made clear that he had some motive for its commission, some strong reason for desiring the death of Cook; unless, in the second place, the symptoms of the deceased before death, and the appearance presented by his body after death, were consistent with the theory of death by strychnia poison, and inconsistent with the theory of death from other and natural causes; unless, thirdly, the circumstantial evidence against him is such as to be inexplicable upon the supposition of his innocence. Now, it is under these three heads that I intend to discuss the evidence that you have heard; and it must be plain to you that if I adhere to that order and method of treating the vast amount of proof which has been laid before you, I must exhaust the whole argument, and leave myself no chance without immediate detection of evading any difficulty in the defence.

Serjeant Shee

Before, however, I proceed to grapple in these close quarters with the case of the Crown, as made by the Attorney-General, allow me, that you may at once see the whole scope of the address with which I have to trouble you, to claim its proper place in the discussion for a fact which, though by no means concealed from you by the Attorney-General, yet appeared to me in that address by which he at once seized upon your judgment to have been thrown too much into the shade, the fact that strychnia was not found in the body of John Parsons Cook. If he died from the poison of strychnia, he died within two hours of the administration to him of a very strong dose of it—he died within a quarter of an hour or twenty minutes of the effects of that dose being visible in the convulsions of his body; the post-mortem examination took place within six days of his death—there is not the least reason to suppose that between the time of the ingestion of the poison, if poison was taken, and the paroxysm in which he died, there was any dilution of it in the stomach, or any ejection of it by vomiting. Never, therefore, were circumstances more favourable; unless the science of chemical analysis is altogether a failure for detection of the poison of strychnia, never was there a case in which it ought to have been so easy to produce it. Now, the fact is, and it is beyond all question, that it was not found. Whatever we may think of Dr. Alfred Taylor, of his judgment, and of his discretion, we have no reason to doubt that he is a skilful analytical chemist—we have not the least reason to suppose, we know the contrary, that he and Dr. Rees, who assisted him, did not do all that the science of chemical analysis could enable man to do to detect the poison of strychnia. They had distinct information from the executor and near relative of the deceased, either personally or through his solicitor, that he, for some cause or other, had reason to suspect the poison of strychnia; they undertook the examination of the stomach, which, I think, upon the whole evidence, without adverting to that part of it now in detail, you will be satisfied was not in an unfavourable condition for a sufficiently accurate analysis, with the expectation that if strychnia had been taken it would be found, and without any doubt as to the efficiency of their tests to detect it; and yet in their letter of the 4th of December they say, "We do not find strychnia, prussic acid, or any trace of opium; from the contents of the stomach having been drained away it is impossible to say whether any strychnia had or had not been given just before death, but it is quite possible for tartar emetic to destroy life, if given in repeated doses; and, as far as we can at present form an opinion, in the absence of any natural cause of death, the deceased may have died from the effects of antimony in this or some other form." Having afterwards attended the inquest, and heard the evidence of Elizabeth Mills and Mr. Jones, of Lutterworth, and the evidence of a person of the name of Roberts, who spoke to the purchase of strychnia poison by Palmer on the morning of the Tuesday, Dr. Taylor came to the conclusion that the pills which were administered to Cook on the Monday and Tuesday night contained strychnia, and that Mr. Cook was poisoned by it; and he came to that conclusion, though he had expressed an opinion in writing that he might—and these are his very words—have been poisoned by antimony, of which some trace was found by him in the body, while no trace was found of strychnia.

Serjeant Shee

Gentlemen, I am not about to discuss that part of the case in detail, but I call your attention to it for the purpose of claiming for it its proper place in this discussion, and that you may know at the commencement of my address what the whole course of my argument will be, and not be under the impression that, because I do not under the three heads to which I have directed your attention advert particularly to that head. I intend to pass it over. I tell you exactly what the case for the defence will be, as to the point that strychnia was not found in Mr. Cook's body. Let me state it as fairly as I can—the gentlemen who have come to the conclusion that strychnia may have been there, though they did not find it, have arrived at that conclusion by experiments of a very partial kind indeed; they contend that the poison of strychnia is of that nature, that when once it has done its fatal work, and become absorbed into the system, it ceases to be the thing which it was when it was taken into the system; it becomes decomposed, its elements separated from each other, and therefore no longer capable of responding to the tests which, according to them, would certainly detect the poison of undecomposed strychnia; that is their case. They account for the fact that it was not found, and for their still retaining the belief that it destroyed Mr. Cook, by that hypothesis. Now, it is only a hypothesis; there is no foundation for it in experiment; it is not supported by the evidence of any eminent toxicologist but themselves—it is due to them to say, and to Dr. Taylor in particular to say, because it will be quite out of my power to speak of Dr. Christison through any part of this discussion except with the respect and consideration which is due to a man of eminent acquirements and of the highest character; it is due to Dr. Taylor to say that he does propound that theory in his book, but he propounds it as a theory of his own; he does not vouch, as I remember, any eminent toxicologist in support of it; and when we recollect that his knowledge on the matter consists—good, humane man!—in having poisoned five rabbits twenty-five years ago, and five since this question of the guilt or innocence of Palmer arose, his opinion, I think, unsupported by the opinions of others, cannot have much weight with you; however, what I have to say now upon that point is, that I will call before you many gentlemen of the highest eminence in their profession, analytical chemists, to state to you their utter renunciation of that theory. I will call before you Mr. Nunneley, a Fellow of the Royal College of Surgeons, and Professor of Surgery at the Leeds School of Medicine, who attended that case of strychnia poison that took place at Leeds, and to which we have agreed that no reference shall be made by name. I will call before you Dr. Williams, Professor of Materia Medica at the Royal College of Surgeons in Ireland, and surgeon for eighteen years to the City of Dublin Hospital, who will tell you that he also entirely rejects that theory, and believes that it has no foundation in experiment or authority. I will call before you Dr. Letheby, one of the ablest and most distinguished among the men of science in this great city, Professor of Chemistry and Toxicology in the Medical College of the London Hospital, and medical officer of health of the city of London, who also rejects that theory as a heresy unworthy of the belief of scientific men. I will call before you Dr. Nicholas Parker, of the College of Physicians, a physician of the London Hospital and Professor of Medicine to that institution, who concurs with Dr. Letheby in his opinion; Dr. Robinson, also of the Royal College of Physicians; Mr. Rogers, Professor of Chemistry to St. George's School; and lastly, I will call before you probably the most eminent chemical analyst in this country, Mr. William Herapath, of Bristol, who totally rejects the theory as utterly unworthy of credence—all of these gentlemen contending, and ready to depose to it on their oaths, that not only if half a grain, or the fiftieth part of a grain, but I believe they will go on to say that if five, or ten, or twenty times less than that quantity had entered into the human frame at all, it could be and must be detected by tests which are unerring. They will tell you this, not as the result of a day's cruelty for ever regretted on five rabbits, but upon a large and tried experience upon the inferior animals, made and created, as you know they were, for the benefit of mankind; upon a very extensive experience in many cases, as to many of them, of the effects of strychnia on the human system. And not to detain you on this part of the case, to which I only now advert, not intending to press it on you later at any length, that you may see what the nature of the defence in point of medical testimony will be, I will satisfy you by evidence which I think must control your judgment, that the only safe conclusion at which you can arrive is that strychnia not having been found in Cook's body, under the circumstances of this case never could have been there. You will find that they all agree in this opinion, that no degree of putrefaction or fermentation in the human system could in their judgment so decompose the poison of strychnia as that it should no longer possess those qualities which in its undecomposed state cause it to respond to the tests which are used for its detection.

Serjeant Shee

Having said so much I will now apply myself to what, in my judgment, is an equally important, if not more important, question in this case, one which I approach with no diffidence whatever except the distrust which I have, under the circumstances in which I speak, of myself, and which, if it were possible for me to write what I think upon it and then to read it to you, I do not entertain the smallest doubt that you must be convinced of the innocence of this man—the question whether, in the second week of November, 1855, he had a motive for the commission of this murder, some strong reason for desiring that Cook should die. I never will believe that, unless it be made clear to you that it was the interest of William Palmer, or that he thought it was his interest, to destroy Cook—I never will believe, till I hear your verdict pronounced, that a jury can come to the conclusion of his guilt. And it seems to me, upon the evidence which has been laid before you, abundantly clear that it not only was not the interest of William Palmer that Cook should die, but that his death was the very worst calamity that could befall him, and that he could not possibly be ignorant that it must be immediately followed by his own ruin. That it was followed by his immediate ruin we know. We know that at the time when he is said to have commenced to plot the death of Cook he was in a condition of the greatest embarrassment. It was an embarrassment which, in its extreme intensity, had come but recently upon him, an embarrassment, too, in some degree mitigated by the circumstance that the person upon whom these bills, which have been stated to you to be forgeries, purported to be drawn was his own mother, a lady of a very large fortune, and with whom he was on the most affectionate terms. Still, he was in a condition unquestionably of great embarrassment. My learned friend has raised the hypothesis of his having a wish to destroy Cook upon the ground of this embarrassment. My learned friend stated to you that the case of the Crown against the prisoner was this, that, "being in desperate circumstances, with ruin, disgrace, and punishment staring him in the face, he took advantage of his intimacy with Cook, when Cook had been the winner of a considerable sum of money, to destroy him and get possession of his money." That is the theory of the Crown. Now, let us test it as a matter of business, relieving, if possible, our minds from the anxiety we must all feel when the fate of a fellow-creature is at stake, as if it was a case in a private room for the decision of an arbitrator. It is my misfortune not to be able at times to speak otherwise than earnestly, but let us look at it as a matter of business and scrutinise it in every corner. Was it his interest that in the second week in November, 1855, Mr. Cook should be killed by a railway accident? If it was not, we have no motive to ascribe to it. If it was not, and more, if the contrary was clearly his interest, no sensible man would believe that he deliberately plotted and committed the murder. A long correspondence has been put in, the material parts of which letters will, in a subsequent stage of the case, be called to your attention. There is evidently a great deal in it that does not touch the point in the case, but the learned judge, before the end of the case, will direct your mind to a correct appreciation of the contents. I watched them with an anxiety which no words can express. Having had the advantage, for which I shall ever honour my learned friend, of reading the correspondence beforehand, I found the history, as told by the correspondence, filled up by the *vivâ voce* testimony which was afterwards given. I was aware, at least I firmly believed, that in that correspondence the innocence of the prisoner lay concealed; and I think that I shall be able to show you that it is demonstrative of this proposition that he not only had no motive to kill Cook, but that the death of Cook was the very worst kind of thing that could happen for him. I shall not apologise to you, you would think it very inopportune to do so, for going into the details of this matter. Allow me, confining myself, as it is my duty, to the evidence in the cause, to call your attention to the position in which these two men stood to each other. They had been intimate as racing friends for two or three years; they had had a great many transactions together; they were jointly interested in at least one racehorse which was training at the stables of Saunders at Hednesford; they generally stayed together at the same hotel; they were seen together on almost all the racecourses in the kingdom, and were known to be connected in betting transactions, and adventurers upon the same horses at the same races. It is in evidence that just before Cook's death he said, in the presence of his friend Jones, addressing Palmer, "Palmer, we have lost a great deal of money upon races this year." And though it is impossible, Cook being dead, and the mouth of the prisoner sealed, and transactions of this character not being recorded in regular books as the transactions in a merchant's counting-house are, to give you in the fulness of evidence the actual state of their relations to each other, yet it is abundantly clear, and I will make it more clear to you presently, that they were very closely connected. When, in the month of May, 1855, money was wanted either by Mr. Cook or Palmer, Palmer applied to Pratt for it. He wanted, I think, £200 to make up a sum for the payment of a debt, he having, I think, a balance of £190 in the hands of Pratt. Mr. Pratt would not lend it him without security, and he proposed the security of his friend John Parsons Cook, a gentleman of respectability and a man of substance.

Serjeant Shee

Now, what the exact state of the affairs of John Parsons Cook at that time was I do not know. Such a fortune as he had might be thrown down in a week by the course of life that he was leading. A young man who is reckless as to the mode in which he employs his fortune, and who has only £13,000, may, if he likes, for a year or two pass before the world as a man of much more considerable means; it is not everybody who will go to Doctors' Commons to ascertain what the exact amount of property he derived from his grandfather was. He was Mr. Cook, of Lutterworth, a gentleman who had a stud of racehorses, who lived expensively, and was known to have inherited a fortune; he was a person whose friendship was at that time probably, and probably continued to be, a matter of considerable convenience to Palmer. You recollect, gentlemen, I am not defending Palmer against the crime of forgery. I am not defending him against the reckless improvidence of obtaining money at the enormous discounts at which he obtained it. The question is, whether he is guilty of murder. Palmer and Cook were then so circumstanced as early as the month of May, 1855. They had had another transaction previously to the date of November, 1855, which I will not advert to now, because it was taken second in the case of my learned friend the Attorney-General; but let us see what their position was in the second week of November, 1855. Respecting that, we have the evidence of Pratt, and from the correspondence which he explained to us there can be no doubt upon our minds. Amongst a mass of bills, amounting altogether to £11,500, which had been repeatedly renewed, there were two bills for £2000 each, which became due in the last week in October; and there was another bill, or two other bills, amounting to £1500 which had become due some time before, but which were held over, as they say, from month to month, Palmer, who was liable upon them, paying for the advantage of having them held over at the end of every month, at what they call interest of about 60 per cent. These three bills, or sums of £2000, £2000, and £1500 were the embarrassments which were pressing upon him in the second week of November; and, be it observed, though pressing upon him, they were pressed upon him by a man, who, no doubt, would have been glad to have got the principal, but who would also upon anything approaching to security have been very well pleased with the interest. How can capital, if it be secure, be better employed than at 40 or 60 per cent. per annum? As long as there was a vestige of good security, Mr. Pratt or Mr. Pratt's clients desired nothing better than that Palmer should continue to hold the money.

Now, in that state of things, on the 27th of October, Palmer, in answer to an urgent demand upon him for money on the ground of the security becoming doubtful, came up to London, and Pratt insisted that, in respect of one of those bills of £2000 which had just become due, as Palmer could not pay it, he should pay instalments upon it in addition to the enormous interest which he charged; and it was agreed at that interview of the 22nd of October that £250 should be paid down, £250 paid on the 31st of October, and that as soon after as possible a further sum of £300 should be paid, making in the whole a payment on account of that bill of £800 to quiet Pratt, or, as Pratt said, to quiet his clients, and induce them to let the bill stand over. On the 9th of November that £300 was paid, and, when paid, a letter was written, which I beg your particular attention to, and you will see how closely and strongly it bears on the point to which I am now entreating your most anxious consideration; a letter of the 13th of November, that is the day when "Polestar" won the race, written by Pratt to Palmer, as follows:—"Dear Sir,—Curiously enough, I find that the great point of the office is, that your brother had delirium tremens more than once, say, three or four times before his life was accepted, and that actually their medical man, Dr. Hastings, reported against the life, as well as Dr. Wardell. I think I shall be able to get a copy of the proposal through a friend." Palmer did not know what the proposal was, and therefore probably it had been made by his brother. "The opinions of several secretaries of insurance offices are that the company have not a leg to stand upon, and from the mere fact of the enormous premium, it is plain that the policy was effected on an extra rate of premium on account of the true statement of the condition of health of the assured. The enormous premium will go a great way to give us a verdict." I do not like to read only one passage from a letter, lest by chance I should mislead, therefore I have read that portion of it; but now attend to this—"I count most positively on seeing you on Saturday; do for both our sakes try to make up the amount to £1000, for without it I shall be unable to renew the £1500 due on the 9th." What does that mean? Pratt told us yesterday the three sums of £300, £250, and £250, and some other small amount, making up the sum of £800, were instalments payable on the bill overdue, and upon which Pratt had threatened to issue writs against Palmer's mother, and Palmer had gone almost down on his knees to beg him not to do so; he said, "For God's sake, do not think of writs." Now, that £800 being paid, Pratt said, "I shall only credit you for £600; I must take £200 for the interest." In his letter of the 13th of November he says, "Do for both our sakes try and make up the amount to a thousand"—that is, make the £800 up to a thousand pounds—"for without it I shall be unable to renew the £1500. I must have a larger instalment, or else I cannot keep this bill afloat for you." He said so, whether it was true or not does not matter in this case; that was the representation which he made, and the duress which he put on Palmer; and, in truth, it meant this—Make it up to a thousand, give me £200 more, or the writ shall be served on your mother. He does not say so, but he said something to the same effect before, and it was a representation that he could not satisfy the people whom he said he represented without that additional sum. Observe, that letter is written on the 13th of November, and Palmer gets it at Rugeley when he arrives on that evening from the race at which "Polestar" won. Palmer, who was at the races the first day, went away in the evening, and went to Rugeley; when he gets to Rugeley, early in the morning of the 14th, the next day probably, he gets this letter of Pratt's pressing on him the necessity of paying a further sum of £200. What does he do? See if it is possible to doubt that at that time Cook's life was of the utmost value to him. He instantly returns to Shrewsbury; he sees Cook. They say he dosed him. We will see how probable that is presently. He gets there on the Wednesday; he sees Cook. Cook goes to bed in a state which I will not at present describe; he gets up much more sensible than he went to bed; goes upon the racecourse, and comes home with Palmer to Rugeley on the next day, Thursday; he goes to bed when he gets to Rugeley; he gets up still ill and uncomfortable, but able to go out, and he dines with Palmer that day, Friday.

Serjeant Shee

Now, I beg your attention to this letter. On that day, the 16th, Palmer writes thus to Pratt—"I am obliged to come to Tattersall's on Monday to the settling, so that I shall not call and see you before Monday, but a friend of mine will call and leave you £200 to-morrow, and I will give you the remainder on Monday." That is written on the 16th, the day they dine together at Palmer's house. Now, you recollect that the person who ordinarily settled Cook's accounts in racing transactions was a person of the name of Fisher, the wine merchant, in Shoe Lane. He was called as the first witness on this trial. That very day Cook writes to Fisher as follows:—"It is of very great importance to both Palmer and myself that a sum of £500 should be paid to a Mr. Pratt, of 5 Queen Street, Mayfair, to-morrow without fail; £300 has been sent up to-night, and if you would be kind enough to pay the other £200 to-morrow on the receipt of this, you will greatly oblige me, and I will give it to you on Monday at Tattersall's." Then there is a postscript which I will read, but make no comment upon it now—"I am much better." What is the fair inference from these two letters? I submit to you that the inference is that at that date Cook was making himself very useful to Palmer. Pratt was pressing him for an additional sum of £200 when he had need of all his money, and Palmer having communicated his difficulty to Mr. Cook, Cook at once comes forward and writes to his agent to pay that £200. And the letter shows more—you may have forgotten that letter, but it was read in the first hour after the speech of my learned friend the Attorney-General; you may have forgotten it, but I read it to you word for word—the passage, "£300 has been sent up to-night," shows that Cook knew all about it, and probably had an interest in Palmer's transactions with Mr. Pratt; it was inserted merely for the purpose of putting a good face upon it to Mr. Pratt, as a man does who, not having a farthing of the sum that he wants to pay, will pretend that he has to pay more, in order to represent that he has got a portion of what he wants to pay, and he says, "Will you lend me a little more; I am not entirely dependent upon you for the sum that I have to pay"; or it means that on that day £300, which had come to their hands in some way or other, was by Cook made applicable to the convenience of Palmer—one of those things it means; whichever way you take it, it proves to demonstration that Palmer and Cook were playing into each other's hands in respect of that heavy incumbrance upon Palmer; and that Palmer could rely upon Cook as a fast friend in any such little difficulty as that; and though his difficulties sound large when we talk of £11,500, the difficulty of the day was nothing like that, because in the spendthrift, reckless way in which they were living, putting on bills from month to month, and paying what sounds an enormous interest per annum, the actual outlay on the day was not always so considerable. I submit to you that letter shows that on the 16th of November, when they say he was poisoning Cook, Cook was behaving to him in the most friendly way, was acquainted with his circumstances, willing to assist in the relief of his embarrassments, and actually to devote a portion of his earnings to the purposes of Palmer. It is perfectly plain, but I will make it plainer if you will attend to me for a moment longer. You will remember that part of the case of my learned friend is this. He says that he intended to defraud Cook; that Palmer having left Cook ill in bed at Rugeley, ran up to town on the Monday, intending to despatch him on the Monday night or the Tuesday; that he ran up to town, went, not to Fisher, who was the agent of Cook, but to Herring, who was his own agent, and told Herring that he was authorised by Cook to settle his Shrewsbury transactions at Tattersall's, thereby getting command over Cook's winnings; that he applied them to his own purposes, and, having done so, determined to put Cook out of the way. That is their case. We had the evidence of Fisher on the first day. Fisher is evidently a shrewd, intelligent man; no friend of Palmer's. He gave, I do not mean to say improperly, I did not wish to throw imputations, but he gave a twist to the dosing at Shrewsbury against Palmer. On the Monday, as on the Tuesday, Cook, though generally indisposed, was during great part of the day quite well, according to the evidence; on the Monday he saw his trainer, Saunders, he saw his two jockeys; he got up and was shaved; he was comfortable the whole day, and the theory is that he was comfortable because Palmer was not there to dose him—you will see how grossly absurd it is presently. He was well on the Monday, quite well on the Tuesday; now, if Palmer had gone up to London, representing that he would do Cook's business for him through Cook's own agent, Fisher, Palmer might be perfectly certain if that was done on the Monday Fisher would write to Cook on that night to say that the thing was done and made straight; Herring, you see, does do it the moment the thing is settled between Palmer and Herring; Herring represents Palmer as saying, "You must write me word about some part of the transactions"; he says, "No, I shall write Mr. Cook word at Rugeley." Do not you think Fisher would have done the same? and if Cook had not known that Palmer intended not to go to Fisher but to Herring, do you not think Cook would have been surprised on the Tuesday morning at not hearing that he had seen Palmer, and that the transactions were settled? Could Palmer, as a man of business, have relied upon Cook's not being alarmed at Fisher's not doing it? We had the evidence of Fisher, who says, "On the 17th of November, at Cook's request, I paid £200 to Mr. Pratt; his account in the ordinary course would have been settled at Tattersall's on Monday, the 19th. I advanced the £200 to pay Pratt; I knew that Cook had won at Shrewsbury, and I should have been entitled to have deducted that £200 from his winnings if I had settled his account at Tattersall's; I did not settle the account." That explains the whole transaction. Cook and Palmer understood each other perfectly well; it was the interest of both of them that Palmer should be relieved from the difficulty of the pressure of Pratt, and accordingly Cook said, "As to the settlement, it shall not go through Fisher; we will have the £200 from Fisher; it shall not be paid to him on Monday; I will let Palmer go up and settle the whole thing through Herring." And that is what was done; and accordingly Fisher has never been paid since.

Serjeant Shee

Now, there is a letter to which I will call your attention, of the 19th November, 1855, from Palmer to Pratt—"Dear Sir,—You will place the £50 I have just paid you, and the £450 you will receive from Mr. Herring, together £500, and the £200 you received on Saturday," that is, the £200 that Fisher paid to Pratt at the express request of Cook "towards payment of my mother's acceptance for £2000, due 25th October, making paid to this day the sum of £1300." Can you doubt when you take all that together—the dining together on the Friday—Cook writing that letter to Fisher, saying it was of the greatest importance to him as well as to Palmer that the £200 should be paid in order to pacify Pratt, can you doubt that on that day Cook was a most convenient friend to Palmer, and that he could not by any possibility do without him. But it does not end there. Cook died on the Wednesday morning early, the 21st; if we want to know what effect that death had on Palmer, and what interest he had in it, Palmer's mouth being sealed, we must get it from Pratt. Nobody else that we know knows anything about it; Cook is gone. On the 22nd November, the day after the death—and I am sure you will make some allowance for a day having elapsed after the death of Cook before he wrote—Palmer writes thus to Pratt—"Ever since I saw you I have been fully engaged with Cook and not able to leave him." Now, unless he murdered him, that is the truest sentence that ever was expressed. He watched the bedside of his friend; he was with him night and day; he attended him as a brother; he called his friends around him; he did all that the most affectionate solicitude could do for a friend that was ill, unless he was plotting his death—"And I am sorry to say after all he died this day, so that you had better write to Saunders; but mind, I must have 'Polestar' if it can be so arranged; and should any one call upon you to know what moneys Cook ever had from you do not answer the question." Then he says, "I sat up two full nights with Cook." That he sat up the whole of the night may not be true, but he was ready to be called if Cook should be ill; and Elizabeth Mills says after the first serious paroxysm, when she went to bed, she left Palmer in the arm-chair, sleeping by the man whom they say he intended to murder. No! murderers do not sleep by their victims in that way. What is the answer? I read it to you in order that you may see what ruin Cook's death brought upon Palmer. The answer of Pratt is—and you will see how much it increased the difficulties of Palmer—"I have your note, and am greatly disappointed at the non-receipt of the money as promised, and at the vague assurance as to any money. I can understand that your being detained by the illness of your friend has been the cause of your not sending up the amount." Attend to this paragraph—"The death of Mr. Cook will now compel you to look about as to the payment of the bill for £500, due the 2nd of December. I have written Saunders informing him of my claim, and requesting to know by return what claim he had for keep and training"; so that the very first effect of Cook's death was, in Pratt's opinion, who knew all about it, to saddle Palmer alone with the sum of £500. He says, "The death of Cook will now compel you to look about as to the payment of the bill for £500 on the 2nd of December." We will investigate the transaction out of which that bill arose, and you will see, I venture to say, that I can satisfy you conclusively that the transaction out of which that bill arose was a transaction for Cook's accommodation, for which Palmer had lent his name to accommodate Cook, and for which upon Cook's death Palmer became primarily and alone responsible. It will be for you to judge, if I prove that to you, whether it suited Palmer at that moment to stand before the holder of that £500 bill—some client of Pratt's—as the only man liable upon it, and whether there was the same chance, supposing it had been for his own accommodation, of putting it on, as they call it, after Cook's death, as there might have been before. But let me be fair to the prosecution, and state to you now the view that the Attorney-General takes of that £500 transaction. As I told you, I mean to meet his case foot to foot, and to show, and I hope to show him, that there is nothing in it; that if he, as the law officer of the Crown, had had the option of taking up this case or not, he would not have taken it up; that the Crown never would have appeared upon it, but because the universal feeling of the country was such as to render it impossible that the case should not be tried after the verdict of wilful murder obtained on Dr. Taylor's evidence; and because the Crown, having seen the absolute necessity of its being tried, felt that it would abandon the duty of protecting every one of the Queen's subjects if it did not take care that a man with so much prejudice against him, that man leading the life that Palmer led, and disgraced by forgeries to a large amount, as it is said, and a gambler by profession, should not have a fair trial. There was no other way of securing a fair trial for this man, as the Attorney-General at once saw—there was no possibility of his being saved but by giving the counsel who defended him all the information that my friend had himself. We will see what his view is. My learned friend states it upon his instruction in this way. He is bound, as I told you in the beginning, in prosecuting this case to prosecute it strenuously; he is bound to put the facts together according to his instructions in such a way that, if they will and ought to establish guilt, it is brought home. Prosecutions must be conducted in that way, or the guilty would escape in nine cases out of ten. And therefore my friend, upon the view of the evidence—a comparatively superficial one— thinks that this is the theory upon which it appears probable that Palmer plotted the death of Mr. Cook. I will read to you from my friend's speech, with reference to the £500 bill transaction; and, as I understand it, it is the greatest mistake that was ever committed, and would not stand for a moment but for the popular prejudice against Palmer. I think I can satisfy you that is so—"Pratt still declining to advance the money"—that is the £1000 which Palmer wanted him to advance—"Pratt proposed an assignment by Cook of two racehorses, one called 'Polestar,' which won the Shrewsbury race, and another called 'Syrius.' That assignment was afterwards executed by Mr. Cook in favour of Pratt, and Cook was entitled to the money raised on that security, which realised £375 in cash and a wine warrant." They twist it in this way, that Palmer, having forged the endorsement of Cook, and being afraid of detection, put Mr. Cook out of the way. That is the view they take of that case. I think I can satisfy you it is impossible that that can be the correct view. It cannot, by any possibility, as it seems to me. It is for you to judge. We know exactly what took place; we had it from Pratt yesterday. What took place was this. Palmer applied for the loan of £1000; Pratt said, "I can't let you have it." Palmer said, "Will you discount a bill for £500?" Pratt said, "Not without security." Palmer said, "What security will you take; it is for the accommodation of Mr. Cook? I have undertaken to get the enclosed bill cashed for Mr. Cook; you had a £200 bill of his." He reminds him that he had been paid a £200 bill, and he says, "He is a very good and responsible man; will you do it, and I will put my name to the bill?" So that it was represented to Pratt as a transaction for the accommodation of Cook; and Pratt's answer is, "If Mr. Cook chooses to give me his security I have no objection, but he must execute a bill of sale of his two racehorses, 'Polestar' and 'Syrius,' and he must execute a power of attorney, and signature to it must be attested by some solicitor in the country, so that I may be quite sure that it is really a valid security; and upon those terms, if you will get all that done, and Mr. Cook will submit to all that, I will give him £375 in money, £65 wine warrant, charging him £10 for expenses, and £50 for discount"— making up the sum of £500; that is what Pratt is willing to do. There is no doubt at all, you know, that Cook attached the highest value to "Polestar"; he was not going to execute a bill of sale with a power of attorney to enable the mortgagee or assignee to enforce it at once; he was not going to do that, and not get any money for doing it; he knew the value of "Polestar" and "Syrius"; "Polestar" was probably backed for the engagements on which he won the money at Shrewsbury. My friend says he never received that £375; it is in the last degree improbable that he never received that money; I put it to you as men of sense that he must have received it; do you think that he remained after executing the bill of sale on the 6th of September the whole time from that day to his death without writing to Pratt—"Why, you have the bill of sale of my two horses, and I have not got any money upon them"? Is it credible, can you believe Cook, who was as much in want of money as Palmer; do you think he would throw away his property in that way, and let Pratt obtain from him a bill of sale and get no money upon it? It is incredible; the only pretence for setting it up is this, it is a perfectly fatal one that will not stand before sensible men for a minute. Along with the cheque for £375 he sent £315 to Palmer for his own purposes; but my friend says Palmer, having got this cheque for £375 payable to order, fraudulently appropriated it to himself; forged the name of Cook upon the back of it, and kept Cook in ignorance of the transaction. Is it credible, that during three whole months Cook, who knew that he had executed a bill of sale of his two racehorses, and I will show you was in want of money, should have allowed it to remain so? Is it not much more probable that the signature of Cook was put on there with his full knowledge? It is not suggested that there was any attempt at imitating his handwriting. Is it not more probable that Cook, who wanted the ready money, and who would probably be put to inconvenience if he did not get the ready money, but only the means of getting it two days later—that Palmer should let him have the £315 cash which was sent up, and Palmer take the cheque? I will show you there is reason for believing that to be the case; I will put it to you, in the first place, whether it is probable he would be silent for three months. Palmer writes, "I will thank you to let me have the £315 by return of post if possible; if not, send it to me by Monday night's post to the post office, Doncaster. I now return you Mr. Cook's paper, and he wants the money on Saturday if he can have it; I have not promised it for Saturday, so please to enclose it with mine in cash in a registered letter, and he must pay for its being registered." So that you see Palmer wanted it to be sent like his own, and Cook wanted it to be sent in cash. "Do not let it be later than Monday night's post." Pratt writes acknowledging the receipt of the document, saying he will send him his money to Doncaster, and endeavour to let Cook have his money at the same time. On the 10th of September Palmer writes to Pratt that he must send him for Mr. Cook £385 instead of £375 and the wine warrant, so that he can hand it to him with the £385. Accordingly, here is an intimation that Cook, who wanted the money on the very day, was inconvenienced by only getting a cheque on London which he could not immediately change, and therefore Palmer gave him the money and took the cheque. It is remarkable, when we look at the banking account of Palmer at Rugeley, the £375 is paid in by somebody to Palmer's account, but the £315 is not paid into Palmer's account at all; that is the only sum paid in on that day, so that I put it to you upon these facts, Pratt saying in a letter which accompanies the money, "I am obliged to send a cheque for Mr. Cook, for I have not received the money, which I shall do no doubt to-morrow"; so that not being able to send cash to the full amount he is obliged to do that which did not suit Cook; he sent him a cheque which he could not cash on the day he got it; he is obliged to send it to London unless he could find some friend down there, and that delays him for a whole day. I submit to you as the true version of the transaction that the bill was accepted for Cook's accommodation; Cook gave as security for it the two horses, "Polestar" and "Syrius"; Cook never complained to Pratt during the rest of his life that he had not received the money upon it. It appears in the correspondence that Cook wanted the ready money, and that he wanted it on Saturday, and it would be probably inconvenient if he had got it a bit later than Monday; though Palmer would not promise to get it sooner than Tuesday. What says Palmer in his letter, which is not written for the purpose of this case, but written at the date of this transaction, that he, Palmer, would let Cook have the cash that was sent, and he himself take the cheque with Cook's authority, and put Cook's name on the back of it; and how else can you account for the silence of Cook, for the fact that the £375 is paid into the account of Palmer at Rugeley, and no trace of the other large sum of £315? That is well worthy your consideration. You cannot account by any reasonable mode for the fact that the security given for that £500 was Cook's horses, and Cook remaining quiet about it for three months after he had executed a regular bill of sale, except the supposition that it was for Cook's accommodation, and Cook got the best part of the money; and, if so, Palmer's name being on the bill, what is the effect of Cook's death? Gentlemen, what Pratt, who knew all about it, says is, "The death of Cook makes you liable for that sum of £500 due on the 2nd December." I submit to you, on the second ground of motive, which my learned friend suggested, the case has altogether failed, and that it is perfectly clear that at the date of Cook's death Pratt was of opinion that the death of Cook threw a further liability on Palmer of £500; he tells him so in that letter. How could it be his interest to kill him? We already find the difficulties which Cook's death brings upon Palmer; the bill of £500, the danger of the loss of "Polestar," which he wanted very much to have, and which Pratt would, of course, unless Palmer paid the £500, send to the hammer, and realise so shortly; we find that inquiries were at once apprehended on the part of Cook's friends as to the money Pratt had paid to Palmer out of those two bill transactions, and the value which Mr. Cook had received for any endorsement which he had given.

Serjeant Shee

Just see another transaction of that date; it is not quite so clear, as it strikes me, but yet it makes it to my mind exceedingly improbable that Palmer should have desired the death of Cook. Exceedingly improbable! Mr. Wetherby told us to-day that though frequently stakes won at a race were sent up by the clerk of the course to the winner's bankers within a week, it was not always so, and it would not be a matter of complaint if it was not. On the 20th of November, the day before Cook dies, and on which he was perfectly comfortable and happy, enjoying the society of his friend Mr. Jones, with whom he was on terms of the greatest intimacy, and to whom he could confide any troubles that he had, and who appears to be a gentleman in every way respectable and intelligent—on that day Cook was well, and Mr. Jones was with him, and there is no doubt that on that day, according to the evidence of Mr. Wetherby, he did sign and give this cheque for £350. If Palmer killed him that night, and by any chance the £350 should not have been sent up by Mr. Frail, so as to be there on the next morning, he (Mr. Wetherby) would not pay that cheque, and would never pay it after notice of Cook's death, though the money should come up. He never did pay it. The end of that transaction was this, that Mr. Frail did not send it up, but made a claim upon Cook in respect of it. Cook's executors disputed that, and Cook's executors finally recovered the money, but they did not send it up to Mr. Wetherby. I do not put it as strong as the other case, because Palmer might think that the money would be there; but he also might think that it would not be there. It is not at all likely that, having got the cheque for £350 from Cook, he would run the risk of losing that money by destroying him in the night, Cook's friends being there, and sure to institute an immediate inquiry into his affairs. Is that probable? I submit to you it is not. It is not likely that Palmer could have got a cheque for £350, or Cook should have given it to him, which should not be payable until the next day, when there might be no funds to meet it; and with that uncertainty, is it likely that Palmer should destroy Cook. That, therefore, is in the last degree improbable. It does not end there—what they have said on the other side is, you know, that he got this cheque fraudulently—he got possession of this money, and then, lest Cook should detect it, he destroyed him. It is not at all probable that that would answer his purpose. The moment the breath was out of Cook's body his friends would surround the corpse. He might be perfectly certain that Mr. Jones would go to Mr. Stevens, that Stevens and Bradford, his brother-in-law, would be down, and that a post-mortem examination would take place, and instead of settling with Pratt as to this £500 bill and the £350 cheque, he would have to settle with hard men of business, men who cared nothing for him, looked upon him as a blackleg, and would care neither for his feeling, his interest, nor anything, but would let him go to ruin which way he liked, not stirring a finger to save him. Do you think that was probable? I submit to you not. It does not end there. We know from Herring that at that very time Herring held one bill for £500 on which Cook's name was.

The ATTORNEY-GENERAL—I do not think there is any proof of that.

Mr. SERJEANT SHEE—Whether it be so or not as to the £500, he had three £200 bills, one of which, I think, was drawn by Cook and accepted by Palmer, and the other two drawn by Palmer and accepted by Cook, or the other way.

The ATTORNEY-GENERAL—You are quite right as to the £500.

<hr>

Serjeant Shee

Mr. SERJEANT SHEE—And another bill of £500, which my friend stated and gave proof was not his mother's signature. So that there was a bill for £500 not in her handwriting to which Cook was a party, for all of which Cook either in whole or in part, unless he rushed upon his own ruin, must provide; in respect of which, for the accommodation of Palmer or not, Palmer could go to Cook and say, "Now, Cook, it is true enough all these bills are for my accommodation, but what is the use of your making a fuss about that? If I cannot pay, you must, or your stud will be sold up; had you not better give your name to some more bills and make it easy?" If he put Cook to death that was gone. Again, in addition to the £500 bill, for which the bill of sale on "Syrius" and "Polestar" was given, the bill for £500 held by Herring was a forgery, according to their case, which there would be no excuse for not meeting; a £500 bill in the hands of a man who wants the money is not so easily put on; that £500 bill would very soon find its way to his mother. It would not have suited Palmer that his mother should know—his mother was a woman of large fortune, a respectable person I am told—she disliked his gambling propensities though she liked her son; neither did the excellent and most honourable man his brother, before me, who stands by him now, but who was estranged from him simply because he disapproved of his gambling, neither would he have given to him any countenance. If Palmer was pressed to pay that £500, and Cook was dead, there was nothing to save him from the exposure. Nothing! If you doubt what I say is the truth, look through the whole of the case—find me in any portion of this most voluminous evidence the slightest trace that there was a man in the world who would lend his name to Palmer to enable him to get money. Is not the fact that he forged, if he did forge, the name of his mother conclusive that he had no other resource? Is there the least trace of evidence that he had any other resource than the good nature, the easiness, perhaps the folly, of Cook, who could have renewed these bills for him—the three £200 bills and the £500—and put them on as they say? And was it not quite certain that if Cook, the acceptor of them, dropped, the claim would come upon Cook's executors, and then the executors would ascertain all about it and sell him up? When you come to think of it, is it credible that the man under those circumstances should desire to bring not merely the creditors and executors of Cook—who might be supposed, though Mr. Stevens is not one of that class, to have some pity for Cook's friend—but men of business, down upon him, who have no right to have any pity? A man dies, his affairs are put into the hands of solicitors; they have a plain duty to perform, they cannot be compassionate, they must be just; they must see the rights of their clients the executors established in due course of law, and compromise and arrangement with them is wholly out of the question. Can you find in any part of this case a single living person who was willing to have done for Palmer what Cook had been doing for him for two or three years? Does it appear that there was one? Does it appear that Cook was a close-fisted fellow, and did not care to do Palmer a turn? When Palmer needed the £200, which the harpy wanted from him, Cook at once wrote and said it is a matter of great importance to him as well as Palmer that this £200 should be paid; and he even risked the displeasure of Fisher in doing it. Then, again, Cook was in his senses perfectly on the Tuesday. He cannot have been very rich at that time. He gave him the cheque for £350. How is it possible to conceive that under those circumstances Palmer should have an interest in the death of Cook, and yet what is the theory of the Crown? That Palmer was convinced that he could settle his affairs as to Cook better with Mr. Stevens than he could with Cook himself—settle these word-of-honour transactions; these things, half of which would not bear inquiry in any way as reasonable business transactions, with a shrewd and probably a penurious man—deliberately thought that it would answer his purpose better to come in contact with his executor, Mr. Stevens, whom Mr. Jones might rush up to town and bring down with him. I submit to you with confidence, though what I say may be inconsistent with the views generally entertained by the public—the public, however, have never had an opportunity of looking at all these letters—but it seems to me as clear as anything can be, that it was the manifest interest of Palmer that Cook should live. But, in addition to its being his interest that he should live, was it safe for him that he should die? Palmer was a man who added to a shrewd knowledge of the world a knowledge of his profession, and, among other things, a knowledge of chemistry. Palmer knew perfectly well, and he had studied his profession sufficiently when he was a young man to know perfectly well, that, if strychnia was administered, it would in all probability throw the victim into horrible convulsions in a very short time, and in a way so striking as to be the talk of a small neighbourhood like Rugeley for a month or two, which would be time enough to alarm everybody, and to provoke inquiries into the circumstances of the death, which must certainly end, or in all probability end, if he was guilty, in his conviction. If that was so, was he so circumstanced at that time as to make it safe for him to run the risk of such suspicions? His brother, Walter Palmer, had died in the month of August, and his only hope, unless his mother forgave him or recognised those acceptances, his only hope of extrication from his difficulties was the getting the amount due by the Prince of Wales Insurance Company to him as the assignee of the policy on Walter Palmer's life; that was his only chance. He had a chance that way, and it is plain that it was so good a chance, as I will show you presently, that he refused an offer of return of premium from the company; it does not appear what the amount was—and Pratt, who was his attorney, believed the chance to be so good that he had actually got the discounts of these large sums of money upon it, and had resolved, under the directions of Palmer, to put it in suit. It was really the only unpledged property he had, and how was he situated respecting it? It is plain from the letters which were put in yesterday, and it is further plain from a piece of evidence to which you will, I am sure, find it worth your while to pay great attention. We had Mr. Deane called yesterday, who is the attorney to the Prince of Wales insurance office; and for some time—though it had ceased just at that time—but for some time previously to this month of November, the insurance company, which, I believe, is not a very old insurance company, were annoyed at being called upon to pay so large a sum, and they determined to do all they could to resist it. They accordingly sent down Inspector Field to Stafford and his man Simpson to make inquiries, which he could not do without talking and insinuating suspicions and raising a cloud of doubt and conjecture about Palmer, and this had been going on for some considerable time. Now, observe the evidence of Deane, and you will see if it is not so. He says, "The name of my firm is Chubb, Deane & Chubb. I had been to Rugeley some time previously to the inquest. I know Field, the detective officer; we were solicitors to the Prince of Wales insurance office; it was in our employment that Field went to Rugeley; he was at Rugeley only a part of one day; he was at Stafford for three or four days altogether; he did not see the prisoner Palmer; this visit had been preceded by that of another officer named Simpson. Simpson went from Stafford to Rugeley with myself and Field; he told me he had seen Palmer; I think he went into Staffordshire in the first week in October." Then my learned friend asked him what they went down for; he said that they went down to make inquiries as to the habits of life of Mr. Walter Palmer, of whose death the Prince of Wales insurance office had shortly before received notice; so that you see just before the death of Cook Palmer knew himself to be an object of suspicion, but he acted as if he thought it was the most unfounded and unwarrantable suspicion, putting the policy of insurance into the hands of an attorney to enforce payment of it, and the office meeting the claim by insinuations and inquiries which were of a nature to destroy his character and to bring around his head the suspicion of another murder.

Serjeant Shee

Gentlemen, that that was so I will show you by the letters which were put in yesterday. You see that the pressure by Pratt upon Palmer to meet the two £1000 bills never took place until the office disputed the payment of that policy. All went as smooth as possible so long as Pratt held what he believed to be a good security, the policy upon Walter Palmer's life, who was dead; but when they began to dispute it, then you will find that Pratt writes to Palmer and tells him the situation of things is quite changed; he could manage the bills very well while that policy was undisputed; but now it is disputed that quite alters the state of things; he says, as he had somewhat anticipated, he finds they can do nothing till the 24th, that is nothing towards compelling the office to pay, because insurance offices generally take three months to pay; and then, stating some other circumstances, he says, "This you will observe quite alters the arrangement, and I therefore must request you to make preparations for meeting the two bills due at the end of this month"; that was where the difficulty was, that was where the pinch was. Then, he says, he shall not flag in his exertions, and so on, and he refers to the circumstances connected with the dispute; Mr. Pratt says—"You, Palmer, know whether they have any ground to dispute that policy upon your brother's life; you are enforcing it, and if you have no right to do it it is at your peril." That is what it means, and then he goes on to say, "We must try and make them pay"—that was the position in which Pratt, who was acting for him, stood as to this Prince of Wales insurance office. He says, "In any event, bear in mind that you must be prepared to cover your mother's acceptances for the £4000 due at the end of the month"; there was the pinch, the office would not pay, the £4000 was becoming due, the holder of the bills saw he was without security, and if anything occurred to increase the suspicions of the insurance office, which was very reluctant to pay, the £13,000 was lost for ever, lost beyond hope. Gentlemen, that £13,000 is sure to be paid unless that man is convicted of murder; and that has a great deal to do with the clamour and alarm which have been excited. So sure as that man is saved, and saved I believe he will be, that £13,000 is paid; there is no defence, no pretence for a defence—the letters of the office make that plain; they took an enormous premium—knowing that the man was only thirty, they took a premium for a man of fifty.

Mr. ATTORNEY-GENERAL—That is not in evidence; do you mean to prove that?

Mr. SERJEANT SHEE—I do not know whether I can show that to be the actual premium, but the letters which were put in show that the premium was enormous; and I say that as sure as he is saved that £13,000 is good for him, and will pay all his creditors.

Now, observe the position in which he was at the moment—all the correspondence turns upon that. This correspondence saves the prisoner, if there is common sense in man.

Serjeant Shee

Now, observe, there is another letter from Pratt containing this passage, "I have your note, acknowledging receipt by your mother of the £2000 acceptance, due the 2nd of October; why not let her acknowledge it herself? You must really not fail to come up at once, if it be for the purpose of arranging for the payment of the two bills at the end of the month; remember I can make no terms for their renewal, and they must be paid. I will, of course, hold the policy for as much as it is worth," and so on. At this time Simpson and Field were making inquiries how a young man of thirty had died, who had had delirium tremens three times, as their own physician, Dr. Hastings, and Mr. Wardell had informed them. Then in a postscript he says he "casts no doubt upon the capability of the company to pay, but that in the nature of things, with so large an amount in question, it is not surprising that, if they think they have grounds for resisting, they should temporise by delay." Does not that show that at that date at least, the 6th of October, suspicions were hanging in menacing meteors about Palmer's head, which would come down with irresistible momentum and crush him upon suspicion of a sudden death by murder? Do you believe that a man who wrote what the effects of strychnia were in his manual would risk such a scene as a deathbed by strychnia, in the presence of the dearest and best friend of Cook—a man whom he could not influence, a medical man, who liked him and loved him well enough when he knew he was ill to sleep with him in the same room that he might be ready to attend to him in case he wanted assistance during the night? Is that common sense; are you going to endorse such a theory as that upon the suggestion of Dr. Alfred Taylor about the effects that strychnia produced upon his five rabbits? Impossible, perfectly impossible! as I submit to you. But to proceed—I will prove to you, most clearly, the position in which he was. On the other side of the letter of the 10th of October Mr. Pratt writes, "Copy of solicitors' reply"; that is, the solicitors to the Prince of Wales insurance office. He says, "I may add that I hear the office have been making inquiries in every direction." To be sure, Field was employed; he is not now in the police, but he is employed as a detective officer; he was at Stafford, and was at Rugeley, and was making inquiries in all directions; inquiries could be made at Stafford as well as Rugeley, and all that had taken place at Rugeley just as easily ascertained there as at Rugeley itself; whatever had taken place there would be known. He says they have been making inquiries in all directions. It is plain, then, that he knew that suspicions were then rife, or that they were endeavouring to create suspicions, against him about the policy on the life of Walter Palmer. Here is the very letter which the company wrote in answer to the claim, dated 8th of October, 1855; it is from Messrs. Chubb, Deane & Chubb, the solicitors to the office, addressed to Thomas Pratt, Esq., acknowledging the application; and shortly afterwards Messrs. Chubb send a reply to the application—there is no date to it, but it is enclosed in a letter of the 18th of October from Pratt to Palmer. After apologising for not answering the letter of the 16th instant, owing to the absence of Mr. Deane, they refer to the "local investigation having been made, and decline to pay the claim upon the ground that the facts disclosed in the course of the inquiry are such as fully to warrant them in doing so." These are letters which my learned friend thought it right to put in yesterday; they are evidence for the Crown, and what is the inference from them? Judge, if you please, from some of the letters to Pratt, and the one which I read first from Pratt to Palmer. Palmer determined that the policy should be paid; he took the advice of Sir Fitzroy Kelly. I see here it is said, "The case will be laid before Kelly to-morrow." This letter came just before the end of the long vacation; the time to take proceedings had only just commenced, in any event, because the three months had only just expired. But so sure as anything happened by foul play to Cook, he had no more chance of getting the £13,000 than £130,000 from the Prince of Wales insurance office—none whatever. That was the only means he had at that time of extricating himself from those incumbrances.

Gentlemen, I have detained you a long time upon this, but not, I trust, too long, if the view I have submitted be one worthy of your consideration. I infer from all this that Palmer had no interest whatever to put Cook to death; that it was contrary to his interest in a pecuniary point of view, and brought claims upon him, some of them small, others of a larger amount, of which he might have shared the liability with Cook, if not have thrown it entirely upon Cook; that it forced an immediate settlement of the affairs of Cook, not with Cook himself, who was an easy man—it is plain he was—and probably their solicitors, and that therefore in a pecuniary sense he had every motive of interest to desire that Cook should live; and further, he had no chance of getting a ready payment from these documents—but with hard and exacting executors of the £13,000, no chance of the sudden death of Cook passing without suspicion and inquiry, and therefore he could not think it safe for him that he should die.

I cannot, I think, be so much mistaken as that a considerable portion of these observations is not well worthy your attention. I humbly contend that the suggested motive altogether fails; and I conclude that head of the observations which I have to address to you by saying that I submit respectfully to you, to the Court, and to my learned friends that that portion of this case has failed. It could not be the interest of Palmer that Cook should die.

I now proceed to the next head, and it is impossible in dealing with this evidence to observe altogether the order of date. I must group the facts as well as I can in order to deal with the whole of the evidence. The question is whether the symptoms of Cook before his death and the appearance presented by his body after death were consistent with the theory of his having died by strychnia poison, and inconsistent with the theory of his having died from other and natural causes. It is under this head, gentlemen, that I shall discuss, I hope not at undue length, the medical evidence in this cause, and present to you such observations as occur to me upon the witnesses who have been called to support the view which the Crown takes of the effect of that medical evidence.

For this purpose let us briefly, in a sentence or two, run over the facts. Cook died on Wednesday morning, the 21st of November, at one o'clock, in violent convulsions; he died in the presence of Mr. Jones. It was no sooner light than Jones posted up to town to see Cook's stepfather and executor,

Mr. Stevens, who came down, and was introduced to Palmer. Palmer took him up to the corpse, and uncovered the corpse to the thighs—brave man he must have been, if he was a murderer, to do that—uncovered the corpse to the thighs before him. Stevens observed the body, and wondered he could have died, he looked so calm, so composed, so well, so little emaciated; he observed, indeed, some slight rigidity about the muscles. I refer to his deposition. I am not sure whether Stevens' deposition was read—but it is evidence supplied to us. He took his hand, and wondered that he should have died; his suspicions were immediately aroused. He dined that day at Rugeley, and asked Palmer to dinner with him, and questioned him about the betting-book; got angry that it was not produced, dissembled with Palmer, cross-examined him, went up to town, met him afterwards at the station at Euston Square, afterwards at Rugby, afterwards at Wolverton, again at Rugeley, and at last threw off the mask, and, addressing him in a tone to which I shall call your attention presently, gave Palmer clearly to understand that he suspected him, and intended to probe the whole matter to the very core. He resolved upon a post-mortem examination, and a post-mortem examination took place. The appearances which were presented at the death of Cook were such as might have been expected by those who had been acquainted with his course of life and his general health, his pursuits—it is a pity to say anything hard of him—his vices—I will not say more than this—his vices, and the company, the drinking, idle, racing company which he kept. His father had died at the age of thirty, his mother about the same age, a year or two after she had married Mr. Stevens; his brother was delicate, his sister was delicate; he was believed by his physicians to have something of a pulmonary complaint, and, when his body was opened, his lungs were found to be emphysematous, that is, their air vessels were distended with air. On further inquiry, for I take both the examinations together, it was found that for a length of time he had been troubled with a very ugly sore throat—a sore throat bad enough to render it necessary that it should be constantly touched with caustic, as well as his tongue; he would not have been able to swallow without it. The tonsils of his throat were at the very time he left for Shrewsbury races, though much better than they had been, sore and inflamed—one of them was very nearly gone, the other was very much reduced in size; and he knew so much better about himself and the cause of it all probably than his medical adviser, that he very much preferred mercury to any other specific for his complaint. He had, besides that, traces about his person which have been so often referred to, the result of disease, that they need not be more particularly mentioned than they have been already, as to the extent of which and the character of which some little doubt exists; but they did not come by an ordinary and chaste mode of life, you may depend upon it; and altogether, as far as it went, he seems to have been about as loose a young man as one is in the habit of meeting, without being utterly lost to all sense of honour and propriety, which I do not mean to suggest that he was.

His body was opened; the soreness of his tongue was manifest; I rather collect that it was not actually sore at the time of his death—yet that there were what they call follicles, and symptoms, if not recent, at least not very ancient, of actual ulcers; the inside of his mouth, too, had been ulcerated, or the skin taken off by some sort of soreness attributed to decayed teeth. We all of us probably have decayed teeth; but that does not happen to us which happened to him—it was sore on both sides. The sores about his mouth he thought himself were syphilitic, and could not be persuaded by the very respectable gentleman, Dr. Savage, to attend readily to his advice. He thought he was not weak enough, I think he said fool enough, to take quack medicines; but weak enough to take the advice of any medical quack who had assurance enough to give advice to him, believing that the best thing for his complaint was mercury; and he was apprehensive, I believe, that what are the worst symptoms of that disease for which mercury is given, namely, spots upon the body, would make their appearance, and that possibly (I believe such things do happen) some day or other he would find on the morning of a race his face covered with large copper-coloured blotches, which would plainly show what life he had been leading. That was the sort of man he was. Many such a man has reformed and become a good and respectable member of society. I should be sorry to say anything unduly harsh upon a man who is gone; but the state of his health is a material subject for our inquiry here. It is plain that he had in his own opinion been affected by virulent syphilis, and that that had not corrected his habits, for he had become recently diseased. The medical men who attended him before concurred in this opinion; and when his body was opened, in addition to all those plainer symptoms of illness to the eye, on the second post-mortem examination, there was between the delicate membrane which covers the spinal marrow, and which is called the arachnoid, I believe—I think I am right—there was pressing upon the arachnoid, and embedded to some extent in the next covering, not so delicate, though still delicate, called the dura mater, granules, as given in evidence, of such an extent as I will satisfy you by men competent to inform you would, if his body had been opened in the dead-house of any hospital in this metropolis, have been said and determined to be the cause of his death.

Such was the condition of Cook, only partially discovered on the post-mortem examination which took place at the desire of the executor, Mr. Stevens. That examination was not conducted with that entirety, so to speak—with that thorough determination to investigate the whole matter—that afterwards was thought to be necessary.

Serjeant Shee

Dr. Taylor attends the coroner's inquest, which is held in consequence, I presume, of his letter. I do not know whether that is so or not, but in consequence of suspicions entertained, and probably in consequence of the letter which he sent in answer to Mr. Stevens' inquiries, and he hears the evidence of Jones, and of Mills, and of Roberts, and of others; but I call your attention to the evidence of those three witnesses, because I think, in fairness to Dr. Taylor, it must be presumed that they principally influenced his opinion. Now, then, I say that upon the loose evidence of chambermaids, and waitresses, and housekeepers, against the opinion of the medical man who attended Cook in his last illness, or, at any rate, with no encouragement, as I will satisfy you presently (for there is an observation to be made upon that)—with no encouragement from the medical man, Mr. Jones, the surgeon at Lutterworth, who was of an age and character, having seen the whole illness, to form an opinion upon the matter—Dr. Taylor, having heard the evidence of Elizabeth Mills, and the evidence of Mr. Jones, and of Roberts, came at once boldly to the conclusion that his notion that antimony was the cause of death was a mistake; and he had the incredible imprudence—an imprudence which has led to all this dreadful excitement—an imprudence which has rendered it necessary that this inquiry should take place in this form and in this place, if at all—to state upon his oath before that jury that he believed that the pills which were administered to Cook on the Monday and Tuesday night contained strychnia, and that Cook was poisoned by it.

Serjeant Shee

Allow me for a moment to ask your attention to what the real character of that opinion was. That opinion as delivered was irrevocable. By it Taylor's reputation was staked against Palmer's life. Instantly followed by the verdict of wilful murder it flew upon the wings of the Press into every house in the United Kingdom. It became known that, according to the opinion of a man whose whole life had been devoted to science, a gentleman of personal character perfectly unimpeachable, a man who stood well with his friends in the medical profession—that on his opinion, not conjectural, not delivered, as an opinion of the kind might properly be delivered, in a private room, to persons on whose discretion reliance was placed, but delivered upon oath in a public room, in the public inn of a little village where everything that took place was known—and he must have known, I cannot but think, that suspicions had been, as I say, and as I think you will be satisfied unduly, excited about the death of Walter Palmer—that, according to his opinion, Cook's death had been caused by strychnia. "In fact," said Dr. Taylor, "though I find no trace of strychnia, and though there is nothing to induce me to believe that there is strychnia in the body, except the suggestion that on the Tuesday Palmer bought it off Roberts" (which would not account in any way, supposing the mere purchase of strychnia could account for anything, for the paroxysm on Monday night), "yet, having heard that evidence, knowing that I have failed to discover the presence of strychnia, I will undertake upon my oath to say, and on my credit publish to the whole world, that the pills which were given to him on Monday and Tuesday night contained strychnia, and that he died from that poison." Observe what it amounts to. It ascertains, not upon scientific, or well-informed, or consistent testimony, but upon testimony ill-informed, of the humblest class, the least fitted to detail accurately the symptoms of such a disease as it is imputed to be, on evidence not consistent with itself, as respects the evidence of Elizabeth Mills in all particulars, or with the evidence of a much better informed person, Mr. Jones, or with the opinion of Mr. Jones—it ascertains, and pronounces positively, that the disease of which Cook died was not simply convulsions of a tetanic form, however violent—not convulsions with many features of tetanus, but that it was actual tetanus, and that description of it which could only be caused by one poison, and that poison strychnia. That is the evidence—he lays that down as a proposition on which he is perfectly satisfied to rest, and on that the verdict goes.

Serjeant Shee

Gentlemen, let me ask you in what position we are placed for the safety of our lives and families if, upon such evidence as this, upon suspicions so excited and so sanctioned by hasty opinions of medical men, we are liable every time a sudden death takes place in a family to be put upon our trials on suspicion of foul play to those with whom we live? In the cases which are usually discussed in this Court, witnesses are called to give evidence respecting processes and means of arriving at truth with a knowledge of the facts in question, with the operation of which processes the prosecuting counsel, the judge, and the jurors are as well acquainted as the witnesses themselves. The witnesses come to speak to facts, a great portion of which are within the ordinary knowledge and appreciation of mankind; but if science is admitted to dogmatise in our Courts—science not exact in its nature—science not successful, but baffled even by its own tests—science bearing upon its forehead the motto that "a little learning is a dangerous thing"—if that is to be introduced to state processes of arriving at truth, conclusive to its satisfaction, but which we cannot follow, and opinions respecting the cause of death which those processes have not discovered, judges and jurors will have an amount of responsibility thrown upon them too great for human nature to bear. This gentleman, Dr. Taylor, if he had found the poison by his own tests, after long experience of their efficacy, would have been a very good witness to have proved unquestionably that strychnia was there; but not having found it, not having seen the patient, and knowing nothing about him but what Elizabeth Mills told him, and what he heard from Mr. Jones, who did not agree with him, or who gave no evidence agreeing with him—with no better means of information than that he thinks himself justified, upon his oath in a public Court, to say that the pills administered by the medical man (of course, he did not mean to impute any misconduct to Mr. Bamford) contained strychnia, that murder was committed, and Cook poisoned by it. If he is allowed to say that, what family and what medical practitioner is safe? Gentlemen, I beg to ask you on what ground does he say that? Not on any peculiar knowledge, for he has not any knowledge as to the effects of strychnia more than any of us—myself, if you please; for when we come thoroughly to look into it he does not appear, of his own knowledge, to have seen a single case of strychnia in the human subject; and yet he has been daring enough, knowing that the consequences would be disastrous to this man—knowing perfectly well that all the world, or, at all events, the great majority of the world, would take for granted that a medical man in his position would not give a hasty opinion—he has the incredible courage to declare, on his oath, that the pills that were given, as far as he knew, by Dr. Bamford, contained strychnia, and that Cook was poisoned by them!

Serjeant Shee

I have said "a little learning is a dangerous thing," and it appears to me that there never was a case in which the adage was so applicable as it is in this. Of all the works of God, the one best calculated to fill us with wonder and admiration, and convince us of our dependence on our Maker, and the utter nothingness of ourselves, is the mortal coil in which we live, and breathe, and think, and have our being. Every minute of our lives functions are performed at our will, the unerring accuracy of which nothing but Omniscience and Omnipotence could have secured. We feel and see exactly what takes place, and yet the moment we attempt to explain what takes place, the instant we endeavour to give a reason for what we know, and see, and do, the mystery of creation—"God created man to His own image; to the image of God created He him"—arrests our course, and we are flung back upon conjecture and doubt. We know in a sense—we suppose—that the soft medullary substance which is within the cavity of the head is the seat of thought, of sensation, and of will. We know that that soft medullary substance is continued down the middle of the back, protected by a bony duct or canal, within which bony duct or canal it lies embedded; and we know that from the sides of this bony duct and from this medullary substance proceed an infinite variety of nerves, the conduits of sensation from all parts of the body to the soul, and of muscles connected and dependent on them, the instruments of voluntary motion. This we know, and we know that by that process all the ordinary actions of our lives, at our own will, are effected with the most wonderful precision. Sometimes, however, these nerves and muscles depart from their normal character, and, instead of being the mere instruments of the will of the soul, become irregular, convulsive, tumultuary, vindicating to themselves a sort of independent vitality, totally regardless of the authority to which they are ordinarily subject. When thrown into this state of irritation and excitement their effects are known by the general name of convulsions. It is remarkable, unlike most other fine names, they are not a modern adaptation. The ancients had them to express the very same thing; the spasmodic and tetanic affections were known then, and as much about them hundreds and thousands of years ago as is known now. Tetanic convulsions have in later times been divided into two specific branches of tetanus—idiopathic and traumatic. We have heard a great deal of these two descriptions of tetanus. One question my lord asked, which was answered by Dr. Todd—it would have been more satisfactory if my lord had asked what the meaning of the English of "idiopathic," viz., self-generating, was; the answer given to the question, What does idiopathic mean? was "constitutional." True, but that means nothing, or, if anything, it means "unaccountable."

LORD CAMPBELL—Without external injury.

Mr. SERJEANT SHEE—Just so, my lord; without external injury, but attributable to no known cause, unless in some few instances, perhaps, where there is some injury in the interior of the body; but the meaning of the word "idiopathic" is unquestionably what I have stated; not that it follows they never can be traced to a cause, but that they constantly occur in which the cause may be attributed to one thing or to another, and in that case we say that it is idiopathic tetanus, because we cannot with certainty say it is traumatic, that is, arising from any external injury.

Serjeant Shee

Now, gentlemen, we have had a great deal of evidence produced by my friends directed to show—assuming that the disease of which Mr. Cook died was tetanus—that it must have been strychnia tetanus. It is a mere assumption they begin with—the merest assumption in the world. I will give you my reasons for saying so, and I think I am justified in so saying. That the deceased died in convulsions is beyond all question, or immediately after convulsions; that they were convulsions that had occurred exactly or about the same hours on the previous night, and something like those which had occurred on the night preceding, something which he described as madness for two minutes, is beyond all doubt. What pretence is there for saying they were tetanus at all? Mr. Jones was examined, and I will read to you presently what the evidence he gave was. Mr. Jones, in the copy of the depositions delivered to me, stated that Mr. Cook died of convulsions, and in the copy of the depositions, which he signed and read over and corrected, there was not a word of tetanus. My learned friend interposed, and said, on looking to the original depositions, it did appear that he had mentioned it, and he said so because in the course of his examination he found a half-written word, "tetinus"—he availed himself of it, not unfairly, to suggest, that though he did not positively say it was tetanus, yet that what he observed was something which put him in mind of tetanus. It bore some of the characteristics of a tetanic convulsion; but, gentlemen, it may do so, and yet not be tetanus; and I submit to you that it is bad reasoning, and I will prove it presently. I put a question to the witness on the subject. It is bad reasoning to say without positive proof of the fact that it was tetanus, and it cannot be traumatic tetanus, because it did not appear it had presented the distinct features of traumatic tetanus, and therefore it must be tetanus by strychnia. That is the argument. They assume it cannot be traumatic tetanus, they have not discovered the poison, but still they say it must be tetanus by poison!

Serjeant Shee

Let us see whether there is any pretence for saying anything of the kind. My learned friends may tell me, if you venture to impeach the authority of a man like Dr. Taylor, who, though he had no knowledge on the subject, undoubtedly is a gentleman of great leading in his profession, and a gentleman who has written a book, which I will not treat as a book not worthy of being attended to because I think it right on this evidence to attack a particular part of it—if you choose to say his opinion is not to be depended upon, it is incumbent on you to suggest some other theory of the cause of Cook's death which will explain the evidence given, and prove not merely negatively it is not what we say it was, but prove affirmatively it is something else. I say I am not called on to do any such thing. The Crown is the party, or rather those out of whose hands this case has been taken by the Crown, who have thought proper to impute the death of this gentleman to the poison of strychnia; they have followed the trail which has been dragged before them by these toxicologists; and, relying on their judgment and discretion, they have made quite sure they will be enabled to establish the fact that it was not either by traumatic or idiopathic tetanus, but by tetanus of strychnia, that he had died. I say I am not bound to suggest any theory upon the subject. It cannot be expected that in the defence I should do so; and, in point of logic, it is not reasonable, when we contradict the fact which it is for them to prove, that our denial of that fact and our reasons should be weakened because we cannot conclusively fix the cause of death, or explain the cause of death in any other way. If we can satisfy you that into any one of the numerous varieties of convulsions this gentleman might have fallen, and might have been either asphyxiated, or by some sudden spasm deprived of life in a way different from asphyxia—it is quite enough for us to prove the probability of that, unless they show conclusively that the circumstances and symptoms which attended his death are irreconcilable with any other theory than that of strychnia poison. Let us see what the symptoms were. I will take the liberty of reading them in the first instance from the depositions, because it is only fair to a person whose judgment I dispute that you should have placed clearly before you the evidence on which they rely.

The Court here adjourned for a short time.

Gentlemen, I have observed in the course of this inquiry, whenever there has been a question of what a witness has said on a previous occasion before a coroner, my lord has thought it right to have the whole of the document read. Now, I propose to read—unless I am corrected by my lord, when, of course, I shall immediately submit—I propose to read, for the purpose of my present inquiry, only that part of the deposition which describes the symptoms.

LORD CAMPBELL—You may read any part of them, completing the sense of the part which you read.

Mr. SERJEANT SHEE—I am much obliged to your lordship; and my object in so doing is this, I will read all the deposition of Mr. Jones, though in truth, in my view of the case, the deposition of Mr. Jones is not so favourable to my case as his evidence in open Court. If there be a difference, the evidence in open Court is more favourable than the deposition; but substantially they are the same. What I propose to do now is to call your attention to the statements of Elizabeth Mills and Mr. Jones before the coroner of the symptoms they observed in Cook on the Monday and Tuesday nights; and having done so, without accepting any challenge which may be made by my friend to account for the symptoms, I will submit to your judgment, on authority which cannot deceive you, whether those symptoms are not more probably accounted for by the convulsions which are not tetanic at all, and certainly not tetanic in its distinct character of strychnia tetanus, but to be classed under those general convulsions by which it constantly pleases Providence to strike man down without leaving a trace of their course in his system.

Gentlemen, what I have to submit to you is this, that the symptoms described in the depositions of Elizabeth Mills and Mr. Jones were such as to make it quite unjustifiable to resort to the hypothesis of tetanus of any kind, much less of strychnia tetanus. You will recollect—I will not repeat it—the peculiarity of the constitution of this young man, and the evidence of occasional functional derangement, not particularly at that time, which involve grave consequences, to which I have already called your attention. I submit to you, on the authorities on matters of this kind, it is much more probable that Cook died in general convulsions, not tetanic at all, than that he died from idiopathic, traumatic, or strychnia tetanus.

I have mentioned all that I intend to say about his bodily infirmities—let us now see what has been the state of his mind. He went to the Shrewsbury races in imminent peril of leaving them a ruined man. Mr. Stevens told Palmer, and we have heard nothing to the contrary, that if anybody had claims upon him, there would not be four thousand shillings to meet them. We know, from the necessity under which he was to raise sums of money at exorbitant interest, that he must have been in circumstances of the utmost embarrassment—that it was impossible, morally speaking, unless some wonderful success on the turf restored his fortunes, that he could stand his ground at all; and it is in this state of mind, and with health, at all events, not strong, and a constitution exceedingly delicate, that he had been for a length of time cherishing the hope that "Polestar," which was hardly his, for it was mortgaged, and which must become another person's if it did not win at Shrewsbury—in all reasonable probability he had been cherishing the hope that "Polestar" would win, and that he by that winning would possess himself at once of the stakes, which my learned friend stated, and I think it was proved, amounted to nearly £400, besides some considerable winnings to the amount of £600 or £700 by bets on the mare—upwards of £1000 altogether. That has been mentioned several times. Fancy the condition in which that young man rose from his bed on the Tuesday morning. He must have known and felt when he went down to breakfast, "This night I am either a beggar, or a man with hopes of recovering myself, and with the means, at least for the time, of keeping up my appearance of respectability." He goes to the races—another race takes place before his mare, "Polestar," is brought to the goal. He waits for it in a state of feverish anxiety and expectation—the hour that intervenes appears to him everlasting. At last the horses start, and his mare wins easily—he is the winner of £1000. We may suppose that to be the sum. What effect has it upon him? Mr. Jones tells us the effect. He is unable to speak for three minutes. He is saved, not merely in purse but in honour and character—saved before his relatives and friends. He will not be a disgrace to them yet, at all events; he may retrieve his fortunes, and become an honourable and respectable man. Conceive him to be a man with right feelings—and it is not because a man falls into the ways of promiscuous licentiousness that he is devoid of all honourable feeling—conceive him to be an honourable man, a man who loved the memory of his father and his mother, who valued the respectability of his family, and who had a desire to appear before his sister, Mrs. Bradford, as an honourable man, instead of being known to her as a levanter and a blackleg, driven from all honourable society. The effect of his success is that for three minutes he cannot speak, though he is with his intimate friend Mr. Jones. He goes back to the inn, though he has to some extent recovered himself, in a state of elation, of which it is my duty to say that one man said he was not more elated than other people when they have won, but still, depend upon it, overjoyed, and with a revulsion from the despair in which he was, which must have convulsed, though not in a sense of immediate illness, every fibre of his frame. His first and his natural inclination was to entertain his friends, and he gives a champagne dinner. The evidence is that he did not drink to excess; that is the evidence—but he had champagne, and we all of us know that when there is champagne there are other things besides, and it very often happens it is not because champagne is drunk the company do not drink as much of other wines. What in ordinary parlance is called a champagne dinner is a good, luxurious entertainment, in which there is no stint and not much self-restraint. I do not mean to say he was drunk. The evidence is he rose from table not drunk, and therefore it is not for me to say, and the evidence will not justify me in saying, he was. That evening he did not spend in the company of Jones. I do not think it is very clear in whose company he spent it after the dinner was over; but we find him the next night, Wednesday, at the Unicorn, with Saunders, the trainer, Mr. Palmer, and a lady. The next morning is cold and wet. He went on the ground, and was observed by Herring standing in the wet, who remonstrated with him for so doing. He was taken ill that night, and you will hear what his symptoms were. I shall call your attention to those under the third head of what I have to address to you. He sent for a doctor, who recommended an emetic. The poor man seemed to know more about it than the doctor. He said he could do it with hot water and a toothbrush. Perhaps he had often relieved his stomach in that way. He was unwell that day, and was ailing till his death at Rugeley. That is the general history, as far as the mental excitement can be referred to—great reason to apprehend ruin when he went to Shrewsbury; immediate, sudden, yet only partial recovery from his embarrassments at Shrewsbury; and home to Rugeley to meet them again in their full intensity, all the winnings and twice the sum, unable to save him from the ruin he had brought on himself. All the property he appears to have had at the time was "Polestar" and "Syrius," and they were mortgaged for debts due to Pratt. He may have had some few hundreds in money. It is with a weakened body and an irritated and excited mind that he is affected with a sickness at Shrewsbury, which clings to a system incapable of being recruited by the ordinary necessary food, without which the strongest man gives way, excites his nerves, and makes him in imminent danger of falling a victim to any convulsive attacks to which his constitution would be likely to be disposed. Depend upon it, the thoughts of that young man, when he retired to bed, were not the thoughts with which you lay your heads upon the pillow. He had much to think of which he regretted, much to deliberate upon which was of a nature to excite in his mind the most serious apprehensions. There was neither credit, nor honour, nor anything in his career which would make him respect himself, or respectable in the eyes of others. His rest was only imperfect at the best, and after the gratifications of the animal appetite to which people in some instances resort to alleviate the unhappy recollections of the moment, he had no resource. He desired no society so much as the society of Palmer. His residence was at the Talbot Arms, which was, in fact, a residence with Palmer. He does not appear to have had a sitting-room to himself; he does not appear to have frequented the coffee-room. He had a bedroom at the Talbot Arms, and his real home, where he often was, and would have been nearly altogether but for his illness, was Palmer's house over the way. That was his condition at Rugeley. He is taken violently ill on Sunday night. We had nothing but his own description of it; but what is that description? He had been poorly for some time. For two nights he had been taking opium pills prescribed by Mr. Bamford. Mr. Bamford is an aged man, but there is no doubt a respectable man, and a man who would be likely, I think we might fairly infer, to consider what the complaint was and prescribe accordingly. In the middle of the night, at twelve o'clock, he was awakened from a dream in a state of affright. He says he was nearly mad; he rang the bell, but nobody would come.

LORD CAMPBELL—He thought they would not hear him; he thought they had gone to bed.

Serjeant Shee

Mr. SERJEANT SHEE—Yes; that is so; I am much obliged to your lordship. He states he was mad for two minutes, and what did he ascribe it to? Nothing but sudden alarm at the noise of a quarrel in the street. Does that happen to us, gentlemen? Does it happen to those of us who live regular lives, and who are of good average constitution? Do we awaken in a state that we can describe as madness, and without any mode of accounting for the paroxysm but a quarrel in the street? It must have been a very high state of nervous excitement. It must have been something violent while it lasted—transient in its character—but something that arose from a disordered state of the stomach and an agitated and anxious mind, probably in some degree weakened by the medicine he was taking, the calomel and the morphia.

The next day, the Monday, he was well the whole day; not well in the sense of being strong and able to take a walk in the fields, or mount his horse and gallop about the country, but well in the sense of being able to get up, after trying to breakfast in bed, to talk of sending for the barber, and, I believe, actually sending for him; of seeing his trainer and his jockeys, and discussing his plans for his next campaign—well to that extent, but not out of his bedroom, taking no substantial food, not vomiting much that day, though a little I think in the morning, which is ascribed by the theory of the Crown, or by those whose case the Crown has been forced by public opinion or by public excitement to take up, to Palmer's absence all that day. We do not hear that Cook took anything solid. We do not hear that he lunched at one o'clock, and then, as most probably he was in the habit of doing, took his beefsteak and his leg of mutton, or his chicken, at five or six o'clock. He had no insuperable dislike to brandy and water; he could, on occasion, take his glass or two, though Palmer was not there; but he does not appear to have been in the condition, ill as he was, to have any gratification in food or drink of any kind; and Palmer was in London all the time. Then, in the middle of the night, at twelve o'clock, he was seized with a paroxysm, which Elizabeth Mills describes. We will take her description. That is the account of Cook's illness on Monday night. It might have been a much less serious fit than the one on the Sunday night. Nothing took place which could justify any man in saying that he was mad for a minute—nothing of the kind. But let us be fair. Afterwards, in talking of it, he says, speaking to Elizabeth Mills, "Did you ever see anybody in such agony as I was last night?" We have the description of Elizabeth Mills, and his own statement afterwards; "I saw him again about seven o'clock, and he asked me whether I ever saw anybody in such agony as he was the previous night." Not to tie the young woman down to a word, the fair inference of the whole of that statement is that for some time during the whole of that paroxysm he was in pain, and in great pain, but that he never lost his senses. He could not very well be in such a state as that which he described on the Sunday night. Now, let us have the statement of Mr. Jones, who is, we must take it, a perfectly competent man, and whose evidence must be attended to. Mr. Jones was requested to go there by Palmer, Palmer having written to him on the Sunday. He was not able to go then, being himself indisposed, and he could not get there till Tuesday. He went there on the Tuesday, and got there by three o'clock, and he was for some time with Cook alone.

Now, just observe the consequence of that, looking at the circumstances of this case. Mr. Jones was the most intimate friend, as far as we can judge, that Cook had. Probably he was. He had a great regard for Mr. Stevens, who had been the husband of Cook's mother, but he was not so intimate with Mr. Stevens. Mr. Stevens was probably a gentleman who did not approve—in fact, he frankly told us he disapproved—of the course Cook was pursuing. Probably he was more austere to him during life than we should imagine from the way he speaks of him after death. His best friend seems to have been Mr. Jones. No doubt Mr. Jones, though he was a respectable man, did not take on himself to rebuke or reprove Cook for what he might think it not correct to do. He lived in his house at Lutterworth, and appears to have been on such good terms with Cook that Palmer knew it would not be disagreeable to Cook if Mr. Jones would come and stay and sleep in the same bedroom, and so long as he required the attendance of a friend; and, as far as we can understand, Mr. Jones has Cook to himself from three to seven o'clock. He has him to himself for some considerable time. You know part of the suggestion in this case for the Crown is that Cook thought that Palmer had played false with him at Shrewsbury; part of the suggestion in this case is that Cook thought at Shrewsbury Palmer laid a plan for circumventing him, and of getting his money. Mr. Jones had the opportunity, during the afternoon, if Cook had wished it, of being the recipient of the whole confidence of Cook; Cook might have said to Mr. Jones, "I am glad you have come; I have been acting the fool with Palmer; I suspect him; I think he means to get my money."

The ATTORNEY-GENERAL—You must not say that. You would not let me ask him any questions about it.

Mr. SERJEANT SHEE—I do not say that it did pass. I use it in this way, it might have passed, and that it did not is clear, because Mr. Jones entertained no suspicion of the kind; he having been with Cook during the whole of the evening shows that it did not pass, and that nothing occurred in the entire and unbounded confidence which may be supposed to have existed between Cook and Mr. Jones to raise a suspicion in the mind of Mr. Jones; and so much was that the case that, at the consultation which took place between seven and eight o'clock on Tuesday evening, between Mr. Jones and Palmer and Mr. Bamford, as to what the medicine ought to be, the fit of the Monday night was never mentioned; it was not alluded to at all.

Gentlemen, that is a very remarkable fact; it is remarkable in two ways; the Crown might say it is remarkable in this sense, that Palmer knew it, and said not a word about it. But it seems it was a matter, in the opinion of Cook, so little serious, that he never said a word of it to Mr. Jones, because, if Cook had thought that those words which he used to Elizabeth Mills were not an exaggerated description of what had occurred, do you not think, when Mr. Jones came to see him, and felt his pulse, and inquired what his symptoms were, that Cook would have said (he being in full possession of his senses), "You cannot judge now from my appearance how I am—I was in a state of madness last night—I was in the greatest possible agony—I do not know what it was—I was attacked in the middle of the night in such a way that I thought I was going to die"? As he had Mr. Jones with him, would he not have mentioned that in the conversation? My inference from that is, that in all probability this first statement of Elizabeth Mills was the correct statement of what occurred; and if we find it is consistent with what Mr. Jones says as to what occurred the next night in its general character, it would be very nearly the same on both nights. We may reasonably infer that anything in excess of that, on which the medical evidence was given, has been the result of imagination, and not so strictly consistent with the truth as the original statement. Let us see what Mr. Jones says. (The learned Serjeant read a portion of the deposition of Mr. Jones before the coroner.) Observe the significance of that. Palmer, in the presence of Mr. Jones, brings up two pills, which it is supposed were the pills that poisoned him—pills containing a substance which sometimes does its work in a quarter of an hour, which has done it in less, but never hardly exceeds half an hour; and so we are to be asked to believe that Palmer, Jones being present, and Cook in his presence objecting to take the pills, positively forced them down his throat, at the imminent peril of his falling down, like the rabbit, in two or three minutes afterwards in convulsions evidently and manifestly tetanic. He states what did take place. (The learned Serjeant read a further portion of Mr. Jones' deposition.) But, as I am reminded by one of my lords, that in the course of the examination of Mr. Jones the word "tetanus" is used, it is right I should say a word on that, lest I should forget it. The word "tetanus" is not in the deposition, and it is very remarkable that the suggestion which has been put forward by the Crown was the suggestion of Dr. Taylor. I do not think it is impossible that Mr. Jones, when he gave that evidence, had in his mind's eye what he had seen that night and not seen very correctly. He had not light enough to see the patient's face. There was only one candle, and he could not tell whether there was any change in his countenance on the Tuesday—a very important symptom. They say it cannot have been tetanic, because there is a peculiar expression in the face—a fact which nobody observed. It was too dark, in this case of Cook's, to take notice. Mr. Jones gave his evidence, and he is a competent professional man, and it is quite clear that the notion of tetanus, tetanic, tetaniform, or something like tetanus, must have entered into his mind, because the clerk has put down "tetinus"; he probably had not heard of the word before, and the probability is something like it was used. He said he did use it, and afterwards it was struck out, and Mr. Jones corrected his deposition, read it all over, and signed it, and left it with the word struck out. There are strong symptoms of "compression," that is, one word struck out; then afterwards there is the word "tetinus," and then those two words are struck out, with Mr. Jones' entire approbation, because otherwise he would have corrected it when he signed it; and he said he read it over, and the words "violent convulsions" were substituted. What is the fair inference from that?—that the man who saw Cook in the paroxysm did not think himself justified in saying it was tetanus. It might be very like; it might have a tetaniform appearance; but it was not tetanus.

Gentlemen, I will call your attention to the features of general convulsions. I cross-examined several of the medical witnesses for the purpose of inducing what I consider to be a true belief as to this case, that the convulsions in which Cook died were not tetanus or tetanic properly speaking; but that they were convulsions of that strong and violent character which are tetaniform, though not classed under idiopathic or traumatic tetanus, but under the head of general convulsions.

Serjeant Shee

Gentlemen, I now propose to read a description of general convulsions from the work of Dr. Copland. I called the attention of the very learned gentlemen who were examined for the Crown to what was laid down in that work, which is admitted to be one of authority, and I cannot conceive how you, to whom this matter of fact is to be submitted, can form an opinion whether or not my theory, or rather my belief, that he died by the visitation of God, in violent general convulsions, be a probable one, unless you hear from what was not written for the purposes of this case what the features of general convulsions are; so, if you please, I will read to you what I have myself copied from the work of Dr. Copland. This, I may say, as I am upon the point, that the only persons in the profession who can be supposed to have any competent or reliable information on the subject of tetanus, not traumatic, are physicians; and not one physician—properly so speaking—not one of that most honourable body of men who see the sudden attacks of patients in their beds, and not in hospitals, has been called to speak to this. Dr. Todd was called, and Dr. Todd gave his evidence in a way to command the respect of everybody; but Dr. Todd is a gentleman whose practice does not appear to have been so much that of a physician as that of a surgeon; he is physician to the King's College Hospital, and has held that office about twenty years; he has lectured on diseases of the nervous system and tetanus, but he does not appear to have been a physician in general practice.

Serjeant Shee

Gentlemen, I am instructed—I shall be able to show—by eminent men that what I am about to read from Dr. Copland's book, as part of my speech, is a true description of convulsions that are not idiopathic or traumatic, but of a general kind. He first gives the definition of "general convulsions," which he says are "violent and involuntary contractions of a part or of the whole of the body, sometimes with rigidity and tension (tonic convulsions), but more frequently with tumultuous agitations, consisting of alternating shocks (clonic convulsions), that come on suddenly, either in recurring or in distinct paroxysms, and after irregular and uncertain intervals." We will see what he says about it—"If we take the character of the spasm in respect of permanency, rigidity, relaxation, and recurrence as a basis of arrangement of all the diseases by abnormal action of involuntary muscles, we shall have every grade, passing imperceptibly from the most acute form of tetanus through cramp, epilepsy, eclompsia, convulsions, &c., down to the most atonic states of chorea and tremor. Also if we consider the affections called convulsions, and which are usually irregular in their forms, with reference to the character of the abnormal contraction of the muscles, we shall see it in some cases of the most violent and spastic nature, frequently of some continuance, the relaxations being of brief duration, or scarcely observable, and in others nearly or altogether approaching to tetanic. These constitute the more tonic form of convulsions, from which there is every possible grade, down to the atonic or most clonic observed in chorea or tremor. The premonitory signs of general convulsions are, *inter alia*, vertigo and dizziness, irritability of temper, flushings or alternate flushing and paleness of the face, nausea, retching or vomiting, or pain and distension of the stomach or left hypochondrium, unusual flatulence of the stomach and bowels, and other dyspeptic symptoms. In many instances the general sensibility and consciousness are but very slightly impaired, particularly in the more simple cases, and when the proximate cause is not seated in the encephalon; but in proportion as this part is affected primarily or consecutively, and the neck and face tumid and livid, the cerebral functions are obscured, and the convulsions attended by stupor, delirium, &c., or pass into or are followed by these states. The paroxysm may cease in a few moments, or minutes, or continue for some or even many hours. It generally subsides rapidly, the patient experiencing at its termination fatigue, headache, or stupor, but he is usually restored in a short time to the same state as before the seizure, which is liable to recur in a person once affected, but at uncertain intervals. After repeated attacks the fit sometimes becomes periodic (the convulsio recurrens of authors). The most common causes are, *inter alia,* all emotions of the mind which excite the nervous power and determine the blood to the head, as joy, anger, religious enthusiasm, excessive desire, &c., or those which greatly depress the nervous influence, as well as diminish and derange the actions of the heart, as fear, terror, anxiety, sadness, distressing intelligence, frightful dreams, &c., the syphilitic poison and repulsion of gout or rheumatism."

Now, do you believe that if Dr. Taylor had read that before he went to the inquest he would have dared to say that this man died of strychnia poison? Is there one single symptom in the statement made in the depositions of Elizabeth Mills and Mr. Jones which may not be classed under one of the varieties of the degrees of convulsions which Dr. Copland describes? Now, it is not for me to suggest a theory, but the gentlemen whom I shall call before you, men of the highest eminence in their profession, not mere surgeons of hospitals who never see anything hardly except it is of that nature, that is, of the traumatic kind—gentlemen, do not suppose that I should be capable of speaking disrespectfully of Sir Benjamin Brodie, or of any of the gentlemen called except in terms of the highest respect; but they are surgeons of hospitals, and obtain a certain experience as to those misfortunes under which, through violence, the human frame suffers; who have not so much opportunity of witnessing and of knowing the symptoms of the class of convulsions which constantly attack people in their own residences in the dead of the night—those convulsions which heads of families and brothers and sisters are most anxious to conceal from anybody but the medical man—those convulsions, the known existence of which deprives a young woman of the hope, or a young man of the hope, of marriage. It is the men who have that sort of experience—the general practitioners—men who enjoy the entire confidence of numerous families, and have the opportunity of visiting, in the way of their profession, the poor at their lowly dwellings, suffering under sudden convulsions when affected by serious disease—those are the men that we want to tell us about convulsions. Do not let me mislead you for a moment—the evidence I have read to you is not the whole of the evidence of Elizabeth Mills. There is her evidence, differing in some material particulars from the evidence given by her before the coroner. As to Mr. Jones, the evidence does not so much differ, though there may be some particulars in which there is a difference—and there is one remarkable one. He said in his depositions, "The body was resting on its head and its heels"; but in his evidence he says, "It was so bent that if it had been turned on its back, it would, or might, have rested on its head and its heels"—that is, if it did not rest on the back; but he in substance says it did. Mr. Bamford says he found it resting on its head, its back, and its heels, thereby excluding the supposition that a part of the body was not supported by the back. However, before I go to that, perhaps you will permit me to call your attention to the symptoms of traumatic disease. My belief is, and I submit it to you, and it is what I shall hope you will confirm by your verdict, that this complaint was not strychnia tetanus at all, but it was, according to this description—the description to which I will call your attention—it may well have been some form of traumatic tetanus or idiopathic tetanus—there being no broad general distinction or certain confine between idiopathic or self-generating tetanus, or tetanus not arising from any extreme hurt or any violence to the interior part of the system; and many forms of convulsions, that is tetaniform, are pretty much the same as idiopathic tetanus, and we have had numbers of medical gentlemen who have told us they never saw a case of idiopathic tetanus. The answer to that is, you have had very limited experience. They are not very frequent; but there are gentlemen here who have seen cases of idiopathic tetanus, and they are not of such unfrequent occurrence by any means. There is one gentleman who is here, and whom I will call before you—a gentleman who attended at the bedside of the lady at Leeds who was suffering under strychnia, who has himself seen four cases of idiopathic tetanus; and there are other gentlemen here who have seen them also—they are not so rare, but they very rarely fall under the notice of surgeons of hospitals; they are not so frequent as traumatic tetanus. Cases of traumatic tetanus do frequently supervene from the operations of the surgeons themselves; sometimes after operations, however skilfully performed, a lockjaw is the consequence. The persons to give you information on the subject are the general practitioners.

Serjeant Shee

Now, we shall see that none of those symptoms which were spoken to on the day of the inquest by Elizabeth Mills and Mr. Jones may not range under one of these forms of tetanus, the idiopathic or traumatic. The idiopathic mingling in all directions with general violent convulsions is not to be distinguished from them, inasmuch as convulsions have constant tetaniform appearances; and the meaning I take it of that is this, it is true, as Dr. Watson says in a passage which I called to the attention of one of their witnesses—it is true that in four cases out of five traumatic tetanus begins with a seizure of the lower jaw, unless, as Sir Benjamin Brodie tells us, it may begin, as it did in two cases which he attended many years ago, in the limbs. He told us so when he was here; it began there before it attacked the jaw; but generally trismus or lockjaw is the first symptom. But there is a fifth case in which it is not, and Mr. Curling told us that that was about the proportion—four out of five; so that even traumatic, or that kind of tetanus which sets in after a wound, does not always begin with some affection of the jaw or neck. Now, gentlemen, having gone so far, and having endeavoured to satisfy you that the symptoms which were spoken to by those two witnesses on the depositions may be the symptoms, as I think—that is to say, as I am told, having no experience of my own in the matter—that these symptoms are rather referable to that violent description of general convulsions than to any form of tetanus, let us go to the question, whether or not the symptoms are consistent with what we know of tetanus produced by strychnia, because if we are satisfied on a full inquiry that they are not consistent with the symptoms unquestionably produced by strychnia tetanus, then the hypothesis of the Crown entirely fails, and John Parsons Cook cannot have died of strychnia poison.

Now, gentlemen, whether that be so or not will depend in a great degree, as it strikes me—but, of course, it is entirely for you—on what you think of the evidence of Elizabeth Mills; but before I go to the evidence of Elizabeth Mills I will call your attention to what the description of strychnia tetanus is, as given us by two very eminent gentlemen who were called the other day for the Crown—Dr. Taylor and Dr. Christison; and if we find on looking at it that that description of the poison of strychnia tetanus, given by them, is a different thing from the picture first given of the complaint, of the paroxysms of John Parsons Cook by Elizabeth Mills and Mr. Jones, I think it would be rather too bad on their mere opinion to say that this is strychnia tetanus. Let us take Dr. Taylor's description of strychnia tetanus—I am not sure whether Dr. Taylor stated he had ever seen strychnia tetanus in the human subject; however, we must be just to Dr. Taylor. Dr. Taylor has had an extensive reading upon the subjects upon which he writes, and it is not to be supposed that Dr. Taylor would hastily set down in his book what he did not find established on high authority; therefore, though having it at second hand, Dr. Taylor knows something upon the subject.

Now, Dr. Taylor, in his work on strychnia poison, has this under the head of strychnia, "that from five to twenty minutes after the poison has been swallowed the patient is suddenly seized with tetanic symptoms, affecting the whole of the muscular system; the body becomes rigid, the limbs stretched out, and the jaws so fixed that considerable difficulty is experienced in introducing anything into the mouth." On both the depositions and the other evidence it is stated that Mr. Cook was sitting up in bed, beating the bed-clothes, frequently telling the people about him to go for Palmer, asking for the remedy, and willing to take whatever was given him; there was no considerable difficulty in introducing anything into the mouth, and the paroxysms, instead of beginning within from five to twenty minutes after the poison was supposed to have been swallowed, did not begin for an hour and a half afterwards. Dr. Taylor further on states, "After several such attacks, increasing in severity, the patient dies asphyxiated." That there were some of these symptoms in this case there can be no doubt, and there will be some of them in every case of violent convulsions, yet it is not the description of such a case as that of John Parsons Cook. Now, let us see what Dr. Christison says—"The symptoms produced by strychnia are very uncommon and striking—the animal begins to tremble, and is seized with stiffness and starting of the limbs. Those symptoms increase till at length the animal is attacked by general spasms." Is that the description of either of these paroxysms? Who can say with any degree of truth that it is? Just observe these last indications of strychnia tetanus, which are consistent with all the cases stated in their books. It is only justice to those gentlemen who have taken pains to look to the authorities to which they refer to say that the statements which they give of their cases are in the main correct, but not in all their details. The books would be five times their size if they were; but they are in the main correct, when we look to the foreign authorities on which they are founded—"The fit is then succeeded by an interval of calm, during which the senses are impaired or are unnaturally acute; but another paroxysm soon sets in, and then another and another, until at last a fit occurs more violent than any that had preceded it, and the animal perishes suffocated." I know exactly what Dr. Christison means by this, because there is a gentleman here who will state an experiment which I saw myself; it was an experiment, and for the purpose of this case, and to assist me; and I disagree with Dr. Taylor that there can be a moment's hesitation in sacrificing ten or twenty dogs for the purpose of ascertaining the truth of this theory when a man's life is involved. These experiments were performed by Dr. Letheby while I was there. I will state them to you, because he will prove it by and by. A dog had some strychnia put in his mouth, one grain, and then for about—I cannot be sure as to the time exactly, but about twenty or twenty-five minutes—I cannot be sure, it might not be so much—the dog was perfectly well. There were two rabbits on the table which were also about to be subjected to the operation, and the dog, when the chain was sufficiently relaxed to enable him to do so, showed all the indications which a dog naturally does to get at the rabbits; he was pulling at his chain, and was smelling and pawing and taking an interest in the rabbits; suddenly it fell down on its side, and its legs were stretched out in a most violent way. It panted, and then it remained for some time—two or three minutes—quiet, occasionally a little jerking, but generally quiet. It recovered again for a time, got up and looked at the rabbits, but was dizzy, seemed afraid to move; and, if you touched it, shuddered and twitched, to use Miss Elizabeth Mills' description; seemed to be afraid, and after another moment down it went again. It got up again, and down it went again, and at last it had a tremendous struggle, and it died. That is what Dr. Christison means by this description; it would be true if the dose had been a strong one. If the dose had not been sufficient to kill the dog it would probably be a longer time—at least, I suppose so—in producing its effect, and the interval between the paroxysms, as stated by Dr. Taylor and Dr. Christison, would get longer and longer, until at last the animal would recover. If the dose is strong enough to kill, the interval between the paroxysms is shorter, till at last the violent one comes which destroys life; the eyes are fixed, and there it lies, and just before its death—and I thought it was dead, but I was told immediately before its death—just before it dies, the limbs become as supple and as free as it is possible to conceive the limbs of an animal to be; whichever way you placed them after the animal is quite dead, if you place them in any form, the rigor-mortis comes on, and they remain in the position in which you place them. Dr. Christison says they assume rigidity. I saw this operation performed, and also on the two rabbits, and their symptoms were substantially the same, and their limbs in both cases were quite as flaccid immediately on death. The animals during the time of the intervals between the paroxysms were exceedingly touchy, and seemed afraid of being touched at all; if you were to touch them they would shrink away. It was more so in the dog; it was, in fact, a sort of shudder—that is what Dr. Christison means.

Now, gentlemen, without going through the whole of these details, I will state to you my reasons for saying, on the authorities and from my study of the books of those two gentlemen, that, according to their principles, this cannot have been strychnia poison. Now, I object to the theory of its being strychnia poison, first, on this ground, that no case can be found in the books in which the patient while the paroxysm lasted has had so much command over the muscles of animal life and voluntary motion as Mr. Cook had on the Monday and Tuesday nights. You heard that Mr. Cook was sitting up in his bed, that Mr. Cook was beating the bed-clothes, that Mr. Cook was talking and crying out for Palmer, and to have the remedy given to him; that Mr. Cook, so far from being afraid of people touching him, asked to have his neck rubbed, and it was rubbed. There is not a single instance in the books of Dr. Taylor, or in the books of Dr. Christison, or any other books of any medical man describing the symptoms of the strychnia poison, in which the well-known symptoms the malasaux took place—not one, and it is inconsistent with their description, and what I tell you will be the proof Dr. Letheby will give of the experiment that I saw, and of many others he had performed.

I will go to the next point on the ground of which I say this is not strychnia poison. I say there is no authentic case of tetanus by strychnia in which the paroxysms were delayed so long after ingestion of the poison as in this case. I will refer, however, to their own statements, knowing that they are here. (Extract from Dr. Taylor's book read.) There was one case to which his attention was called; it was not a fatal one, but it got better, and still he says the symptoms were those which he described, and thought it was too late to get the poison out of the stomach, as in half an hour it had got into the circulation—what can be more clear? it is a broad, distinguishing feature in the strychnia. The interval which took place between the ingestion of the poison in Mr. Cook's case and the time when the paroxysm commenced was much too long, three times too long, to indicate the effect of poison by strychnia. It cannot be pretended it was a similar case, if the symptoms are properly described, as I will presently call your attention to them, by Elizabeth Mills in her statement in this Court. Now, gentlemen, thirdly, I submit, and I will prove, that there is no case in which recovery from a paroxysm of strychnia poison has been so rapid as in Cook's case on Monday night, or in which a patient has enjoyed so long an interval of repose or exemption from its symptoms after they had once set in. It is a very remarkable feature, if it be true—if I am right in saying that there is no case in which recovery has been so rapid as in Mr. Cook's case on Monday night, followed by so long an interval of relief from the paroxysm. In fact, in the case of Mr. Cook's, on the theory of the Crown, it would not have come on again if a second dose had not been given. There was an end of it when Elizabeth Mills left Palmer sleeping by the side of his friend in the arm-chair. How easy it would have been for him then, if he had been disposed, when Elizabeth Mills had gone to bed and had retired to her room, to have called out to her that Mr. Cook was in another fit, and to have killed him, almost without suspicion on the part of anybody. Dr. Christison tells us in general terms that these convulsions are succeeded by intervals of calm, during which the senses are unnaturally and unusually acute; another fit then begins, it subsides, and is succeeded by another and another, till at length a fit takes place more violent than any before it, and the animal dies suffocated. Here, I submit to you, is a distinction between the case of Mr. Cook and that which these gentlemen state to be the distinguishing feature, in that there is no recurrence.

Now, I will come to another feature of the disease, the post-mortem symptoms of the disease. I saw three animals killed, of which I have spoken to you, and Dr. Letheby was good enough to have dug up from his garden a rabbit which had been killed by strychnia, and to open it before me, to examine the heart, and the heart was full; the heart of the dog was quite full, and the hearts of the two rabbits which I saw killed were quite full—as full as they could possibly be. I am told that the result of an enormous proportion of such examinations has been, and, if properly conducted, of all of them, that the heart is full on the right side invariably. We will prove to you that the heart of the animal which was killed by strychnia poison is invariably full, and it stands to reason it would be so.

Serjeant Shee

Now, I have discussed what may be said for this purpose to be the theory of the matter, but I have not yet met the strong point which will be made for the Crown on the evidence of Elizabeth Mills. I am, on all occasions, most reluctant to attack a witness examined on his or her oath, and particularly if she be in a humble position. I am very reluctant to impute perjury to such a person. Let me point out to you what occurs to me to be the right opinion to be formed of the evidence of Elizabeth Mills. I submit to you in this case of life and death, or in any one case involving any question of real importance to liberty or to property, that that young woman's evidence cannot and would not be regarded in the ordinary administration of justice when on material points she has stated two different stories. A jury can really hardly believe such a witness, and in criminal cases the learned judges are, without altogether rejecting the evidence and withholding it from the jury, in the habit of pointing out to the jury the discrepancies between the statements given at different times, and saying that under all the circumstances of the case it would not be safe to rely on the testimony in the last instance, if it differ from, and probably is more strongly adverse to, the party accused than the statements made when the impression was fresh in the witness's mind. Now, observe that since the first time that she gave her evidence she has had the means of knowing what the case of the Crown is. She has had the means of knowing—I do not mean to say she has been tutored by the Crown—it would be a gross injustice to say so; and I know if my learned friend thought that had been done he would not have called her—or by any of the gentlemen who act for the Crown; but since she was examined at Rugeley she has had the means of knowing, by interviews she has had with different people, that the case of the Crown is, that Palmer, having first prepared the body of Cook for deadly poison by the poison of antimony, afterwards despatched him with the deadly poison of strychnia. She has learned that their case is, that there was an administration of something which did not eventually kill him, that is, antimony, but which had the effect of producing retching, and nausea, and irritation of the stomach, which is attributed, according to the hypothesis of the Crown, to the deliberate, persevering intention of the prisoner at the bar to reduce him bit by bit—making him reject everything off his stomach, so that when once the ingestion of the poison occurred he was certainly dead; that is the case. In her first evidence before the coroner she was asked whether she had tasted the broth, and she said that she had tasted the broth, and thought it very good; she did not say a single word about any ill effects that broth had produced upon her—not a single word. She has since learned it is part of the case for the Crown, or of those out of whose hands the Crown has taken this prosecution—in fact, the theory of Dr. Taylor—that all this retching and vomiting was the result of a constant dosing with antimonial poison, in order to prepare him for an utter inability to resist the fatal dose of strychnia which it was intended to give him. Accordingly, when she is examined here, fitting her evidence to the case, and probably after having been asked many times whether she had not been sick on some Sunday or another, she has persuaded herself, if she has not been persuaded—I do not wish to use the word suborned—that her sickness on some Sunday afternoon took place on the Sunday afternoon that broth was sent, and was caused by her having taken two spoonfuls of it. She did not say so in the first instance before the coroner, but that "she tasted it, and it was very good." I ask you to consider for a moment whether it is not to the last degree improbable that a man like Palmer—a shrewd, intelligent, clever man—would expose himself to such a chance of detection as the sending of poisoned broth made at the Albion to the Talbot Arms, at the imminent risk of its finding its way to the kitchen, where, sure as fate, the cook would taste it. Can you conceive a cook not tasting broth made by another cook, and sent over as particularly good? I submit to you it was such a risk as no man in his senses could by any possibility run. A cook is, in the nature of the thing, a taster; she tastes everything; she does not know, of course, if it be her own making, whether it is good until she tastes it; she gets the habit of tasting—and as sure as Palmer sent the broth to the Talbot Arms, and any part of it reached the kitchen, so sure, if it contained antimony, would the cook be ill. Is it credible? I submit to you, it is not credible; and when you find she did not say a word about it in the first instance, and that an ample opportunity was afforded for her so to do in the way I have described, I submit you cannot rely upon her evidence here, as it differs with her evidence before the coroner. Again, she said that on the Saturday Cook had coffee for breakfast about eight o'clock. "He ate nothing but he vomited directly he had swallowed it. Up to the time I had given him the coffee I had not seen Palmer." When she gave that evidence she was not aware it was part of the theory of the Crown that the traces of antimony (which Dr. Taylor says might have killed him) were to be made to fit into the theory of the strychnia poison—that it was a gradual preparation, by vomiting, for strychnia. That chart of the country over which she was to travel had not been laid before her. She did not then know what at the time she came here she did know—that it was part of the case for the Crown.

The Attorney-General opened the case in that way distinctly, that that was the theory for the Crown; "that Palmer had ordered some coffee for Cook on the Saturday morning; it was brought up by the chambermaid, Elizabeth Mills, and given to Cook by Palmer, who had an opportunity of tampering with it before giving it to Cook." That was the statement which the Attorney-General was instructed to make. There is all the difference between her first statement, that up to the time she had given the coffee to Palmer for Cook, and that Palmer had an opportunity of tampering with it. The young woman would not go so far as that, but she went to this extent—"Palmer came over at eight o'clock—ordered a cup of coffee for Cook—I gave it to Cook—I believe Palmer was in the bedroom—I put it into Mr. Cook's hands, but I did not see him drink it—I observed afterwards the coffee had been vomited." The statement thus made by her before you was not so strong as that of the Attorney-General, but, on the other hand, it was a great deal stronger than the statement she made before the coroner, because, according to her story then, Palmer had not an opportunity of dealing with it—she "did not see Palmer up to the time she had given him the coffee." From the statement which she made here you might suppose that Palmer, if he had chosen, might have got the coffee from Cook—but that is in the last degree improbable—and have done what he wanted to do with it; for she says, "Palmer came over at eight o'clock and ordered a cup of coffee, and that when it was made she took the coffee up into the bedroom and gave it into Cook's hands" (she believed Palmer was there), "but she did not see him drink it, and afterwards she observed the coffee had been vomited." These two statements, the one before the coroner and the other before you, are essentially different, and the difference between them consists in this, that the last one supports the theory now set up on the part of the Crown, while the first one is totally inconsistent with it. Can you rely on a woman who has altered her testimony to such an extent? But that is not all; the case for the Crown is that Cook was reluctant to take the pills which were given to him, and that he expressed a reluctance which Palmer of his own head overruled, and that Palmer knew that Cook was angry with him, or, at all events, displeased with him, for forcing him to take the pills. In the first statement of Elizabeth Mills before the coroner she said Cook said it was "the pills that made him ill, and that he had taken the pills about half-past ten." When she came here she swore that Cook said "the pills which Palmer gave him at half-past ten made him ill"; thereby, you see, fixing the fact that Palmer gave him the pills, and fixing the time at which Palmer gave them to him, she having had an opportunity of learning that the later the pills were given the more favourable it would be to the suspicion that death had been occasioned by this poison. Before the coroner she did not say that Palmer was in Cook's bedroom between nine and ten o'clock on the Monday night, but she did when she was here. You will see that makes him more about the bedside of Cook, having more opportunity of dealing with the pills. By these variances from her first statement she shows the animus which now, for some reason or other, actuates her. Perhaps it has been the result of the persuasion that Palmer was the murderer of Mr. Cook, as Dr. Alfred Swayne Taylor swore he is, and of her horror of so great a crime; that gives it the just, charitable construction; still, I say, she is not to be relied upon. I have mentioned the particulars in which her statements vary, but these are nothing to the important particulars to which I will now call your attention. I impeach her testimony on the ground that she adopted here a manner and a gesticulation in describing the symptoms under which Cook laboured which, if true, would have exhibited itself at the inquest, and would have at once attracted the attention of Dr. Taylor. The contortions into which she put her hands, and her neck, and her mouth, before you, could not by any possibility have escaped the attention of Dr. Taylor. If anything like it took place there it would have been observed by him, and questions would have been put to reduce, so to speak, those gesticulations into verbal expressions, that they might be recorded in the depositions. But that is not all. I am told, and you will have an opportunity of hearing it from Mr. Nunneley, Dr. Letheby, Dr. Robinson, and other eminent medical men, that the description of the symptoms which she gave to you is inconsistent with any known disease— that they were grouped by her in a manner so extraordinary as to be quite inconsistent with strychnia tetanus.

Serjeant Shee

Let me call your attention to this part of the evidence. You are aware that in the months of February (the last week of February) and March a very frightful case of strychnia poisoning occurred at Leeds. It was a case in which a person, having constant access to the bedside of the patient, was supposed to have administered repeated small doses of strychnia so as not at once to strike her down, but gradually to destroy her; and that after having kept her in a state of irritation for a lengthened period, he at last consummated the work and killed her. That was the case. It appeared in all the newspapers. The nurse who attended the patient and the medical gentlemen spoke of symptoms which she exhibited from the 24th or 25th February to the 1st of March, and they described it in this way—She had "prickings" and "twitchings" in the legs, coming on without any violent paroxysms or spasms, and was alarmed at the thought even of being touched by anybody in the intervals of the spasms which occurred from time to time. Now, let me call your attention to the evidence before you of Elizabeth Mills. She says, "He said, 'I cannot lie down'; his body and neck were moving and jerking; he would throw himself up, jumping and jerking all over his body all the time; he asked me to rub his hands; I noticed him to 'twitch' while I was rubbing his hands." (The learned serjeant read a portion of the evidence.) Now, I submit to you that some of these expressions, particularly the twitching, are very remarkable; and it may well have been that, this case coming before the public and exciting no little degree of attention, although not to the same extent as this Rugeley case, persons who had been in the habit of going to see her and conversing with her may have been asking her questions about this case, of which she admitted she had heard, "Did you observe in Cook any such symptoms as these?" her attention being called to them in such a way as to induce her to alter the statement made by her at the inquest. You cannot, indeed, account, as I submit to you, for so remarkable a difference between the first and second statements, without supposing something of that kind. Now, is it improbable that that did take place? From the time she left the Talbot Arms till she came here she seems to have been a person of very remarkable importance. She went to Dolly's, and Mr. Stevens visited her six or seven times. Why did he visit here? What for? Mr. Stevens is unquestionably—and if under proper self-restraint, no one can blame him for it—very indignant at what he fears to have been the foul play of Palmer with Cook. He is not in the same condition of life as Elizabeth Mills. Why should he have gone to visit her six or seven times, conversing with her in a private room? She says, "He only came to see whether I liked the place; he called to inquire after my health." Gardner also, his attorney, saw her once, but only asked her how she was, and they talked about other things. She said she gave the last authentic account of her evidence to a man she did not know—whom she had never seen before; and when I found out, after much questioning, that Mr. Stevens was with him, and asked her why she had not told me so, her answer was, "Because you never asked me." That raised a laugh, and she enjoyed her triumph. All this looks like having been tutored. I put it to you that you cannot, with any degree of satisfaction, rely on the evidence of the young woman; and you will learn that the confusion and the variety of the symptoms she has put together, taking them partly from her depositions and partly from this new version, have made the case which she described not only not a case of tetanus, but not of any known disease.

Serjeant Shee

Now, on this part of the case I have this observation to make; the illness of the Sunday night appears to have been a very remarkable occurrence. It came out in the course of the examination, as a fact spoken to by Cook, and it will be for you to judge, after you have heard the evidence of the medical gentlemen, whether the periodicity of the attacks does not militate against the theory of death by strychnia poison. The illnesses of Cook take place three nights running, exactly at the same time, or if not exactly at the same time, very nearly. I find that is a symptom of very frequent occurrence, that about the same hour of the night, or of the week, or of the month, and very often after the patient has got to bed, the thing occurs. It is about the same hour in this case of Mr. Cook's. On the question whether the symptoms were such as are consistent with the theory of strychnia poison, and inconsistent with the theory of death from other and natural causes, I have only now further to state what I intend to prove. I will not go through in detail what will be better stated by the gentlemen who will be called; but I shall call a number of most respectable physicians, surgeons, and general practitioners, having extensive experience in our large cities, who all support the view I have to submit to you, and which they have suggested to me as the probable one—that these fits of Mr. Cook were not tetanus, but violent convulsions, the result of the weak habit of his body, which had been increased by his mode of life.

I propose now to discuss the question whether the circumstantial evidence against Palmer be such as to be inexplicable on the supposition of his innocence, and if I show you on the broad and salient features of the evidence that it is not (you will not expect me to go into the more minute details), and I have succeeded in satisfying you on any considerable portion of the points to which I have directed your attention, and if the evidence comes up to what I have been instructed to say it will, you will be too happy, recollecting that you are the country in the language of the law—that the country out of doors, in a case of crime, of life and death, is uninformed, without the opportunity of hearing the witnesses examined or cross-examined on their oaths to decide between the Crown and the Queen's subject on the evidence alone. Every word of this evidence will be carried to all the ends and corners of the earth, and it will remain to be seen whether this great country of England, in a paroxysm or convulsion of prejudice, created by the rashness of one scientific man who had no knowledge of his own about the matter, has made up its mind to sacrifice the life of a fellow-creature under circumstances which would expose any person who has ever been present at deathbed convulsions liable to the same charge.

I say the circumstantial evidence in this case is not such as to justify you in coming to a conclusion of the guilt of the prisoner. I will endeavour in this part of the discussion to address myself to those portions of the case which seem at the first blush of them, and on judicial consideration of them, to require notice. I will not avoid anything that is difficult or that may seem to you difficult, so that when I sit down you will see that I have discussed this great argument fully and fairly in every branch of it, and ask yourselves, what ground is there for any verdict but a verdict of "not guilty"? I will avoid nothing, and proceed at once to one of the most salient points. I will pass over, after an intimation that was made from the bench, the point about pushing the man at the inquest, or the accident of a slit in the covering of the jar, which, sharp instruments being used by the operators, may easily have occurred, or the putting it in a further corner of the room, from which there was no possibility of its being removed. I do not believe that any such circumstances as these would induce you to come to a conclusion against the prisoner.

LORD CAMPBELL—No member of the Court, I think, has intimated any opinion as to the other portions of the case; merely as to the pushing.

Serjeant Shee

Mr. SERJEANT SHEE—I do not wish to suggest anything which is not strictly correct, and perhaps I ought not to use what was intimated from the bench in any way, but rather submit that, where everybody perfectly well knew Palmer, in any little apparent shove, so to speak, during the course of the post-mortem, is not to be taken as an evidence of his guilt. It was in leaning over, if at all, to observe an examination of considerable interest to all persons present, and I cannot conceive that anything of this kind can be taken into consideration. No serious complaint was made at the time. Mr. Devonshire said nothing was lost by it. He said also the jar was removed to a corner of the room. It was not removed out of sight. It was in the broad daylight. It was impossible it could be taken away without observation. It would be absurd that Palmer should be suspected of having done so with an improper object. This we know, that he was very reluctant to have the jar removed out of the possession of those on whom he could rely. That is very true; there were some persons who did not want to pay him £13,000; there were some persons who had been doing all they could to undermine his character for a very considerable time, imputing to him the most wicked conduct respecting a near relation, which none of his own relations ever joined in, knowing that there were many persons at Rugeley much prejudiced against him, and it was in his judgment of the last importance that anything which could be brought against him (and it was clear that this post-mortem, from the conduct of Stevens, was intended to found a charge against him), should be kept in unsuspected custody, and that nobody should have an opportunity of tampering with it and its contents. When told that Dr. Harland is coming to make the post-mortem, he says, "I am glad of that, for there is no knowing who might have done it; and it is a satisfaction that you, whom I do know, are coming to superintend it." I say that was the conduct of a respectable man, who knows that his conduct would bear investigation if it were properly inquired into. But we know also that in a town like Rugeley there were a great many serious people, who could not approve of his habits of life, to whom his running about to races would not much recommend him, and whom he has reason to know would not very much regret any injury which might happen to him.

Is there any other part of his conduct connected with the post-mortem which requires explanation? When the jar was going to be sent to town he objects to its going to Frere's. He had some reason for that. He had an assistant in his service who had been in the service of Frere. We know the jealousies that exist in country towns between professional men. We will not do Mr. Frere the injustice to suppose he would do so great a wrong to Palmer as might result from tampering with the contents of the jar; but still it was right to be cautious, and Palmer told Dr. Harland, "I want you to take it with you to Stafford, and not let it go to Frere's house." In these minor incidental matters his conduct appears to me perfectly consistent with innocence. Let me call your attention to this more important matter, on which my learned friend in his instructions was told to rely—and accordingly he did, in the discharge of his duty, rely upon it. I will call your attention to what has been stated by Myatt, the postboy. His evidence was pressed into the case; it could not well be excluded from it as an evidence of guilt. Now, what did it amount to? Before I have done, under the general head of Palmer's conduct, I will call your attention to what passed between him and Stevens. You will find the conduct and deportment of the latter were such as would make some men almost kick him; it was so very provoking, supposing Palmer was innocent. He dissembled with him—pretended to take his advice—cross-questioned him—changed his tone upon him—now speaking to him mildly, now in a voice of menace—threatened him with a post-mortem examination—and evidently did the whole thing hostilely to him, as if he thought something wrong had taken place, and it was his duty not only to protect the property, but to see any person who had been guilty of foul play towards Cook brought to condign punishment. Stevens, after poring over the remains of the dead man at the post-mortem examination, was ready to leave Rugeley, and a fly was ordered for him and his companion, Mr. Boycott, in which they were to proceed with the jar to Stafford, and thence by rail to London. Now, if there were anybody base enough, either in support of a theory, in support of a reputation—God forbid that I should suggest that to the prejudice of Dr. Taylor!—if there were anybody capable of so great a wickedness as tampering with the jar, it might easily be done; and he was anxious to have it kept by Dr. Harland and not committed to the custody of Stevens. His conduct to Palmer had been vexatious and annoying in the last degree; the fly was being got ready after Palmer, we may suppose, had dined; and meeting the postboy Myatt, he asked him, according to Myatt, whether he was going to drive Mr.

Stevens to Stafford. "I told him," said Myatt, "I was. He asked me if I would upset them?" Now the word "them" was first used in this Court to designate the jars. There was only one jar at that time, so it could not be meant to apply to the jars; if used at all, which I think very doubtful for the reason I tell you—at least in a bad sense—it must have been applied to Mr. Stevens and his companion. And now just see if the facts in this case which are undoubted do not give a reasonable colour to that. Palmer (though I will show you his conduct to Stevens was exemplary in every respect, by putting the dialogue between them before you without making any comment on it) must have felt outraged beyond all expression if—knowing himself to be innocent, that he had acted as a friend and brother to Cook, and had called his relations about him when he was ill—he found himself suspected of stealing a trumpery betting-book, which he knew was of no use to any one, and charged of playing falsely and foully with the life of Cook. He had great cause to be vexed and irritated with Stevens, and that he was so is plain from what he said to Dr. Harland—"There was a queer old fellow," he said, "who has been down making inquiries, who seemed to be suspicious of my having stolen the betting-book, which everybody knows can be of no earthly use to anybody." It shows that his mind was impressed with the idea that he was wronged. He may be supposed, communing with himself, to say, "He has ill-treated me; he has encouraged suspicions which have been excited against me already, and which, if he persists in his course of bringing another charge against me in this matter, will probably render it impossible to get the money from the insurance company in time to rescue me from a position which may involve in ruin myself and some members of my family." That was evidently the tendency of what Stevens was about. He meets this postboy and asks him if he is to be ready to drive the fly to Stafford; the boy says, "Yes, I am." He said, "If I would upset them there was a £10 note for me." He has been asked, "Had anything been said about the jars?" I submit to you the true construction of the story, if it occurred at all, is, that being under a feeling of irritation against Stevens, and using strong expressions with regard to Stevens, hearing he was going to Stafford, he said, "I should not mind giving £10 to upset him." He had been vexed at his conduct, and irritated by the perpetual suspicions and inquisitiveness which he had displayed, even when he went up with him, like a friend, to show him the corpse, uncovering it down to the thighs. Some previous suspicion must have existed in Stevens' mind; but Palmer had no suspicion of this thought that he was guilty of so foul a crime as that which was imputed to him. If that evidence be throughout true, it is only true in the milder and innocent sense, and I have this reason for saying so. This man was in the service of the landlord of the Talbot Arms, and was always about the yard; he was driving to and from the Talbot Arms every day of his life; he must have been there on the day of the post-mortem examination; he must have been a constant companion of the stable boys and labourers about the yard; and his observation must have been drawn to a thing so striking and remarkable as a post-mortem examination on account of a suspicion of murder. He was not called before the coroner; and nobody knew, at the time the inquest was held, that he had ever said anything which could be fairly taken in a sense which would make it evidence of a guilty mind in Palmer. But if he had said that Palmer said, "I should not mind giving a £10 note to have him upset; it is a humbugging concern," and in that manner, and with the feeling I have stated, it would not have excited any observation or suspicion, and no one would have summoned Myatt to the inquest. I submit that is the true version of this story. It is not to be supposed that a medical man, knowing that he had given a large dose of strychnia, would suppose that, by the accidental spilling of a jar, the liver and spleen and some of the tissues continuing untouched, he could have escaped the detection of his guilt.

Serjeant Shee

Next I shall call your attention to the evidence of Charles Newton; he is a person who has sworn before you that he saw Palmer at Mr. Salt's surgery at nine o'clock on the Monday night, and that Palmer asked for three grains of strychnia; that he weighed it, and gave it to him in a piece of paper; that is the first part of what he swore before you and my lords. Now, I should tell you how this case has been conducted. As soon as my learned friend the Attorney-General, as counsel for the Crown, was made acquainted with the illness of my learned friend Mr. Serjeant Wilkins, with his inability to conduct the defence and that I was to supply his place, he desired that every scrap of evidence against the prisoner should be forwarded to me, and to my learned friends near me; and, accordingly, as soon as he received this evidence of Newton he forwarded it to me, and I received it on the day this Court met. I believe it was sent to me late on the previous night, but I did not see it until the morning you were sworn; so that this witness Newton did not bring this matter that was in his knowledge of the fact of the purchase by Palmer at Mr. Salt's surgery at nine o'clock on the Monday night of three grains of strychnia—he did not bring that to the knowledge of the Crown until the night before this trial commenced. Now, he had been examined at the inquest, and he did not tell before the coroner the rest of the story which he told when he was examined here. (The learned serjeant read the examination of Charles Newton.) He did not tell that to the coroner. All he told the coroner was that he was present when Palmer bought some strychnia off Roberts on the Tuesday night in the shop of Mr. Hawkins; he did not speak to the purchase of the strychnia on the Monday night; he knew that he was called to corroborate a statement which Roberts had made as to the presence of Palmer at the shop, and the purchasing of the strychnia on the Tuesday, yet he never said one word at that time either of the fact of Palmer having bought strychnia off him on the Monday night or of his having asked him what appearances, if a dog were killed by strychnia, would be exhibited on its post-mortem examination. A man who so conducts himself is utterly unworthy of credit. There is one honest, laudable motive in a Court of justice, and that is to assist in the administration of the criminal law of the land. If any man had the least hesitation when in Court, or to come into Court and take the oath to depose to what he knew were the facts, we should not be safe against crime for a moment. But you cannot justify the fact of swearing away another man's life, except under a sense of duty, and for that object; and if a man, knowing that he is to be sworn touching so grave a subject as that of murder, the first time he takes the oath omits a considerable portion of what he knows, and three weeks afterwards tells another portion, and at a further interval comes forward and tells more—enough, in his opinion, to drive the guilt home to the man who is accused—the witness, I say, who conducts himself in that manner ought not to be believed. The prisoner who is convicted upon the evidence of such a man as that is sacrificed by a jury. But there are other circumstances in that statement which render it in the last degree improbable. That Palmer should, once in a week, purchase strychnia in the town of Rugeley is not to be wondered at. Strychnia is sold for many purposes, to kill dogs and vermin, and Palmer, as you may recollect, had often occasion to complain of the dogs from the slipping of the foals and the galloping of the mares. In the course of the evidence in this case it has been mentioned that strychnia was purchased by Palmer twice within the week, when the first time he had bought quite enough, and more, for the purpose imputed to him. But that a person should go and buy strychnia twice in a week in a small country town, having bought enough for all purposes the first time—that he should go and buy more the next day at the shop of a rival tradesman, with whom he was on bad terms—is to the last degree improbable. Common sense revolts at it; nobody can or ought to be believed who makes any such statements. Again, observe he had been to London on the Monday. In London there is no difficulty for a medical man to get anything of the sort which he may require. He has only to write it down in the technical way, so as to give evidence of a medical education, and it is given to him at once, without a word. He had been to London; and, again, if he could not get it there, he could get it at Stafford. Why should he get it at Rugeley? that is the last place that he would have gone to for it. It seems to me that it is equally impossible he ever could have bought it for such a purpose as the purpose attributed to him, and that he would have been, if really guilty, so unwary as to allow the paper in which the strychnia had been not to be found with the full quantity he had purchased in it; he would not have been such a fool as not to take care that the paper in which it was wrapped was full of strychnia before his house was searched, so as to make sure that it should be found that nothing should appear to have been used out of it, and that the exact quantity was in the paper. I submit, therefore, it cannot be believed—it is not credible!

I am now in a condition to satisfy you that Palmer was undoubtedly in town, and that he could not have been there at nine o'clock; that he was in London at a quarter-past three o'clock, and that he could not have been there by nine o'clock—the hours at which the trains start rendered it impossible. The thing is false—downright false. It is impossible to have got to Rugeley before a quarter-past ten, and we will account for what he did in a way that will entirely satisfy you. He attended the post-mortem examination, and is it credible that a skilful medical man, who has studied at the London hospitals, would have gone to that dolt Newton to ask him as to what would be the effects of strychnia on a dog's stomach? Is it credible that he should go to that stupid sort of fellow, who gave his evidence in that dogged, mulish, sullen manner, which often is indicative of something else besides the want of understanding, and that he would have gone and asked a chap like that, "What are the effects of strychnia?" and then, when he had been told, he would snap his fingers and say, "All right." It cannot be—it is impossible. No one would believe it; and I submit to you confidently that unless there is much stronger evidence than that, it is evidence on which you cannot rely for a moment. To show the animus of this Newton against Palmer, I will remind you of what he stated. Palmer said that "you will find that he has taken a great deal of mercury; you will find this 'fellow' died from a diseased throat." When he is questioned about it mildly and quietly by my friend Mr. Grove as to what was the exact term used, he answers, "I do not know whether he said poor or rich"; just as if it could be a question of that kind. What we wanted to know was whether he had spoken of the poor dead man in a pitying way, or whether he had spoken of him as a disreputable person, unworthy of all consideration. As to that part of the case I will say no more, and I will proceed to other matters taking you back again to what occurred at Shrewsbury.

Serjeant Shee

The case for the Crown is, that as early as the 14th November, at Shrewsbury, the scheme—the plot—of poisoning commenced. That is the supposition of those from whom the case has been taken by the Crown. Now, it is suggested that on the night of Wednesday, the 14th, Palmer dosed this man Cook with something that he put into his brandy, and the witness Fisher told us that Cook told him so. If you remember the early part of my address to you, I read a few words at the end of a letter from Cook to Fisher, in which, after telling him it was of vast importance to him, as well as to Palmer, that £500 should be paid to Mr. Pratt, he adds in a postscript "I am better." These words must have referred to his illness at Shrewsbury. The letter relates to another matter which is of great importance to him and to Palmer, and he does not seem to treat it as one having in his own mind a belief that Palmer had drugged him with poison for the purpose of destroying his health at Shrewsbury. Then, again, on the evidence, what does Palmer say himself about what occurred at Shrewsbury? He says, when it is mentioned, "Cook says I have put something in his glass; I do not play such tricks with people"—taking it as if it had been never understood otherwise than as a loose expression of a man, perhaps not actually drunk—the evidence does not go to that extent—though I think you will be of opinion he was very nearly approaching to that condition. I could not help being a little amused by a version which I read some time ago of this portion of the Shrewsbury plot. I will read it to you—"After indulging freely in the foreign wines of an English country town, 150 miles from London, the owner of 'Polestar' took to brandy and water to restore his British solidity. Tossing off his glass, he complained that there was something in it, for it burned his throat. Perhaps those who have drunk strong brandy and water with similar haste may have experienced the same sensation; perhaps also, like Mr. Cook, they may have vomited afterwards. He bolted his brandy and water down at Palmer's challenge, and bolted it up again when it encountered the cold champagne. That night he was very drunk, and very sick, and very ill. His dinner he cast up into a basin; his money he deposited with his friend Mr. Ishmael Fisher, a sporting wine merchant, of Shoe Lane, Holborn. To this Mr. Ishmael Fisher the owner of 'Polestar' gave £700 to keep till next morning, expressing his belief, at the same time, that Palmer had dosed him for the sake of the money. If such had been Palmer's intention, would he have left Cook at such a moment? He neither followed him from the room when his stomach rebelled, nor did he go near him all that night. This neglect showed, indeed, how hollow was his friendship, but it proves his innocence; guilt would have been much more officious. Next morning Cook looked very ill, as men are apt to do after excessive vinous vomiting; but his drunken suspicions of Palmer had evaporated with the fumes of the brandy, and they were again friends and brother sportsmen."

Serjeant Shee

I believe that is the true version of the matter, and that Cook believed it to be so. He breakfasted with Palmer the next morning; he was good friends with him the whole of the day, and went with him to Rugeley, and there remained on Palmer's invitation. In consequence of the letter which Pratt wrote on the 13th, and which Palmer got on the 14th, in which they both had an interest, Cook wrote to Pratt to say that somebody would call on him with £200, and he wrote to Fisher to tell Fisher to do so. Did anybody at that time believe that there was any intention to drug and poison this man? Does not the explanation that Mrs. Brookes gave, which I must say was exceedingly creditable to her, the readiness with which she stated to me that her husband did not approve of her attending races, that it was disagreeable to him; and the dignity, if I may say so, with which she answered the question put to her by my learned friend—"Are you intimate with Palmer?" by this other question, "What do you mean by intimate with him? I am friendly," seemed to me to entitle her to all due respect. And when she, being called for the Crown, tells you, "That night I heard in several directions of a great number of people who were purged and vomited; there was a general affection of the kind amongst strangers visiting Shrewsbury on that occasion"—I submit to you it was to the last degree improbable that anything of that kind occurred. About the tumbler which she saw in Palmer's hand I cannot suggest any reason, because it is not in my instructions, but it might probably be accounted for in this way, when he came back from Rugeley and found all the people indisposed he would naturally look at the water to see if there was anything to account for its unwholesomeness. Mrs. Brookes said, and that is the point to which I wish to call your attention, that he was in a passage under a chandelier; that the waiter pointed to him when he showed her upstairs; that he spoke to her while holding up the glass to the light, and said, "Wait a minute, and I will come to you." Nothing can be more natural than that; and I submit to you it is impossible to say that there is anything to justify a suspicion of poison in it. With regard to the money he gave to Fisher, I can suggest no other reason than that, just before being sick, he gave his money to Fisher, feeling that it was coming upon him, and that his stomach was revolting at the liberties he had taken with it. He had the good sense to place his money, when he was still very sick, in the hands of Fisher, and he afterwards went to bed. It may have been that he had been guilty of excess in eating and drinking, and it was necessary to send for the doctor, who, when he came, wished to send him an emetic. The young man knew so well what to do that he said, "Oh! I can make myself sick without an emetic; I will put my tooth-brush down my throat; I can be sick without your emetic." He took a pill when it was recommended to him and a black draught, and the moment he laid his head on his pillow he was perfectly free from any alarm, and he got up the next morning perfectly well. Gentlemen, that is really too ludicrous to be worthy of a moment's consideration. Now, let us go to certain other matters, and more particularly to the conduct of the prisoner himself. I would just mention that there was a person there of the name of Myatt in the room at the time they say the brandy and water was drugged. Why was he not called? The others came in just before going to bed, but Myatt had been there the whole evening, and was not a mere accidental visitor in the room. You will hear his version so far as it is necessary. They have now got back to

Rugeley, and then the history of the slow poisoning continues. Cook and Palmer go back together, and probably they talk all the way about Pratt and their difficulties, and the way of getting out of them, and of the small way that the winnings of Shrewsbury will go to effect the object. They both see ruin staring them in the face unless the Prince of Wales office can be forced to pay the money due upon the policy of insurance, and they can remain free from all suspicion of insolvency or misconduct in the meantime. When they get to Rugeley, by sending up the £200 to Pratt, they provide for the temporary difficulty. They are on friendly terms, Palmer making use of Cook's things, and probably both attaining their own objects, as it would appear that Palmer said directly Cook died that he had some interest in bills which were outstanding; and that might well have been, considering they were engaged in racing transactions; that they were joint owners of one horse; that they had the same trainer, betted for each other at races, and that they were confederates and friends on the turf, in that sort of relation to each other which gave them a joint interest in the same ventures. Cook sat at the table of Palmer on the 16th, and wrote up that night to Pratt. Cook goes to bed late on that evening, well enough, not so drunk as to prevent his asking the chambermaid to give him a longer candle, in order that he might read in bed. He seems to have had a little champagne, not so much as to have made him drunk, yet perhaps too much for a stomach weakened by the excess, if it was excess, at Shrewsbury, or by the vomiting which was occasioned by the illness there, and the hot water which he had taken. He gets up the next morning poorly; he eats nothing that day; ails enough for Mr. Bamford to be called in by Palmer, and Palmer is unremitting in his attention to him on that day and the Sunday following.

Serjeant Shee

Now, it is said that that very attentiveness is evidence of the prisoner's guilt. What, as my friend here (Mr. Grove) says, what is a man to do? Here is a young fellow's health in very considerable danger. Cook, having a joint interest in racing transactions with Palmer, thinks it convenient to stop at Rugeley, where he has no friend but Palmer. They are not flush of money, and Palmer has a house and an establishment on a moderate scale immediately opposite the inn in which Cook is staying. He is enabled to send such things over as can be got in a private house, not at hotel prices, but at a very trifling expense. He was on a visit to Palmer, and he knew nobody there but Palmer. He was ailing; and as it is very dull for a man who has no intellectual pursuits to be alone all day when out of health, Palmer goes over and talks to him, and attends to him, and gets him what comforts he can. That is what a man would do to a friend; it is precisely what a man would do. If he had not done it, but merely attended to him at night when he was taken ill on the Monday night, without visiting him during the day, it might have been said that he was neglecting him, and only attended to him when he wanted to give him another dose of poison. That is the way the Crown would have put it then! He is laboriously attentive to him under circumstances which can well be accounted for by the reason that he had actually, if not a sincere friendship for him, at least a friendly kind of liking for him, and an interest with him on betting and racing transactions, and could supply him with several things from his house at little or no expense. If Cook had been well he would probably have had his meals at Palmer's house. He was ill, and Palmer sends Dr. Bamford to him. He saw him at eight o'clock on Sunday morning, and again at six or seven o'clock. Cook told him his bowels had been moved twice or thrice. That is what he told to Dr. Bamford; it may have been known to Palmer that it was oftener, and that the truth was he was slightly suffering under some symptoms of diarrhœa, as he afterwards stated in the letter to Jones. It was Cook himself who told Dr. Bamford about his bowels having been moved; and on the same day Palmer wrote a letter to Jones, intending to bring Jones there, he being about to go to London, and stated "Cook had been suffering from diarrhœa." It was at Shrewsbury, where everybody else had diarrhœa. He took the pill and black draught, and their effects continued, probably to some extent when he was at Rugeley. It is absurd to pretend that the suggestion of diarrhœa could have any sinister object, as Jones must have ascertained the truth as soon as he arrived at Rugeley.

Serjeant Shee

I now beg to call your attention to the next important fact in this case. It seems to me to be, though I touch upon it briefly here, one of the very last importance, and one which ought to decide it in the prisoner's favour. The supposition of the Crown is, that Palmer intended to dose Cook with antimony, to keep his stomach in a perpetual state of vomiting, in order the more easily to despatch him by strychnia; that he began the plot on the Wednesday at Shrewsbury and continued it at Rugeley, and that during the Sunday Cook was under the influence of that treatment—Sunday was the day Palmer attempted, as was said, to force the broth upon him. Now, being bent, as it is supposed, upon destroying Cook, there is one man in the world who would be the very last witness he would select as a witness of his proceedings. He was a medical man, in the prime of life, intimately acquainted with Cook, living in the same house with him, much attached to him, at all events sufficiently attached to him to come to him as soon as he had heard that he had had an attack of diarrhœa—Mr. Jones, of Lutterworth. Palmer, intending to go to London, and not wishing to leave Cook alone, wrote on the Sunday to Mr. Jones, telling him that Cook was then ill with diarrhœa, a statement which is not altogether inconsistent with the evidence of Dr. Bamford and what Cook stated, and begs of him to come over. I beg of you to pause here for a moment in order to appreciate the full importance of this fact; the more you think of it the more profound will be your conviction that it affords evidence irrefragable of Palmer's innocence. The imputation upon Palmer is that he intended to kill Cook to possess himself of his winnings. Who was with Cook when the race was won? Who was by his side on Shrewsbury racecourse for the three minutes that he was speechless? Who saw him take out his betting-book and count his winnings? Who but Jones—Jones who was his bosom friend, his companion, his confidant, and who knew to the last farthing the amount of his gains? Jones was, of all men living, the most likely to be the recipient of Cook's confidence, and the man bound by every consideration of honour, friendship, and affection to protect him, to vindicate his cause, and to avenge his death. Yet this was the man for whom Palmer sent, that he might converse with Cook, receive his confidence, minister to him in his illness, and even sleep in the same room with him! How, if Palmer is the murderer they represent him, are you to account for his summoning Jones to the bedside of the sick man? If Cook really suspected—as we are assured he did—that Palmer was poisoning him, Jones was the man to whom he would most willingly have unbosomed himself, and in whose faithful ear he would have most eagerly disburthened the perilous stuff that weighed upon his own brain. Jones, as well as Palmer, was a medical man, and it is not improbable that, in the course of his studies, the former may have noted in his class-book the very passages respecting the operation of strychnia which had attracted the attention of the latter. Is it conceivable that, if Palmer meant to slay Cook with poison in the dead of the night, he would have previously ensured the presence in his victim's chamber of a medical witness, who would know from his frightful symptoms that the man was not dying a natural death? He brings a medical man into the room, and makes him lie within a few inches of the sick man's bed, that he may be startled by his terrific shrieks, and gaze upon those agonising convulsions which indicate the fatal potency of poison! Can you believe it? He might have despatched him by means that would have defied detection, for Cook was taking morphia medicinally, and a grain or two more would have silently thrown him into an eternal sleep; but instead of doing so, he sends to Lutterworth for Jones. You have been told that this was done to cover appearances. Done to cover appearances! No, no, no! You cannot believe it—it is not in human nature—it cannot be true—you cannot find him guilty—you dare not find him guilty on the supposition of its truth—the country will not stand by you if you believe it to be true—you will be impeached before the whole world if you say that it is true—I believe in my conscience that it is false, because, consistently with the laws that govern human nature, it cannot possibly be true.

Gentlemen, there are other facts to be adverted to before I sit down to which it is necessary your attention should be drawn. There was a great stir at the hotel at Rugeley after Mr. Jones had returned from London with Mr. Stevens, the executor. Mr. Stevens arrives at the inn with Mr. Jones, has been in conversation all the way down with Mr. Jones, and has heard from Mr. Jones all that Mr. Jones knows, and does not appear to have had anything communicated to him by Mr. Jones which could justify any suspicion on his part. Mr. Jones, when they arrive at Rugeley, introduces him to Palmer, and Palmer at once takes him up to the room of the dead man, and uncovers the body down to the thighs, and Mr. Stevens looks at the corpse and sees there are no convulsions about the body except the clenching of the hands. He sees there is no emaciation, no signs as he thinks of illness, and, wondering within himself, says, "How can you have died?" or something to that effect; "How grievous a thing it is that your young life should have passed away!" I think he said he did not look as if he were dead. After seeing the corpse they went down to dinner, and he asked Palmer to dine with him, and Jones, and Mr. Bradford, the husband of Mr. Cook's sister. He has not been called; he could have told us if there was anything suspicious in the conduct of Palmer, anything that could justify such conduct on the part of Mr. Stevens. They have their dinner, and when their dinner is over, see what takes place. It is important you should know it, because I think you will see from the way it occurred that the conduct of Palmer was the conduct of a man certainly apprehensive of any sort of vexatious inquiry which might involve him in pecuniary troubles, and was therefore anxious to conciliate Mr. Stevens, still comporting himself like one who could firmly and freely maintain his equality with Mr. Stevens unabashed, with a clear brow and the appearance of an innocent man. (The learned serjeant read a portion of the dialogue which took place between Mr. Stevens and Palmer.) He said, "with a spasmodic convulsion of the throat," which was perfectly apparent; he could not see his face, but there was a spasmodic convulsion of his throat. Who could believe such a testimony of guilt as that? He expects that Palmer is to be bound to look after everything of every kind that was in the hotel belonging to Cook, and because he could not find a trumpery book, which anybody might have taken away, thinking and probably having heard it was of very little use, which could not be of the slightest service in any way to Palmer for any purpose whatever, or to anybody, simply on that account, he is to indulge in this vexatious proceeding. The last time the book was seen was on the Monday. The last person who saw it was Elizabeth Mills, on the Monday, and on that day there were several people there with Cook—Saunders the trainer, and the jockeys; after his death the two servant-maids and the housekeeper, the three undertaker's men, the two women who laid Cook out, and some other persons; the barber who shaved him might have taken the book, and having taken it could not return it; for here again is the effect of dishonesty as well as falsehood. Once done, you cannot repair it; without admitting it you cannot set it right again. I throw imputation on nobody; I simply say, that as many people had access to the room, it is not fair, it is not right under the circumstances when a man is charged in such a case of momentous importance without any assignable reason for his purloining the betting book, to fix it on him without any proof that he ever had it in his hands, when nothing like a proper search was made for it until some time after Cook's death. I asked whether the drawers were not full of linen and clothes, the answer was that they were. It was not seen immediately after the death, nor was there any search made for it, nor was it set aside and taken care of in the room, so that it could not have been removed by Palmer with a guilty intention of purloining it. Let us go on for a moment with this dialogue—(the learned serjeant then read a passage from the dialogue as detailed in the evidence)—and at last, after goading and irritating the man for all this time, though Palmer was willing to make explanations and provoke inquiries into anything or circumstance which if inquired into would at once have led to a discussion of matters in a fair and gentleman-like manner, Stevens snubs him by asking him whether he intends to be at the post-mortem; and at last, when he says, "It is a matter of indifference to me," goads the poor man into saying, "So it is to me." That is the only word of irritation that Palmer—who kept his ground during the whole time and stood up to this man—that is the only word of irritation that he used. Mr. Stevens speaks to him in a very warm manner, yet Palmer manifests the composure of a gentleman, of a man of feeling and consideration to the father—as he called himself—but the stepfather of the young man, and that is to be turned into evidence of guilt.

There is another story made against him, that he was found searching in the pockets of Mr. Cook shortly after his death—it is the most absurd suggestion on their own showing. The facts were these. Mr. Jones, I think, told the servants to tell Palmer to come into the room. I think that was it—to tell Palmer to go into the room; and then I think Mr. Jones told another servant to follow him into the room. Elizabeth Mills is the witness to that. She says, "I went in, and I saw him looking about seeing if there was anything in one of the coats, and he also looked under the bolster of the bed, just as a gentleman might be looking for a watch; and he went on doing so after I got into the room." It was quite clear she suspected nothing, and I submit it is not fair that any suspicion should attach to him on the subject.

Serjeant Shee

One other circumstance there is on which reliance has been placed; and although it has been said great reliance is not intended to be placed upon it, I cannot tell what effect it will produce on your minds. I am sure that when those who have promoted this prosecution first undertook it they intended to rely, as proof of damning guilt, on the manuscript extracts about strychnia in these medical books. I think it will be within your experience that in youth and early manhood the best protection that a man can have for his honour and integrity is the company and society of a wife whom he loves. If you find a man in early youth attached to a virtuous young woman, whom he loves with a sincere and heartfelt attachment, depend upon it he is of a gentle nature, and little prone to deeds of violence. They have put in these books to show that Palmer had a knowledge of strychnia poison, and they are the books which he used when a student attending lectures in London, as must have been known to his deceased wife. I find, in what I am in a condition to prove to be her own handwriting, proof positive that this was his student's book, and that he then and long after loved that young woman in the way in which it is God's will, under the sanction of His holy ordinance, young men should love their wives. His marriage was a marriage of affection; he loved her for herself and for her person; he loved her as ardently as he now loves her first-born, his only surviving child, a boy of seven years old, who waits with trembling anxiety for a sentence which will restore him to his father's arms, or drive that father to an ignominious death upon the scaffold. He loved her with a pure, generous affection. There is proof positive in this letter, copied in her handwriting into his notebook, that such a man was William Palmer when only a few years younger than he is now—

"My dearest Annie,—I snatch a moment to write to your dear, dear little self. I need scarcely say the principal inducement I have to work is the desire of getting my studies finished, so as to be able to press your dear little form in my arms. With best, best love, believe me, dearest Annie, your own William."

Now, this is not the sort of letter that is generally read in Courts of justice. It was no part of my instructions to read it to you, but that book was put in to prove that this man was a wicked, heartless, savage desperado, and I show you from it what he was when that letter was written—what his deceased wife knew him to be when she copied it—a young man who loved a young woman for her own sake—loved her with a pure and virtuous affection, such an affection as would in almost all natures be a sure antidote against guilt.

Such, gentlemen, is the man whom it is my duty to defend. Upon the evidence which is before you I cannot believe him guilty. Do not suppose for a moment that he is abandoned in this dreadful strait by his family and friends. An aged mother, who may have disapproved of some parts of his conduct, expects in an agony of grief your verdict. A dear sister can scarcely sustain herself under the suspense which presses upon her. A gallant and devoted brother stands by him to defend him, sparing neither time nor labour to save him from an awful doom. I call upon you to expand your minds to a capacity for estimating the high duty that you have to perform. You have to stem the torrent of prejudice; you have to vindicate the honour and character of your country; you have with firmness and courage to do your duty, and find a verdict for the Crown, if you believe that guilt is proved; but if you have a doubt upon the point, depend upon it the time will come when the innocence of this man will be made apparent, and when you will deeply regret any want of due and calm consideration of the case which it will be my duty to lay before you.

The Court then adjourned.

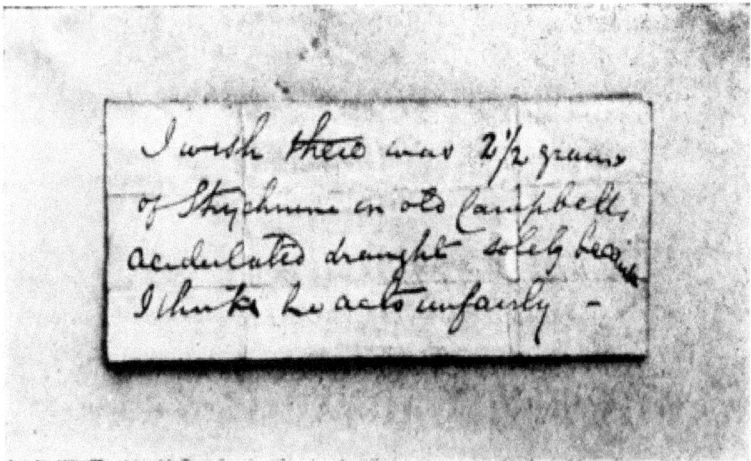

Note written by Palmer to his Counsel while in the dock at the Old Bailey

Eighth Day, 22nd May, 1856.

The Court met at ten o'clock.

Evidence for the Defence.

T. Nunneley

Mr. THOMAS NUNNELEY, examined by Mr. GROVE—I am a Fellow of the College of Surgeons, Professor of Surgery at the Leeds School of Medicine, and a member of several foreign and English scientific societies. I have been in practice between twenty and thirty years. I have seen cases of both traumatic and idiopathic tetanus. One of the four cases of idiopathic tetanus I have seen did not commence with the symptoms of lockjaw, nor did lockjaw occur sufficiently to prevent swallowing during the whole period of illness. I have been present during the evidence given here as to the symptoms of Mr. Cook. I had previously read the portions of the depositions as to the scientific and medical part of the case. Judging from the symptoms as described, and confining myself to the evidence as to the scientific part of the case, my opinion is that Mr. Cook died from some convulsive disease. I found that upon the difference of the symptoms described in the deposition and on the evidence before the Court.

LORD CAMPBELL—This is not satisfactory; we cannot ask witnesses what faith they give to the evidence of the witnesses as contrasted with the depositions. This witness's opinion ought to be founded on the *viva voce* evidence of the witnesses given during the trial.

Examination resumed—The previous state of health of Mr. Cook had some effect on my judgment.

State your own grounds in your own way for that opinion?—If I take the evidence which has occurred in Court—

By LORD CAMPBELL—The evidence of the symptoms of John Parsons Cook as stated by the witnesses?—Not merely the symptoms, but the general state of health.

But we have nothing to do with that. The witness should give his opinion on the symptoms described, and then state what influences the other facts may have had on his mind.

By Mr. SERJEANT SHEE—Do you remember the accounts that were given of what was said or supposed to be syphilitic sores?

The ATTORNEY-GENERAL—But there was no such thing said.

Mr. BARON ALDERSON—Supposing a person had syphilitic sores, what would you say then? That is the proper way of putting it.

LORD CAMPBELL—We must take it that medical men are not to be substituted for the jury.

T. Nunneley

Mr. JUSTICE CRESWELL—If I were to suggest a mode of meeting the thing it would be this—let the gentleman describe what he assumes to be the state of the deceased's health at the time, then the Attorney-General may say he is not justified in assuming.

Examination resumed—Will you do that having heard the evidence?—I assume him to have been a man of very delicate constitution; that for a long period he felt himself to be ill, for which he had been under medical treatment; that he had suffered from syphilis; had disease of the lungs; had an old-standing disease of the throat; led an irregular life; was subject to mental excitement and depression; that after death traces were found in his body which show this to have been the case; there was found an unusual appearance within the stomach; the throat was in an unnatural condition; the back of the tongue showed similar indications; the lungs were in an emphysematous condition, that is, the air cells dilated; in the lining of the aorta or large artery of the body there was an unnatural deposit; and there was a very unusual appearance in the membranes of the spinal marrow. These are the indications which are unnatural in the post-mortem examination. I should also state it is described by one of the witnesses that there was a loss of substance of the penis. The symptoms on the root of the tongue and the throat I ascribe to syphilitic inflammation of the throat. From these symptoms I have described I should infer that his health had not been good for long, and that his constitution was delicate. It was also stated that his father and mother had died young, and that the brother and sister were both delicate. That being the state of health of Mr. Cook, he would be liable to nervous irritation. Excitement or depression might bring it on. Exposure to wet and cold would have a greater effect than on a healthy person. It is a condition of the constitution when a convulsive disease is more likely to supervene.

What would you infer from the fact, supposing it to have occurred, that three days before death he suddenly woke up in the middle of the night in a state described as madness, for two or three minutes? I understand that he had three attacks on succeeding nights, each occurring about the same hour. Would you draw any inference from that circumstance?—Yes, that they were of a convulsive character, in the absence of other causes to account for it. Convulsive effects are extremely variable in their forms and degrees of violence. It is not possible to give a definite name to every convulsive attack. There are some forms of violent convulsions, such as hysteria, in which the patient retains his consciousness. It is stated that there are forms of convulsions, epileptic in their character, in which the patient retains his consciousness.

By LORD CAMPBELL—Have you met with any?—No, not during a fit.

T. Nunneley

But it is during a state of fit we are inquiring?—I have not.

Examination resumed—I know by my reading as a medical man that that does occur sometimes. The degree of consciousness in epilepsy varies very much; in some attacks the consciousness is altogether lost. Convulsive attacks are sometimes accompanied by violent spasms and with rigidity of portions of the body. Convulsions arising from a convulsive disease, either from infancy or from other causes, but not exactly tetanus, sometimes assume something of the complexion of tetanic affection. Such convulsions might arise from any cause—worms in children, affections of the brain in adults, hysteria, administration of chloroform to some persons. Indigestible food will sometimes produce convulsions in adults. I agree with Dr. Copland, whose book was referred to yesterday, that these convulsions sometimes end immediately in death. Asphyxia is frequently the cause of death when a man dies in one of these convulsions. I have seen convulsions of the character I have described recurring at various intervals, sometimes in hours, in other cases days. The time also varies very much when a patient, suffering from a violent paroxysm of such convulsions, becomes easier; it may be hours or minutes. When death takes place in the paroxysm of such convulsions it sometimes happens in post-mortem examinations that there is no trace of organic disease in the body.

Have you known at all or frequently in persons, not further advanced in years than the age of twenty-eight, granules between the dura mater and the arachnoid?—They are not common to any age that I am aware of.

Do you know whether granules have been part of the symptoms of tetaniform convulsions?—I have seen three preparations in St. Thomas's Hospital museum where granules are found in the membranes of the spinal cord, in which patients are said to have died of tetanus. In order to ascertain with satisfaction the nature and probable extent of the injury of such granules the spinal cord should be examined immediately after death. Not the most remote medical judgment could be formed if the examination was made two or three months after death. If an examination of the spinal cord is made so long after death, if there had been a large tumour or some similar change, it might have been discovered; but neither softening nor induration of the minute structure of the cord could be detected. The minute nervous structures change within two hours after death.

T. Nunneley

I have in the course of my experience had cases of traumatic tetanus. It generally begins by an attack of the jaw. I have had under my personal observation four cases of idiopathic tetanus. One of them was my own child. In three cases the symptoms commenced with lockjaw. In the fourth case the symptoms commenced in the body; the power of swallowing easily was retained to the last. Within the last twelve months I have made a post-mortem examination of two women who have died from the poison of strychnia. In both cases it was by chemical analysis that I ascertained the deaths had been caused by strychnia. In one case the post-mortem took place forty-two hours after death, in the other case thirty hours.

(The witness produced his report to the coroner on these two cases.)

I have not seen a fatal case, but several of taking too large a dose. One, a middle-aged man, took one-sixth of a grain of strychnia, given in solution. In a very few minutes the symptoms manifested themselves by the want of power of controlling the muscles, by twitching and rigidity, with some cramp, more violent in the legs than any part of the body. He was up and walking about. It was not a severe case. In six hours the spasms entirely disappeared. They were intermittent in character, every two or three seconds at first. The other case was similar with one-twelfth of a grain.

I have experimented on upwards of sixty animals—dogs, cats, mice, rats, guinea pigs, rabbits, frogs, and toads. After the ingestion of the poison the symptoms appear from two minutes to thirty, more generally about five or six. The symptoms in their order are—a desire to be quite still; hurried breathing; slavering at the mouth when given at the mouth; twitching of the ears; trembling of the muscles; inability to walk; convulsion of all the muscles of the body; the jaws generally being firmly closed during convulsions; these convulsions followed by a total want of power in the muscles, which, in the last attacks, were thrown into violent spasms with a galvanic-like shock running through them. Spasms come on if the animal is either touched or attempts to move. These spasms occur at various periods. The animals die at various periods up to three and a half hours. In every case before death the rigidity ceases, and the muscles are quite soft and powerless. The longest intervals between the violent convulsions in the animals to which strychnia has been administered has been about half an hour, but that is not common. After death the hearts of the animals have been invariably full on the right side, very generally the left ventricle firmly contracted, and the blood usually dark and often fluid. There is no particular appearance attached to the spine. I have attended to the evidence as to the symptoms of Mr. Cook on the Monday and Tuesday nights.

By LORD CAMPBELL—What do you assume the symptoms to have been on the Saturday night?—A state of great excitement in a less severe form; that Mr. Cook described himself to have been very ill.

T. Nunneley

Examination resumed—What else?—In a condition that he considered himself mad for two minutes, caused, he stated, through some noise in the street.

Now, adverting to the symptoms described on these three occasions here in the Court, is it your opinion that they could have been produced by the poison of strychnia?—They did not resemble what I have seen to follow it. He had more power of voluntary motion—sitting up in bed, moving his hands about, freely swallowing, and asking to be rubbed and moved, and a greater length of time occurred from the taking of the pills supposed to contain strychnia and the occurrence of the symptoms, much greater than any period that has occurred in my experience.

Does any observation occur to you on the screaming?—The screaming foreran the vomiting. I have never seen an animal vomit after taking strychnia, nor scream as an expression of voluntary exercise. Where there is so much spasm there is an inability on the part of the patient to vomit. I have a case, which is related in the 10th volume of the *Journal de Pharmacie*, in which attempts were made to give emetics without success.

With reference to the post-mortem observations of animals poisoned by strychnia, could you form any opinion on the post-mortem examination of Mr. Cook whether he had been under the influence of poison?—They differ materially in the particulars I have mentioned. The heart is stated to be empty and contracted, the state of the lungs not congested, the state of the brain not congested.

In the case of the paroxysms of the animals what has been the course of the subsiding of the paroxysm?—Gradual. I have never known a case of a severe paroxysm return, and then a long interval of complete repose for several hours. I have known it for half an hour.

I have experimented on the bodies of animals poisoned by strychnia with a view of discovering the strychnia poison from a few hours up to the forty-third day, the body being perfectly putrid in the latter case. In no one case have I failed to discover the poison.

Suppose a person to have died under the immediate effects of strychnia poison, in the first paroxysm after its administration, and his stomach to have been taken out and put into a jar on the sixth day after death, in your opinion must strychnia have been found in the body on proper chemical analysis?—If it were there.

T. Nunneley

Adverting to the statement about the stomach being put in a jar, brought up to London, and then immediately submitted to examination, in your judgment was that in an unfavourable or favourable condition for ascertaining whether the strychnia was there?—It would give a little more trouble; I do not see anything else. It is not my opinion that the analysis may be defeated or confused by the existence in the stomach of any other substance which would produce the same colours.

Supposing death to have been caused by a dose of strychnia poison sufficient, but not more than sufficient, to destroy the animal, in your judgment would it be so decomposed by the process of absorption as that you would not be able to detect it by those tests in any portion of the system?—No.

By LORD CAMPBELL—It is a question on which toxicologists have entertained a different opinion?—I believe they have.

Examination resumed—Have you studied the question sufficiently to be able to state reasons for thinking the minimum dose, after having done its work, continues in the system?—I believe the illustration given was that as food undergoes a change on being taken into the body, these substances also do.

By LORD CAMPBELL—It has been said that the decomposition of food affords an analogy?—It has. I believe not. The change in food takes place during digestion, consequently these elements are not found in the blood, or, if the change does not take place there, they remain unchanged in the blood. These alkaloids are absorbed without digestion, and may be obtained unchanged from the blood.

Cross-examined by the ATTORNEY-GENERAL—About half of the experiments on the sixty animals I spoke of were made in conjunction with Mr. Morley, the gentleman who was called for the prosecution. A few of these experiments were made in connection with this case, but the great bulk certainly not.

You have not told us what may be material, the general dose given?—The general dose given in the experiments has been from half a grain to two grains. I have seen a cat and a dog die from half a grain, not always. There are varying degrees of susceptibility both in animals of different species and in individuals of the same species.

You say that the symptoms generally appear in from two to thirty minutes; Mr. Morley states two minutes to an hour; will you undertake to say there have not been cases in which the first appearances have been delayed an hour?—I do.

Have you not known instances in which you have had to repeat the doses of poison?—When the dose has not been sufficient to kill, but to produce symptoms, there is a wide difference. I have given it three times. The quantity I gave was half a grain. That in the solid state would be a small dose to kill an old strong cat; a small dose will suffice in the fluid form. Where the half-grain dose has been given three times the reason was that the cat did not swallow the doses.

T. Nunneley

With regard to the symptoms you have described to us, can you tell me whether the result of your observations is that these symptoms occur uniformly, or at uniform periods of time, or whether they vary occasionally?—They certainly do not occur at uniform periods of time. I have not observed considerable variation in the order, but I have in the time.

When the convulsions have once set in have you found considerable difference as to the periods at which they take place?—Some difference, with greater or less intervals.

Have you also found that one animal will have a succession of attacks before it dies, and another will die after a much less amount of convulsion?—Yes. An animal seldom dies after one convulsion, generally four or five, and often a great many more. I have known one or two instances in which the animals have died after one convulsion.

From a dose which in the same quantity has not produced the same effect in other instances?—Yes.

Does the order in which the muscles of the body are convulsed vary also?—To some extent it does. The convulsions are generally simultaneous in the muscles of the trunk and those of the extremities. I think the limbs are generally affected first; they may be simultaneous; but the limbs are more easily observed.

Have you known any instance in which rigidity greater than is due to the ordinary rigor-mortis has occurred after death?—I do not think there is any difference. I have known instances in which they were very rigid, but I have known instances in which the muscles were flaccid. I may state I do not think there is any peculiar rigidity produced by strychnia.

With regard to the lady whose case we do not name, was it not the fact that, although the muscles of the body were flexible, the hands were curved and the feet arched and muscles contracted?—Not more than is usual from ordinary causes. I have said the hands were curved and the feet arched by muscular contraction.

Do you mean to say that when you spoke of the feet being decidedly arched that you meant no more than is due to the ordinary rigidity of death?—I do; that is what I mean by muscular contraction.

Do you mean to say that when you signed this, "The hands were incurved and the feet decidedly arched by muscular contraction," you meant no more than is due to the ordinary rigidity of death?—I do, and stated so at the time, not in the report I have signed, but in conversation with the parties engaged.

You made a report which did not include the whole?—It is stated in the former part of the report that the other muscles of the body were so; that there was a distinction between the two portions of the body—a statement of fact, but nothing more.

T. Nunneley

Mr. Morley stated here the other day that in the experiments he made with you on animals killed with the poison, that after death there was an interval of flaccidity, after this rigidity commenced, more than if it had been occasioned by the usual rigor-mortis; you do not agree with him as to the statement of the fact?—I do not; it is a difference of opinion entirely.

You say you generally found the heart full?—Yes, the right side. The fact of the heart having been found empty in this case, amongst other things, leads me to the conclusion that it was not a death by strychnia poison.

Did you hear the evidence given here the other day of the post-mortem?—I did. I also heard this stated, "that the heart was contracted and empty." I believe I was in Court when the gentleman who conducted it gave his evidence of the post-mortem examination of Mrs. Smyth, who died from the unfortunate administration of strychnia.

In those two cases does the fact of the heart having been found empty exercise any influence on your judgment?—Not unless I know how the post-mortem was made. If the post-mortem was commenced in the head, the explanation is given by Mr. Morley and myself in the case at Leeds. We had no doubt of the heart being full, the blood being fluid, but the head being first opened, and the large vessels cut, the consequence was that the blood by mere natural physical causes drains away.

Are you aware how the post-mortem was made in this particular case of Mr. Cook?—It is stated that the chest and abdomen were opened before the head.

What effect would that have?—If there were blood in the heart it ought to be there.

That would not make the difference. The head was not opened there in the first instance?—No; that is my explanation of it.

How do you account for the emptiness and contraction of the heart in Mr. Cook's case?—The heart, if empty, is usually contracted. I cannot account, from the appearance of the body after death, for the emptiness of the heart, any more than it might be the usual effect of death. It varies very much, but, as a general rule in post-mortem examinations, we find, if the heart is empty, it is contracted.

If I understand you, the post-mortem appearance of Cook's body, which you say differs materially from those you have seen after death from strychnia, were the emptiness of the heart, the state of the lungs, and the want of congestion in the brain. What do you say as to the state of the lungs?—The lungs are described as not being congested.

T. Nunneley

Do you attach any importance to the emphysema?—It is of two kinds. One consists in a dilatation of the cells, the other in a rupture by which the air, not being in the cells, passes amongst them.

I suppose you say it was not from the rupture of the cells here?—That I inferred from the description given.

Have you not found emphysema in the cases of the animals that have died?—Yes. It has always been from a rupture of the cells. It could be in no other way.

What is there in the statement of witnesses which makes you think there was emphysema of the other sort?—There was during life a diseased condition of the lungs.

I am speaking of the appearance of the lungs after death?—I must put the whole together.

Would it not have been desirable to know whether this emphysema was natural or whether it was from rupture? We heard the witnesses here who made the post-mortem examination?—If the question had been put to them.

But you were advising my friends throughout, while Dr. Harland was here, and you heard what he said. Did it occur to you it was proper to ask him what was the nature of those?—No, because I heard (which was sufficient to my mind) that disease had existed. The question was put, as to the disease, to Dr. Savage.

I am speaking of this emphysema?—It did not occur to me.

You have told us the various symptoms about this gentleman, from which you gather he was of a delicate constitution. To which do you ascribe these convulsions of which he died?—Not to any.

I understood you to say that the fact of his having syphilis was an important ingredient in your mind?—Yes, but you ask for convulsions.

You have no doubt he died of convulsions?—No.

You entered into a long detail of the various ailments under which this unfortunate man suffered, and you say that this would predispose him to convulsions. I ask you which of them?—The whole; the continuation of them.

Amongst others you mentioned excitement?—Yes, and depression of spirits.

What evidence is there, on which you rely, of his being a man subject to depression of spirits?—It is stated by Mr. Jones that he was subject to depression of spirits—mental depression. There was a good deal of mental depression at Rugeley.

Would you expect excitement to produce its effects recently in its existence, or after it was totally and entirely gone?—It may induce that state of brain in which convulsions will follow at some distance.

Did you find from the evidence that the brain was perfectly healthy?—No, not perfectly healthy. Mr. Bamford said it was not.

T. Nunneley

Do you mean, as against the reputed testimony, and the testimony here of Dr. Harland and Dr. Moncton, as well as Mr. Devonshire, to set up the testimony of that old gentleman, Mr. Bamford?—The evidence stated at the inquest itself is put in the depositions.

Do you mean to say, in your opinion, that excitement, producing disease of the brain, would bring on these convulsions?—I mean to say this, that in the condition of the brain, and the statement that has been made, I believe it to be quite probable that convulsions might come on and destroy a person, and leave no trace behind.

Do you believe that this man died of apoplexy?—I do not. You must bear in mind he had taken doses of morphia.

Do you ascribe his death to morphia?—No, except that it would assist in the convulsive attack, and it would affect the spinal marrow.

Brought about by the morphia?—No.

In your opinion was morphia right treatment or wrong?—I should think not very good in the state of excitement he was in then.

Do you mean that there has been anything to show any excitement at Rugeley?—You will not allow me to furnish an answer. There was no excitement at Rugeley, but morphia, when there is sickness, will sometimes disagree with a patient when there is an irritable state of the brain.

The stomach was irritated, I will allow, but where is the evidence that there was any excitement at Rugeley?—There is none.

Then why was morphia a wrong treatment?—Because it is after sickness, and there is evidence of there being an irritable state of the brain. From what he said himself, he must either have been delirious on the Sunday night, or he must have had some attack similar to what he had on the Monday night.

Do you mean the attack of the Sunday night was similar to that on the Monday night?—Less intensity, but I think very probably of the same character.

You do believe there were convulsions on the Sunday night, then?—No, I do not.

He died of convulsions?—Yes, but I say of the same character.

Then you do believe he had convulsions?—To a certain extent, but less in intensity. There was a great deal of mental and bodily excitement.

On the Monday night?—I have stated to you that he was in that condition which very often precedes convulsions.

Will you admit if a man so under the influence of morphia and he is suddenly disturbed by a noise, it is likely to have a depressing effect upon him?—I will; but there is no proof of a noise.

T. Nunneley

There is no proof, except his own statement, of any illness?—Precisely; that is part of my opinion—that he did not state what had occurred accurately.

Do you mean to say that he did not state that thing?—No; that he was mistaken. That is one of the symptoms. I believe the man to have been delirious then.

Now, be so good as to tell me what are the convulsions of which you gave some statement to my friend which will produce convulsions of a tetanic form?—Any irritation will produce it.

Ending in death?—It may end in death.

Will you tell me of any convulsions which you have known end in death accompanied with what my friend calls tetanic symptoms?—I have known them in children. I have never had such a case in an adult.

Has your reading furnished you with any?—The general statement of all writers is that such cases do occur.

Have you ever known or read of a case in which the patient was conscious to the last?—No, I have not. I have seen it stated so, but I have never met with it.

In epilepsy you have these tetanic symptoms?—Yes, but before death consciousness is gone.

You have had considerable experience in idiopathic tetanus, and some five or six, perhaps, of traumatic. (An extract from the evidence of Mr. Jones was read.) I have read to you the description of Cook's symptoms as witnessed by Mr. Jones. I ask you to point out any distinction between those symptoms and the symptoms of tetanus?—Do you mean the one paroxysm or the disease which is called tetanus?

I am speaking of the paroxysm of tetanus?—It is very like.

By LORD CAMPBELL—You say this is not tetanus at all?—It is not. I never saw a case of tetanus in which the rigidity continued at the time of death and afterwards.

Cross-examination resumed—I am asking you as to symptoms of the paroxysms. I understand you to say the symptoms of the paroxysms are not distinguishable from those of tetanus?—Some of them are at the moment of death.

Give me any of them?

By LORD CAMPBELL—This is not tetanus, but, as far as they go, they coincide with the symptoms of tetanus at the moment of death?—Yes.

Cross-examination resumed—Observe, you have here consciousness to the last. That before the man dies he says, "Turn me over," and as soon as they turn him over he dies. Tell me of any case you know of in which death has ensued from convulsions, where the death was not from tetanus, in which the patient was conscious?—I have already said I do not know of such a case.

Let me call your attention to strychnia tetanus. Would you call the symptoms tetanic?—They are called so very properly.

T. Nunneley

Do you agree with Sir Benjamin Brodie that while the paroxysms of tetanic convulsions last there is no difference between those which arise from strychnia and those which arise from tetanus properly so called, but the difference is in the course of them?—I think there is. I think that the hands are less violently contracted and affected in ordinary tetanus, and that the whole effect of the spasms is less in ordinary tetanus.

You would expect to find the hands more firmly and tightly closed in tetanus from strychnia than in ordinary tetanus?—I think it is so. There is another difference, that in tetanus the convulsions never entirely pass away.

That is one of the reasons Sir Benjamin Brodie gave for distinguishing the course?—In the case at Leeds it was the same.

I believe you felt perfectly prepared in that case, on the description of the symptoms, to come to the determination that it was a death from strychnia?—I thought it possible and probable. I did not come to a determined opinion. I expressed an opinion. I did not say I had no doubt as to the cause of death. We had ascertained at that time that there was strychnia.

After the opinion you expressed in that case, is it possible that you can represent this case of Mr. Cook as one of idiopathic tetanus?—I never did, and you have not heard from me that I infer that.

I have heard it said in this case that this may have been something arising from a syphilitic affection?—Idiopathic or traumatic tetanus was mentioned. I do not think it was a case of tetanus in any sense of the word.

Why not?—I have given the description. Because it differed from the course of tetanus from strychnia in the particulars I have already described.

Repeat them once more?—The very sudden acquisition of the convulsions after the first rousing of Mr. Jones; his power of talking.

Did you not know that Mrs. Smyth begged to have water thrown upon her, and talked throughout?—It did not occur to me.

Are you judging of the one incidental case, and coming here with conclusions founded on that?—I think it is an element, the time.

Then let me add the element, that the lady continues to the last conscious, and asks to have her legs stretched just before she died; does that shake your faith?—Yes.

Do you not know in that case her last words were to turn her over?—Not at the last moment. I do not dispute it if it is said so.

Were there not here the premonitory symptoms; the animals are affected about the jaws and the ears, and Mr. Cook has stiffness in his neck, and asks to have it rubbed?—It is a premonitory symptom.

Was it not a symptom of the convulsions, which are not distinguishable from tetanus?—I have said so. I have stated here that I believe in cases of poison from strychnia it is first developed in the legs and feet.

You have told us the animals began to feel twitching in the ears. This gentleman had, before the convulsions came on, stiffness in the muscles of the neck and jaw, and begged to have them rubbed?—That might be if it were anything else.

I ask you now, is not the difficulty of breathing one of the premonitory symptoms? He sat up in bed and complained of feeling suffocated?—Yes.

And felt a stiffness about the neck and asked to have it rubbed, and, as far as we know, this was the case in all the animals, though they could not ask to be rubbed. I ask you what were these but premonitory symptoms?—In no one single instance could the animal bear to be touched, and it evidently was most painful to it to be touched. I know that Mrs. Smyth asked to have her legs and arms straightened.

Let me ask you this, have you not often found that it was prior to the occurrence of the paroxysm, and not after the paroxysm?—No, I have seen a paroxysm brought on by it.

In all cases?—No, not in all cases. But in the other case, for two hours before she died, when she could speak, she begged them not to touch her.

Did she not ask to have her legs rubbed?—That was when the attack was slight, not during the fatal attack.

After the paroxysms had set in, did she not request to be rubbed?—She did before the convulsions came on; she liked to have her feet and legs rubbed.

Afterwards she could not bear it, because it caused a recurrence?—Yes.

That was in consequence of the twitchings, was it not?—I think not. It is stated by all the witnesses she begged she might not be touched.

But for that one thing, that the paroxysms came on so soon after the first premonitory symptom, is there one single point in which this differs from strychnia tetanus?—The power of swallowing so lately.

On what does it depend, the inability to swallow?—From the inability to move the jaw.

I ask you whether it is not a fact that, unlike as in natural tetanus, in tetanus from strychnia lockjaw is not the last symptom, and very often never sets in at all?—I have never seen an instance in which it does not make its appearance.

T. Nunneley

Is it the last?—I do not deny that it may be.

At what stage did it come on in the Leeds case?—Very early, more than two hours before death.

How long did the paroxysms continue before death took place?—Two hours and a half.

That was in a case in which very large doses of strychnia were administered?—We supposed four or five times repeatedly.

In the case of Leeds there were four animals killed afterwards from the contents of the stomach?—There were.

You state that you have succeeded in every case where you have tried in your experiments in finding the strychnia?—Yes.

Did not Mr. Morley differ from you in two cases?—In one he did. We divided the poison which we found in the stomach into two portions, and we adopted two different processes for extracting it, and by the one process we were both rather doubtful, but by the other we produced it.

Now, you thought you found it, and he thought you did not?—Not that I recollect.

Do not you know that Mr. Morley has been rather doubtful as to the results of these experiments?—No. Mr. Morley stated differently in his own examination.

In his examination here?—Yes; if you refer to it, except in one case, and that is the explanation I give of it.

Re-examined by Mr. SERJEANT SHEE—The Attorney-General directed your attention to your report on one of these cases that the hands were rigid and the feet incurved. In reports of this kind do you state only extraordinary appearances, or ordinary appearances as well?—Ordinary appearances also. It is a statement of a fact without anything more.

W. Herepath

Mr. WILLIAM HEREPATH, examined by Mr. GROVE—I am Professor of Chemistry and Toxicologist at the Bristol Medical School. I have been occupied in chemistry forty years and in toxicology probably thirty. I have experimented on the poison of strychnia. I have examined the contents of the stomach of a patient who died from strychnia. I discovered the strychnia in the contents of the stomach three days after death. I have experimented upon eight, nine, or ten animals. In the case of a cat, to which I gave one grain of strychnia in solid form, I could not get the animal to take it voluntarily, and I left it in meat at night. I found the animal dead next morning. The body was dreadfully contorted—extremely rigid, the fore limbs extended, the head turned round to the side, the eyes protruding and staring, the iris expanded so as to be almost invisible. I found in the urine which had been ejected strychnia, and also in the stomach. I gave the same quantity of strychnia to another cat. It remained very quiet for fifteen or sixteen minutes, with but few symptoms until thirty-five minutes. It merely seemed a little restless with its eyes, the breathing a little quickened, and at thirty-five minutes it had a terrible spasm, the four extremities and the head being drawn together. I watched it for three hours more. After this it had a second spasm. A frothing saliva was dripping from its mouth, and it forcibly ejected its urine. It had another spasm a few minutes after, when I thought the animal would die. It soon recovered itself, and then remained quiet, with the exception of a trembling all over. The slightest breath of air would affect it. It continued in this state for some time longer. During this three hours and a half, or nearly so, the animal was in a peculiar state. Touching it appeared to electrify it all through, even blowing upon it produced the same effect. Touching the basket, the slightest thing that could affect the animal, produced a sort of electric jump. I left it then, thinking it would recover, but in the morning I found it dead, in the same indurated and contracted condition in which the former animal was found. About thirty-six hours afterwards, by chemical examination, I found strychnia in the urine, the stomach, and upper intestines, in the liver, and in the blood of the heart. In my search for strychnia I took extraordinary means to get rid of the organic matter.

In all cases which you have seen where strychnia has been taken has the examination been successful?—Not only strychnia, but nux vomica, has been extracted. In one case the animal had been buried two months. I have detected strychnia in cases where it has been mixed purposely with putrid remains.

Are you of opinion, as a chemist, that where strychnia has been taken in a sufficient dose to poison, it can be detected, and ought to be detected?—Yes, up to the time the body is decomposed completely. Even where there is putrefaction—where the body has become a dry powder. I am of opinion that strychnia ought to have been detected if it had existed in the jar containing the stomach, even in the state it then was.

Cross-examined by the ATTORNEY-GENERAL—Until lately my experiments for the purpose of finding strychnia have been principally in the stomach. In two cases I found it in the tissues of the animals. One was the second cat, the other a dog to which I gave the large dose of one grain. Judging from reports in newspapers, I have said in conversation that strychnia had been given, and that "If it was there, Professor Taylor ought to have found it."

W. Herepath

Re-examined by Mr. GROVE—What is the smallest quantity you have detected in the tissues of the stomach?—I am satisfied that you could discover the fifty-thousandth part of a grain that is unmixed with organic matter. I dissolved the tenth part of a grain in a gallon of water, that is 1 in 70,000. I can take the tenth part of a drop of the water and demonstrate the presence of strychnia.

What is the smallest portion of strychnia when mixed with organic matter you can detect?—I took about an eighth part of the liver of a dog, and from that I had enough to make four distinct experiments with the four tests.

So that you experimented on a thirty-second part of the liver?—Yes.

J. E. D. Rogers

Mr. JULIAN EDWARD DISBROWE ROGERS, examined by Mr. GRAY—I have been sixteen years Professor of Chemistry at St. George's School of Medicine, in London. I made an experiment with one dog with a view of extracting strychnia from the body. I gave it two grains of pure strychnia between two pieces of meat. Three days after it was dead I removed the stomach and its contents, and took some of the blood. I analysed the blood ten days after its removal from the body, when it was putrid, and found strychnia by the colour tests. About a month or five weeks afterwards I analysed the stomach and its contents, and strychnia was separated in a large quantity. Having heard the evidence as to the stomach and its contents in this case being put in a jar and sent to London, in my judgment strychnia, if it had been administered, must have been found in the contents of the stomach.

Cross-examined by the ATTORNEY-GENERAL—I have only made one experiment with strychnia on this dog.

Do you think it would make any difference if the contents were lost?—If there were no contents spread over the intestines, then that would make a difference. If they had been spilt and shaken, then it would make no difference.

But, supposing they were not there?—There would be the washings of the stomach. If the stomach was sent me with no contents, I would wash the stomach and proceed with that.

If you had tried on the tissues of the deceased's body I suppose you would have been able to ascertain whether there had been any strychnia?—That is my opinion.

So that the time that has elapsed since Cook died would not matter. If you had an opportunity to operate on it, you would have found the strychnia?—If it had been there, I feel satisfied I should find it.

LORD CAMPBELL—Do you mean then or now?—I do not see that the time would prevent it.

H. Letheby

Dr. HENRY LETHEBY, examined by Mr. KENEALY—I am a Bachelor of Chemistry and Professor of Medicine in the London Hospital; also a medical officer of health to the city of London. I have for a considerable time studied poisons. I believe in every case of this kind tried in this Court during the last fourteen years I have been engaged on behalf of the Crown. I have been present during the examination of the medical witnesses at this trial and heard them describe certain symptoms attending the death of Mr. Cook. I have seen many deaths by strychnia in the lower animals. I have seen several cases of nux vomica in the human subject, one of which was fatal. The symptoms in the animals do not accord with the symptoms in this case. In the first place, I have never known such a long interval between the administration of the poison and the coming on of the symptoms. The longest interval has been three-quarters of an hour, and then the poison was given in a form not easy of solution, and when the stomach was full. I have seen the symptoms begin in five minutes after the poison was administered. A quarter of an hour would be the average. Another reason is that in all the animals I have seen, and the human subject also, when under strychnia, the system has been so irritable that the very slightest excitement, as an effort to move, a slight touch, a noise, or a breath of air, will set them off in convulsions. I do not think it at all probable that a person to whom a dose of strychnia had been given could rise out of bed and ring a bell violently. Any movement at all would excite the nervous system, and there would be spasms. It is not likely a person in that state of nervous irritation could bear to have his neck rubbed. Where poisoning by strychnia does not end fatally, the paroxysm is succeeded by other paroxysms, which gradually shade themselves off. They generally become less and less, over a period of some hours. My experience agrees with Dr. Christison, that it would last over a period of sixteen or eighteen hours before the man gets better. I do not hesitate to say that strychnia is of all poisons the most easy of detection. I have detected it in the stomach, in the blood, and in the tissues of animals in numerous instances. The longest period after death that I have examined a body has been one month. The animal was then in a state of decomposition, and I succeeded in detecting very minute portions of the strychnia. When the strychnia is pure it can be detected in a very small portion of a part, at least the twentieth part of a grain. When mixed up with other matter it is a little more difficult. I can detect the tenth part of a grain in a pint of any liquid that you put before me, whether the liquid was pure or putrefied.

You have succeeded in detecting it in animals which have been killed a month, and were in a state of decomposition. What is the dose you have given them?—I gave the animal, a rabbit, originally half a grain, which killed it, and I have the strychnia here within a fraction of what I gave. I lost about a tenth part of a grain in the course of the investigation.

H. Letheby

Supposing a person had taken strychnia eight or ten days before, and that he died of strychnia poison, should you be able positively to say that you could detect it?—I do say so positively. I have never failed. In the post-mortem examinations I have always found the right side of the heart full of blood. The reason for that is that the death takes place by the fixing of the muscles of the chest in spasm. In my opinion this is invariably so. At that time the blood is unable to pass through the lungs, and the heart cannot relieve itself of the blood that is flowing into it. It therefore becomes gorged. I have also observed that the lungs are congested, filled with blood.

Do you agree in the opinion of Dr. Taylor that where strychnia is administered as a sort of pill or bolus it kills from about six to eleven minutes?—It may do so. I do not say it would always. I agree with him that the jaws are spasmodically closed, and also that the slightest noise reproduces another convulsive paroxysm. I do not agree with Dr. Taylor that the colouring tests for the discovery of strychnia are fallacious. They always succeeded with me.

Dr. Taylor has given as a reason for the non-finding of the strychnia that it is absorbed into the blood and becomes changed?—I agree with its absorption, but I do not agree with its being changed.

Have you turned your attention to the theory that strychnia is decomposed after the poisoning?—I have examined the tissues of the body and I have found it; and my opinion is that it is not changed so as not to be discoverable.

Supposing the contents were put into a jar and jumbled up with the intestines and a portion of the stomach, would that prevent the discovery of strychnia?—It would not.

Supposing that all the contents of the stomach were lost, ought the mucous membrane, in the ordinary course of things, to exhibit traces of strychnia?— I think so.

I have also studied the poison of antimony.

Supposing a quantity of antimony were placed in some brandy and water, and it was drunk off at a sudden gulp, would the immediate effect of that be to burn the throat, or anything of that kind?—No. Not in the form of tartar emetic.

H. Letheby

Cross-examined by the ATTORNEY-GENERAL—I am neither a member of the College of Physicians nor of the College of Surgeons. I do not now carry on business in the medical line, but have done so in general practice for not more than two or three years. I have destroyed about fifty animals by strychnia, some within the last two months. I have never given more than a grain. In recent cases I have always administered the poison in a solid form— sometimes made into a pill with bread, and at other times put on the tongue of the animal. In one case I gave it under very disadvantageous circumstances; the dog had had a very hearty meal, and it was kneaded up into a hard mass with some bread, and it took three-quarters of an hour before the action came on. There was one other case which took about half an hour, but the poison, half a grain, was not given in sufficient quantity. We gave it another dose, which acted in about ten minutes.

Dr. Nunneley describes the symptoms—first, a desire to be still, then a difficulty in breathing, a slobbering of the mouth, twitching of the ears, trembling of the muscles, and, after that, convulsions; did you observe all these?—I cannot say all of them in that order. There is an excitement manifested in the animal, an indisposition to touch, and trembling on being touched.

I am speaking of the symptoms before the convulsions. The touching, did that occasion a tremulous action of the muscles?—Yes, I have noticed that.

Have they come on in regular order?—No, I think not. There are some little variations.

After the convulsions have once commenced, is there an interval?—Yes. A breath, a sound, or a touch will cause a recurrence of the convulsive symptoms after they have been seized. This does not apply where the animal dies in the first paroxysm, and I have known many cases where an animal has so died.

You mentioned a distinctive feature in this case of Cook. You were surprised at his manifesting so much power as to be able to sit up in bed and ring the bell. Are you aware that that was at the commencement, before any of the convulsive symptoms had set in?—Yes, I apprehend that was at the onset or beginning of the paroxysm.

Do you know that he sat up in bed and rang the bell, and it was not till Palmer had been and had gone back and brought the pills that the convulsions came on?—Yes, I do; and I have noticed in animals that the mere touch sends them into convulsions, and they show an indisposition to move.

In the case of the lady who died near Romsey, did you hear what the maid said, that she discovered, when her mistress' bell rang violently, that she had got out of bed and was sitting on the floor?—It struck me as inconsistent with what I have seen. I have no doubt that was a death from strychnia.

If that evidence be true, and it is a fact that she got up and rang her bell, does not that shake your faith?—No, it does not. You must compare it with what I have seen. Both are irreconcilable with what I have seen.

H. Letheby

Speaking of the Tuesday night, with the exception of the ringing of the bell, and that in this case it was an hour or an hour and a half after the supposed administration of the poison, can you point to anything to distinguish the symptoms and death of Mr. Cook from death by tetanus of strychnia?—No, I cannot. It is inconsistent with what I have seen, but it is not inconsistent with what I have heard in the case of Mrs. Smyth.

Is not one of the symptoms hard breathing?—It is a panting respiration. It is excitement of the breathing rather than difficulty. It is in the convulsions that there is a difficulty of breathing. If a man were to breathe hardly it is a position naturally assumed for him to sit up. Until the convulsion of the muscles comes on there is nothing to prevent the patient sitting up.

If I understand you, if I except the delay and the fact of his sitting up in bed and crying for help on the Tuesday, is there anything to distinguish the convulsions under which this man suffered and died from the convulsions of tetanus of strychnia?—It is not perfectly consistent with strychnia, because I say that the account which is given of Mrs. Smyth is what I cannot reconcile with what I have before observed.

With regard to the abrupt termination instead of the gradual subsidence?—I have observed the gradual subsidence in man as well as in animals.

In the case of the man—what dose had he taken?—Nearly a grain and a half.

This is a strongish dose?—Yes.

You might expect a recurrence of the paroxysm?—Certainly. The subsidence will not depend on the strength of the dose; it will depend on whether the individual is to recover or not. I have seen four or five instances of recoveries.

Is it not generally known that the effect of strychnia is very varied in different individuals?—No, I do not think so. There would be a little variation in time, but in the main features of the case there is no variation.

Do not you find this difference, that from the same dose in the same species you get no paroxysm, or you get a series of paroxysms ending in death?—Yes, that is true; but the attacks are the same for all that. The symptoms are the same.

What do you say about the Sunday night fit?—I was disposed to think it was a fit. I cannot tell you what it was; I have formed no opinion.

What do you ascribe Mr. Cook's death to?—It is irreconcilable with everything I am acquainted with.

By LORD CAMPBELL—Is it reconcilable with any known disease which you have ever seen or heard of?—No, my lord.

H. Letheby

Re-examined by Mr. SERJEANT SHEE—Do you mean to say it could not be the result of any variety of convulsions, however violent, though not classed under a particular description of convulsion?—We are learning new facts every day, and I do not conceive it to be impossible that some peculiarity of the spinal cord, unrecognisable except the examination be made immediately after death, may produce symptoms like these.

When you say it is irreconcilable with anything you have heard of, do you include anything you have heard of strychnia poison as well as anything else?—Certainly I do.

Is the vomiting of the pills just before death inconsistent with what you have known and observed of strychnia poison?—It is not consistent with anything I have observed.

Have you ascertained whether, if you touch an animal which is beginning those minor premonitory symptoms, but which as yet has had no paroxysms, this brings the paroxysms on?—Yes.

Was not the Romsey case exceptional from the manner in which the strychnia was administered and the quantity of the dose?—Yes, it was. It is quite consistent with all I am saying that the ringing of the bell by the lady the moment she felt anything of uneasiness would produce the paroxysm which ultimately was observed. In my judgment, it is not safe to argue from the symptoms of a case in which the paroxysm took place only a few moments after the ingestion of the poison, and it was in a fluid state, to what may be the probabilities in another case.

R. E. Gay

Mr. ROBERT EDWARD GAY, examined by Mr. SERJEANT SHEE—I am a member of the Royal College of Surgeons. In 1855 I attended a person named Foster suffering under tetanus. He had an inflammatory sore throat, muscular pains in the neck and the upper portion of the spinal vertebræ. He was feverish, and had the usual symptoms attending catarrh. On about the fourth day the muscular pains extended to the face. A difficulty of swallowing came on, the pains in the muscles covering the spinal vertebræ and in those of the lower jaw increased. In the evening of that day the jaw became completely locked; the pain came on in the muscles of the bowels, the same in the legs and the arms. He became very much convulsed throughout the entire muscular system. He had frequent and violent convulsions of the arms and hands, and afterwards of the legs. The difficulty of swallowing increased up to the ninth or tenth day. Not a particle of food, either solid or liquid, could be taken or introduced to the mouth. An attempt to swallow the smallest portion brought on the most violent convulsions. The convulsions were so strong throughout the whole system that I could compare him to nothing more than a piece of warped board in shape. The head was drawn back, the abdomen was forced forward, and the legs were frequently drawn upwards and backwards. The attempt of feeding with the spoon, the opening of the window, or placing the fingers on the pulse frequently brought on violent convulsions. He complained of great hunger. He was able to speak. He repeatedly cried out he was very hungry, what would he do if he could not eat? and he was kept alive till the fourteenth day by injections of a nutritive character. He screamed during these convulsions, and the noises he made were more like those of a dying man. About the twelfth day he became insensible. The convulsions, although very weak, continued till the fourteenth day, when he died. He was by business an omnibus conductor. He had been ill some few days—it might be a week. He had no other hurt or injury to his person of any kind which would account for these symptoms. His body was not examined after death.

By LORD CAMPBELL—What do you call the disease?—I call it inflammatory sore throat from cold and exposure to the weather. The symptoms became tetanic in consequence of an extremely nervous and anxious disposition. He had a very large family, and was a very hard-working man. I did not hear the evidence of the witnesses who described the symptoms of Mr. Cook.

Cross-examined by the ATTORNEY-GENERAL—That is what you call idiopathic tetanus?—Yes, decidedly so. I have had a vast number of cases of inflammatory sore throats and a great many anxious, nervous patients. That is the only case I have ever seen of idiopathic tetanus.

If I rightly apprehend your history of the symptoms, the disease was altogether progressive in its character, and, although there was an occasional cessation of the more painful symptoms, there never was a full cessation of the symptoms?—He was not suffering from tetanic affection. There was a twitching of the muscles going on, but there was not that violent convulsion. The lockjaw was the first of the more aggravated symptoms that presented itself, the muscular spasms about the trunk of the body progressing onwards to the extremities. He was conscious till the tenth day, when insensibility supervened while the convulsions were upon him. I consider the brain had been affected and congestion had taken place, and that produced insensibility.

After that was there some diminution in the severity of the convulsions?—Very great diminution, but they still continued.

Would that be likely to take place from the constant recurrence of the convulsions?—From the constant recurrence of the convulsions the brain would be congested.

You would expect to find a difference in that respect in a case where a man died very early in such a disease, and where it was spread over a longer period?—That would depend greatly on the violence of the convulsions.

By LORD CAMPBELL—And the repetition?—And the repetition.

The Court then adjourned.

Ninth Day, Friday, 23rd May, 1856.

The Court met at ten o'clock.

J. B. Ross

Mr. JOHN BROWN ROSS, examined by Mr. GROVE—I am house surgeon to the London Hospital. On 22nd March a labourer, aged thirty-seven, was brought to the hospital about half-past seven in the evening. He had had one paroxysm in the receiving room of our hospital before I saw him. He had a rapid but feeble pulse, breathing quickly though not laboriously. The jaws were closed and fixed, there was an expression of anxiety about the countenance, and the features were sunken. He was unable to swallow, the muscles of the abdomen and back were somewhat tense. After he had been in the ward about ten minutes he had another paroxysm and opisthotonos, which lasted about one minute. He was then quiet for a few minutes; he had then another, and died. He had only been in the hospital about half an hour. An inquest was held on the body, but no poison was found. I attribute the cause of death to tetanus. There were three wounds, two on the back of the right elbow, about the size of a shilling each, and one on the left elbow, about the size of a sixpence. The man told me he had had them about twelve or sixteen years. They were old, chronic, indurated ulcers, circular in outline, the edges thickened round, undermined, and covered with a dirty white coating without any granulations. I am unable to say what produced those ulcers. I have seen old, chronic syphilitic wounds in the legs similar to those in the elbow, but I cannot say that these were so. These wounds were the only things to account for tetanus. There was no other cause found.

Cross-examined by the ATTORNEY-GENERAL—I learned from the man's wife that a linseed meal poultice had been applied to this ulcer a day or two before. The jaws were completely fixed when he came, so as to render him incapable of swallowing anything. He said he had just been taken with strange symptoms about the jaws at dinner that morning about eleven o'clock. He was able to speak, though he could not open his jaw. That is the case in tetanus.

Were there also symptoms of rigidity when he was brought in about the abdominal and lumbar muscles; did you learn from him how long this rigidity had been coming on?—Not further than that the first symptoms of the illness he had felt were that morning. He did not say how long he had felt this rigidity about the neck. He was seen by the parish surgeon in the afternoon before coming to the hospital. I have no doubt that the disease had been coming on from the morning.

Though you cannot speak as to the precise character of these sores, were they ugly sores?—Yes; sores of a chronic character—ulcers. The two on the right elbow were perfectly running into one another. A piece of integument connected the two, so that they would be likely to run into one another eventually. By saying that those sores were undermined I mean that the wounds continued under the skin. There were no signs of healing, and they had the appearance of old, neglected sores.

Were they near the site of any particular nerve?—They were near the ulnar nerve, a very sensitive nerve connected with what we call the "funny bone."

How soon was he seized with the first paroxysm after he came in?—He had one directly he came into the hospital, but I did not see it. Half an hour from that time he died.

Had he had any paroxysms before he came to the hospital?—I believe he had, all the afternoon.

That was not one continuous paroxysm?—No; there was a twitching of the muscles of the legs and arms.

What are the particular symptoms of the case to which you refer as indicative of death from tetanus?—From the tetanic symptoms and from having wounds.

Put aside for the moment the fact of his having the wounds that would lead to that inference; what were the symptoms that manifested themselves previous to, or concomitantly with, death which you would call tetanic?— The tetanic symptoms there are the lockjaw and the muscles of the abdomen and the back also being rigid; and he complained of pain in his stomach, just over the stomach. I did not hear the account given of the symptoms of Mr. Cook's death.

Re-examined by Mr. GROVE—Strychnia was suspected in this case before the body was examined. The nerves of the tongue are very delicate ones. There are very delicate nerves at the throat and fauces.

Were you here yesterday when a case was described of an injury in the throat—a sore throat that caused tetanus?—I was.

Are you of opinion that an irritation of the nerves of the throat would cause tetanus as well as the other nerves?—That was produced by exposure to cold; it was therefore idiopathic.

Would any injury to any delicate nerves be a cause of tetanus?—Decidedly.

F. Wrightson

Dr. FRANCIS WRIGHTSON, examined by Mr. KENEALY—I was a pupil of Liebig. I am an analytical chemist and teacher of chemistry at the School of Chemistry at Birmingham. I have studied and made experiments in various poisons, including strychnia. I have not found any extraordinary difficulties in the detection of strychnia. It is detected by the usual tests. I have detected strychnia pure, and I have also discovered it when mixed with impurity, such as bile, bilious matter from putrefying blood, after having separated it from the impurities. Strychnia can be discovered in the tissues. I have discovered it in the viscera of a cat poisoned by strychnia, also in the blood of a dog poisoned by strychnia, also in the urine of another dog poisoned by strychnia. I have heard the theory propounded by Dr. Taylor as to the decomposition of strychnia by the act of poisoning.

Are you of opinion strychnia undergoes decomposition in the act of poisoning?—I am of opinion that it does not. If it were decomposed in the act of poisoning I should say it would not be possible to discover it in the tissues. Portions of strychnia can be discovered in extremely minute quantities indeed. In the first case I mentioned of the detection of strychnia in the blood, 2 grains were given to the dog. One grain was given to the second dog, in which we detected it in the urine. Half a grain was attempted to be administered to the cat, but a considerable portion of it was spilt.

Assuming that a man was poisoned by strychnia, and that his stomach and a portion of his tissues were sent within eight, or nine, or ten days after death for analytical examination, do you say you could discover the poison of strychnia in his remains?—I should have no doubt whatever in saying so.

Cross-examined by the ATTORNEY-GENERAL—Suppose the whole of this poison to be absorbed, where would you expect to find it?—In the blood.

In its progress to its final destination, the destruction of life, does it pass from the blood, or is it left by the blood in the solid tissues of the body before it produces that effect?—I cannot tell.

If it has passed from the stomach by absorption in the blood, the whole dose, into the circulation, do you say you would still expect to find any of it?— Decidedly so, because I believe it exists as strychnia in the blood.

Do you say you would still expect to find any of it in the stomach?—In order to be absorbed it must be dissolved, and in that portion of the fluid which surrounds the coats of the stomach I should expect to find it.

Suppose the whole to be absorbed?—Then I should not detect it.

Suppose the whole of it has been eliminated from the blood and passed from the system?—Certainly not.

LORD CAMPBELL—You would expect to find it elsewhere, not in the stomach?—Yes. I would expect to find it in the blood and in the tissues.

F. Wrightson

Cross-examination resumed—My question only supposes the minimum of the dose that will destroy life to have been given; and, supposing that to have been absorbed into the circulation, and there deposited in the tissues, or part of it eliminated by the action of the kidneys, would you know where to search for it?—I should search for it both in the blood and in the tissues, and in the ejecta of the kidneys; and from my experiments I should expect to find it in each of them, in case the urine was not ejected during the time of poisoning.

Re-examined by Mr. SERJEANT SHEE—If a man had been killed by strychnia, administered an hour and a half before he died, the poison would certainly be detected in the stomach in the first instance.

Supposing it to have been administered in the shape of pills, would it by that time have been all absorbed and circulated in the system so as to get out of the stomach?—I cannot tell. If it were so I would find it in the blood, the liver, and the spleen.

Could you form an opinion whether it could be detected under these circumstances on the coats of the stomach?—Not knowing the dose administered and the powers of absorption, I cannot say with absolute certainty it would be detected, but I should think it in the highest degree probable if a moderate dose had been administered.

Could you form any opinion from the fact that death had taken place after one paroxysm, and in an hour and a half after the ingestion of the poison, whether it was a considerable or an inconsiderable dose?—I cannot give a decided opinion.

LORD CAMPBELL—I cannot allow this gentleman to leave the box without expressing my high approbation of the manner in which he has given his evidence.

Mr. RICHARD PARTRIDGE, examined by Mr. GROVE—I have been for many years in practice as a surgeon, and am Professor of Anatomy at King's College. I have heard the evidence as to the symptoms of Mr. Cook and as to the post-mortem examination. In my opinion it is most important in a case of convulsion that the spinal cord should be examined after death. The gritty granules that were found would be likely to cause inflammation of the arachnoid membrane, which would be discoverable if the spinal cord had been examined shortly after death. If examined nine weeks after it is not likely it would be discovered. Although I have not seen such a case, there are cases on record that such inflammation, if it existed, would be capable of producing tetaniform convulsions. The medical term for such inflammation of the arachnoid is arachnitis, or inflammation of the membrane. That disorder produces convulsions and death. I should not say universally; sometimes it does not result in death. I could not form any positive judgment as to the cause of death in Mr. Cook's case. I have heard the evidence as to the state of contraction after death. No inference at all can be formed of the degree of contraction, or the kind of contraction, that I heard described. If I find the back curved and the body resting on its back and feet after death, I should infer that he died of that form of tetanus which convulses the muscles of the back. Various degrees and varieties of rigidity occur after a natural death. The clenching of the hands or the semi-bending of the feet are not uncommon in cases of ordinary death.

Cross-examined by the ATTORNEY-GENERAL—The granules from which arachnitis might have proceeded were, I understand, situated in the inner surface of the fibrous investment of the cord. They are occasionally found in these parts; not commonly. They are signs. Arachnitis, producing convulsions, has never come under my personal observation, nor has it satisfactorily come under my observation without producing convulsions. It is a very rare disease.

Are you enabled to state from the recorded cases the course of the symptoms of the disease?—No.

Do not you know it to be a disease of considerable duration?—The cases have varied in duration; commonly days at the shortest. Arachnitis is accompanied with paralysis if they live.

Would it, considering the connection that there is between the spinal cord and the brain, affect the brain by sympathy, or otherwise, prior to death?— No.

In these cases, where granules have produced arachnitis, do you happen to know whether the granules have been considerable in point of size?—It has varied in different cases.

Suppose them to be very small and minute?—I should think there would be less likelihood of their producing inflammation.

Suppose an examination at a longer interval than nine days after death failed to detect the inflammation of the arachnoid, that the spinal cord and its integuments had not undergone any decomposition, and that the appearance was perfectly healthy, should you be warranted in inferring there was inflammation?—I should not conclude there was inflammation. Prior to decomposition I should not.

The examination was made by four medical men; are you of opinion that they would be competent judges as to decomposition?—[The question was objected to.]

Does arachnitis not sometimes extend to a matter of months, even where it extends to death?—It might go on for months.

Does it not affect the patient by a series of convulsions at recurring intervals?—That varies.

Did you ever know, or hear of, or read of a case in which the patient died after a single convulsion of arachnitis?—Not a single one.

What would be the concomitant symptoms; would it affect the rest of the patient or affect the general health?—I cannot say.

R. Partridge

Do you believe that a man could have twenty-four hours of complete repose?—No.

In the interval between the convulsions could he be quite well?—No; he would have pain and uneasiness according to the situation of the muscles convulsed, the back usually.

You have heard the symptoms, and I presume you have heard from the midnight of Monday till Tuesday Mr. Cook had complete repose. I now ask you if, in the face of the Court and of the profession, you will undertake to say that Mr. Cook's death proceeded from arachnitis?—I should think not. The majority of the symptoms do not show arachnitis.

You have mentioned that there were one or two of the appearances after death in Cook's case which would be common to other cases, the semi-closing of the hand. Did you ever know, except in a case of tetanus, the hand so completely clenched as to require force to take the fingers away from the hand?—No, I do not.

Have you ever known the feet to be so distorted as to be described by a medical man as assuming the form of a club foot?—Never.

Did you hear the description given by Mr. Jones that when this man died the body was bowed so that, if he had turned it from its side upon its back, it would have rested on its head and on its heels?—I did.

Have you any doubt that that indicates death from tetanus?—Not from some form of tetanic symptoms. I am only acquainted by reading and hearsay with the symptoms that accompany death from tetanus resulting from the administration of strychnia.

From your knowledge of the subject, having attended to the symptoms described by Mr. Jones from the moment the paroxysm set in of which Mr. Cook died, and the symptoms and appearances attending his death, does it appear that these symptoms are consistent with death by strychnia?—Some are consistent and some are inconsistent. The long interval which occurred after the taking of the poison is inconsistent.

What I am asking you is, whether these symptoms on the Tuesday night, from the time the man was taken with the paroxysms of convulsions of the muscles of the trunk, of the legs, of the arms—the bending of the body into a bow—the difficulty of respiration—are consistent with what you know of death by strychnia?—Quite.

Do you agree that the symptoms in tetanus come on gradually and progressive; that, although they are intermitted, the disease is never wholly remitted?—I do.

What is the shortest period in which you have ever known the disease of traumatic tetanus run its course to death?—Never under three or four days.

R. Partridge

Suppose a case could be described as of shorter duration, such as a day or a few hours, would your medical experience lead you to infer that the premonitory symptoms had very likely been neglected?—I should consider that probable.

Bearing in mind the distinction between traumatic and idiopathic tetanus and a case such as has been here described, have you ever seen such a death as this was with the symptoms mentioned proceed from natural causes?—No.

Re-examined by Mr. GROVE—What are the other symptoms which you consider inconsistent with strychnia?—The sickness manifested before the attack came on; the beating of the bed clothes with the arms, want of sensitiveness to external impression, and the sudden cessation of the convulsions, and apparent complete recovery.

You mentioned previously the time that occurred between the ingestion of the poison and the paroxysm coming on. What inference do you deduce from that?—That it is inconsistent with strychnia.

As to the mode in which it came on without premonitory symptoms, do you consider that is inconsistent with strychnia?—There was apparently an absence of the usual condition that is described.

You stated that the bent form indicated some tetaniform symptom. Did that answer apply to natural tetaniform as well as to tetaniform convulsions caused by strychnia?—Yes. The bent form of the feet indicated tetanic spasm. That would be the case whether it was a tetaniform spasm with poison or without poison.

By LORD CAMPBELL—And the other symptoms of rigidity?—It is rather a question of degree.

They would be more violent if from poison?—No doubt.

You have stated in the cases of tetanus you have seen there was no intermission. Do you know, from your reading, that the intermission of the disease is a frequent thing?—I know it occurs, but it is not frequent.

As to decomposition of the spine. Do you think it could remain for nine weeks undecomposed?—I do not.

The ATTORNEY-GENERAL—I have one question which I would put (this gentleman spoke as to vomiting), whether, if the stomach had been brought by any other cause into a state of irritation, would he think those causes inconsistent?

LORD CAMPBELL—I intended to put the question myself.

WITNESS—I should think it not inconsistent.

John Gay

Mr. JOHN GAY, examined by Mr. GRAY—I am a Fellow of the Royal College of Surgeons, and have been for eighteen years a surgeon of the Royal Free Hospital. In the year 1843 I had under my care in the hospital a case of tetanus in a boy eight years old. He was brought in on the 28th of July. The accident occurred a week before. I saw him on the 28th of July. He could not open his mouth at that time. He complained of great pain and stiffness about the neck. During the first three days I saw him he had unusually severe paroxysms.

By LORD CAMPBELL—During the first night of his admission he started up convulsed, and spasmodically closed his jaw. During the following night he was a good deal convulsed at times. The abdominal muscles, as well as the muscles of the neck and back, had become rigid during the night. The muscles of the face were also in a state of great contraction. On the following day I found the muscles remained in the same state. In the morning of that day, at two o'clock, on visiting him I found there was much rigidity of the muscles, especially those of the abdomen and back. The following morning the muscular rigidity had gone. He opened his mouth as usual, and was able to talk. The lad appeared to be thoroughly relieved. He had no return of the spasms till the following day. At that time he asked the nurse to change his linen, and she was lifting him up in bed to do so when violent convulsions of the arms and face came on, and he died in a few minutes.

Examination resumed—About thirty hours elapsed from the time the convulsions of which he died came on and the last preceding convulsions. The last paroxysm before he died lasted a few minutes. Before it came on the rigidity which I have described had been completely relieved. At the time he was convulsed the nurse was lifting him up to put on his linen.

By LORD CAMPBELL—The second day I gave him small doses of tartar emetic to produce vomiting, but without effect. I repeated them in larger doses of 2 grains, but without effect. I did not repeat the dose after the third day.

Cross-examined by the ATTORNEY-GENERAL—What was the accident?— A large stone had fallen on the middle of the left foot and had completely smashed it. The wound had become very unhealthy. When I first saw it it had portions of bone and cartilage adhering to the surface. I amputated the toe. When the boy was brought in his mother said he could not open his mouth so wide as usual. When I saw him his mouth was almost closed up.

On 29th July he slept but little during the night, and during sleep started up convulsed and spasmodically closed the jaw. The jaw remained closed until the 1st of August. It was closed when I administered tartar emetic to him. In all these cases so trifling a remedy as the tarter emetic is easily given.

By LORD CAMPBELL—The tongue seems to retain its powers?—Yes. The case is recorded in the *Lancet*.

Cross-examination resumed—After the 29th of July did the convulsions continue throughout the 30th and part of the 31st?—The convulsions came on during the night, and they appear to have remitted during the day, except a muscular rigidity. The tetanus did remain.

But were there no spasms during the daytime?—I believe not.

In the daytime, although there were no convulsions, were the muscles of the body, of the chest, and of the abdominal back and neck all rigid?—Yes. That continued throughout the two days I administered tartar emetic. The rigidity of the muscles and of the stomach would go far to prevent sickness.

You have no doubt that your tartar emetic would have produced its effect but for the rigidity of the muscles?—I suppose it would have done so.

When did the symptoms begin to abate?—On the 1st of August, on the fourth day, and they gradually subsided. They appeared to have subsided during the night. I saw the child during the middle of the day, and I found that they had subsided, and in fact had entirely gone off. I thought he was going to get well.

You told us the woman set him up in bed for the purpose of changing his linen. Would that in any way have brought the toe, that part that had been attacked, into any friction with some parts of the bed?—It must have done so. But I do not think the simple irritation of the toe at that part would have any effect.

But there not having been, in your judgment, nervous irritation set up from the original seat of the disease, can you account in any way for the nervous or muscular disease of tetanus?—If the cause had not entirely gone the symptoms were brought back by the act of sitting up in bed. My impression is there must be some action about the spinal cord as the immediate cause of the symptoms.

Action set up in the spinal cord by irritation of the nerves in the immediate site of the laceration or wound?—Quite so.

May it not be reasonable to infer that any irritation of the part originally injured, exciting or irritating the nerve or the nerves connected with the part, may support its action over the whole system, and so produce convulsion?— I had removed the end of the diseased part, so I cannot conceive that the same cause could exist.

If you imagine you feel yourself justified in saying that the irritation of the spinal cord once set up continues, why should you infer that the irritation of the nerve may not also continue?—There must be some peculiar irritation of the nerve to give rise to the affection of the spinal cord from which tetanus arises. There appear to be some particular circumstances which produce it.

You have no doubt the state of the toe was the original cause of the convulsions?—I have not.

And that death took place by something or other distinct from the first cause?—Yes.

Re-examined by Mr. GRAY—I think you told my friend that, with regard to the convulsions which end in death, you thought they arose from some irritation set up in the spinal cord?—I did, from that and other causes.

May the causes of such irritation be very various in different cases? May the cause of the irritation in the spinal cord which would end in tetaniform be very various?—I think so.

Suppose in one you have a death accompanied with tetaniform symptoms and opisthotonos, and the various symptoms of a tetanic character; in the absence of any knowledge of the case—of the cause you state, probably the irritation of the spinal cord—do you think it is possible to ascribe them to any particular cause?—I think it would be extremely difficult to do so.

Will you give me the proposition you lay down?—In the event of a given set of symptoms, tetanic symptoms I should say, being proposed, it would be extremely difficult, if not impossible, without some other evidence, or collateral evidence, to assign it to any given disease.

LORD CAMPBELL—Or cause?—Or cause.

W. M'Donnell

Dr. WILLIAM M'DONNELL, examined by Mr. KENEALY—I am a licentiate of the College of Surgeons of Edinburgh, and have been in practice for about eight years. I have had practical as well as theoretical knowledge of idiopathic and traumatic tetanus. Tetanus will proceed from very slight causes. Almost any internal disorder or alteration of the internal secretions will produce idiopathic tetanus. Exposure to cold or damp would produce it. Mental excitement would be a probable cause.

By LORD CAMPBELL—Mental excitement would be the proximate cause of tetanus. The presence of gritty particles or granules in any part connected with the nervous structure, in either the spine or the brain, might produce tetanic convulsions. I have seen small deposits or tubercles in the brain, the only assignable cause for death terminating in convulsions.

W. M'Donnell

Examination resumed—In addition to those slight causes, I believe that tetanic convulsions arise from causes as yet quite undiscoverable by science. I have had many post-mortem examinations of patients who have died of tetanus, and no trace of any disease whatever could be discovered beyond the congestion or vascularity of some of the vessels surrounding the nerves. Though tetanus is not easily discoverable, strychnia is easily discoverable by scientific men. I had a case of idiopathic tetanus—a female, Catherine Watson. I was fortunate enough to restore her, and she is here. (Dr. M'Donnell read his notes of the case of Catherine Watson.) In her case lockjaw set in about the middle of the attack. She was able to speak. In acute idiopathic tetanus, ending fatally, trismus is generally a later symptom. I had a case of tetanus which ended fatally, a man named Copeland. It must have been idiopathic, as there was no external cause. Death took place in somewhat less than half an hour. I cannot say precisely. He was dead before I could reach the house.

By LORD CAMPBELL—Do you know what the cause of the disease was?— Yes. I examined the patient carefully, and made inquiry as to the symptoms.

Examination resumed—I have made a number of experiments on animals with reference to strychnia poison. I have found the muscles of the brain highly congested, the sinuses gorged with blood, and in one case hæmorrhage from the nostrils. That would indicate a very high state of congestion. I have found extravasation of the blood in some cases, likewise in the brain. I have cut through the substance of the brain and found numerous red points. I have found the lungs of these animals either collapsed or congested. The heart has been invariably filled in the right side with blood, and very often on the left. The liver has been congested, the kidneys normal generally, the spleen in its ordinary condition. I have found the vessels of the stomach on the outer surface congested, and on the mucous or inner surface highly vascular. In the spinal cord I have found the vessels of the membranes congested, and also red points seen on cutting it through, not invariably, but sometimes. I have experimented in many cases for the discovery of strychnia. You may discover the smallest dose that will kill the animal. If you kill an animal with a grain of strychnia you may discover traces of it.

What do you mean by a trace of it?—Evidence of its appearance.

Does that mean an imponderable quantity?—It may.

Do you mean by traces to convey the idea that you can discover the smallest quantity?—That will kill.

What is the smallest quantity you can discover?—The fifty-thousandth part of a grain.

Have you actually experimented so as to discover that quantity?—Yes.

W. M'Donnell

You have heard a theory propounded in the course of this inquiry by Dr. Taylor—I mean the destruction by the supposed decomposition of strychnia—to your knowledge has any scientific man of eminence ever propounded that theory at all?—I never heard of it until mentioned in this Court. In my opinion there are no well-grounded reasons for that theory. I have proved that that theory is false by numerous experiments. I have taken the blood of an animal poisoned with 2 grains of strychnia, about the least quantity which would kill an animal, and have injected it into the abdominal cavities of some animals, and have destroyed them, with the symptoms and post-mortem appearances of strychnia. It should not make it any more difficult to detect if the strychnia is administered in the form of pills. If the pills were hard, and not readily solved, you would find it much easier, because you might find some remains of the pill. I do not agree with Dr. Taylor's opinion about the fallacy of colour tests. I believe a colour test is a reliable mode of ascertaining strychnia. I agree with Mr. Herepath that it is found in urine that has been ejected. I have found it invariably.

Does it first pass into the blood and then into that watery excretion?—Part of it may be drawn off by that means. It is not true that strychnia can be confounded with pyroxanthine. In these animals which I have killed with strychnia I have generally observed an increased flow of saliva; that was a very marked symptom. The animals were very susceptible to touch. A stamp of the foot, a slight touch, or a breath, or a sharp word, would drive them into tetanic convulsions. We recognised them by the straightened condition of the muscles.

Supposing that a dose of strychnia sufficient to kill a man were administered to him, do you think he could bear to have his neck rubbed?—I think it would be very likely to throw him into convulsions before the paroxysm came on.

By LORD CAMPBELL—As soon as the poison is taken into his system?—No. It requires a certain time. You must have the first symptoms of poison developed. It would be after the first symptoms.

W. M'Donnell

Examination resumed—What would be the effect of a man pulling a bell violently if he was poisoned by strychnia?—I think it would be extremely probable, if the dose had been sufficient, to destroy life, provided the symptoms had made their appearance. I quite agree with Mr. Herepath that, if a sufficient dose to poison has been administered, it can and ought to be discovered. I have heard the medical evidence that was given in this case and the evidence as to the symptoms. The symptoms I attach very little importance to as the means of diagnosis, as you may have the same symptoms developed from many different causes. There is one principal reason I have, which is this—a dose of strychnia sufficient to destroy life in one paroxysm would hardly require an hour and a half or two hours. The cause of death was from convulsions, epileptic convulsions with tetanic symptoms.

Does the interval of repose from the Monday night to the Tuesday at all operate on your judgment in coming to that conclusion?—If my opinion that it was of an epileptic character were correct, it would.

It is your opinion that if that were of an epileptic character—then what follows?—The intermission from the Monday night would be considered important, as epilepsy seizures very often recur about the same hours, as I have seen them.

Assuming that a man was in such an excitable state of mind that he was silent for two or three minutes after his horse winning a race, that he exposed himself to cold and damp, that he excited his brain by drinking, and he was attacked by violent vomiting, and after his death gritty granules were found in the neighbourhood of his spine, could not, in the present instance, such a death as it was arise from these causes?—Any of these causes might aggravate or hurry it.

You say any one of those causes?—Might cause it.

Cross-examined by the ATTORNEY-GENERAL—I am a general practitioner at Garnkirk, near Glasgow, general surgeon to the ironworks, and parochial medical officer. I have had personal experience of two cases of idiopathic tetanus—this one I have recorded and another.

What you have been telling us about mental excitement, sensual excitement, is not within your own observation?—This case might have arisen from those causes.

Have you any reason to think it did?—I have no reason to do so.

Then do not tell us what it might have done. Now, in the case of Catherine Wilson?—I saw her about half-past ten at night. She had been ill very nearly an hour before I saw her. She had convulsions. She had gone about her usual duties up to the evening. She felt a slight lassitude previous to that time. It was only by close pressing that she could call it to mind. The lockjaw, I think, came on in an hour or two; I could not be positive.

In the other case, of Mr. Copeland?—It was a young child between three and four months old.

Was that the person of the name of Copeland?—Yes.

What was the matter with the child?—I saw it in good health half an hour before the attack came on. It had an attack of convulsions and opisthotonos. I rode away from the house, and they supposed I had not gone a couple of miles when it died.

W. M'Donnell

It was seized with a fit?—Apparently a spasm, which I consider to be of the tetaniform character. I had seen the child half an hour before. There was nothing the matter with it then. It was in bed, I believe, with the mother, who was laid up. I did not see its face. I saw it lying in bed, but did not examine it. I judged it to be asleep.

With regard to the animals that you experimented on with strychnia, when did you begin with them?—I began this series of experiments for this case in January.

Had you ever made any before?—Yes; I think eight or ten years ago. The dose by which I killed the animals was from 1¾ to 2 grains. The animals experimented upon were dogs, cats, rabbits, and fowls. These experiments will relate to dogs. A grain is the smallest dose I administered. In four cases I used a grain, in five 1½ grains, in one, I think, 1¼ grains, and in two 2 grains.

You never tried them with half a grain?—Yes, I did; I did not mention it before. I gave half a grain for the purpose of ascertaining the least dose that would kill.

Did you try if you could detect it afterwards?—How could I try before I killed the dog?

Do you mean on your oath you do not understand my question? Show me one instance where you have given half a grain?—I did not make a note, because it did not kill. I have never destroyed a dog with half a grain; I tried it, and it did not answer.

Now let us come to your symptoms. You say you have always found the brain highly congested?—By the stoppage of the circulation in the system.

Have you not found in some cases that the brain was not congested?—No; I think in every case there were more or less congestion.

Is that greater in proportion to the length of the paroxysm?—No; it is greatest where the animal was young and in a full state of health.

Have you ever seen any case of traumatic tetanus?—I think two in my own practice, but I have seen a few others in hospital.

Have you ever seen a case of strychnia in the human subject?—No, I have not.

I understand you to say that, in your opinion, this was a case of epilepsy with tetanic complications?—As far as I can judge from hearing the evidence in Court.

What does epilepsy proceed from?—Nobody can answer that question.

You have no theory upon the subject?—I have not exactly arrived at any distinct theory, not quite as distinct as strychnia or tetanus. I have seen one case of death from epilepsy. The patient was not conscious when he died.

Can you find me any case in which consciousness has preceded death?—I cannot recollect.

W. M'Donnell

You have studied on purpose for these cases?—No; I am pretty well up in most branches.

Being so universally proficient in the science of your profession, do you know of any single recorded case of consciousness at the time of death?—I do not from my own knowledge. I have heard what Sir Benjamin Brodie said on this subject.

You mean deliberately to state that you believe this to have been from epilepsy?—I do state so.

Without being able to refer to any cause whatever as producing the disease?—When I have told you before that deaths often take place in idiopathic tetanus without leaving any trace behind, I think I may say——

That is idiopathic tetanus?—They are all of the same class. I think all forms of convulsions arise from a decomposition of the blood, and, if a person has probably an incipient tendency to disease of the brain, that it always may be affected, and that the decomposition of the blood might set up the diseased action.

Do I understand you that mental excitement had anything to do with this?—I do not say it had. I said it might have caused it.

Do you find any excitement in this case?—I find at Shrewsbury he was excited, and wherever you have excitement you have a consequent depression.

Do you find he was depressed?—When you find a man in bed sick, he must be depressed.

I was speaking of the depression consequent on these symptoms. Where do you find any symptom of illness until he begins to vomit?—If I have much excitement, if I am up all night, it upsets me the next day, and I generally vomit the food I take. Cook was overjoyed at winning his race.

And you think he vomited in consequence?—He might.

Do you mean to swear that you think the excitement of the three minutes on the course on the Tuesday accounts for the vomiting?—I do not mean to say anything of the kind.

Do you find any excitement or depression from that time till the time he died?—There is nothing reported that I can recollect just now.

On the contrary, do you not recollect that the man, when he was not vomiting, on that very night, was joking and laughing; was that sufficient to make him vomit?—That may well be where a man is subject to bilious fits.

We are talking of excitement—of epilepsy with tetanic complications; I want to know on what you can put your hand in the way of excitement or depression which will account for the remarkable symptoms?—I have told you that almost any one of them is sufficient.

W. M'Donnell

Where is there one which you say might have occasioned death?—These white spots in the stomach might have caused death by an inflammatory condition of the stomach.

But there was no inflammation of the stomach, was there?—I have given you my opinion.

If there had been any, would not the gentlemen who examined it have seen it?—If those white spots were present you would have had inflammation.

They say there was none?—I do not believe them.

Sensual excitement is a cause of epilepsy with tetanic complications; is that what you say?—Yes, it might be.

Do you find a tittle of evidence of any such excitement?—I think so—the syphilitic spots. There was no doubt about it.

Do you mean to say that you attribute this to some excitement at some anterior period long before?—I am not called upon to say that. I take my opinion from what was seen.

Supposing the man had any such excitement a week before, do you mean that is sufficient?—Yes; we have instances on record of convulsions in the very act you allude to.

Have you any instance a fortnight afterwards?—It is quite within the range of possibility.

Would epilepsy, with tetanic complications, set in from that cause? Do you mean to stand there, as a serious man of science, and tell me that?—Yes, the results of sensual excitement—chancre in one of them, and syphilitic sore throat.

Did you ever hear or know of such a thing as chancre or any other form of syphilis producing epilepsy?—Not epilepsy, but tetanus. You are forgetting the tetanic complications.

If I understand it rightly, it stands thus: the sensual excitement produces the epilepsy, and the chancre produces tetanic complications?—You are quite mistaken. I say the results of a sensual excitement.

You have just now said that your reason for thinking and referring it to epilepsy was that, amongst other things, an hour or an hour and a half intervened between the taking of the poison and the appearance of the first symptoms. Do you mean that in your reading you have not met with cases quite as long as that when the death has arisen from strychnia?—I cannot recollect where death has followed.

Would the fact of morphia having been given for an hour or two previously in any way touch your opinion with regard to poison?—No; I have seen opium bring on convulsions very nearly the same.

Will opium bring on convulsions?—Yes, but a different form of convulsions from epilepsy.

Because opium brings on convulsions, you assume in this case that morphia accelerated the disease?—Drawing the inference, I should say it might.

W. M'Donnell

Suppose not a case of epilepsy, but of strychnia; what would be the action of morphia? How would it attack the disease?—In some cases it stimulates. It is exceedingly apt to cause congestion of the brain.

In which disease does it cause excitement?—It depends on the idiosyncrasy, on the habit of body, if I might use a common term.

Having taken it on the Saturday and Sunday night, and having been free from nervous excitement on the Sunday and Monday, what would you assume judging from the result?—If it were opium, yet it is only presumed to be opium, it appears to have soothed him.

And why, when the man was tranquil on the Sunday and Monday, did you, after that, venture to say that these pills irritated him?—I do not mean to say they did.

Re-examined by Mr. SERJEANT SHEE—You stated that, though you had seen no case of epileptic convulsions with tetanic complications, your reading informed you that there had been, and you mentioned Dr. Mason Goode?—Yes. He is a well-known author on the subject of convulsions. There is a class of convulsions called epileptic—not, strictly speaking, epilepsy—though they resemble it in some of its features. Epilepsy, properly so called, is sudden in its attacks. The patient falls down at once with a shriek. Within my knowledge, the disease constantly occurs at night and in bed.

Are the convulsions which the authors do not class as properly epilepsy, but as convulsions of an epileptic character, sometimes attended with premonitory symptoms?—Sometimes the patient is thrown into tetanic and tetaniform convulsions. Pending the struggle or the convulsions, actual epilepsy may come on in this way, and the patient die. In epilepsy and in convulsions of an epileptic character, a patient may have suffered in the night and be well the next morning, and as well the next day as if he had had no fit at all, more especially where adults are seized for the first time. When an adult is seized for the first time it is in my experience that several fits follow each other during a short period.

If it were true that Cook's mind appeared distressed and irritable the afternoon before he died, would you infer from that, considering the former excitement and elation, he was in a state of depression or not?—Yes.

What would you infer from what happened in the middle of the Sunday night, supposing it were true that he represented himself to be mad for ten minutes, and it was occasioned by a quarrel in the streets?—That he had been seized with some sudden cramp or spasm.

W. M'Donnell

Supposing there was no such cramp, and that he meant to tell the truth, would you refer what he said to any nervous and mental excitement?—Yes, decidedly.

With regard to the spots on the stomach, which you mentioned when my friend was examining you, you stated you differed from some gentlemen of your profession?—Yes.

The ATTORNEY-GENERAL—He said he did not believe them?—I did not. I did not believe that inflammation could be absent and these spots present.

Re-examination resumed—Have you known any serious consequence of a convulsive character reasonably imputed to spots of that description?—I have. There was a case about twenty years ago. It was published. I saw a case myself, about eighteen months ago. I examined the body after death. It was a case of fever, I thought. I did not know what the spots were, and consulted all the authors who had treated on the mucous structure of the stomach, and could find no account of it but in one which I have here, an essay by Dr. Sproshoid, a medical man practising in Edinburgh, but now deceased.

J. N. Bainbridge

Dr. JOHN NATHAN BAINBRIDGE, examined by Mr. GROVE—I am a doctor of medicine and medical officer to the St. Martin's Workhouse. I have had considerable experience of convulsive disorders. They admit of a very great variety of symptoms. There are causes of them varying from what are called chronic diseases to rigid opisthotonos. Hysterical convulsions are very frequently accompanied with opisthotonos; convulsions of the muscles of the back and of the limbs. The different cases vary very much as to the frequency of the recurrences, and as to the muscles attacked. Periodicity is very common, that is, occurring at the same hour, the same day, and at an interval of a year. I have known this very common at shorter periods, such as twelve or twenty-four hours. These disorders run so imperceptibly one into the other that it is almost impossible for the most experienced medical man to decide where one kind of convulsion terminates and the other begins. Epileptic attacks are frequently accompanied with tetanic complications, or tetanic spasms.

Cross-examined by the ATTORNEY-GENERAL—Do hysterical convulsions ever end in death without being attended by these tetanic symptoms?—Very rarely indeed. I have known one case within the last three months.

Can you undertake to say that that was not a death by apoplexy?—No. The symptoms were somewhat of the same character, but more of the character of epilepsy. It would be very difficult for any man to define the difference in some instances between hysteria and epilepsy.

J. N. Bainbridge

In fact, had not the man been subject to these fits for a long series of years, and at last he died in one of them?—Yes, he had.

In attacks of this nature is there in the fits a loss of consciousness?— Sometimes. I have seen several cases in which there has been, and in others they can almost understand anything you say to them, not perfectly perhaps, but you may rouse them.

Have you ever known an instance in which a man was able to speak when the paroxysm has set in?—They will scream, and recollect what we have said to them. I never knew any of them, in the actual violence of the paroxysm, ask to have their position changed. Epilepsy, when it is very bad, is sometimes attended with opisthotonos.

When the convulsions are so violent that opisthotonos is produced, have you ever known patients conscious?—Partly conscious. If they were asked subsequently they would recollect what had occurred. I have seen cases of traumatic tetanus. As far as I have observed the patient always retains his consciousness. I have frequently known epilepsy end in death, and also hysteria with tetanic complications end in death.

Because you tell me you have known of hysteria ending in death, I wish you to inform me what in your opinion is the distinction between them?—The less consciousness more especially found in epilepsy, and the sudden falling down.

Did you ever know a case of death in epilepsy where consciousness was not destroyed before death?—No, I do not know one.

Mr. SERJEANT SHEE—I think it is an assumption that Mr. Cook was conscious between the last shriek and his death.

E. A. Steady

Mr. EDWARD AUSTIN STEADY, examined by Mr. GRAY—I am a member of the Royal College of Surgeons, and am in practice as a surgeon at Chatham. In June, 1854, I attended a person for trismus and pleurosthotonos, the head depending on one side, and not backwards as is the case in opisthotonos. Convulsions came on in paroxysms. The first attack continued for a fortnight. She had trismus all the time. For twelve months there were remissions of the pleurosthotonos. She appeared to get better to a certain extent, and walked about, but the tendons of one knee were contracted. About twelve months after she was again seized. The seizure continued about a week.

Did you ascertain the cause which had brought about this disease?—It was detailed to me as excitement. A passion, I believe, brought it on. I believe she had had some quarrel with her husband. I discovered no other cause.

E. A. Steady

Cross-examined by Mr. JAMES—I do not know how long before I was called in she had this quarrel. I learned that during the quarrel she had had a blow given her on her side by her husband. I observed the setting in of the lockjaw at that time. I saw her in March, 1855, when she was under my care for about a week. The locking of the jaw continued the whole week. She has never got thoroughly well. She has tetanic extensions of the limbs in any case of excitement. In my opinion the disease is in action in her system at the present time.

G. Robinson

Dr. GEORGE ROBINSON, examined by Mr. KENEALY—I am a Licentiate of the Royal College of Physicians and Fellow of the Royal Medical Chirurgical Society of London, and physician to the Newcastle-on-Tyne Dispensary and Fever Hospital. I have devoted considerable attention to pathology, and have published essays on it. I have practised as a physician for ten years. From the symptoms I have heard described my opinion is that Mr. Cook died from tetanic convulsions, by which I mean, not the disease of tetanus, but convulsions similar to those witnessed in tetanus. Convulsions of that kind occasionally assume the nature of epilepsy. I know of no department of pathology which is more obscure than that of convulsive diseases. I have been present at post-mortem examinations of persons who died from convulsive diseases. I have sometimes seen no morbid appearance whatever, and in other cases the morbid appearances which were visible were common to a variety of diseases. Convulsive diseases undoubtedly depend very much on the state of the nerves. They are all connected with disorders of the nervous action. The brain has great influence in producing convulsive diseases, but the spinal cord has a greater influence. The presence of gritty granules in the neighbourhood of the spinal cord would be likely to produce convulsive diseases. There is such a disease as spinal epilepsy, which is accompanied by strong convulsions, which might resemble in a great degree those described in the present case. Periodicity would belong to convulsions arising from spinal epilepsy. I should think from the evidence I have heard that Mr. Cook's mode of life would predispose him to epilepsy.

Cross-examined by the ATTORNEY-GENERAL—In all cases of epilepsy there are violent convulsions. I cannot tell you how many I have seen assume a tetanic character; perhaps twenty.

Has it gone as far as opisthotonos?—Not the extreme opisthotonos of tetanus. The whole body has been straightened out and the head thrown back. I heard Mr. Jones describe Mr. Cook's symptoms, that the body was so bowed that he could not raise it, so bowed that it would lean upon its heels and the back of its head if it had been turned over.

G. Robinson

Have you ever seen anything in epilepsy approaching to these symptoms?— I have never seen anything approaching to it. I have never seen a body so stiffened that it would rest on the head and heels.

Is that symptom peculiar to tetanus?—You may have convulsions of the same character occurring from other causes—tetanic convulsions from the operation of various poisons.

Keep to natural diseases. Did you ever know these symptoms of opisthotonos, in that shape or to that extent, arise from anything but tetanus?—Not within my own experience. I have read of epilepsy being accompanied with tetanic convulsions. Epilepsy, when it assumes that marked character, is accompanied with unconsciousness. I have read in a case of Dr. Marshall Hall's that sometimes unconsciousness is not present. He does not mention whether death took place in this case or not. That would make all the difference.

You said that gritty granules would be likely to produce convulsive diseases. What extent of development, in your judgment, must such granules reach to produce an action in the spinal marrow?—I should say there is no relation between the size of the granules and the extent of the effect produced.

Would you expect when they began to get to the size that they would have any effect on the nervous system—that they would begin to show their effect more or less gradually?—No, in epilepsy I have myself observed several granules in the membrane of the brain; and any disturbing cause in the system, I think, would be likely to produce convulsions. I believe that the granules in this case were very likely to irritate the spinal cord, and an attack might very likely come on at once in a fit of epilepsy. There would be pain during the continuance of the violent spasms of the patient, not necessarily pain merely from the spasms. These granules might or might not produce arachnitis.

You would expect to find inflammation in that case?—Not necessarily. Irritation, not inflammation. Granules of that description do not often exist in healthy spines. In the dissections of epilepsy in the large hospitals, these small granules have been found very frequently. The granules, in my opinion, would be likely to produce epilepsy. In my experience I have never known epilepsy unaccompanied by unconsciousness, nor have I known epilepsy producing the marked symptoms of tetanic character which occur in Mr. Cook's case.

G. Robinson

Do you feel yourself warranted in giving an opinion that these granules caused epilepsy in this case?—I think I might have done so. If I put aside the hypothesis of poisoning by strychnia I would. Several of the symptoms described by Mr. Jones, the severe paroxysm, the stiffening of the body, the convulsions of all the muscles of the trunk and limbs, and the complete opisthotonos, are also common to other convulsions. The symptoms are certainly consistent with death by strychnia.

They are the symptoms that you would expect after strychnia?—I think there would have been some slight premonitory symptoms. If I had no other cause to which I could ascribe the death I would ascribe it to epilepsy.

But in this case you admit some of the symptoms are inconsistent with your experience of epilepsy?—Yes.

Re-examined by Mr. SERJEANT SHEE—They are consistent with the possibility of epilepsy. They are consistent with convulsions of an epileptic form ending in death, though perhaps not actually amounting to epilepsy.

Supposing it to have been actual epilepsy, at what period of the last attack should you say the epilepsy commenced?—When Mr. Cook sat up in bed and cried out. I should imagine that would be the sense of suffocation which would be the premonitory symptoms.

After the final shriek, and throwing himself back in his bed, is there any symptom from which you would infer consciousness after that moment?—Except that he swallowed some pills.

The ATTORNEY-GENERAL—Allow me to remind you he asked them to turn him over.

By Mr. SERJEANT SHEE—Would you consider that a body which immediately, or within ten minutes after death, when it is quite warm, lay perfectly straight, the hands extended, resting on its heels and its back and its head, was in a state of opisthotonos?—Not if it rested on its back. In my judgment it might be that the body might assume, without actual rigidity, the bow-like shape and appearance which has been spoken of, and yet, when turned over, lie flat in the bed, resting on the head, back, and heels.

B. W. Richardson

Dr. BENJAMIN WARD RICHARDSON, examined by Mr. SERJEANT SHEE—I practise in London, and I am a licentiate of the Faculty of Physicians and Surgeons in Glasgow and a member of the College of Physicians in London. I have never seen a case of idiopathic or traumatic tetanus, but I have seen a considerable number of deaths by convulsions, and I have known these cases, when they have ended in death, sometimes assume tetaniform appearances without being, strictly speaking, tetanus. The patient, if conscious, generally desires to sit up. I have known persons to die from a disease called angina pectoris. The symptoms of the disease, when it is fatal, resemble closely the symptoms of the paroxysms in which Mr. Cook died. It is classed amongst the convulsive or spasmodic diseases, and has no distinctive feature in post-mortem examination.

B. W. Richardson

Will you state what symptoms you particularly refer to?—I could not do better than describe a case which I myself saw. A child, ten years of age, was under my care in November, 1850. I supposed she had suffered from scarlet fever. She had a slight feverish attack. She recovered so far that my visits ceased on 20th November. I left her merry in the morning, and at half-past ten I was called to see her dying. She was supported upright at her own request. The face was pale; the whole of the face and arms rigid, the fingers clenched, the respiratory muscles completely fixed and rigid, and, with all, complained of an intense agony and restlessness such as I had never witnessed. There was perfect consciousness. The child knew me, and explained her intense agony; eagerly took from my hands some brandy and water from a spoon. I then left to get some chloroform for the purpose of producing relaxation by chloroform vapour. On returning, I found the head was thrown back. I could detect no respiration. The eyes remained fixed open, and the body just resembling a fit. She was dead. I did not observe whether the rigor-mortis came on at its usual time or later. I made a post-mortem examination the following day. Unfortunately I left the body in the arms of the sister, and, of course, it was laid out afterwards. At the post-mortem examination I observed that the brain was slightly congested; a portion of the upper part of the spinal cord seemed normal and healthy, the lungs were collapsed, the heart was in such a state of firm spasms and so empty that I remarked it might have been rinsed out, it was so perfectly clean and free from blood. There were no appearances of functional disturbances except a slight effusion of serum in one pleural cavity, I believe the right side. The other part of the spinal cord was in a normal state. They told me the child was unusually well and merry at supper; that she then went to bed with her sister, and in lying down suddenly jumped up and said, "I am going to die," and begged her sister to rub her.

Cross-examined by the ATTORNEY-GENERAL—This case accords with all the descriptions of angina pectoris by the best authors—Latham, Watson, Boyeau, Pratt, and Sir Everett Holme.

What is the true nature and cause of angina pectoris?—It has been laid down as disease of the valves of the heart. There have been many cases in which there has been no discovered cause.

Are the symptoms of angina pectoris not those that would be produced by taking strychnia?—Not exactly. In angina pectoris the patient requests to be rubbed to give relief.

Did you hear the Leeds case?—Assuming that that was a case of strychnia, I must say that the two forms are so strictly analogous that there would be great difficulty in detecting angina from strychnia, with this difference, that angina is paroxysmal, it comes and goes, and strychnia would not be so likely to do that. You would not expect it for many months.

B. W. Richardson

But in this case you are speaking as if it ended in the first paroxysm?—Yes.

How then can you be justified, in cases where you discover no abnormal conditions of the heart or its arteries, in setting down the death to angina?—Precisely as if I saw the symptoms of epilepsy I should accept them as such.

Supposing the disease was referable to two causes, in the absence of all evidence, what is your reason for setting it down to one in preference to the other?—I quite admit that if I had known as much of the nature of strychnia as I do now I should have gone on to make analysis.

Is the disease of angina pectoris attended with painful symptoms before it terminates in death?—Most painful. The paroxysms terminating in death may run on for more than eight minutes. It comes on suddenly. It does not always kill at the first attack. It generally spreads itself over a certain period of time.

You said that the head was somewhat bent back. Was that opisthotonos?—There was rigidity, not amounting to opisthotonos, but still very marked. The neck was so stiffly bent back that if the body had been laid down, and the lower limbs, which I did not see, had been the same, I have no doubt the body would be resting on its head and heels.

You say in epileptic convulsions you have seen the hands clenched firmly till death. Did you ever see them so long after death?—I have seen them firmly clenched, not in epilepsy only.

In what cases have you seen them firmly clenched after death?—In cases where there has been violent convulsion. I saw them once from hæmorrhage.

In other cases have you?—I can only say, in a general sense, I have seen the hands clenched over and over again, and have paid no attention to it. My belief, from seeing people die, is that the clenching of the hands is, in many cases, mere matter of accident.

Re-examined by Mr. SERJEANT SHEE—Have you known cases personally or from your reading where patients recover from angina pectoris, and whether within a short time afterwards they sometimes have another attack?—They do, sometimes in so short an interval as twenty-four hours.

During the interval between the two attacks what is the condition of the patient?—Perfectly healthy, to all appearance.

Are the symptoms described in the evidence more like the symptoms of angina pectoris or strychnia poison?—I should certainly say angina pectoris.

You had no reason to suspect poison of any kind in that case, either before or now?—Not the slightest.

Dr. WRIGHTSON, recalled, examined by Mr. SERJEANT SHEE—In your opinion, when the strychnia poison is absorbed into the system, does it become diffused by the circulation of the blood through the system, or does it collect in the tissues?—I should think it is diffused throughout the entire system by circulation if it be wholly absorbed, and it would depend on the rapidity with which death takes place after complete absorption, and on the quickness of circulation.

Cross-examined by the ATTORNEY-GENERAL—Would the absorption be more complete if a longer time were given for the process between the administration and the death?—Certainly, it would be.

Is that supposing a minimum dose given sufficient to destroy life; if a long interval elapses between the taking of the poison and the death, the more complete the absorption the less the chance of finding it in the stomach?—*Cæteris paribus* that would be so.

By Mr. SERJEANT SHEE—Would you have a very good chance of finding it in the kidneys and spleen and in the blood?—Yes.

C. Watson

CATHERINE WATSON, examined by Mr. GROVE—I live at Garnkirk, in Scotland. Last October I was affected with a fit. I had no wound nor injury on my body before. I had taken no poison.

Cross-examined by the ATTORNEY-GENERAL—I was not ill during the day. I was in low spirits, but not in pain. A few minutes before eleven at night I took a pain in the stomach, then two cramps in my arms, then I was very ill. I have never had cramps like this before nor since.

The Court then adjourned.

Tenth Day, Saturday, 24th May, 1856.

The Court met at ten o'clock.

O. Pemberton

Mr. OLIVER PEMBERTON, examined by Mr. SERJEANT SHEE—I am Lecturer in Anatomy at Queen's College, Birmingham, and surgeon to the General Hospital at Birmingham. I was present at the examination of the body of the late Mr. Cook after it had been exhumed in January or February. I observed the condition of the spinal cord. In my judgment it was not in a condition to enable one to state with confidence in what state it had been immediately after death. The upper part, where the brain had been separated, was green in colour from the effects of decomposition. The remaining portion, though fairly preserved for a body buried two months, was so soft as not to enable me to form any opinion as to its state immediately after death.

Cross-examined by the ATTORNEY-GENERAL,—I did not see the body till the day after the bony canal had been opened, which, to a certain extent, would expose the interior substance of the cord to the atmosphere. So far as I recollect, it was still covered with a very hard, dense membrane. Mr. Bolton, the professor at Queen's College, was also present on Palmer's behalf.

Mr. SERJEANT SHEE—My lord, this closes the medical testimony.

H. Matthews

HENRY MATTHEWS, examined by Mr. GROVE—I am an inspector of police at Euston Station. I was there on 19th November last. The two o'clock afternoon train is the last that stops at Rugeley. The express for Stafford leaves at five, and is due at Stafford at 8.42. On 19th November it arrived at 8.45. From Stafford to Rugeley it is nineteen miles by railway. I do not know how far by road. After the two o'clock train to Rugeley, the quickest way to get there is by the five o'clock to Stafford, and then by road.

Joseph Foster

JOSEPH FOSTER, examined by Mr. GRAY—I have known the late John Parsons Cook for many years, and, from what I saw of him, he was of weak health and constitution. I have been with him when he has had a bilious attack and sick headache.

Cross-examined by Mr. JAMES—He hunted regularly about three days a week. He was a member of the Welford Cricket Club, but I have not seen him playing for three or four years.

GEORGE MYATT, examined by Mr. GROVE—I am a saddler at Rugeley. I was at Shrewsbury races, and saw Palmer and Cook at the Raven Hotel there on the Wednesday evening of the race week. It was about twelve at night, and Cook seemed the worse of liquor. We had some brandy and water together. Cook drank most of his, and remarked that it was not good, and thought there was something in it. Cook proposed having some more, but Palmer told him to finish what he had first. Cook then drank his up. We all then went to bed. I slept in the same room as Palmer. The brandy we had was brought in a decanter and poured out. I did not leave the room from the time Palmer and Cook came in till we went to bed. Had anything been put in the brandy and water I should have seen it. As far as I can remember, when Palmer and I went to our bedroom we left Cook in the sitting room. I locked our door, and Palmer never left the bedroom during the night. In the morning Palmer asked me to call Mr. Cook, which I did. Cook then told me how ill he had been during the night. He said he had been obliged to send for a doctor, and asked me what was put in the brandy and water. I told him I did not know that anything was put in. He then asked me to send Palmer to him, which I did. After Palmer and I had finished our breakfast, I next saw Cook, who came into the sitting room and had his breakfast. That night the three of us had dinner at the Raven, and left for Rugeley about six o'clock. We went by express from Shrewsbury to Stafford. Palmer took the three tickets and paid. We took a fly from Stafford, there being no train. In the fly from Stafford to Rugeley Palmer was sick, and vomited through the window. They could not account for it, unless it was cooking in some brass utensil, or the water. I heard other people speak about being ill at Rugeley, and they could not account for it. It is 9 miles by the road from Stafford to Rugeley.

Cross-examined by Mr. JAMES—I have known the prisoner all my life, and he deals with me for his saddlery at his racing stables. I am not in the habit of going to racing meetings with him, although I attend them myself. He paid my expenses at Shrewsbury races, but never at any other race meeting. About four or five weeks ago I went with Mr. Smith to Stafford gaol, and was with Palmer for about two hours. I have now and then stood in half a sovereign or a sovereign with Palmer when betting on his horses. On the Wednesday night in which I saw Palmer and Cook I dined at home at Rugeley, and reached Shrewsbury between eight and nine. I went straight from the station to the Raven Hotel, and up to Palmer's room, where I saw Cook. Palmer was out, and I went to the town for about an hour, and returned to Palmer's room. He was not in; I waited about two hours, when he came in with Cook, about twelve o'clock. Cook was drunk, but not very drunk. The decanter of brandy and the tumblers were brought in directly. The water, I think, was on the table. I do not remember Mrs. Brooks calling, or Palmer being called out of the room to speak to her. I remember Mr. Fisher coming in. I will swear that Palmer did not at any time that evening take out a glass of brandy and water and leave the room. He never left the room from the time I joined him till we went to bed. When Cook drank his brandy and water he made a remark to the effect that it was not good, and that there was something in it. I will swear that he did not say, "It burns my throat dreadfully," or anything to that effect. The brandy and water was then given to some one to taste. I think there were but four people in the room when Cook drank the brandy and water. Palmer sipped from the glass Cook had drank from, and said he could not taste anything the matter. He held the glass to Mr. Fisher. I do not remember whether Fisher said, "It is no good giving me the glass, it is empty." I will not swear he did not. Palmer and I went to bed about half an hour after, and left Cook in the room. That I will swear. The first I heard of Cook being ill during the night was when he told me of it next morning.

John Sargent

JOHN SARGENT, examined by Mr. SERJEANT SHEE—I frequently attend race meetings, and knew Mr. Cook intimately. I was with him at Liverpool on the week previous to the Shrewsbury meeting. We slept in adjoining rooms, and in the morning he called my attention to the state of his throat and mouth. The back part of his tongue was in a complete state of ulcer. I said I was surprised that he could eat and drink in the state his mouth was in. He said he had been in that state for weeks and months, and took no notice of it now. He had frequently before then shown me his throat when it was in that state. On one occasion, when he took a ginger nut with cayenne by mistake, he told me that it nearly killed him. Before Shrewsbury races Cook was very poor. He owed me £25, and paid £10 on account, saying he had not sufficient to pay his expenses at Liverpool. Cook and Palmer were in the habit of betting for each other on particular horses. I have heard Cook apply to Palmer to supply him with a lotion called blackwash. This is a mercurial lotion of calomel and lime water.

Cross-examined by Mr. JAMES—He applied for it at the latter end of last year. Having seen the state of his throat, I was surprised at his eating and drinking so well.

JEREMIAH SMITH, examined by Mr. SERJEANT SHEE—I am an attorney at Rugeley, and knew the late Mr. Cook. I saw him at ten o'clock on Friday morning, 16th November, 1855. He was having breakfast in bed—a cup of tea with a wineglassful of brandy in it. I dined with him and Mr. Palmer about two o'clock. We had a beefsteak and some champagne. After dinner we had three bottles of port wine, of which Cook drank his share. We rose from the table between five and six, and Cook and I went to my house, and then to the Albion Hotel, which is next door, and had a brandy and water each. Cook left me there between seven and eight. He said he felt cold. During that day I asked Cook for £50 he was due me. He gave me £5, and when he took the note out of his case I said, "You can pay me the whole £50." He said, "No; there is only £41 10s. due to you." Then he said he had given Mr. Palmer money, and he would pay me the remainder when he returned from Tattersall's on Monday after the settling. On the Saturday night following I slept in the same room with him, as he was not well. We went to bed about twelve o'clock. In the early part of the night he got some toast and water, and he was sick. I saw him using a night-chair in the room. He tried to vomit, but I do not know whether he did so or not. After that I slept until Mr. Palmer and Mr. Bamford came in the morning to see him. He said, "I am rather better this morning. I slept from about two or three o'clock, after the confounded concert was gone." Mr. Bamford said, "I will send you some more medicine." I then got up and left the house. I know Mrs. Palmer, the mother of the prisoner. She asked me to see her on Monday evening, and, in consequence of that, I went about two o'clock to see if I could find Palmer, but could not. About ten minutes past ten I saw him in a car coming from the direction of Stafford. I asked him, "Have you seen Mr. Cook to-day?" He said, "No; we had better just run up and see." We went up, and Cook told Palmer he was late, and that he had taken the medicine. We only stayed two or three minutes. Cook said he had taken some pills Mr. Bamford had sent him. He also said he had been up that day, and Palmer said he ought not to have been up. Palmer and I then went to his mother's house, about 400 or 500 yards. We stayed about half an hour, and then left for Palmer's house. I left him at his house and went home. On the Saturday I asked Cook to dine with me, but he did not. He said he was not well. I got for him a boiled leg of mutton and some broth from the Albion, which was taken to him by Ann Rowley, a charwoman. In the May before his death I borrowed £100 from Mrs. Palmer and £100 from William Palmer for Cook. I also negotiated a £500 loan through Mr. Pratt. I know that Palmer and Cook were jointly interested in one horse, "Pyrrhine," and that they were in the habit of betting very frequently for each other. Shortly before Mr. Cook's death I had seen Mr. Thirlby, Palmer's assistant, dress Cook's throat with caustic. I have seen this four or five times, chiefly before Shrewsbury races. I know Mr. Cook's signature. [Some papers were handed to witness.] Here are two notes, instructions for the £500. One is signed "J. P. Cook" and the other "J. Parsons Cook." I saw that signed. Some weeks before Mr. Cook's death he was served with a writ. [The following letter was read:—]

My dear Sir,—I have been in a devil of a fix about the bill, but have at last settled it at the cost of three guineas, for the damned discounter had issued a writ against me, and I am very much disgusted at it.

JOHN PARSONS.

I destroyed the envelope in which that was contained. [Another letter was read, dated 25th June, 1855—]

Dear Jimmy,—I should like to have the bill renewed for two months more. Can it be done? Let me know by return; 4 Victoria Street, Holborn Bridge. I have scratched "Polestar" for the Northamptonshire and Wolverhampton Stakes. I shall be down on Friday and Saturday. In haste.—J. Parsons Cook. Fred tells me "Bolton" or "Arabus" will win the Northumberland Plate.

J. P. COOK.

I saw that "J. P. Cook" written. [The following paper was read:—]

"Polestar," three years; "Sirius," two years, by way of mortgage, to secure £500, advanced on a bill of exchange, dated 29th August, 1855, payable three months after date.

These were the instructions to prepare the mortgage.

J. Smith

Cross-examined by the ATTORNEY-GENERAL—I am the Mr. Smith that took Mr. Myatt to Stafford gaol. I have been employed a good deal by Mr. Palmer as his attorney. I do not recollect that he applied to me in December, 1854, to attest a proposal on the life of his brother Walter for £13,000 at the Solicitors and General office. Nor do I recollect that I was applied to by Palmer to attest a proposal for £13,000 to the Prince of Wales office on his brother Walter's life. I knew that Walter Palmer had been a bankrupt six years before, but not that he was in great distress for money. I believe he had an allowance from his mother. I do not recollect that I was called upon to attest another proposal in the Universal office for £13,000 upon the life of Walter Palmer. If I could see any document or any letter to remind me of the circumstance I would not deny it. [An assignment of this policy by Walter Palmer to William Palmer was handed to witness. He was asked if he received £5 for attesting the assignment, and answered he might have, he did not recollect.] This is very like my signature. It is a good imitation. I have some doubt that it is not my handwriting. That is Walter Palmer's signature, and the attestation, "signed, sealed, and delivered," is in Mr. Pratt's handwriting. I got the document from Mr. Palmer. I still do not think that what bears to be my signature is in my handwriting. In October, 1855, I applied to the Midland Counties office to be appointed their agent. Bates and Palmer came together to my office with a prospectus, and asked me if there was any agent in Rugeley. I said I never heard of one. They asked me to write and get an appointment, as they wanted to raise money. I did so. The reason I became an agent was to get an insurance effected upon Bates' life for £10,000. Bates at that time was the superintendent of William Palmer's stud and stables. After this I went to the widow of Walter Palmer to get her to give up her claim upon the policy of her husband. She refused. This document, the signature to which I doubt whether it is my handwriting or not, is signed by Walter Palmer. I do not know that he got nothing for the assignment. I understood he got a house furnished for him. I do not recollect being applied to by William Palmer in December, 1854, to attest a proposal on his brother's life for £13,000 in the Solicitors and General office. I have no doubt I might. The body of the document [handed to witness] is in the handwriting of William Palmer. The signature is mine. I may have signed it blank. I do not remember getting £5 for attesting the execution of that deed of assignment by Walter Palmer to his brother. [The witness gave similar answers to questions put as to his attestation of proposals for policies of £13,000 on Walter Palmer's life in two other offices.] With reference to that £200 which I got for Mr. Cook, £100 from Mrs. Palmer and the other £100 from William Palmer, Cook gave £10 for the accommodation to William Palmer. William Palmer was the drawer of the bill and Cook the acceptor. He received £100 less £10 in cash. When the bill was given I handed it over to Mr. Palmer. What he did with it I do not know. I do not know if he discounted with Mr. Pratt. I have never seen the bill since. Palmer was not short of money at this time, as he lent £100 to Cook. I do not know that he wanted some money to make up the sum of £500 payable to Mr. Sargent.

Proof closed.

Attorney-General's Address to Jury.

Attorney-General

Mr. ATTORNEY-GENERAL—May it please your lordships—Gentlemen of the jury, the case for the prosecution and the case for the defence are now before you; and it becomes my duty to address to you such observations upon the whole of the materials, upon which your judgment is to be founded, as suggest themselves to my mind. I have a solemn and an important duty to perform. I wish that I could have answered the appeal made to me the other day by my learned friend, Mr. Serjeant Shee, and have felt that I was satisfied with the case that he submitted to you on the part of the defence. But, standing here as the instrument of public justice, I feel that I should be wanting in the duty that I have to perform if I did not ask at your hands for a verdict of guilty against the accused. I approach the consideration of the case in what, I hope, I may term a spirit of fairness, of moderation, and of truth. My business is to convince you, if I can, by facts and legitimate argument, of the prisoner's guilt. If I cannot establish it to your satisfaction, no man will rejoice more than I shall in the verdict that you will pronounce of not guilty.

Gentlemen, in the vast mass of materials which the evidence in this case has brought before you, two main questions present themselves prominently for your consideration—— did the deceased man, into whose death we are now inquiring, die a natural death, or was he taken off by the foul means of poison? And if the latter proposition be sanctioned by your approbation, then comes the important—if possible the still more important—question of whether the prisoner at the bar was the author of his death? I will proceed at once without further observation to the discussion of those questions, taking them in the order in which I have proposed them. Did John Parsons Cook die by poison? I assert and maintain the affirmative of that proposition. The case which is submitted to you on behalf of the Crown is this, that having been first practised upon by antimony, he was at last killed by strychnia; and the proposition which I have to establish is that the death of the deceased was occasioned by that poison. The first question, with a view of seeing what is the conclusion at which we shall arrive upon that point, is, what was the immediate and proximate cause of his death? The witnesses for the prosecution have told you one and all that he died, in their judgment, of tetanus, which signifies a spasmodic convulsive action of the muscles of the body. Can there be any doubt that that opinion is correct? Of course, it does not follow that because he died from tetanus it must be tetanus from strychnia; that is a matter for after consideration; but inasmuch as strychnia produces death by

Attorney-General

- 215 -

Sir Alexander Cockburn.

tetanus, we must see, in the first place, whether it admits of any doubt that he did die of tetanus. I have listened with attention to every form in which that disease has been brought under your consideration, whether by the positive evidence of witnesses, or by reference to the works of scientific authors; and I assert deliberately that no case either of a human subject, or of any animal, has been brought under your notice in which the symptoms of tetanus have been so marked as they are in this case; from the moment the paroxysm came on, of which this unhappy man died, the symptoms were of the most marked and of the most striking character. Every muscle, says the medical man who was present at the time, of his body was convulsed; he expressed the most intense dread of suffocation; he entreated them to lift him up lest he should be suffocated, and when they stooped to raise him every muscle of his body, from the crown of his head to the sole of his foot, was so stiffened that the flexibility of the trunk and limbs was gone, so that they could have raised him as you would raise a dead corpse or a lifeless log. It was found to be impossible, and the man prayed to be turned over in order to escape from the sense of the imminent risk of suffocation; they turned him over, and in the midst of doing so a fearful paroxysm, one mighty spasm, seems to have seized upon his heart, to have pressed from it the life blood, so that in a moment vitality ebbed, and the man was dead before them; when dead, the body exhibited the most marked symptoms of this most fearful disease; it was bowed from head to foot, and it would have rested, if it had been so placed, says the witness, upon the back of the head and the heels; the hands were clenched with a grasp which it required power to overcome, and the feet were curved till they assumed the appearance of a natural malformation. It is impossible to conceive symptoms more striking of tetanus; nor is it possible to conceive evidence more dishonest than that which has attempted to represent it as any other than as a case of tetanus.

Attorney-General

Well, then, if it was a case of tetanus, as to which I will not waste your time with any further observations, was it a case of tetanus from strychnia? I will confine myself for the moment to the exhibition of the symptoms as they have been described by the witnesses. Tetanus may proceed from natural causes as well as from the administration of poison. While the symptoms last they are the same, but in the course of the symptoms before the disease reaches its consummation in the death of the patient the distinction between the two is marked by characteristics which will enable any one conversant with the subject to distinguish between the two. We have been told upon the highest authority that the distinctions are these—Natural tetanus is a disease not of minutes, not even of hours, but of days. It takes, say several of the witnesses, from three to four days, and will extend to a period of even three weeks, before the patient is destroyed. Upon that point we have the most abundant and conclusive evidence. We have the evidence of gentlemen who have made it their especial study, like Mr. Curling and Dr. Todd. We have the evidence of one of the most eminent practitioners who ever adorned that profession or any other, I mean Sir Benjamin Brodie. We have the evidence of Mr. Gordon, who for twenty-eight years was surgeon to the Bristol Hospital; we have the evidence of Mr. Daniel, who saw twenty-five or thirty of these cases of natural tetanus; we have the evidence of a gentleman who practised for twenty-five years in India, where, owing to the particular character of the climate, those cases are infinitely more frequent than they present themselves here, and he gives exactly the same description of the course of symptoms through which this disease runs. Idiopathic or traumatic tetanus are therefore, upon the evidence, out of the question; but traumatic tetanus is out of the question for a very different reason. Traumatic tetanus is tetanus brought on by lesion of some part of the body. What is there in this particular case to show that there was lesion in any part of the body at all? We have had the most singular representations upon the subject of Mr. Cook's health made by the witnesses who have come here on behalf of the defence, and who appear to have come into that box with the determination as far as possible to misconceive every fact which they could pervert to their purpose. We call before you for the purpose of showing what Cook's health was an eminent physician who had had him under his care. It seems that in the spring of 1855 Cook, having found certain small spots manifest themselves in one or two parts of his body, and having something of ulcers under his tongue, or in his throat, conceived that he was labouring under symptoms of a particular character, and he addressed himself to Dr. Savage, who found the course of medicine he had been pursuing, founded upon this belief, was, in his judgment, an erroneous one; he altered it altogether; he enjoined the discontinuance of mercury, and was obeyed in his injunction; and the result was that the deceased, who was suffering, not from disease, but from the treatment, rapidly grew well. Nevertheless, lest there should be the possibility of mistake, Dr. Savage made him come to him from time to time that he might see that things were going on right, and he sees, long before the summer had advanced, the very unsatisfactory symptoms had entirely gone, and that there was nothing about him except that affection of the throat to which sometimes people are subject, some abnormal condition of one of the tonsils, but in other respects the man was better than he had been, and might be said to be perfectly convalescent. On the very day he left London to go into the country about a fortnight before the races, his stepfather accompanied him to the station, and congratulated him upon his healthy and vigorous appearance, and the young man, in the consciousness of the possession of health, struck his breast, and said he was well, and he felt so.

Attorney-General

Well, he goes to Shrewsbury, and shortly afterwards came those matters to which I shall have to call your attention presently, more particularly that ended in his death. I want to know upon what part of this evidence there is the slightest pretence for saying that this man had any affection about him from which traumatic tetanus could ensue. It is said at some former time he had exhibited his throat to some of the witnesses who were called, and that he had applied to Palmer for some mercurial wash to apply to his throat, or some of those ulcers. The precise period of it is not fixed, but it is perfectly clear that though he had at one time adopted that course, under the recommendation of Dr. Savage, he had got rid of it; and there is not the slightest pretence for saying that this man was suffering under a syphilitic affection of any kind; nevertheless that fact was distinctly and unequivocally negatived by a man of the highest authority—a medical gentleman of eminence—under whose treatment the man got so rapidly well. That fact is assumed by the witnesses for the defence as the ground upon which to suggest that there was traumatic tetanus in this case. It is a pretence, gentlemen, which has not the shadow of a foundation, and which I should be shrinking from my duty if I did not denounce as altogether unworthy of your attention. There was nothing about the man, according to the statement of all those who were competent to give you an opinion, which would warrant for a single moment the supposition that there was anything in any part of the man's body which could justify the notion of traumatic tetanus; even if there were, the character which his symptoms assumed when the tetanus set in is utterly incompatible, according to the evidence of all the witnesses, with a case of traumatic tetanus. One or two cases of traumatic tetanus have been adduced in evidence on the part of the defence. We had the case of a man who was brought to the London Hospital in the evening, and who died the same night. Yes, but what were the facts of that case? The facts are that he had had before he was brought in repeated paroxysms; that he felt premonitory symptoms early in the morning; he was suffering from ulcers of a most aggravated description; and that the symptoms had run their course, rapidly it is true, but still the disease was not a matter of minutes, but a matter of hours. There is no other case that I am aware of. There is the case of the boy who was brought in, if it be necessary to allude to it. But there again we have the disease existing for some time before it ends in death. It is a matter there again of hours, and not of minutes, and not a single paroxysm like this was observed. But it is then suggested that this may have been a case of idiopathic tetanus. Idiopathic tetanus proceeding from what? They say that Mr. Cook was a man of delicate constitution—subject to excitement—that he had something the matter with his chest—that in addition to having something the matter with his chest, he had this diseased condition of the throat—and, putting all these things together, they say that the man, if he took cold, might get idiopathic tetanus. We are launched into a sea of speculation and of possibilities. Mr. Nunneley, who comes forward here for the purpose of inducing you to believe that there was anything like idiopathic tetanus, goes through a bead-roll of the supposed infirmities of Mr. Cook and talks about his excitability—talks about his delicacy of chest—talks about the affection of his throat—goes through those various heads, and says that those things may have predisposed him to idiopathic tetanus if he took cold. What evidence is there that he ever did take cold? Not the slightest in the world. The man, from the beginning to the end of the symptoms, was never treated for cold by anybody, or ever complained that he had taken cold. I cannot help saying, to me it seems that it is a scandal upon a learned, a distinguished, and a liberal profession, that men should come forward and put forward such speculations as these, perverting the facts, and drawing from them sophistical and unwarranted conclusions with the view of deceiving a jury. I have the greatest respect for science—no man can have more; but I cannot repress my indignation and abhorrence when I see it thus perverted and prostituted to the purposes of a particular cause in a Court of justice. Do not talk to me about excitement, as Mr. Nunneley did the other day, being the occasion of idiopathic tetanus. You remember the sorts of excitement he spoke of. They are unworthy of your notice, and they were topics discreditable to be put forward by a witness as worthy of the attention of sensible men constituting such a tribunal as you are.

But suppose for a single moment that excitement of this kind could produce any such effect or influence, where is the excitement manifested by Cook as leading to this supposed disease? They say that the man, when his mare won at Shrewsbury, was full of excitement; and well he might be—his fortunes depended upon the result of that race; and I do not deny for a few minutes he was overpowered by the emotions that the joy of the moment excited in his breast. But that subsided, and we have no further trace of it from that time to the moment of his death. The man passed the rest of the day with his friends in ordinary conversation and in ordinary enjoyment. No trace of emotion was left about him. He is taken ill; he goes to Rugeley; he is taken ill there again; is there the slightest symptom of excitement about the man, or, on the other hand, of depression? Not the slightest in the world. When he is ill, like most other people, he is low; but as soon as he gets a little better he is cheerful and happy; he admits his friends, and he converses with them; the very night of his death, so far from any excitement, his conversation is full of cheerfulness and mirth—he is laughing and happy, little thinking, poor wretch, of the fate that was impending over him. He is cheerful and happy, talking of the future, not in the language of excitement on the one hand, or of depression on the other. What pretence is there for this idle story of excitement and depression? Not the slightest shadow of foundation in the world. But if there were—if those things were capable of producing that form of tetanus which goes by the term "idiopathic," the character of the disease is so essentially different that it is impossible to mistake the two. What are the cases which they attempt to set up against it? They have brought you the case of Mary Watson, which a gentleman came all the way from Scotland to tell us about. The girl had been ill all day. She was taken with cramps in the night, probably originating in the stomach, extending to all other parts of her body. She gets well in a very short time, and goes about her business. Is that case to be compared for a single instant to the death agony of that wretched man, and the paroxysm that destroyed him? Those are the sort of cases with which they attempt to meet such symptoms as those which are spoken to by the witnesses as accompanying the decease of Mr. Cook.

Gentlemen, I venture, upon the evidence, to assert boldly that the cases of idiopathic tetanus and traumatic, or what I may call natural tetanus, are marked by clear and distinct characteristics, distinguishing them from the tetanus produced by strychnia; and I say that the tetanus which accompanied Mr. Cook's death is not referable to either of those forms of tetanus. You have upon that point the evidence of witnesses of the highest competency and of the most unquestionable integrity; and upon their evidence I am quite satisfied you can come to no other conclusion but that this was not a case either of idiopathic or of traumatic tetanus. But, then, they say it may have been something else; and various attempts have been made to set up different causes as capable of producing this tetanic disease. And, first, we have the theory of general convulsions; and Mr. Nunneley, having gone through the bead-roll of the supposed infirmities of Mr. Cook, says, "Oh, this may have been a case of general convulsions. I have known general convulsions to assume a tetanic character." "Well, but pause a moment, Mr. Nunneley, have you ever seen one single case in which death arising from general convulsions, accompanied with tetanic symptoms, has not ended in the unconsciousness of the patient before death!—No, I never knew such a case—not one. But in some book or other, I am told that there is some such case reported"; and he cites, not for that purpose, I think, but he cites, with reference to general convulsions being sometimes accompanied with tetanic symptoms, and ending in death, a very eminent author of the present day. I mean Dr. Copland. Dr. Copland is living, and Dr. Copland might have been called. The author of the book, I apprehend, would stand before you as a higher authority than a man who merely quotes the book as the foundation of his knowledge. Dr. Copland might have been called. Dr. Copland was not called, notwithstanding the challenge which I threw out. Why? Because it is infinitely better in such a case to call together from the east and from the west practitioners of more or less obscurity, instead of bringing to bear upon the subject the light of science which is treasured up in the breasts of the eminent practitioners with whom this great city abounds. Dr. Copland is not called; but I say, as regards general convulsions, the distinction is plain, that where they destroy the patient they destroy consciousness; and here it is unquestionably the fact, that to the last moment of Mr. Cook's existence, until his burst heart ceased to beat, his consciousness remained.

Attorney-General

But then comes another supposed condition from which death in this form may be said to have resulted, and that is the case which was intended to be set up by a very eminent practitioner, I mean Mr. Partridge. It seems that in the post-mortem examination of Mr. Cook, when the spinal marrow was investigated, certain granules were found, and this is seized upon. It is said, "Oh, those granules may have occasioned tetanic convulsions similar to those which were found in Mr. Cook's case," and a very eminent gentleman is called to give his opinion upon that subject. I admit him to be not only a man of great eminence, but a man of the highest honour and the most perfect veracity. I allude to Mr. Partridge. I must distinguish between him and other of my learned friend's witnesses. Some there were who would not be induced, for any consideration in the world, to swerve from what they believed to be the truth. Mr. Partridge is called here to prove that this was a case of what he called arachnitis—inflammation of the arachnoid in consequence of the granules, or some other abnormal condition. I asked him the symptoms which he would find in such a case. I called his attention to what evidently had not been done before, namely, the symptoms of Mr. Cook's case; and I asked him, in simple, straightforward terms, whether, looking at those symptoms, he would pledge his opinion, in the face of the medical world and the Court, that this was a case of arachnitis, and he candidly admitted that he would not assert that this was in his opinion a case of arachnitis.

Then we have the gentleman who comes all the way from Scotland to inform us, as the next proposition, that Mr. Cook's was a case of epileptic convulsions with tetanic complications. Now, I asked him this question, "Did you ever know a case of epilepsy, with or without tetanic convulsions, in which consciousness was not destroyed before the patient died?" He said, "No; I cannot say that I ever did, but I have read in some book that such a case has occurred." "Is there anything to make you think that this was epilepsy?—Well, it may have been epilepsy, because I do not know what else to ascribe it to; but I must admit that epilepsy is characterised generally by a loss of consciousness." "Well, then, what difference would tetanic complications make?" That he is unable to explain. I remind you of that species of evidence in which the witnesses resorted to the most speculative reasoning, and put forward the barest possibilities without the shadow of a foundation. But this I undertake to assert, and I refer to the evidence to prove it, that there is not a single case either to which they have spoken as coming within their own experience, or of which they have spoken as the result of reading, in which there were the formidable and decisive symptoms of marked tetanus which existed in this case of Mr. Cook.

Attorney-General

Having gone through this evidence, I think we have four sets of diseases—general convulsions, arachnitis, epilepsy proper, and epilepsy with tetanic complications. I expected that we had pretty well exhausted the whole of those scientific theories, but we were destined to have another that assumed the formidable name of angina pectoris. I do not know whether it struck you as remarkable that when my learned friend opened this case for the defence he never ventured to assert what would be the nature of the disease to which he would endeavour to refer the symptoms of Mr. Cook; and it must, I think, have struck you as a very remarkable thing that no less than four or five distinct and separate theories are set up by the witnesses who appear on the part of the defence—general convulsions, arachnitis, epilepsy with tetanic complications, and, lastly, angina pectoris. My learned friend had, however, this advantage in not stating to you what was the theory that his medical witnesses would endeavour to set up, because, one after another, I must admit they took me entirely by surprise. The gentleman who was called yesterday at the last moment, and who talked of angina pectoris, would not have escaped quite so easily if I had had the books to which he referred under my hand, and had been able to expose, as I would have done, the ignorance or the presumption of the assertion which he dared to make. I say ignorance or presumption, or, what is worse, an intention to deceive. I assert it in the face of the whole medical profession, and I am satisfied I shall have their verdict in my favour.

Attorney-General

But it is a fact which I am entitled to dwell upon, that all those medical witnesses, one and all, differed in the views which they take in this case. There is this remarkable coincidence between the views of some of them and the views of the witnesses whom I called—Mr. Partridge and Dr. Robinson, two of the most respectable witnesses they called, ay, and Dr. Letheby himself, strongly as he was biassed in favour of the defence, being three of the most eminent of the witnesses whom my learned friend brought forward, agreed with the statement made by Sir Benjamin Brodie, and supported by other witnesses whom I brought before you, that in the whole of their experience, in the whole range of their learning and information, they knew of no known disease to which the symptoms of Mr. Cook could possibly be referred. When such men as those tell us such a fact, I cannot but submit to you that it is impossible to exaggerate its importance. But, then, if it be the fact that no known disease can account for such symptoms as those of Mr. Cook, and that they are referable to poison alone, can any one entertain a doubt that that poison was the poison of strychnia? The symptoms, at all events from the time the paroxysm set in, are precisely the same. Distinctions are sought to be made by the subtlety of the witnesses for the defence between some of the antecedent symptoms and some of the appearances after death; but I think I shall show you beyond all possibility of contradiction, that those distinctions are imaginary, and have no foundation in fact. I think I may take this, however, along with me as I go on, that the witnesses called for the defence admit this fact, that from the time the paroxysm set in, of which Mr. Cook died, until the time of the death, the symptoms are precisely similar to the symptoms of tetanus from strychnia. But, then, they say, and this is worthy of your most attentive consideration, that there are points of difference which have led them to the conclusion, or some of them at all events, that those symptoms could not have resulted from strychnia. Let us see what they are. In the first place, they showed that the period which elapsed between the supposed administration of the poison and the first appearance of the symptoms was longer than they have ever observed in animals upon which they have experimented. Now, the first observation which arises there is this, that there is a known difference between animal and human life, in the power with which specific things act upon its organisation, and it may well be that the poison administered to a rabbit will produce its effect in a given time; it by no means follows that it will produce effect in the same time upon an animal of a different description, and still less does it follow that it will exercise its baneful influence in the same time upon a human subject. The whole of the evidence on both sides tends to establish this fact, that not only in individuals of different species, but between individuals of the same species, the same poison and the same dose will produce effects different in degree, different in duration, and different in power. But, again, it is perfectly notorious that the rapidity with which the poison begins to work depends materially upon the mode of its administration. If it is administered as a fluid, it acts with great rapidity; if it is administered in a solid state, its effects come on more slowly; and if it is administered in some indurated substance, it will act with still greater tardiness; and if that substance is difficult of solution, then the period will be still longer before the substance, having become dissolved, is acted upon by the absorbents and taken up into the system.

Attorney-General

Now, what was the period at which this poison began to act after its administration, assuming it to have been poison for the purpose of argument? It seems, from Mr. Jones' statement, that the prisoner came and administered these pills; he saw him administer the pills somewhere about eleven o'clock, so that they were not administered upon his first arrival. The patient, as though with an instinctive sense of the peril which impended, strenuously resisted the attempt to make him take them, and no doubt those remonstrances and the endeavour to overcome them occupied some period of time. The pills at last were taken, and, assuming them to have contained strychnia (which I only do now for the purpose of argument), how soon did they begin to operate? Mr. Jones says he went down after this and had his supper, and came back about twelve o'clock. Upon his return to the room, after a word or two of conversation with Cook, he proceeded to undress and go to bed; and he had not been in bed ten minutes before the warning came that another of these paroxysms was about to take place. The maid-servants put it still earlier; they say that about ten minutes before twelve the first alarm was given, which would make the interval little more than three-quarters of an hour from the taking of the pills and the first manifestation of the symptoms. When, therefore, my learned friend's witnesses tell us that it took an hour and a half or two hours, we have here another of those exaggerated determinations to see the facts only in the way that will make most for the view which they think proper to put forward. I say it certainly was not more than an hour, and I find in some of the experiments that have been made that the duration of time before which the poison began to work has been little less, if any less, than an hour. Mr. Morley, who is as much entitled to your attention as Mr. Nunneley—indeed, when I contrast the way in which the two men gave their evidence, I am paying him but a poor compliment when I say that he is as worthy of attention as Mr. Nunneley—Mr. Morley says in his evidence that five or six minutes, or something less than an hour, is the period which he observed the poison required to produce its effects upon animals, and in every one of the cases which we have got it will be seen that more than an hour was necessary. In the case of the girl at Glasgow, though I see the medical gentleman speaks of twenty minutes when he was called in, he could have only had that information from the statement of some of the people about. I see the nurse says it was three-quarters of an hour before the pills began to work upon the girl. There may have been some cause for the pills not beginning to take effect within a certain time after their administration; it would be very easy to mix them with some substance that should render them difficult of solution; nay, which might retard their action. I cannot for a single moment bring myself to believe, if in all other respects you are perfectly satisfied that the symptoms, the consequences, and effects were analogous and similar to those produced by strychnia, it is not because those pills may have taken a quarter of an hour or a longer time to manifest their working, it is not on that account you will hesitate to come to the conclusion that strychnia was administered in this case. But then they say, yes, but the premonitory symptoms were wanting here. They tell us in animals they observed that the animal manifests first some uneasiness, shrinks, and gathers itself into itself, as it were, avoids movement, and then certain involuntary twitchings about the head come, those being the premonitory symptoms before the paroxysms set in. They say there were no premonitory symptoms in Cook's case; I utterly deny that proposition—I say there were premonitory symptoms of the most marked character, though he did not describe them in language. He is lying in bed—he suddenly starts up in an agony of alarm. What made him do that? Was there nothing premonitory, nothing that warned him that the paroxysm was coming? It is clear there must have been. He jumps up in his bed, and says, "Fetch me Palmer, I am going to be ill, as I was last night." What was it but that he knew the symptoms that attended him on the previous evening were now warning him of what he might expect in a short period, unless succour could be obtained? He sits up, and he prays to have his neck rubbed. What was the feeling about the neck but a premonitory symptom which was to precede the paroxysm which presently supervened? He says, "Rub my neck, it gives me comfort to have it done."

But here again they take exception, and they say this could not have been tetanus from strychnia, because animals cannot bear to be touched; a touch brings on the paroxysm; not only a touch but a breath of air, a sound, a word, a movement of any one near, will bring on a recurrence of the paroxysm. True; but that is after the paroxysm has once been set up, or when it is just about to begin. It is quite clear that those witnesses who come and say that the fact of Mr. Cook having desired to have his neck rubbed is a fact to prove that this could not be a death from tetanus, have either wilfully suppressed the knowledge in their own minds of the evidence they had heard, or they had paid no attention to it; because in two cases of death from strychnia we have shown the patient endured the touching of the limbs, and found satisfaction from it. In Mrs. Smyth's case, when her legs were distorted, in the agony of the convulsion she prayed and entreated to have them straightened; she found no additional pain from that operation. The lady at Leeds, in the case which Mr. Nunneley himself attended, implored her husband, between the spasms, to rub her legs and her arms, in order to overcome and subdue their rigidity. That case was under his own knowledge, and, in spite of it, although he detected afterwards strychnia in the body of that unhappy woman, he dares to come forward here and say that the fact of Mr. Cook having before the paroxysm tolerated rubbing, and found comfort in it, proves that this could not have been a death from strychnia. What think you of the honesty of such a witness? But there is a third case, which is the case of Mr. Clutterbuck, spoken to by Mr. Moore. That gentleman had taken an overdose of strychnia, and he suffered from all the pains of tetanus; his only comfort was having his limbs rubbed; and therefore, I say, to contend and to endeavour to persuade a jury that the fact of Cook's having had his neck rubbed proved that this was not tetanus from strychnia, proves, I say, nothing but the dishonesty and insincerity of the witnesses who can dare to put forward such a pretence.

But, then, they go further, and they say that Mr. Cook was able to swallow. So he was, before the paroxysm came on. Nobody ever pretended that he could swallow after the paroxysm came on. He swallowed the pills, and, what is very curious, and, as they think, bears out and illustrates a part of their theory, is this. It was the act of attempting to swallow the pills—the sort of movement that must have taken place in raising his head and neck for the purpose—that immediately brings on the violent paroxysm of which he died. So far from that in the slightest degree militating against the supposition that this was a case of poisoning by strychnia, it is strongly and decisively conclusive in its favour.

But then they take us to the appearances after death, and they say that there are circumstances to be found which militate against this being a case of strychnia poisoning. Let us see what they are. In the first place, they say the limbs became rigid either at the time of death or immediately after, and that ought not to be found in a case of tetanus from strychnia. Mr. Nunneley says, "In all cases upon which I have experimented I have found the animals become flaccid before death, and they do not become again rigid after it." I can hardly believe that statement, and I certainly was not a little surprised when the very next witness who got into the box (Mr. Herapath, of Bristol) told us he had made two experiments upon cats, and killed them both. He described them as "indurated and contorted." Those were his expressions when he found them some hours after death. The presence of rigidity in the body at or immediately after death here is put forward on the part of Mr. Nunneley as one of the grounds upon which he says this was not a death by strychnia, although Dr. Taylor had told us that in the case of one of the cats he killed the rigidity after death was such that upon taking the animal by the hind legs and holding it up in the air, the body maintained its horizontal natural position, as though the animal had been upon its four legs upon a plain surface. Notwithstanding that evidence, Mr. Nunneley had the audacity to say that he did not believe this was a case of poisoning by strychnia, because there had been rigidity of the limbs—because the feet were distorted, the hands clenched, and the muscles rigid as the unhappy man exhibited prior to his death. The very next witness called upon the other side produced two instances in which the animals were indurated from one end of their bodies to the other. As he says they were contorted in all their limbs, and so they remained, it shows what you are to think of the honesty of this sort of evidence, in which facts are selected because they make in favour of the particular hypothesis of the party who brings them forward.

Then the next thing that is said is that the heart in this case was empty. In the animals Mr. Nunneley and Dr. Letheby have operated upon I think the heart has been found full. I do not think that applies to all the cases; I think they make some exceptions; and, as I said at the outset, it is a remarkable fact connected with the history of this particular poison, that you never can rely upon the precise form or order which the symptoms before death and the appearances after it will assume. There are only certain great, leading, marked characteristic features—the collateral incidents are capable of infinite variety. We have here the main marked characteristic features, and we have, what is more, collateral incidents similar to the cases in which the administration of strychnia and the fact that death was caused by it are beyond the possibility of dispute. In the very evidence which has been adduced of two cases of poisoning, Mrs. Smyth's and the Glasgow girl, in both the heart had been found contracted and emptied; and it is obvious to any one who reflects for a single moment that the question whether the heart shall be found congested or the lungs congested must depend upon the immediate cause of death, and we know that in cases of tetanus death may result from more than one cause. All the muscles of the body are subject to the exciting action of this powerful poison, but no one can tell in what order those muscles will be affected, or where the poisonous influence will put forth the fulness of its power. If it act upon the respiratory muscles, and arrest the play of the lungs, and with it the breathing of atmospheric air, the result will be that the heart will be left full; but if some spasm seizes on the heart, contracting it and expelling from it the blood that it contains, and so produces death, why the result will be that the heart will be found empty, and the other vessels gorged with blood. So that you have never perfect certainty as to how those symptoms will manifest themselves after death; but that is again put forward as if the fact of the heart having been found empty is a conclusive fact against death having in this case taken place from strychnia. Yet those men who came here to make those statements as witnesses under the sanction of scientific authority must have heard both those cases spoken to by the medical gentlemen who examined those two unfortunate patients after death, and who told us that in both cases the heart was found empty. That gets rid of that matter. And so again with regard to the congestion of the brain and other vessels the same observation applies. If instead of being killed by the action of the poison upon the respiratory muscles or by its action upon the heart, death is the result of a long series of paroxysms exhausting the vital power of the victim, then you expect to find the brain and other vessels congested by those series of convulsions and spasms. As death takes place from one or other of those causes, so will be the appearance of the heart, the brain, and the body after death. There is nothing, I say, in this for a single moment to negative the conclusion which you would otherwise arrive at from the symptoms which appeared in this man's body at the time of his death and immediately afterwards—that those are the symptoms of tetanus of the strongest and most aggravated kind; that is a proposition about which, I think, you can entertain no doubt. If so, are they referable to tetanus of any other description? Certainly not; because, as Sir Benjamin Brodie told you, the course of the symptoms is marked by characteristics of unquestionable difference.

Is it not then preposterous to contend that this was not a case of tetanus? And if every one of the distinctions they have attempted to set up I show you to have really nothing to do with the case (because I produce you at once an undoubted case in which the administration of strychnia is beyond the reach of question, in which those particular symptoms and appearances were manifested and observed) I get rid at once of all those vain, futile attempts to distinguish this case, either in its premonitory symptoms or in the appearances either before or upon post-mortem examination. I get rid of all those difficulties, and I come back to the symptoms which attended this unhappy man's demise. I ask whether you can doubt that, when I have excluded all those cases of tetanic convulsions, epilepsy, and arachnitis, or angina pectoris, which occurred, you recollect, in a young girl after an attack of scarlet fever—in all human probability the scarlet fever had been thrown back upon the system, and had produced all those consequences—when I exclude all those cases, and then, lastly, exclude traumatic or idiopathic tetanus, what remains? The tetanus of strychnia, and the tetanus of strychnia only. I pray your attention to the cases of which evidence has been given, in which there was no question as to strychnia having been administered, there not being the shadow of a doubt about it, and in which the circumstances were so similar, and the symptoms so analogous, that I think you cannot hesitate to come to the conclusion that this was death by strychnia. Medical witnesses of the highest authority, both on the part of the Crown and on the part of the defence, agree that in the whole range of their experience and knowledge they know of no natural disease to which these remarkable symptoms can be referred. If that be so, and there is a known poison that will produce them, how strong, how cogent, how irresistible becomes the inference that to that poison, and to that poison alone, are those symptoms and this death to be ascribed!

Nevertheless, gentlemen, on the other hand, the case is not without its difficulties; and I will not shrink from the discussion of them, nor from the candid recognition of these difficulties, so far as they in reality exist. Strychnia was not found in this body; and we have it, no doubt upon strong evidence, that in a variety of experiments which have been tried upon the bodies of animals killed by strychnia, strychnia has been detected by the tests which science places at the disposition of scientific men. If strychnia had been found, of course there would have been no difficulty, and we should have had none of the ingenious theories which gentlemen from a variety of parts have been brought forward to propound in this Court. The question for your consideration is, whether the absence of its detection leads conclusively to the view that this death could not have been caused by the administration of that poison. Now, in the first place, under what circumstances was the examination made of which Dr. Taylor and Dr. Rees have spoken? They tell you that when the stomach of this man was brought to them for the purpose of analysis, it was presented to them under the most unfavourable circumstances. They say that its contents had been lost, and that they had no opportunity of experimenting upon them. It is very true that those who put up the jar make a statement somewhat different. They say that the contents of the stomach were emptied into the jar, but there appears (at all events I will not put it higher than accident), by accident, to have been some spilling of the contents; and there is, I think, the clearest and most undeniable evidence of very considerable bungling in the way in which the stomach was cut, and the way in which it was emptied into the jar. It was cut from end to end, says Dr. Taylor. It was tied up at both ends; it had been turned inside out into the contents of the intestines, and lay there in a mass of fœculent matter, and was therefore in a condition the most unsatisfactory for analysis and experiment. It is very true that the witnesses upon the other side—Mr. Nunneley, Mr. Herapath, and Dr. Letheby—say that, no matter how contaminated or how mixed with impurities, they would have been able to ascertain the presence of strychnia in the stomach, if strychnia ever had been there. I own I should have more confidence in the testimony of those witnesses if their partiality and partisanship had not been so much marked as they are. I should have more confidence in the testimony of Mr. Herapath if he had not been constrained to admit to me a fact which had come to my knowledge, that he has again and again asserted that this case was a case of poisoning by strychnia, but that Dr. Taylor had not known how to find it out—he admits that that is a statement he has again and again made.

Mr. SERJEANT SHEE—It was in the newspapers, he said.

Mr. ATTORNEY-GENERAL—He did not venture to say that the newspaper statement in any way differed from the fact which he admitted in this Court. I have seen that gentleman not merely contenting himself with coming forward, when called upon for the purposes of justice, to state that which he knew as a matter of science or of experiment, but I have seen him mixing himself up as a thoroughgoing partisan in this case, advising my learned friend, suggesting question upon question, and that in behalf of a man whom he has again and again asserted he believed to be a poisoner by strychnia. I do not say that alters the fact; but I do say that it induces one to look at the credit of those witnesses with a very great amount of suspicion. I reverence a man who, from a sense of justice and a love of truth—from those high considerations which form the noblest elements in the character of man—comes forward in favour of a man against whom the world may run in a torrent of prejudice and aversion, and who stands and states what he believes to be the truth; but I abhor the traffic in testimony to which I regret to say men of science sometimes permit themselves to condescend. I ask you therefore to look at the statements of those witnesses with dispassionate consideration before you attach implicit credit to them. But let me assume that all they say is true, that it is the fact that they in their experiments have succeeded in discovering strychnia when mixed with other impurities, and contaminated, no matter by what cause—they say that no extent of putrefaction, no amount of decomposition, will alter the character of that vegetable matter, so that it may not be detected if it is in the human stomach. Be it so. But then must it always be found in every case where death has ensued? Professor Taylor says no; and he says it would be a most dangerous and mischievous proposition to assert that that must necessarily be so—that it would enable many a guilty man to escape who, by administering the smallest quantity whereby life can be affected and destroyed, might by that means prevent the possibility of the detection of the poison in the stomach of the individual. All the witnesses seem to agree in this, or, at all events, the great bulk of them agree in this, that the poison acts after it has been absorbed into the system; taken up by the absorbents of the stomach, it is carried into the blood; passing by means of the circulation through the tissues, it is deposited there; at some stage or other of its progress it affects the nervous system; and as soon as the nerves affecting the muscles of motion become influenced by its baneful power, then come on those muscular spasms and convulsions of which we have heard so much. If the minimum dose be given, and that operates by absorption, it is perfectly clear—and must be clear—that the whole must be taken up by absorbents and pass into the blood, and that none therefore will be found in the stomach. Nay, a further proposition is also clear. If it is necessary that it should be first passed by means of the circulation into the solid tissues of the body, before it acts upon the nervous system, it will cease to be found in the blood. Again, a portion of it, if in excess, will be eliminated in the kidneys, and pass off in watery excretion. You do not know, therefore, in what part of the human body to put your hand upon it. But this is undoubtedly the fact, if there has been an excess over the quantity necessary to destroy the life of a particular individual, then, as soon as the absorbents have taken up the necessary quantity, the nervous system will at once be affected and life destroyed; you will find the excess in the stomach, if you adopt the proper means of seeking for it. Now, what did these gentlemen do? They gave never less than a grain—often as much as two grains; and yet we now know that a quarter of a grain is enough to destroy a small animal like a rabbit, and that no man could venture to hope for life who took half a grain or three-quarters of a grain of it. Therefore in the cases of their experiments, and experiments made, allow me to say, for the purpose of this case, after those parties had been retained—I use the word "retained," for it is the appropriate word; no parties can be more thoroughgoing partisans than scientific men who have once taken up a case—after they have been retained for this case, and desire that their experiments should have a certain result, they take good care to have doses large enough to leave a small portion in the stomach. But be this as it may, I have only now to deal with the experiments of Professor Taylor and Dr. Rees; they may, for aught I know, be a pair of bunglers; it is no part of my business to uphold them if their professional reputation will not do it; but they tell us that they tried its effects upon four animals of the same species with fully adequate doses. Where they administered two grains they reproduced the poison in abundance; where they administered one grain they found a small indication of it; and when they administered half a grain to two rabbits they found no traces of the poison at all. It may well be that that may result, as Mr. Herapath says, from Professor Taylor not knowing the right way of going about it. It may be, if Mr. Herapath had had the stomach under his more scientific manipulation, he would have produced the strychnia. It is enough for my purpose when, as I show, the man who did in this case experiment upon the stomach of Mr. Cook, in two cases out of four when he had given a smaller dose to rabbits failed to reproduce the poison. What is the conclusion I draw from it? Why, that although I cannot have the advantage here which the positive detection of the strychnia would have afforded if it had been found, there is no room for the opposite conclusion— the converse of the proposition for which my learned friend and his witnesses contend—that the fact of the strychnia not having been reproduced or discovered affords negative conclusive proof that the death was not produced by strychnia. I have no positive proof on the one hand, but on the other hand my learned friend is in the same predicament—he cannot say that he has negative proof conclusive of the fact of this death not having taken place by strychnia.

Attorney-General

But now is there no other evidence in the case? Do I ask you to come to the conclusion that he administered strychnia to his friend, simply because the symptoms of that friend's death are reconcilable with no known form of disease which the most enlarged experience or knowledge can supply? No, gentlemen, it does not rest there. Not because those symptoms are precisely those which show themselves in cases of poisoning by strychnia. No, the case does not rest there; I wish it did. But, alas! it does not. I must now draw your serious attention to a part of the case which has not been met, and has not been grappled with. My learned friend said that he would contest the ground with the prosecution foot by foot. Alas! we are upon that ground upon which, as it were, is centred the crisis of this momentous question; and, alas! my learned friend has not grappled with it for an instant. We have here a death of which the dread manifestations bore upon their face the character of strychnia poisoning. Was the prisoner at the bar possessed of that poison? Did he obtain it upon the eve of the death into which we are inquiring? These are matters of fearful moment. They are matters with which it behoved my learned friend, indeed, to have grappled with all the vigour of which he was capable and with all the means that his case afforded. But I grieve to say that this part of the case is left untouched as regards the defence. Did the prisoner at the bar obtain possession of strychnia on the Monday late? Did he get it again upon the Tuesday morning? The fact of his having got it on the Monday night rests, it is true, upon the evidence of an individual whose statement, as I said to you at the outset, and as I repeat now, requires at your hands the most careful and anxious attention before you adopt it easily. Newton tells us that on that night when Mr. Palmer came back from London, he came to him and obtained from him three grains of the poison of which, supposing it had been administered, the symptoms and effect both in life and death would have been precisely the same as those which have been described in Cook's case. Is Newton speaking the truth, or is he not? It is open to observation—I said so from the beginning, and my learned friend has done no more than reiterate the warning I gave you—it is, I say, open to serious observation, that Newton never made that statement until the day previous to the commencement of the trial. He has explained to you the reasons which induced his silence. His employer had been for a long time upon unpleasant terms with Palmer. The young man, who knew him, however, and who appears to have been more or less upon familiar terms with him, did not hesitate to give him the three grains of strychnia. Palmer was a medical man, and strychnia is often used by medical men. There was nothing extraordinary therefore at that time of night, when chemists' shops might be expected to be shut up, that, upon Mr. Palmer's coming to him for three grains of strychnia, he gave them to him, and probably thought little more about it. But when afterwards the question of the mode by which this man's life had been taken away became rife in Rugeley, and suspicions arose of strychnia, and Roberts came forward and said that upon the Tuesday morning Mr. Palmer had bought strychnia off him, and this young man was called to confirm the circumstance of Mr. Palmer having been at the shop, he heard that this question of strychnia was involved, and it began to occur to him that it might seriously implicate him with his employer, might cast even the shadow of doubt and suspicion upon himself, if he came forward and voluntarily stated that he had supplied Palmer with the poison the night before. Then he locked this secret in his breast. But when the eve of the trial came, and he knew that he was to be subjected to examination here, he felt a sort of oppression at having this secret locked up in his breast, and he voluntarily came forward and made the statement which he has repeated here. It is for you to say whether you are satisfied with that explanation. It is unquestionably true that it detracts from the otherwise perfect credibility which would attach to his statement. But then, gentlemen, on the other hand, there is a consideration which I cannot fail to press upon you. What possible conceivable motive can this young man have, except a sense of truth, for coming forward to make this statement? My learned friend, with justice and with propriety, has asked for your most attentive consideration to the question of motives involved in this case. Before you can charge a man with having taken away the life of another by aforethought and deliberate malice, it does become important to see whether there were motives that could operate upon him to do so foul a deed. That does not apply to this witness, for, even though the hideous crime of taking life by poison is not perhaps so horrible to contemplate as the notion of judicial murder effected by false witness against a man's neighbour, can you suppose that this young man can have the remotest shadow of a motive for coming forward upon this occasion, under the solemn sanction of an oath, in a Court of justice like this, to take away the life—for, alas! if you believe his evidence, it must take away the life—of the prisoner at the bar? If you believe that on the night of Monday, for no other conceivable or assignable purpose except the deed of darkness which was to be done that night upon the person of Mr. Cook, the prisoner at the bar went to Newton and obtained from him the fatal and deadly instrument whereby life was to be destroyed, it is impossible that you can come to any other conclusion than that the prisoner is guilty, and that your verdict must pronounce him so.

What says my learned friend? He says that Newton does not speak the truth—first, because he did not come forward till the last minute; and, secondly, because he lays the time of his communication with the prisoner, and affording him the strychnia, at nine o'clock, and the prisoner was not in Rugeley until ten.

Attorney-General

Now, in the first place, I must remark upon this that the young man does not say nine o'clock. He says, "about nine," and every one knows how easy it is to make a mistake as to time with reference to half an hour or three-quarters of an hour, or even an hour, when your attention is not till perhaps a week or a fortnight or three weeks afterwards called to a particular circumstance. A man may be sitting working in his study or his surgery, and have no clock before him, and have nothing particular to impress upon his mind the precise hour of time at which a certain transaction took place; and to say afterwards, when he comes to speak to it under the sanction of an oath, that because he makes some slight difference as to the time therefore he must be taken to be speaking untruly, appears to my mind a most untenable and unsatisfactory argument. It is due to my learned friend to say that he has sought to meet this part of the case. He has produced to-day a witness of whom all I can say is this, that I implore you, for the sake of justice, not to allow the man who stands at the bar to be prejudiced by the evidence of that most discreditable and unworthy witness who has been called to-day on his behalf. I say that not to one word which that man has uttered will you attach the slightest value. Before I come to him, however, I must make this remark—that, if Newton could not be mistaken as to the time, how is it possible that the prisoner could be mistaken as to the time? Yet he clearly was. He told Dr. Bamford (and we have it from Dr. Bamford himself) the next morning that he visited Cook between nine and ten o'clock the night before. And now there comes a witness who tells us that it was a quarter past ten that he had with him alighted from the car that brought them from Stafford, and he could not till after that have gone to visit Cook. My learned friend reminds me that it was ten minutes past ten. Then he had to go to Cook. One of the maid-servants, Lavinia Barnes, like every other witness, may be mistaken; but she asserts that on that night, the Monday evening, Mr. Palmer came to the hotel, and went to see Mr. Cook before nine o'clock. It is clear that she must have been mistaken. It is clear that he could not have been there much before ten. I am told that they get over in about an hour. There was a carriage waiting for him, and he would come over to Rugeley with as much rapidity as he could, which would not be before ten o'clock. As to the fact of the witness pretending that he saw him alight from the car, and that he went to Cook and stayed a certain time so as to cover the whole evening, I ask you not to believe a single word, and I do so because in my heart I do not believe a single word of it.

Attorney-General

It is a remarkable fact, which has not escaped your attention, I dare say, that my learned friend did not open a single word of the testimony that he was going to call. He said he hoped and thought he should be able to cover that whole period at Rugeley. Did he tell us what the witness was going to prove, that Jeremiah Smith had been upstairs in the inn, and seen by some of the people at the inn going upstairs to Cook's room? No, he did not. If he had we should have had plenty of time between that and this to ascertain how the fact stood, and I believe have been ready to meet Mr. Jeremiah Smith with contradictory evidence. It was well to follow that course when you were uncertain what your witness would say, or what your case might be, because you might be met and confronted by contradictory evidence. I need not say that any evidence would have been better than the evidence of that miserable man whom we saw exhibited to-day. Such a spectacle I never saw in my recollection in a Court of justice. He calls himself a member of the legal profession. I blush for it to number such a man upon its roll. There was not one that heard him to-day that was not satisfied that that man came here to tell a false tale. There cannot be a man who is not convinced that he has been mixed up in many a villainy which, if not perpetrated, had been attempted to be perpetrated in that quarter, and he comes now to save, if he can, the life of his companion and his friend—the son of the woman with whom he has had that intimacy which he sought to-day in vain to disguise. I say, when you look at the whole of those circumstances, balance the evidence on both sides, and look at the question of whether Newton can by any possibility have any motive for coming here to give evidence which must be fatal to a man who, if that evidence be not true, he must believe to be an innocent man—when you see that he can have no motive for such a purpose—to suppose that he would do so without a motive is to suppose human nature in its worst and most repulsive form to be one hundred times more wicked and perverse than experience ever yet has found it—I cannot but submit to you that you ought to believe that evidence, and I cannot but submit to you deferentially, but at the same time firmly and emphatically, that if you do believe that evidence it is conclusive of the case.

Attorney-General

But it does not stop there. On the morrow of that day we have the clearest and most unquestioned evidence that Mr. Palmer bought more strychnia. He went to Mr. Hawkins' shop, and there purchased six grains more, and the circumstances attending that purchase are peculiar in the extreme. He comes to the shop, and he gives an order for prussic acid, and, having got his prussic acid, he gives an order for strychnia. Before the strychnia is put up, Newton, the same man, comes into the shop. What does the prisoner do? He immediately takes Newton by the arm, and says he has something particular to say to him, and takes him to the door. What was it he had to say to him? Was it anything particular? Was it anything of the slightest importance? Was it anything that might not have been said in the presence of Roberts, who was putting up the strychnia? Certainly not. It was to ask a most unimportant question, namely, when young Mr. Salt was going to the farm which he had taken at Sudbury. In that question there could be nothing which might not be put in the presence of anybody, no matter who. He takes him to the door, and then puts this question. At the same time a man of the name of Brassington, a cooper, comes up, and Brassington had something to say to

Newton upon business, having some bills against Newton's employer, Mr. Salt. Upon that Brassington and Newton get into conversation at some little distance from the door. The prisoner immediately takes advantage of those two being in conversation, and he goes back and completes the purchase of the strychnia. But while the strychnia was being made up he stands in the doorway with his back to the shop, and his face to the street, where he would have a perfect command of the persons of Newton and Brassington, and where, if Newton had quitted Brassington to return into the shop, the prisoner would at once have been in a position to take every possible step for not letting Newton go in, by renewing the conversation with him until the strychnia had been taken away. I ask you, having this description of the transaction given to you by Roberts, in the first place, confirmed by Newton afterwards, can you entertain any reasonable doubt that the prisoner was desirous of not letting Newton know that he was purchasing strychnia there? You can very well understand that he would be desirous of keeping that fact from Newton, because, if it be true that Newton had let him have three grains the night before, Newton's attention would be naturally immediately aroused by so strange a circumstance, because nine grains of strychnia were enough—three grains were enough—to kill three, perhaps six people. What could a man want with nine grains of strychnia in so short a space of time? It would attract Newton's attention, and it did; for Newton immediately went and asked what he wanted there, his attention being, in the first place, directed, not so much to what he had come to purchase as to the singularity of his coming there at all, because for two years past the prisoner never bought an article of any sort or kind at the shop of Mr. Hawkins. His former assistant, Mr. Thirlby, had two years before set up in business as a chemist, and from that time, naturally enough, Mr. Palmer had withdrawn his custom from Mr. Hawkins, and had given it to his former assistant, Mr. Thirlby. It was a remarkable thing that he should go to Mr. Hawkins' shop upon this occasion to get strychnia. Why did he not go to Mr. Thirlby? I will tell you. Mr. Thirlby would have known perfectly well that he could have no legitimate use for such an article. Mr. Thirlby had taken his practice. Mr. Palmer was no longer in practice, except in the circle of his relatives and his own immediate friends; and if he had gone to Mr. Thirlby for strychnia, Mr. Thirlby would have said, naturally enough, "What are you going to do with it?" and therefore he did not go to Mr. Thirlby. Why he should have gone to purchase strychnia (I agree with my learned friend it is one of the mysteries of this case) on two successive days I cannot tell; but that he did is undeniably true; and if on the one hand some little difficulty arises, on the other hand is not the difficulty infinitely greater in accounting for the motive that induced him to go and get this strychnia either on the Monday night or upon the Tuesday? If it was for the purpose of professional use for the benefit of some patient for whom small doses of strychnia might have been advantageous, where is the patient, and why is he not produced? My learned friend did not even advert to the question of the second purchase of strychnia in the whole of his powerful observations. He passes it over in mysterious but significant silence. Account for that six grains of strychnia, the purchase of which is an undoubted and indisputable fact. Throw doubt if you please—I blame you not for it—upon the story of the purchase on the previous night; but on the Tuesday it is unquestionably true that six grains of strychnia were purchased. Purchased for whom? purchased for what? If for any patient, who is that patient? Produce him. If for any other purpose, at least let us have it explained. Has there been the slightest shadow of an attempt at explanation? Alas! I grieve to say, none at all. Something was said, in the outset of this case, about some dogs that had been troublesome in the paddocks where the mares and foals were, but that proved to have been in September. If there had been any recurrence of such a thing, where are the grooms who had the care and charge of those mares and foals, and why are they not here to state the fact? If this poison was used for the purpose of destroying dogs, some one must have assisted Mr. Palmer in the attempts which he resorted to for that purpose. Where are those persons? Why are they not called? But, not only are they not called, they are not even named. My learned friend does not venture to breathe even a suggestion of anything of the kind. I ask, gentlemen, what conclusion can we draw from these things, except one, and one alone? Death, with all the symptoms of strychnia—death in all the convulsive agonies and throes which that fatal poison produces in the frame of man—death with all the appearances which follow upon death, and mark how that death has come to pass—all these things, in the minds of those who can discuss and consider them with calm, dispassionate attention, who do not mix themselves up as advocates, partisans, or witnesses, leading to but one conclusion; and then the fact of the strychnia being purchased by the prisoner on the morning of the fatal day, if not obtained by him, as was sworn to, on the night before, is left wholly uncovered and wholly unmet, without the shadow of a defence. Alas! gentlemen, is it possible that we can come to any other than one painful and dread conclusion? I protest I can suggest to you none.

It is said by my learned friend, "Is it likely that Mr. Palmer should have purchased strychnia at Rugeley when he might have got it in London?" I admit the fact. I feel the force of the observation. If he could have shown that he had done anything with this strychnia—if he could have shown any legitimate purpose to which it was intended to be applied, and to which it was afterwards applied—then I should say that it would be an argument worthy of your gravest and most attentive consideration. But just see on the one hand how the fact may stand. He was in town on the Monday, and he had the opportunity, as my learned friend suggests, of purchasing strychnia there. But on the other hand he had much to do; he had his train to catch by a certain time; he had in the meanwhile his pecuniary embarrassments to solve if he could. Time may have flown too fast for him to be able to go and obtain this strychnia; and even if he had had time, I do not believe it is sold in chemists' shops in London without the name of the party purchasing it as a voucher. If he had given his name, of course, it would have been still worse if he had bought strychnia in London than if he had bought it in Rugeley. I do not say that it is not worthy of your consideration, that it is not a difficulty in the case; but I say there is plain, distinct, positive proof of the purchase of strychnia, and under circumstances which cannot fail to lead to the conclusion that he shrank from the observation of Newton at the time he was buying it; and there is a total absence of all proof, nay, of all suggestion, of any legitimate purpose to which that fatal poison was to be, or was in point of fact, afterwards actually applied.

Attorney-General

Then, gentlemen, it is said that there are two other circumstances in the case which make strongly in favour of the prisoner, and negative the presumption of a guilty intention, and those are, the fact that he called in two medical men. Here, again, I admit that this is a matter to which all due consideration ought to be given. He called in Dr. Bamford on the Saturday, and he wrote to Mr. Jones on the Sunday, and desired his presence to attend his sick friend. It is perfectly true that he did. It is perfectly true, as medical men, they would be likely to know the symptoms of poisoning by strychnia, and they would be likely to suspect that death had ensued from it; and yet even here it strikes me that there is a singular inconsistency in the defence. See the strange contradiction in which the witnesses called for the defence involve my learned friend who puts them forward, if all those symptoms were not the symptoms of strychnia. If they are referable to all the multiform variety of disease to which those witnesses have spoken, why, then, should Mr. Palmer have the credit of having selected medical men who would be likely to know from those symptoms that they were symptoms of strychnia? I pass that by; it is not a matter of very much importance. It is true that he did have those two medical men. He called in old Dr. Bamford. I speak of that gentleman in terms of perfect respect; but I think I do him no injustice if I say that the vigour of his intellect and his power of observation have been impaired, as all human powers are liable to be impaired, by the advancing hand of time. I do not think he was a person likely to make very shrewd observations upon any symptoms exhibited to him, either immediately after death or upon the subsequent examination of the body; and the best proof of that is to be found in that which he has actually done and written with reference to this case. As regards Mr. Jones the same observation does not apply. He was a young man in the full possession of his intellect and the professional knowledge which he had acquired. Nevertheless, about him the observations I am about to address to you I think are not unworthy of notice. The prisoner at the bar selected his men well, for what has come to pass shows how wisely he judged of what was likely to take place. This death occurred in the presence of Mr. Jones, with all those fearful symptoms which you have heard described; yet Mr. Jones suspected nothing; and if Mr. Stevens had not exhibited that sagacity and firmness which he did manifest in the after parts of this transaction, and if Mr. Palmer had succeeded in getting that body hastily introduced into the strong oak coffin that he had had made for it, the body would have been consigned to the grave, and nobody would have been aught the wiser. The presence of Mr. Jones, and the presence of Dr. Bamford, would not have led to detection, would not have frustrated the designs with which I shall presently contend before you this death was brought about.

Attorney-General

On the other hand, gentlemen, the matter is perhaps capable of this aspect, it may have been that a man whose cunning was equal to his boldness may have thought it the best course to adopt to avoid suspicion—to prevent its possibility—was to take care that medical men should be called in and should be present at the time of death; nor is there anything to show that the prisoner had the most distant notion that Mr. Jones intended to sleep in this room that night; and if he had not the man would have been found dead in the morning; he would have gone through his mortal struggle and intense and fearful agony; he would have died there alone and unbefriended; he would have been found dead the next morning; the old man would have said it was apoplexy, and the young man would have put it down to epilepsy. If any one had whispered a suspicion, the same argument would have been used which has been used now with so much power and force by my learned friend. Can you imagine that the man would have called in medical men to be the witnesses of a death which he himself was bringing about? But, gentlemen, as I have already said, if you believe the evidence of Newton, and if you believe that that same night pills were administered to Cook by Palmer—and that, I believe, will be your opinion and conclusion, notwithstanding that wretched witness to-day said he heard Cook say to Palmer that he had taken the pills already, because he, Palmer, was late, whereas the woman witness, Mills, told you that the next morning Cook reminded her that his agony was such as she never could have witnessed in any human being, and he told her he ascribed it to the pills which Palmer had given him at half-past ten—if you believe that statement, and that the pills were given him by Palmer at half-past ten, and you find that Palmer a few short minutes, perhaps, before went to Newton, and got the poison from Newton, and you find upon that night the first paroxysms, though not so violent and not fatal, yet similar and analogous in character to those which preceded the death, can you doubt on the first night the poison was administered to him? though with what purpose I know not; I can only speculate—whether it was to bring about by some minute dose convulsions which should not have the complete character of tetanus, but would bear a resemblance to natural convulsions which should justify his saying afterwards that the man had had a fit, and so prepare those who should hear of it on the next night, when the death was to ensue, for the belief that it was merely a succession of the same description of fit that he had had before. That is one solution. The other may be that he attempted on that Monday night to carry out his fell purpose to its full extent, but that the poison proved inefficacious. We hear that an adulterated form, or, at all events, an inferior form, called bruchsia, is occasionally sold, and it may have been that it failed in its effect. It is only one-tenth of the strength. We know that he purchased poison on Tuesday, and that on that night Cook died with all the symptoms of poison; and why he purchased that poison is not in any way accounted for. The symptoms were the same on the Tuesday night in character, though greater in degree, than they were on the Monday; and there is found a witness who comes forward and says, with no earthly motive to tell so foul a falsehood, "I found the character of the convulsions the two succeeding nights the same." I cannot resist the conclusion to which my reasoning impels me that poison was administered upon both nights, though it failed upon the first. I can only speculate as to what was the cause of failure. There are the facts, and you must deal with them.

Attorney-General

Alas! gentlemen, it does not stop there; there is another part of this case which, though it may not have been the means of death, is of the highest value in estimating the credit that is to be given to the point which we advance of this death having been produced by strychnia—I allude to the antimony. We have had medical men and analytical chemists who have told us a great deal about strychnia, but not one has said a word about antimony. On the Wednesday night, at Shrewsbury, when Cook drinks his glass of brandy and water he fancies there is something in it that burns his throat; he exclaims at the time, and he is seized immediately with vomiting, which lasts for several hours. On that same night Mrs. Brookes sees the prisoner shaking something in a glass, evidently dissolving something in fluid. A man has been called here to-day, the boon companion, the chosen associate, the racing confederate of the prisoner, to come and tell you that all that story is untrue—that the woman never came down stairs—that Palmer never carried out the brandy and water—that there is not a word of truth in it—and the fact is that Palmer and Cook only came in at twelve o'clock, when Myatt, forsooth, had been waiting for two hours. Mrs. Brookes' story is, according to him, an entire invention from beginning to end; he swears that he must have seen if anything had been mixed with the brandy and water, and nothing was mixed with it. I think you will be more disposed to believe Mrs. Brookes than to believe any of those persons who were the associates of the prisoner, and who had been partners in his transactions. It is a remarkable fact that Cook drinks that brandy and water and a few minutes after is taken ill. There were other persons taken ill at Shrewsbury; it may be within the verge of possibility—although ten minutes after he had drunk the brandy and water he was taken with vomiting—that it was the same form of complaint to which other persons were subject in Shrewsbury; I do not want to press it one jot further than it ought to go, but it is a remarkable circumstance that the man is seen with a glass and with a fluid which he is mixing up and holding to the light, and shortly afterwards his friend who is drinking with him or drinking at the same table at which he is drinking, who, if Myatt be telling the truth, was somewhat in liquor, and ought not to have been pressed to take brandy and water—Palmer says that he will not take anything until Cook has exhausted his portion—and then immediately afterwards the man is taken ill. These are circumstances not altogether incapable of producing certain impressions upon one which it is difficult to shake off.

Attorney-General

Nevertheless, I pass on from that, and go to Rugeley. From the Saturday morning until the Monday morning I find this poor man suffering under the influence of constant vomiting; that was not the Shrewsbury disease—he had got rid of it; he was well on Thursday and he was well on Friday. On Saturday morning, after dining at Mr. Palmer's, he is taken ill; and then we have the fact of Mr. Palmer administering his food, administering his remedies, sending over toast and water, sending over broth; and, no sooner has this poor man taken those things than he is seized with incessant vomitings of the most painful description. What about the broth? The broth is said to-day by Smith to have been sent from the Albion. Yes; and where does it find its way to? It is taken, not to the Talbot Arms, but to the prisoner's kitchen. After that, instead of leaving it, as one would suppose he would leave it, to the woman to take to the Talbot Arms, he takes it himself from the fire, puts it into the cup, gives it to her, it is taken over, and the man vomits immediately after he has drunk it. On the Sunday the same thing is done again; the broth is brought from the same quarter, and attended with the same results. Of that broth the woman takes a couple of spoonfuls, and she is sick for several hours. She vomits twenty times, and is unable to leave her bed for some hours. My learned friend said she did not state that before the coroner. Nevertheless, it is sworn to by the other servant that the woman was ill. I can quite understand why the woman did not state it before the coroner. It shows the honesty of the woman's character. It did not occur to her to connect the sickness from which she suffered with the taking of the broth; but afterwards, when the story of the antimony came up, and Cook's sickness was connected with it, then she remembered perfectly well, after the evidence had been given, how she, having taken the broth, immediately became ill. The fact is not one capable of dispute, although it may be that she did not mention it before the coroner. And I think you will regard it as a very important and significant fact in the case, that, on the Monday when Palmer is absent, Cook is better. On the Tuesday he vomits again, though not in the same degree. But after death—now comes the important fact—antimony is found in the tissues of that man's body, and his blood shows the presence of it; the blood shows distinctly that it must have been taken recently, within the last eight-and-forty hours previous to his death. How came it there? The small quantity that is found does not form the slightest criterion of the quantity that had been administered to him. Part of it, you know, would be thrown up by the act of vomiting which it provokes; part of it would pass away in other forms, but none would be there unless he had taken some. When did he take it? If you find that he is suffering from vomiting for days before his death—that a person is constantly administering things to him, and after taking those things he vomits—when the prisoner sends him over a basin of broth he vomits, and when the servant takes a couple of spoonfuls she is reduced to the same condition—what other conclusion can you come to, knowing that antimony is an irritant that will produce vomiting and retching in the human system, than that the antimony must have been administered to him by some one? By whom? Who but the prisoner at the bar could have done it? My learned friend says Cook might have taken antimony at some former time—that he might have taken James' powder for a cold. There is not the slightest trace of evidence from the beginning to the end of the case that he ever had a cold, or ever took James' powder over the whole period we are now ranging. Moreover, as I have even now said, it was in his blood, it must have been administered eight-and-forty hours before death; who could have administered it but the prisoner at the bar? I ask you to form your own judgment upon that matter, but I cannot resist the conclusion, it is irresistible. If so, for what purpose was it administered; it is difficult to say with anything like precision; one can only speculate upon it. It may have been, however, to produce the appearance of natural disease, to account for the calling in of medical men, and to account for the catastrophe which was already in preparation; but it may also have had another and a different object, and it is this—if we are right as to the motives which impelled the prisoner at the bar to commit this great crime, it was, at all events in part, that he might possess himself of the money which Cook would have to realise upon the settling day at Tattersall's on Monday. If Cook went there himself the scheme was frustrated; Mr. Cook intended to go there himself, and if he had done so the prisoner's designs would have failed of accomplishment. To make him ill at Shrewsbury—to get him in consequence to go to Rugeley, instead of going to London or anywhere else—to make him ill again and keep him ill at Rugeley might be part of a cleverly contrived and organised scheme. It might have been with one or other of those motives, it might have been with both, that the antimony was administered, and so sickness produced, but that the sickness was produced and that the antimony was afterwards found in the body are incapable of dispute. Put them together and you have cause and effect; and if you are satisfied that antimony was introduced into that poor man's body for the purpose of producing vomiting and sickness, then, I say there is no one who could have given it to him within that recent period but the prisoner at the bar. Neither the doctor at Shrewsbury nor the doctor at Rugeley ever gave him one fraction of antimony which had those natural effects which as a cause it was certain to produce; then it will be for you to ask yourselves whether it can have been with any other than a fell purpose and design—with a view of paving the way for the more important act which was afterwards to follow.

My learned friend has dealt with this case of antimony in no other way than that which I have suggested, namely, casting out some loose, floating, imaginary notion that at some period or other, for which no precise date is given, he may have taken James' powder for the purpose of getting rid of a cold. Alas! gentlemen, I feel that so idle an objection cannot stand between you and the conclusion which, I submit to you, arises from the fact that this antimony was given to Mr. Cook with a wicked design. If it was, just see the important influence which it exercises upon the other question. If antimony was found—if antimony can have been given with no legitimate object, and if it can only have been given by the prisoner at the bar—how great does it render the probability that to carry out the purpose, whatever it may be, that he had in his mind, he gave him this strychnia, of which the deadly effects and consequences have been but too plainly made manifest.

Attorney-General

Then, gentlemen, let us take the conduct of the prisoner into consideration in the after stages of the case, and also in one remarkable particular—in an incident that took place on the day of the death, on the evening of the preparation of the pills—and in his conduct taken in all its circumstances I fear you will find but too cogent proofs of his guilt. I begin with the Tuesday, the day of the death. Mr. Cook had had what every one will admit to have been a most severe fit on the night before. Dr. Bamford comes upon the Tuesday, but not a word is said to him about it. He comes, and the prisoner is solicitous that he shall not see Cook; and twice in the course of that morning, when old Mr. Bamford is desirous of coming up to see the man, the prisoner said, "He is tranquil and dozing; I wish him not to be disturbed." That may have been innocent, but on the other hand, if Dr. Bamford had come at that time when the fit was fresh in Cook's mind, the probability is great that Cook would have told him what had happened the night before. Cook does not see him till seven o'clock, when Mr. Jones had arrived. One would have expected that, having been invited to come by the prisoner, the first thing Mr. Palmer would have done would have been to mention how he found him the night before. He talks of nothing but about the bilious symptoms—bilious at Shrewsbury, bilious to Dr. Bamford, and bilious to Mr. Jones; and thus he is represented throughout by the prisoner at the bar, yet all this time the medical men agree in saying that there was not a bilious symptom about him from beginning to end; no feverish skin, no loaded tongue, and none of the concomitants of a bilious condition. The moment Mr. Jones sees him, considering he had heard that this man was suffering under a bilious affection, he says, "That is not the tongue of a bilious patient." The only answer he gets is, "You should have seen it before." When? When the man saw him at Shrewsbury, or when Dr. Bamford saw him, they both found his tongue perfectly clean; the irritation in the bowels was not the result of natural action, but of the antimony; and not one single word does he say to Mr. Jones of the fit that had taken place the night before. It is a remarkable circumstance, when the three medical men are consulting at the bedside, the patient says, "I will have no more pills—no more medicine to-night," intimating that his sufferings of the night before he ascribed to the pills which he had taken. There is no observation made by Mr. Palmer as to what had been the nature of the man's attack the night before, he having been called up in the dead of the night. They go into an adjoining room to consult as to the best thing to be done. The man had declared his aversion to taking any pills or medicine; and Mr. Palmer immediately proposes that he shall take the same pills that he took the night before. He says to Mr. Jones, "Do not tell him the contents, because he has a strong objection to them." It is arranged to have the pills made up; he does not wait to have the pills sent by Dr. Bamford, though it was early in the evening, but he accompanies Dr. Bamford down to his surgery. I cannot for the life of me understand why Dr. Bamford should have made up those pills at all. The prisoner had a surgery of his own close by, and he could have made up the pills in two minutes, he knew perfectly well their contents, instead of which he goes down with Dr. Bamford to his surgery. One would have supposed it would have been quite enough, as he was the person who every night administered the pills to Cook, if Dr. Bamford put the pills in a box and handed them over to Mr. Palmer, who knew what was to be done with them, instead of which Mr. Palmer asks Dr. Bamford to write the direction. He does write the direction, and then Mr. Palmer walks away with the pills. An interval occurs of an hour or two, during which time he had abundant opportunity of going home to his surgery and doing what he pleased in the way of substituting other pills. He comes back, and before he gives the pills he takes care to call the attention of Mr. Jones, who was present, to the remarkable handwriting of the old gentleman, Dr. Bamford, as being worthy of attention in a man of his advanced age. What necessity was there for all that? Was not it, think you, part of a scheme, that in case there should afterwards be any question as to the cause of this man's death, or the possibility of his having had poison administered to him, he should be able to say to Mr. Jones, "Why, you know they were Dr. Bamford's pills. You were present at the bedside of the deceased, you saw that I administered nothing except pills, and you must be clear they were Dr. Bamford's pills. Did not I show you the address written, and call your attention to the excellence of the handwriting?" Who knows but all that prevented the possibility of suspicion being excited and presenting itself to the mind of Mr. Jones.

Attorney-General

Now, any one of those circumstances in itself would not be such as I could venture to submit to you as conclusive of the prisoner's guilt, but I ask your attention to a series of things following one upon the other, which, at the same time, are of a most remarkable character, and, taken as a whole, lead but to one conclusion. The death having taken place (I am passing over for a moment other circumstances which have no reference to the immediate cause of death, I shall come back to them in another part of the case), we find the father-in-law comes down to Rugeley upon the Friday. Let us see what the conduct of the prisoner is then. The father-in-law applies to him for information on the subject of his stepson's affairs. I pass that over, because that, too, will come under a different head; but having done so, and it appearing from the representation which the father-in-law made that the man had died in comparative poverty, something is said about his being buried. "Well," says Mr. Stevens, "rich or poor, poor fellow, he must be buried." Mr. Palmer immediately says, "If that is all, I will bury him myself." "No," says the stepfather, and the brother interposes. Mr. Stevens says, "No, I am his stepfather and his executor, and it is my place to bury him." Well, there is nothing in all that. Palmer may have said, with regard to his friend, that he would see the last respect paid to his memory. But there is this remarkable thing, when the stepfather says that nobody shall bury him but himself, and makes the observation that perhaps it will be inconvenient to the people at the inn to have him lying there for two or three days, because he intended to have him buried in town, so that the poor man might lie in the same grave with his mother—immediately after this Palmer says, "There will be no harm in that, he can stay as long as you like; but the body ought to

- 246 -

be put in a coffin immediately." After that Mr. Stevens gets into conversation with Dr. Bamford about his son-in-law, and while they are in conversation Mr. Palmer slips away, goes out into the town, and comes back in about half an hour, when Mr. Stevens asks him for the name of some undertaker in order that he may go and give the undertaker directions about the funeral, and he finds to his surprise that Mr. Palmer has gone out, and has himself, without any authority, ordered a shell and a strong oak coffin in order that the body may be immediately put away. This, again, is a circumstance not unworthy of consideration. Why should he interfere and meddle in a matter which did not concern him, and which it was the business and province of another man to attend to, except this, that he had made up his mind that that body should be consigned to its last resting-place and removed from the sight of man with as much rapidity as circumstances would permit of? You have heard what took place in the course of conversation upon the subject of the betting book. I pass that by for the present.

I now come to Saturday, when, returning from London, Mr. Stevens and Mr. Palmer met in the railway train, and at the different stations when the train stopped had conversations with one another; and it appeared at that time Mr. Stevens had fully made up his mind to have the body examined—there were circumstances which had engendered suspicion in his mind; he had seen the attitude of the corpse; he had seen the clenched hands; and, being a man of sagacity and shrewdness, upon putting things together, there was a lurking suspicion in his mind that he could not overcome, and he was determined that he would be satisfied, and he made known his intention of having the body examined before it was consigned to the grave. It is due to Mr. Palmer to say that he did not flinch from the trying ordeal of Mr. Stevens' scrutinising glance when he mentioned the subject of post-mortem examination; he makes no objection to the post-mortem examination; he is anxious to know who shall perform it, but Mr. Stevens will not inform him of the fact. It is to take place, and it is appointed to take place on the Monday. On the Sunday we have that remarkable conversation to which Newton speaks, and which has been in the possession of the Crown (it is not, like the other part of his evidence, brought forward at the last moment) and in the possession of my learned friend. It is true he did not state it before the coroner, but the explanation is extremely easy. Before the coroner, Roberts was the man who came forward to prove the purchase of strychnia, and vouched Newton being there. Newton was immediately fetched, and his deposition will be found immediately following that of Roberts; not for the purpose of giving a general statement, but for the purpose of corroborating Roberts, which he does. Hence it came to pass, in answering only the questions which were put to him by the coroner, nothing was said upon the subject of that Sunday's conversation, but it was given immediately afterwards to the Crown.

I think you will not believe that Newton comes forward for the purpose of making a false representation as to this conversation. What was the conversation? He is sent for by Mr. Palmer to his house, and he is treated with a glass of brandy and water, and when he has a glass of brandy and water they get into general conversation, and then, I think, the prisoner says, "How much strychnia would you give if you wanted to kill a dog?" "Why, I should give from half a grain to a grain." "Would you expect to find any appearances in the stomach after death?" "No inflammation or erosion, no appearances." Upon which a sort of half-uttered ejaculation comes from the prisoner. "That is all right," and a sort of action of the hands. Was that entirely an invention? Was nothing said about a dog? Was nothing said about strychnia? Now, it may have proceeded from two causes, if you believe the conversation. It may have been that the prisoner was in a state of great anxiety when he found the post-mortem examination was to take place, and he was anxious to know whether the views of another medical man confirmed his own with regard to the appearances in the body after death, where death had been occasioned by strychnia. It may have been that he meditated some trickery, some jugglery, that involved the real destruction of a dog, which may have given rise to those questions which were suggested on the part of the defence to one of the witnesses who were called; it may have been that something was in contemplation to destroy or attempt to destroy a dog, to account for the purchase of the strychnia, which he knew was likely to be brought up in evidence against him, and which it would be a difficult matter to explain. Whether any such attempt was afterwards made I know not; I imagined that we were going to have some evidence to that effect, from the questions that were asked, but no such evidence has been afforded—not the slightest as to what purpose this quantity of strychnia has been applied. It has not been found upon the prisoner's premises. What has become of it? I cannot solve precisely the secret of that conversation. Like many other matters in this case, it remains a mystery; but this I know, I can look at it in no aspect in which it does not reflect light upon the guilt in which this transaction is involved; if you can solve the difficulty, for heaven's sake do, but I can suggest to you no solution. From that man Newton, then, he got his strychnia on the Monday night, and for that man he sends on the Sunday. With that man he holds a conversation—was it with the view of leading Newton to believe that it was for the purpose of killing a dog he had got it? These are speculations and surmises, into which I do not deem it necessary further to go. It will be for you to say whether you can entertain any doubt upon all these facts, when they are before you, that this death was occasioned by strychnia, and that that strychnia was administered by the prisoner, either from what he obtained upon the Monday night, or from that which, beyond the possibility of question, he obtained upon the Tuesday, for which he has failed to account, and for which, indeed, he has not attempted to account.

But, then, my learned friend says that the man had no motive to take away the life of his friend, and it is right we should see how that matter stands. Gentlemen, if, indeed, I have satisfied you, beyond the reach of reasonable doubt, by the evidence I have adduced, and by the failure on the part of the evidence for the defence to neutralise its effect, that the death here was occasioned by strychnia—that the strychnia could have been administered by no one, and, in fact, was administered by no one, save Mr. Palmer—the question of motive becomes a matter of secondary consideration. It is often difficult to dive into the breasts of men, to understand the motives that have been working there, and by those motives to account for their actions. Omniscience alone can exercise that faculty and that power; and therefore, where acts are proved against a man beyond the reach of reasonable doubt, it is not because we may not be able to exercise a sufficiently scrutinising power to ascertain the motives that we are to doubt the facts, the existence of which is brought beyond the reach of reasonable doubt; but nevertheless it is always an important element in a case, and it is, above all, an important element in a case upon which any reasonable doubt can by possibility rest, to see whether there was an adequate motive to lead to the perpetration of the act which is charged. On the other hand, gentlemen, we must not be too precise in weighing the question of adequacy of motive; that which, to the good, would appear of no influence, however remote or minute, in inducing them to commit crime, oftentimes, with the wicked, is quite sufficient to impel them into crime, and it may have been so here.

Attorney-General

But let us see, before I make any further observations upon that point, how the matter stands upon the proof which is before us. I told you that Mr. Palmer was a man in circumstances of the direst embarrassment, with ruin actually staring him in the face, and that nothing could avert that ruin save pecuniary means at once obtained for his purpose. The proof which I have offered to you has fully come up to the proposition with which I started. The fact has been proved beyond the possibility of doubt. It appears that in the month of November, 1855, Mr. Palmer was in this position. He owed upon bills, all of which were forged, the sum of £19,000; he had bills to the amount of £12,500 standing in the hands of Mr. Pratt; he had bills to the amount of £6500 standing in the hands of Mr. Wright; and he had a bill for £2000 in the hands of Mr. Padwick. Although it is true that £1000 upon that account had been paid off to Mr. Pratt, yet the bills still remained for the full amount in Mr. Pratt's hands. Although £1000 had been paid to Mr. Padwick, he held a warrant of attorney and a bill of sale upon the stud for the remaining £1000. All those bills, without exception, were forgeries. A correspondence took place between Mr. Pratt and himself with regard to the £13,000 policy upon his brother's death, through which he hoped to liquidate Mr. Pratt's demand; he had been disappointed of that money, and upon the office declining to pay the money, as early as the middle of October, Mr. Pratt gave him to understand, in the most distinct and positive terms, that the bills must be met. Bills for £4000 were due, or were coming due, at the end of that month—one upon the 25th for £2000, and another upon the 27th for £2000. Bills already renewed were coming due from month to month, and there was £5500 which it was necessary immediately to provide for. Mr. Pratt gave him notice that he could give him no longer delay, inasmuch as the office had resolved to dispute this policy. It was no longer an existing valid security, and consequently Mr. Pratt could not be a party to representing to his clients, with whose money those bills had been discounted, that it was in any respect a valid security, therefore the bills must be met.

Attorney-General

The matter was coming to a crisis; the bills must be paid at maturity; he sends him up three small sums, first a sum of £300, and then two sums of £250 each, making the sum of £800. Of that sum £200 was to come off other bills to fall due in January, leaving only £600 applicable to the principal. He is told at once that he must do a great deal more; he is told, late in October, that unless he does a great deal more writs will be issued against his mother and against himself, which would at once bring the matter to a termination by showing that those bills were forgeries. He entreats that time shall be given; he obtains this concession from Mr. Pratt, that the writs shall not be served until a given day, and he in the interval must make further payments on account of the principal bill due. That being the state of things upon the 13th, Mr. Pratt writes and presses him for further payment. On that day "Polestar" won. Cook was, as you have heard, in an ecstasy of delight, feeling that his difficulties were, at all events for a time, removed; that he should now get through the winter and live happily till the next racing season. He little thought what was about to take place. If this accusation is well founded, the mare winning, and his being entitled to a large sum of money, was the most fatal thing that could have befallen him. Alas! how great is the shortsightedness of mortal man! When we have the highest cause of joy and exultation, often while the sunshine of our prosperity warms and gladdens our heart for a moment, there is lurking beneath our feet a fatal abyss, into which we are about to fall. This poor man, if this charge be true, might have been living now, had it not been that upon that fatal day his mare won, and he became entitled to a large sum of money, which afforded temptation to his murderer.

Now, it becomes perfectly clear that at this moment matters were approaching an immediate crisis. What was Mr. Palmer to do? He had no source to which to turn for money. It is clear that he could not go to his mother. I presume that source had long since been exhausted, or he would not have forged her name. What was he to do if he could not get money to satisfy Pratt's demand? You know, although a moneylender is considerate and indulgent enough as long as he is certain of his payment, and gets his heavy usurious interest paid down on the nail, if he once becomes doubtful of the security and uncertain of payment, you may as well ask mercy of a rabid tiger, or you may as well ask pity of stones, as hope to find bowels of compassion in him. Pratt gave him fair warning that the money must be paid, or something must be paid by way of instalment on the principal, and to keep the interest down. Where was Mr. Palmer to get money from? My learned friend says Cook was his best friend, and that Cook was the man he was to look to; and that as long as he kept Cook alive he had a friend in need to whom he could resort for assistance. In what way? Was Cook to give acceptances to Pratt? Is anybody weak enough to suppose that Pratt would have taken Cook's acceptances to keep those bills alive, unless there was a part payment of the principal and interest? It is quite clear that he would not. When even for the sum of £500 he was asked to take Cook's security, he refused to do so, unless there was the collateral security of an assignment of his horses. Cook had assigned to him all the property he possessed. All that Cook had in the world was his winnings upon that day's race at Shrewsbury, and what little money he may have obtained by his winnings at the races at Worcester. If you believe the witness Myatt, those winnings were exhausted, and therefore this man had nothing except his winnings at the Shrewsbury races; and you are asked by my learned friend to believe that it would have been of use to Palmer to keep this man alive. The reverse is proved by the evidence. With Pratt his personal security would have been unavailing. Pratt tells you that he would not take anything from him unless it was the real security of an assignment of his horses or other property. Just see the interest which Palmer had in securing all Cook's effects. My learned friend says they were mixed up together in transactions in which they had a joint and common interest—they were confederates upon the turf and had joint bets together. Yes; but one man putting another on does not mean that when A puts B on and says we are likely to make a good thing, and we will share it, that B is to pay A's losings if they do not win. They might be confederates on the turf, but that did not make Cook responsible for Palmer's liabilities.

Does any one suppose that Cook intended to find the means to enable Palmer to meet Pratt's insatiable demands, to stave off the difficulties in that quarter? Was Cook to deprive himself of his winnings, and leave himself without money, for the benefit of his friend? That is the proposition, for the whole of which my learned friend must contend before you before he can establish anything like a case to show that if Cook had lived it would have been better for Palmer than that he should die. My learned friend says there is proof that they were mixed up closely together to be found in this, that Cook writes to his agent, Fisher, and says to Fisher, writing on the Friday after he had dined with Palmer, "There is a matter which is of importance to Palmer and to me, that £500 should be paid to Mr. Pratt to-morrow; £300 has been sent down to-night, and I request you will be so good as to pay Mr. Pratt £200 to-morrow on my account, and charge it to me." My learned friend thought that that transaction would be favourable to his client, and he put it prominently forward. To my mind he could have adduced nothing more fatal. The explanation of it is to me as clear as the sun at noonday. Cook had brought with him some £600 or £700; at least at Shrewsbury he was seen by Fisher with a roll of notes amounting to some £700 or £800. On the same evening the parties came to Rugeley, when he had not had time to spend the money. He speaks of a £500 transaction, in which he and Palmer have a joint interest. There is only that one transaction with Pratt in which they had a common interest, that was the £500 raised by the assignment of "Polestar," and a bill, of which we say Cook never got the proceeds; and he says, writing on that night to Fisher, "£300 have been sent up to-night, and I will be obliged to you to pay the other £200 to make up the whole." No £300 were ever sent up that night. Mr. Pratt has given an account of the whole transaction. £300 were to be sent that night; by whom were they to be sent? Can you doubt? Where is all Cook's money gone? I can quite understand that he handed over £300 to Palmer to send up to Pratt, and directed Fisher to pay another £200. What followed in respect to the joint transaction? What was the joint transaction? they never had but one, and that was for £500. What was it? Why, it was the money which had been got by the assignment of "Polestar" and "Sirius"; "Polestar" had just won at Shrewsbury—it was natural that the man should desire to redeem his mare; moreover, the bill was coming due; he had the cash in his pocket, and he knew that he was going to receive money at Tattersall's, which he never did; and he says, "£300 will be sent up to-night." It is the only matter in which they have a common interest, not only as to the £500, but in any respect; Pratt had no other dealing whatever with them jointly or with Cook, if we except the bill for £500— what does it show? It shows that £300 had been sent for the purpose—he sends up £300, but how is it applied? Pause for a moment; the £300 is not sent up, Palmer keeps it in his pocket; what is done with the other £200? Is it carried to the account of the matter in which they had joint interest with

Pratt? No such thing; it goes as part of the payment made by Palmer to Pratt on account of the bills which Pratt then held—it never went to any matter of joint interest—it is an idle and false pretence to say that Cook was in any way responsible to Pratt; it may have been the intention of Palmer when Cook should be no more to represent him as so, but there is no foundation in reality and in fact for the statement. I say the transaction of the £500, so far from helping the prisoner's case, shows conclusively that the £200 advanced by Fisher, and the £300 to be sent up that night to satisfy this bill for £500, and the assignment to release "Polestar" and "Sirius," was £500 more taken from this young man and appropriated by the prisoner to his own use.

But the matter does not rest there—would it did. I come now to the transaction of the Monday, and I find £1020 of Cook's money applied to the prisoner's use. He goes up to London; he had ascertained by some means or other the amount that Cook was entitled to receive on the Monday—possibly Cook had told him; Fisher was Cook's agent, and the probability is that Cook desired the prisoner to hand an account of his bets which he had won to Fisher, who would go and settle with the parties at Tattersall's; Fisher would have to pay himself back the £200; we know that he intended his accounts should pass through Fisher, because he asked Fisher to advance the £200 upon the credit of it; but it is suggested that under the guidance of Palmer he now meditated a fraud, and that he intended to pass his account through Mr. Herring, in order to avoid paying Fisher the £200 for a time. Is it charitable to Mr. Cook to ascribe to him a fraud of this description, which, so far as we know, he was not in the habit of doing? I ask you this question as reasonable men, supposing he had disposed of his ready money, and we find none left— that he had given the prisoner £300 to send up, you cannot suppose that this man who had nothing of his fortune left, who sees ruin staring him in the face—he was not a ruined man as long as he had this money, but having parted with this money he was a ruined man—you cannot suppose that he intended to deprive himself of the whole of the money that he had won, to leave himself destitute and naked for the coming winter; the thing is out of the question—besides, if the prisoner's representation is true which he made to Mr. Cheshire, that he had got the genuine cheque of this man for very nearly the amount, through his agents, Messrs. Wetherby, of the stakes at Shrewsbury, you are asked to believe on the one hand that he had given him his ready money, and on the other hand that he had given him a cheque to receive of Messrs. Wetherby, and that he had given him £1020, which constituted absolutely the whole that the poor man possessed—you are asked to believe that he hands it over to the prisoner to go and dispose of as he pleases—that is my learned friend's proposition, but I do not think you will adopt it.

Then, if that be not so, what does the prisoner do? He goes to London, but does not go to Fisher, who was the agent of Cook, who would, in the first place, have paid himself back the £200, and, in the second place, would not have paid the sums which he received except upon Cook's authority and instruction, but would have sent the money to Cook, or have paid it upon Cook's written direction as to what was to be done with it. He takes the account, therefore, to a comparative stranger, who never had acted for Mr. Cook before, feeling that that stranger would have no hesitation or repugnance in paying the money according to the direction of the man from whom he had the direction to receive it, supposing that both emanated from Mr. Cook, the person interested in the money. Accordingly he says to Mr. Herring, "Here is a list of bets which Cook will be entitled to be paid at Tattersall's; they are so much, you dispose of it in this way; pay yourself £200"; it being the fact that Mr. Cook and the prisoner had before raised the sum, I think, of £600; £200 had been raised by Mr. Cook on his acceptance, and £400 had been raised on the acceptance of the prisoner. Mr. Cook's portion had been paid off, but that of the prisoner remained unpaid. Palmer says to Mr. Herring, "Pay yourself £200, then go to Pratt's and pay him £450; then go to Padwick and pay him £350." Now, it is perfectly clear that the £450 was a debt due from Palmer to Pratt, and it is untrue that Cook had anything to do with it. The debt of £350 to Padwick was for some bet, and although it is not proved, I have reason to believe that the minor part of it was a debt of Cook's, but the larger part was a debt of Palmer's upon a matter in which they stood in together. There is evidence that Mr. Palmer treated the debt due to Padwick as his. He says, "I will pay you my bet of £350 at such a time." I am giving him credit for what I believe was the fact, that a part of it was Cook's. Why was Cook's debt paid then? There was a warrant of attorney in the hands of Mr. Padwick, and Mr. Padwick was getting impatient for his £1000, and if this bet had not been paid to Mr. Padwick, Mr. Padwick would have resented the non-payment of the debt of honour which he had no means of enforcing, and would have come down upon Mr. Palmer, no doubt, at a very early period in respect of the £1000 due upon the bill dishonoured twelve months before. Exactly that came to pass—in consequence of Mr. Herring not receiving the whole of the money, he was not able to pay Mr. Padwick, and the result was that Mr. Padwick put the process of the law in motion against the prisoner on that bill, and brought an action against his mother. The bill for £1000 was the bill of Mr. Palmer, upon which Mr. Cook was not primarily liable. I say here was a distinct interest which the prisoner had to appropriate this money to himself, because it was the means for the moment, and the only means he could resort to, of staving off the evil hour which was rapidly approaching. The degree of difficulty in which he was placed must not be measured simply by the amount of his pecuniary liabilities. It was not merely that he had these large bills upon which at any moment process might be issued, but he had made his mother answerable for those bills, and the moment the first of them was put in motion in the Courts the fraud and forgery would come to light, and he would be exposed not merely to the consequences of his inability to pay his debts, but to the consequences of the law which he had violated. The former might have been got rid of in the Insolvent Court or the Bankruptcy Court, but the crime of forgery could not have been got rid of; for that he would have to answer at the bar of a Court of criminal justice, and would have incurred the penalty of transportation, or of penal servitude in an aggravated form. But there is a further sum besides the £1000; he appropriated a further sum of £350, which was to be got from Messrs. Wetherby. It is said that he got a genuine cheque from Cook to entitle him to receive that money, but it is not for a moment suggested what induced Cook to give it to him. Was it a genuine cheque? That matter might have been solved by its production. It is not produced; yet it is quite clear that it was returned to the prisoner's hands by Messrs. Wetherby when they could not get the money. It is quite clear that it was of great importance to him to get the money, because there was £100 to be paid to Pratt, which must be paid in order to stave off the evil day upon the bill of £1500, which was due on the 9th of November. Where is that cheque? If it had been produced we could have seen whether it was a genuine cheque or not. It is not forthcoming. What are the circumstances under which he presents that cheque to Mr. Cheshire? He goes to Mr. Cheshire upon the Tuesday, and, having shown the cheque to Mr. Cheshire, he asks Mr. Cheshire to be so good as to fill up the body of it. I suppose he saw some manifestation of surprise in Mr. Cheshire, and he said, "Cook, poor fellow, is ill, and I am apprehensive if I fill up the body of the cheque Wetherbys will know my handwriting." Why should not they know his handwriting? What objection was there, if the cheque was genuine, and if the transaction was an honest one, to Messrs. Wetherby knowing that the handwriting was his? Does not it pretty plainly indicate that there was some fraud going on which he was afraid might be detected? Why, in heaven's name, should he send for Cheshire? He had to send for Cheshire from the post office when Cheshire was busily engaged in the business of the evening, at seven o'clock in the evening. Just about that same period, a little before or a little after, as the case may be, he had to meet Dr. Bamford and Mr. Jones in consultation as to Cook's case. Mr. Jones was his intimate friend—the trusty friend that came over that afternoon. If poor Cook intended to give him the cheque, and was at the same time so ill that he could not write, why not have said to Mr. Jones,

"Jones, I do not want to bother Cook to fill up this cheque, fill it up in my favour for £350, and we will get Cook to sign it?" Why should he send to the post office to get Cheshire down to his house, alleging at the time that he was apprehensive that if he filled it up his own handwriting might be known. Does not that transaction bear fraud upon the face of it? On the other hand, it may be a genuine cheque; but, I ask again, where is it? Between the time when these matters were called in question and the time when Mr. Palmer was finally arrested, not upon the criminal but upon the civil process, which came down unluckily for him before the coroner's inquest, which secured his bodily presence to answer not only the pecuniary matters but these charges, in the interval he had undisturbed possession of his own papers. From the moment when that freedom of action and possession ceased, we have traced the possession of the papers; and it is clear that at the time those papers were taken possession of that cheque was not amongst them; it is clear that the prisoner, who had possession of it, must have dealt with it in some manner. What has become of it? Why is it not produced? Can you help drawing the inference from its non-production that there is something in the transaction that will not bear the light? It is clear that he intended to get possession of the £350, which ought to have been given to Cook, upon false pretences. He had not a farthing himself, for when he went to Shrewsbury races he borrowed £25. As I have shown, a person made a bet for him upon the races, and, having won £200, pressed him for the debt, but could not get another shilling from him. I show you that he comes back to Rugeley, and is from that moment in the possession of money. Where could he have got that money? It is clear that he must have got it from Cook, who had not any left himself; it is clear that he had all that money to the extent of £350, probably much more, and besides that he gets £1020 as the proceeds of the betting at Tattersall's, and he attempts to get, but does not get, £375, which ought to have been paid into Messrs. Wetherbys' hands. This was the whole of the worldly possessions, the whole sum of the wealth of this poor young man.

But he is not satisfied with that—it is clear that he meditated another fraud of a different description. On the Friday, almost as soon as the breath is out of the man's body, he intimates that he has a claim upon him for £3000 or £4000 in respect of bills which had his (Palmer's) name or acceptance upon them, but which, in fact, had been negotiated for Cook's purposes. He tells the same story to the father-in-law, but it is as clear as the sun at noonday that he endeavoured to fabricate an instrument to give a show of colour to those representations. He goes on the Thursday or the Friday to Mr. Cheshire, and brings to him a document which he asks him to attest, that document bearing the signature "J. P. Cook." The man having left the body, and living only in the spirit eight-and-forty hours before that signature had been brought to be attested, who can fail to see that here was some great fraud and design meditated? What was the document? It was a document which purported to be an acknowledgment from Cook that certain large bills which had been negotiated were for Cook's benefit, and for Cook's benefit alone, and that he (Palmer) had had no part of the proceeds. Now, there are no such bills in existence. We have exhausted the bills pretty well, I think, and none such are proved to exist; but if there be any such bills in existence, who would know it better than the prisoner at the bar? He could have no difficulty in satisfying you of the fact, and of removing this great stumbling-block in the way of his defence; but he produces this document; and on the same day, the day that followed this poor man's death, he writes to Pratt, and says, "Mind, I must have 'Polestar' if it can be arranged." What was this scheme? Having got every shilling of the man's money, his purpose was to secure the little property that remained in "Polestar," the value of which he may perhaps to himself have considerably exaggerated. The mare had just won, and she might be supposed to be worth more than she had been, or he had in view speculating at other races to bring about results of benefit to himself. Further, he may have intended to pay out of Cook's estate some of those bills, under the pretence that Cook had had the money for them. For all these purposes, from the beginning to the end, it was necessary that Cook should be put on one side. Then with this document in his hand he goes to Cheshire, and he asks Cheshire to attest the signature of a man who was then dead. If Cheshire had had the weakness and wickedness to comply he would have had him in his power; and the next thing would have been that he would have brought him trembling and reluctant into the witness-box of some Court of justice to swear to the fact that he had seen the dead man put his signature to that piece of paper. But it may be suggested that, after all, the document was a genuine one, and that the signature was not a forgery. Then produce it and we can judge. Here, again, I point out, and there is no escape from it, that the papers of the prisoner were in his possession till the time of his arrest, and they have been taken care of since then, and are here one and all, either to be answered for or produced in his presence, or they have been handed over to his brother. Who would not fail to notice that this paper has never been found or asked for? Who can doubt that that paper brought to Cheshire remained in the possession of the prisoner? Who can doubt that it is either destroyed or is purposely withheld? Under these circumstances who can doubt that in it is to be found proof of some meditated act—of some vast design of a fraudulent and flagitious character, for the full completion of which the death of Cook was a necessary thing?

Now, gentlemen, I have gone through that part of the case which relates to the motives of the prisoner, and it will be for you to say whether you are satisfied that this was a death by strychnia—that the prisoner was in possession of strychnia—that he had access to the dead man's bedside, and that he administered pills to him at a period short enough to be capable of being connected with the catastrophe that afterwards happened; and it will be for you to say whether you do not find that the state of things with reference to pecuniary matters to which I have been just alluding is sufficient to account for the act which is ascribed to the prisoner.

But there is another part of his conduct as throwing light upon this matter to which I cannot fail to refer. What has become of Cook's betting book? What has been the conduct and the language of the prisoner with reference to it? On the night when Cook died, ere the breath had hardly passed from that poor man's body, the prisoner at the bar was rummaging his pockets and searching under his pillow. That may have been for a perfectly legitimate purpose. But let us see what takes place. He calls to Mr. Jones, and he tells Mr. Jones that it is his duty, as the nearest friend of the dead man, to take possession of his effects, and Mr. Jones does take possession of his watch, and afterwards, at the suggestion of the prisoner, of his rings. At the same time Mr. Jones asks for the betting book. My learned friend endeavoured to explain away this most awkward part of the case by saying, "There were other persons who had access to the place. The undertaker came there with his men, the women came to lay out the dead body, and the servants were there; any one of those might have stolen the book." But all this is met by the fact that, on that same night, before the women had had anything to do in the room—before they came to lay out the corpse—before anybody made their appearance—that very night, when Mr. Jones is seeking to gather up the effects of the dead man, he asks for the book. What is the answer? "Oh," says Palmer, adopting the language which he afterwards repeated, "the betting book will be of no use to any one." Does anybody doubt in his own mind where that betting book had gone to? The father-in-law came down on the Friday, and he begins to discourse about the affair, and he is not satisfied with the answers he gets. The day passes away. He says to Mr. Jones, "Be so good as to collect my son-in-law's betting book and papers and bring them away." Mr. Jones goes upstairs; he is immediately followed by the prisoner—up they go, but there is no betting book to be found. Down comes Mr. Jones, and says to Mr. Stevens, "We cannot find the betting book." "Not find the betting book! surely you must be mistaken"; and, turning round, he says, "Why, Mr. Palmer, how is this?" Upon which Mr. Palmer says, "Oh, the betting book is of no use." "No use! I am the best judge of that. I think it will be of a good deal of use." The observation is again repeated, "It is of no use." Mr. Stevens said, "Why?" "Because a dead man's bets are void, and because he received the money himself upon the course at Shrewsbury." A dead man's bets are void! Yes, that is true; they are void, but not when they have been received in his lifetime. Who received the dead man's bets? The prisoner at the bar. Who appropriated the proceeds of the dead man's bets? The prisoner at the bar. Who was answerable for them? The prisoner at the bar. Who had an interest in concealing the fact that he had received them? He had. What was the best mode of doing it? The destruction of the betting book. What was the best mode of calming the determination of the man who was the executor of the dead man, when he wanted to know what he was entitled to receive and what he had received, and to see the record of his pecuniary transactions? Why, to tell him that the record, even if found, would be of no use, for a dead man was not entitled to any bets, he having died before they were received—yet at that very moment he had received the proceeds of the bets which he was representing as void, and was applying the proceeds to his own purpose. Does not that throw light upon the real nature of the transaction? What possible motive could he have for representing that the bets were void, having himself received them, unless he knew that he had received them fraudulently and wrongfully? See what would have taken place if the truth had come out. Mr. Stevens, if he had seen that book, would have seen that his stepson was entitled to receive £1020. He would have inquired who was his agent, to see whether by any possibility those debts could be realised; he would have learned what everybody knew, at least that portion of the turfites with whom Cook was in the habit of communicating, that Fisher was his agent. Fisher would have told him, "I ought to have received the money to repay myself £200, but Mr. Herring received the money." He would have gone to Mr. Herring, and he would have found that every shilling of the money found its way into the prisoner's pocket, and was appropriated for his own purposes. How was all this to be done? By the removal of Cook, and then by the destruction of the only record which could have afforded to his representative, who was entitled to stand in his place and realise his pecuniary rights, the information of the money having been received by a wrongdoer, by a man who had no right to it. Gentlemen, I submit these things to your consideration, but I submit them to you as leading, unhappily, but to one conclusion, and that the conclusion of the prisoner's guilt.

Attorney-General

But, gentlemen, the matter does not even rest here; there is more of the prisoner's conduct yet to be commented upon, on which I must say a few words before I conclude. Mr. Stevens determined upon having a post-mortem examination. Let us watch the conduct of the prisoner in respect of that most important part of the history of this case. Dr. Harland comes over to perform this most important office; the prisoner is on the watch to see who comes; he meets him as he alights at the inn; he accompanies him to Dr.

Bamford's; they get into conversation about this death, and Dr. Harland says, naturally enough, speaking to a brother medical man who he supposed had been attendant upon the patient, "What is this case? I hear there is a suspicion of poisoning." "Oh, no," says Palmer, "not at all; no suspicion of poisoning; the man had two epileptic fits upon the Monday and Tuesday, and you will find old disease, both of the head and of the heart." Well, there was no disease found of the head or of the heart, unless that very wise gentleman, whom I should have liked to have asked a few questions of to-day, was right about his story of angina pectoris, which I doubt was ever accompanied by tetanic symptoms in this world, or that any other man in the universe would declare that it was. "You will find disease of the head and the heart." They opened him, and found neither. He said, "He had two epileptic fits on the Monday and Tuesday." That very same man the day before had gone to Dr. Bamford, and asked Dr. Bamford to fill up the certificate, and Dr. Bamford said naturally enough, "He is your patient, not mine; I have only attended him at your request." "No, I would rather you did." He gets Dr. Bamford to fill in "apoplexy"; the next day he tells Dr. Harland that it is a case of epilepsy. This is not an ordinary individual, but a medical man, possessing full knowledge and information with regard to medical matters. However, the post-mortem examination took place; before they go to it there is some conversation with Newton which I will not again more particularly refer to; it is not satisfactory, nor does it show the state of mind in which you would expect to find a man whose friend had just died, from the way in which he speaks of the examination about to take place. Let us come to the examination itself. The stomach and its contents are, as we understood, removed; there is some story about his having pushed against the parties who were performing the examination; I think that is carrying the matter too far; it may have been an accident, and we will look at it in that light; at last the stomach, we say without its contents, and a portion of the intestines are put into a jar, and the jar is fastened with a parchment covering doubled over it; it is tied and sealed, and then it is placed upon a table while the post-mortem examination, with reference to other parts of the body, is made. Dr. Harland has this done; when Dr. Harland turns round he finds the jar removed; he immediately makes an outcry, and then at the other end of a long room, and at a door which was not the proper entrance, but a door which led into a different apartment, which apartment led into the passage, the prisoner was found with the jar in his hand, and when Dr. Harland exclaims, he says, "I thought it would have been more convenient to you when you were going out." That might have been his motive, though it was an awkward circumstance that the jar containing the stomach should be in the hands of the man against whom there rested a suspicion of having deprived the deceased of life by unfair means. That is not all; two slits were found in the parchment cover when it was tied and sealed up; who could have made them except the prisoner? What did he do it for? There, again, we are lost in conjecture, but the only conclusion at which we can arrive is against the honesty of the purpose and the integrity of the transaction; whether it may have been for the purpose of introducing something which might be capable of neutralising the poison, I cannot tell you; all I know is the fact, and it is a fact of very significant importance in the consideration of the case.

It does not end there—we find that he is restless and uneasy as to what is going to be done with the jar, and objects to its being taken away; he remonstrates with Dr. Bamford at letting it go away, as if Dr. Bamford had any interest in the matter, and as if any one would suspect Dr. Bamford of having had any hand in the taking off of this poor man. The jar is taken away, and then that occurred which must have made a painful impression upon all who heard it in this Court—then comes the story of his going to the post boy, and asking him to upset the carriage which was conveying those who had possession of the jar to Stafford or London, for the purpose of its contents being analysed. My learned friend sought to give a comparatively innocent complexion to this transaction; he says that this bribe of £10 to upset the carriage arose simply out of resentment against the officious stepfather who had dared to interfere in this matter—to insist upon a searching investigation—he had been guilty, my learned friend says, in return for the civility, courtesy, and kindness with which he had been treated by the prisoner, of "prying, meddling, insolent curiosity." A man who had seen his poor stepson, to whom he was tenderly attached, lying dead under circumstances which raised in his mind a suspicion—and I think I am fully justified, at all events, whatever may be the result of this inquiry, in saying that the very inquiry we are now upon—the gravity and importance of it— at least fully justify Mr. Stevens in the suspicions which he entertained for having insisted upon the inquiry, and that ought to have protected him against the suggestion of "insolent curiosity." It was known that Mr. Stevens insisted upon inquiry—was it a reasonable motive operating upon this man's mind that it should occasion such a sense of resentment and anger that he should desire the destruction or mutilation of this man, and offer £10 to the post boy to upset him upon the road? I believe the other to have been the true version—if you upset him you may break the jar, and then the contents never could be found, and there would be no danger of strychnia being discovered.

Attorney-General

But it does not stop even there; the inquiry takes place, and the post-mortem examination having been made, a coroner's inquest is insisted upon and becomes inevitable, and then we have the prisoner seeking to tamper with the administration of a most important office; sending presents to the coroner at the time the inquest was sitting; presents, unquestionably, of game and things of that description, and if the evidence does not very much mislead us a present of money also. For what purpose was all that done? We find him, with uneasy restlessness, obtaining through Cheshire information of what is taking place between the professional man who was employed to analyse the contents of the stomach and the attorney at Rugeley who was instructed on behalf of Mr. Stevens; is that the conduct of innocence or of guilt? Why should he be desirous of knowing whether strychnia, above all other things, should be found in the intestines of the deceased? Let me call your attention to the letter which he writes to the coroner—"I am sorry to tell you that I am still confined to my bed; I do not think it was mentioned at the inquest yesterday that Cook was taken ill on Sunday and on Monday night in the same way that he was on Tuesday night when he died; the chambermaid at the Crown Hotel can prove this; I believe a man of the name of Fisher is coming down to prove that he received some money at Shrewsbury; now, here he can only pay Smith £10 out of £41 he owed him. "Does he tell what had become of the rest of the money that the man had at Shrewsbury? "Had you not better call Smith," that is, Mr. Jeremiah Smith whom we saw here to-day, "to prove this?" What a witness Jeremiah Smith would have been in the hands of the coroner, Mr. Ward, the friendly coroner of Staffordshire! And, again, "Whatever Professor Taylor may say to-morrow, he wrote from London last Tuesday night to Gardner to say, we (that is, Dr. Taylor and Dr. Rees) have this day finished our analysis, and find no traces of either strychnia, prussic acid, or opium; what can beat this from a man like Taylor, if he says what he has already said of Dr. Harland's evidence? Mind you, I know it, I saw in black and white what Taylor said to Gardner; but this is strictly private and confidential, but it is true. As regards his betting book, I know nothing of it, and it is of no good to any one"; the repetition of the same story. "I hope the verdict to-morrow will be that he died of natural causes, and thus end it"; but the verdict was not so, and it did not end it; and it is for you to say whether upon a review of the whole of this evidence you can come to any other conclusion than that of the prisoner's guilt. Look at his restless anxiety; it may possibly, it is true, be compatible with innocence, but I think on the other hand it must be admitted that it bears strongly the aspect of guilt; if it stood alone, I would not ask you upon that to come to a conclusion adverse to the prisoner, but it is one of a series of things, small perhaps, each individually in themselves, but, taken as a whole, as I submit to you, leading irresistibly to the conclusion of the guilt of this man.

Attorney-General

Now, gentlemen, the whole case is before you. It will be for you to determine it. You have, on the one hand, a man overwhelmed by a pressure almost unparalleled and unexampled of pecuniary liabilities which he is utterly unable to meet involving the penalties of the law, which must bring disaster and ruin upon him. His only mode of averting those consequences is by obtaining money; and, under those circumstances, with a bad man, a small amount, if that amount will meet the exigencies of the moment and avert the impending catastrophe and ruin, will operate with immense power. Then you find that he has access to the bedside of the man whose death we are now inquiring into; that he has the means of administering poison to him, and you find that, within eight-and-forty hours, he has twice acquired possession of the very poison, the traces of which are found in the death, and after the death; and then you have the death itself in its terrible and revolting circumstances, all of which are characteristic only of death by that poison and of no other. You have then the fact that, to the uttermost of his ability, he realises the purpose for which it is suggested to you the death was accomplished. You have all those facts, and the undoubted and undisputed fact, that a subsidiary poison was also used, of which traces have been found in the man's body, although no traces may have been found, for the reasons and from the causes I have suggested, of the principal poison, whose possession by the prisoner we have traced, and whose presence we show in the symptoms which accompanied the death of the deceased. It is for you to take all those circumstances into your consideration.

Gentlemen, you have, indeed, had introduced into this case one other element which I own I think would have been better omitted. You have had from my learned friend the unusual, and I think I may say unprecedented, assurance of his conviction of his client's innocence.

Mr. SERJEANT SHEE—Not unprecedented.

The ATTORNEY-GENERAL—I can only say I think it would have been better if my learned friend had abstained from so strange a declaration. What would he think of me if, imitating his example, I at this moment stated to you, upon my "honour," as he did, what is my internal conviction from a conscientious consideration of this case. The best reproof which I can administer to my learned friend is to abstain from imitating so dangerous an example. My learned friend in that address, of which we all admired the power and ability, also adopted a course sometimes resorted to by advocates, but which I cannot help thinking is more or less an insult to a jury, the endeavouring to intimidate them by the fear of their own consciences and the fear of the country's opinion from discharging firmly and honestly the great and solemn duty which you have to perform upon this occasion. My learned friend told you if your verdict should be "Guilty," one day or other the innocence of the prisoner would be made manifest, and you would never cease to repent the verdict you had given. If my learned friend was sincere in that—and I know he was—there is no man in whom the spirit of truth and honour is more keenly alive—he said what he believed; but all I can say in answer is, that it shows how when a man enters with a bias upon his mind upon the consideration of a subject he is led into error; and when my learned friend said that he had entered upon this case with an unbiassed and an unprejudiced mind, who could have failed to feel that never in anything could he have been more deceived than in thinking that? For who that has to give his best energies to a defence upon such a charge as this would not shrink in his own mind from the conclusion that he was to advocate the cause of one whom he believed to have been guilty of the foulest of all imaginable crimes? I say, therefore, I think my learned friend had better have abstained from making any observations which involved the assurance of his own conviction. I say, further, I think he ought, in justice and in consideration for you, to have abstained from reminding you or telling you that the voice of the country would not sanction the verdict which you were about to give. I say nothing of the inconsistency which is involved in such a statement, coming from one who but a short hour before had complained in eloquent terms of the universal torrent of passion and prejudice by which he said his client was oppressed and borne down. Why, gentlemen, in answer to my learned friend, I have only to say, pay no regard to the voice of the country, whether it be for condemnation or acquittal; pay no regard to anything but the internal voice of your own consciences, and the sense of that duty to God and man which you are to discharge upon this occasion. Seek no reward, except the comforting assurance when you shall look back to the events of this day, that you have discharged to the best of your ability and to the uttermost of your power the duty that it was yours to perform. If, upon a review of this whole case, comparing the evidence upon the one side and upon the other, and weighing it in the even scales of justice, you can come to a conclusion of the prisoner's innocence, or even entertain that fair and reasonable amount of doubt of which the accused is entitled to the benefit, in God's name acquit him. But if, on the other hand, all the facts and all the evidence lead your minds, with satisfaction to yourselves, to the conclusion of the prisoner's guilt, then, but then only, I ask for a verdict of guilty at your hands. For the protection of the good, and for the repression of the wicked, I ask for that verdict, by which alone, as it seems to me, the safety of society can be secured, and the demands, the imperious demands, of public justice can alone be satisfied.

The Court then adjourned.

Eleventh Day, Monday, 26th May, 1856.

The Court met at ten o'clock.

Charge to the Jury.

Lord Campbell

LORD CAMPBELL—Gentlemen of the jury, we have at length arrived at that stage of these solemn proceedings when it becomes my duty, as the chief judge presiding in this Court, to explain to you the nature of the charge brought against the prisoner, and those questions and considerations upon which your verdict ought to be found. And, gentlemen, I must begin by conjuring you to banish from your minds all that you have heard with reference to these proceedings before entering into that box. There is no doubt that a strong prejudice elsewhere did prevail against the prisoner at the bar, in the county of Stafford, where the offence for which he has now to answer is alleged to have been committed; that prejudice was so strong that the Court of Queen's Bench made an order to remove the trial from that county. The prisoner, by his counsel, expressed a wish that the trial should take place in the Central Criminal Court. To enable that wish to be accomplished an Act has been passed by the Legislature authorising the Court of Queen's Bench to direct the trial to take place in the Central Criminal Court, where it was believed and known that the trial would be fair and impartial. I must not only warn you, gentlemen, against being influenced by what you may have before heard, but I must likewise warn you—although I am sure it is an unnecessary caution, but one which it is my duty to offer—against being improperly influenced by the evidence that has been laid before you; because there has been evidence which certainly implicates the prisoner in transactions of a very discreditable nature. It appears that he had forged a great many bills of exchange, and that he had entered into transactions not of a reputable nature. These transactions, however, would have been excluded from your consideration altogether had it not been necessary to bring them forward to assist you in arriving at your verdict. By the law and practice of some countries it is allowed to raise a probability that the party accused has committed the offence which he has to answer, to show that he has committed other offences, with a view of showing that he is an immoral man, and not unlikely to commit other offences, whether of the same or of a different nature; but the law of England is different, and, presuming every man to be innocent until his guilt is established, it allows his guilt to be established only by evidence directly connected with the charge brought against him.

Lord Chief-Justice Campbell.

Gentlemen, it gives me great satisfaction to find that this case has been so fully laid before you. Everything has been done that could be accomplished for the purpose of assisting the jury in coming to a right conclusion. The prosecution has been taken up by the Government of the country, so that justice may be effectively administered. The Attorney-General, who is the first law officer of the Crown, has conducted the prosecution as the Minister of Public Justice. Again, I am much pleased to think that the prisoner appears to have had ample means to prepare for and conduct his defence. Witnesses very properly have been brought from all parts of the kingdom to assist in his defence; and he has had the advantage of having his case conducted by one of the most distinguished advocates at the English bar. Gentlemen, I most strongly recommend to you to attend to everything that fell so eloquently, so ably, and so impressively from that advocate, with the exception of his own private personal opinion. It is my duty to tell you that that ought to be no ingredient in your verdict. You are to try the prisoner upon the evidence before you, according as that evidence may be laid before you upon the one side and on the other, and by that alone, and not by any opinion of his advocate. I feel also bound to say that it would have been better if his advocate had abstained from some of the observations which he made in his address to you, in which he laid great stress upon his own conviction of the prisoner's innocence of the crime imputed to him and of his apprehension that if you returned a verdict of guilty you one day would have to regret your verdict. The fact of the prisoner saying "Not guilty" is a mere form; it goes for nothing, and it may lead to the most disastrous consequences if that formal answer is to be dwelt upon with too much importance, as it may lead a jury to believe that a prisoner is not guilty because his advocate expresses his perfect conviction of his innocence. And, upon the other hand, if the advocate withholds an opinion, the jury may suppose that he is conscious of his client's guilt, whereas it is the duty of the advocate to press his argument upon the jury, and not his opinion.

Lord Campbell

Gentlemen, I will now in a few words give you the allegations upon the one side and on the other. On the part of the prosecution it is alleged that the deceased, John Parsons Cook, was first tampered with by antimony, that he was then killed by strychnia, and that his symptoms were the symptoms of poison by strychnia. It is then alleged that the prisoner at the bar had a motive for making away with him; that he had an opportunity of administering the poison; that suspicion fell upon no one else; and that on two days, when the poison was supposed to have been administered, he actually purchased strychnia, the poison employed; and that, as they allege, his conduct before that transaction, before the deed, while it was going on, and afterwards, was that of a guilty, and not of an innocent, man. On the other side it is contended (and you are to say whether or not truly contended) that the prisoner at the bar was really the victim of prejudice; that he had no interest in the death of the deceased; and, on the contrary, that the death of the deceased was to his prejudice; further, that Cook did not die from poison by strychnia, but from natural disease; that his symptoms were those of natural disease, and not of poison by strychnia; and, further, it is contended that no part of the evidence which has been given shows anything which is at all consistent with the guilt of the prisoner. Gentlemen, it is for you to determine between the allegations on the one side and the other according to the evidence. A most anxious task is imposed upon you, knowing that the life of the prisoner is at stake; and, if you find him guilty, he must expiate his crime by an ignominious death. It is of the last importance that you should be convinced of his innocence or his guilt; and, if you are not convinced of his guilt, you will rescue him from the fate with which he is threatened. On the other hand, when you have heard the statements which were given in evidence—if you are satisfied of his guilt—it will be your duty to return a verdict of guilty; for if the poisoner were to escape with impunity, there would be no safety for mankind, and society would fall to pieces. Gentlemen, the burthen of proving the guilt rests on the prosecution; and unless that is fully sustained, and you are not convinced upon the evidence that he is guilty, then it will be your duty to acquit the prisoner; but in a case of this kind you cannot expect that witnesses should be called to state that they saw the deadly poison administered by the prisoner or mixed up by the prisoner openly before them. Circumstantial evidence as to that is all that can be reasonably expected; and if there are a series of circumstances leading to the conclusion of guilt, then, gentlemen, a verdict of guilty may satisfactorily be pronounced. With respect to the alleged motive, it is of great importance to see whether there was a motive for committing such a crime, or whether there was not, or whether there is an improbability of its having been committed so strong as not to be overpowered by positive evidence. But, gentlemen, if there be any motive which can be assigned, I am bound to tell you that the adequacy of that motive is of little importance. We know from the experience of criminal Courts that atrocious crimes of this sort have been committed from very slight motives, not merely from malice and revenge, but to gain a small pecuniary advantage and to drive off for a time pressing difficulties. It seems to me, gentlemen, you will have to consider well whether the symptoms of Cook's death are consistent with a poisoning by strychnia. If they are not, if you believe that death arose from natural causes, the prisoner is at once entitled to a verdict of not guilty at your hands; but if those symptoms are consistent with a poisoning by strychnia, then you will have another and an important question to consider, whether the evidence which has been adduced is sufficient to convince you that it was a death by strychnia, and by strychnia which the prisoner administered. In cases of the sort the evidence has often been divided into medical and moral evidence, the medical being that of the scientific men, and the moral the circumstantial facts which are calculated to prove the truth of the charge against the party accused. Gentlemen, they cannot be finally separated in the minds of the jury, because it is by combination of the two species of evidence that their verdict ought to be found. In this case you will look at the medical evidence to see whether the deceased, in your opinion, did die by strychnia or by natural disease; and you will look at what is called the moral evidence, and consider whether that shows that the prisoner not only had the opportunity, but that he actually availed himself of that opportunity, to administer to the deceased the deadly poison of which he died.

Now, gentlemen, with these preliminary observations I will proceed to read over to you the evidence which has been given in this long trial; and I must implore you earnestly that, in any observations I may make upon its effect, you will be guided only by your own judgment. To assist you from time to time I may make observations, but you will not be in the slightest degree influenced by them unless so far as your own judgment concurs in them. The verdict must be yours, and in your hands the life of the prisoner must rest.

[His lordship then began with and took the jury through the story of Palmer's financial transactions; next the evidence of Cook's illness at Shrewsbury; and then that of Elizabeth Mills and Lavinia Barnes, and of Mr. Jones as to the illness at Rugeley; and passed to the evidence of Newton.]

Now, gentlemen, comes a witness of the greatest importance, Charles Newton. (His lordship read a portion of Mr. Newton's evidence.) I may notice to you that Roberts swears, and is, I think, not contradicted, that he had sold strychnia, among other drugs, to Palmer; and you are called upon to observe the demeanour of Palmer at that time, and the way in which he tried to prevent Newton from observing that he had been obtaining this drug at the shop of Mr. Hawkins. (His lordship then read a further portion of the evidence of Mr. Newton.) Then the deposition of Newton was read, and it had better be read again. (The deposition of Mr. Newton, taken before the coroner, was then read, and his lordship concluded reading the evidence of the witness.) Now, gentlemen, this is the evidence of Newton, and most important it is for your consideration. It certainly must be recollected that he did not mention the furnishing of the strychnia to Palmer on Monday before the coroner, and that he did not mention it till the Tuesday morning, when he was coming up here. That certainly requires consideration at your hands; but then, gentlemen, you will observe that in his deposition, which has been read before you, although there is an omission, which is always to be borne in mind, there is no contradiction of anything that he has said. Well, then, you are to consider what is the probability of his inventing this wicked and most abominable lie. He had no ill-will towards the prisoner at the bar; he had nothing to gain by injuring him, much less by saying anything to affect his life. I see no motive that Mr. Newton could have for inventing a lie to take away the life of another person. No inducement could be held out to him from the Crown; he says himself that no inducement was held out to him, and that he at last disclosed it from a sense of justice. If you believe him, certainly the evidence is very strong against the prisoner at the bar. Now I will take you to the evidence of the next witness, whose evidence is closely connected with the witness Newton—who did furnish strychnia to the prisoner—I mean Joseph Roberts. (The learned judge read the examination-in-chief of Mr. Roberts.)

Now comes the cross-examination, which consists in this, and this only, "I did not make an entry of any of those things in our books; if articles are sold over the counter and paid for at the time, we do not enter them in our books." Now, gentlemen, this is the evidence of Mr. Roberts, which is most important, for he is not cross-examined as to the veracity of his testimony, nor is it contradicted at all. It is not denied that on this Tuesday morning the prisoner at the bar got 6 grains of strychnia from Mr. Roberts. If you couple that with the evidence of Mr. Newton, believing that, then you will have positive evidence of strychnia being procured by the prisoner at the bar; that the symptoms of strychnia were exhibited in Mr. Cook, the deceased; and you have the evidence of Mr. Roberts, undenied and unquestioned, that on the Tuesday the 6 grains of strychnia were supplied. Now, gentlemen, if you believe both, a very serious case is adduced, supposing you should come to the conclusion that the symptoms of Mr. Cook were consistent with that poison. If you think the symptoms are accounted for by merely ordinary tetanus, of course the fact of strychnia being obtained by the prisoner at the bar is entitled to very little weight; but if you should come to the conclusion that the symptoms which Mr. Cook exhibited on the Monday night and Tuesday night are consistent with strychnia, then a fearful case is made out against him. Gentlemen, I have listened with the most anxious attention to know what explanation would be given respecting the strychnia that was purchased on the Tuesday morning. The learned counsel for the prisoner told us that we must believe nothing, that he would combat and disprove everything, and no doubt, according to his instructions, he very properly denied that Mr. Newton was to be believed; and, disbelieving Mr. Newton, you have no evidence of any strychnia being obtained on the Monday evening; but, disbelieving Mr. Newton and believing Mr. Roberts, you have evidence of 6 grains of strychnia having been obtained on the Tuesday morning, and no explanation is given of it. The learned counsel did not favour us with the theory which he had formed in his own mind respecting that strychnia, and how he considered it to be consistent with the view that he suggested. There is no evidence of the intention with which it was purchased; there is no evidence how it was applied, what became of it, or what was done with it.

Then I say, gentlemen, that it will not at all influence your verdict unless you come to the conclusion that the symptoms of Mr. Cook were consistent with a death by strychnia; but if you come to that conclusion I should shrink from my duty, and I should be unworthy to sit here, if I did not draw to your consideration the importance of the testimony and the inference it may afford of the death having been occasioned by strychnia, and that that was administered by the prisoner.

[The evidence as to the post-mortem was then read, and that of the postboy, of Cheshire, the postmaster, and several others, without comment of material importance. Passing to the scientific witnesses, his lordship said—"Now, gentlemen, you are called upon to form your opinion as to the opinion of scientific men respecting the appearance of the symptoms that Cook exhibited, and how far they can be accounted for by natural disease, and how far also, upon the evidence, they are consistent with strychnia. Whether they agree with traumatic or idiopathic tetanus, whatever it may be, or whether the symptoms correspond with a natural disease, and do not correspond with strychnia, is a matter that is of very great importance for you to consider." Until his lordship reached Dr. Taylor the scientific evidence was read to the jury with no material comments.]

Lord Campbell

The next witness is Dr. Taylor. Now, gentlemen, here is something most important for your consideration. You see it is very properly relied on, on the part of the prisoner, that, though strychnia may be found in the body by analysis, none was found upon the analysis which was made by Dr. Taylor and Dr. Rees, for they, and they alone, experimented upon it, and they could find none. We know that experiments were made by those two individuals, and they say that, so far as their skill goes, there may be death by strychnia and yet that strychnia cannot be detected. But Dr. Taylor and Dr. Rees state experiments that they made where the death had been by strychnia which they themselves administered; and in at least two of those cases where there had been death by strychnia they could discover none. Now, it is possible that other chemists and other medical men might have discovered strychnia in those animals, and might have discovered strychnia in the body or in the jar which contained the stomach of Cook, but they found none in their analysis. They found none also in at least two cases where they killed animals by strychnia, and afterwards did all their skill enabled them to do for the purpose of discovering the strychnia. I thought at one time that these examinations were made with a view to show that, if the pills prepared by Mr. Bamford had been taken as he prepared them, mercury ought to have been found in the body of Mr. Cook; but I think that was not pressed, and I should think that it ought not to have any influence upon your verdict— there was no mercury found. There was mercury in the pills which Mr. Bamford prepared, and which Cook ought to have taken, but the simple fact of no mercury being found in those parts of Cook's body that were examined ought not to have any influence upon your verdict; but that, of course, you will judge of for yourselves. Then the learned counsel, in cross-examination, read a passage from Orfila about a dog who had taken antimony, and some few minutes afterwards antimony was found in the bones, in the fat, and in the liver. (His lordship read the letter written by Dr. Taylor to Mr. Gardener.) You will bear in mind, gentlemen, that was written before the symptoms were known to Dr. Taylor and Dr. Rees, but they had been informed that prussic acid and strychnia and opium had been bought by Palmer on the Tuesday. They search for all these poisons and they find none; but they swear distinctly that they found antimony in the body, and therefore, in the absence of the symptoms, they do not impute the death to strychnia, but they say it may possibly have been produced by antimony, because the quantity they discovered in the body was no test of the quantity that had been administered to the deceased. Then a letter was read which Dr. Taylor wrote to the *Lancet*, and I must say that he would have done better to have abstained from taking any notice whatsoever of what was said about him, but you will say whether what he did write materially detracts from the credit which would otherwise be due to him. I think the passage in this letter in the *Lancet*, which was relied on, is the last passage which I will read to you. He explains what his evidence had been, and complains of the reports that had been spread abroad respecting him, and then he concludes his letter thus—"In concluding this letter I would observe that during a quarter of a century which I have now specially devoted to toxicological inquiries, I have never met with any cases like those suspected of poisoning at Rugeley. The mode in which they will affect the person accused is of minor importance compared with their probable influence on society. I have no hesitation in saying that the future security of life in this country will mainly depend on the judge, the jury, and the counsel who may have to dispose of the charges of murder which have arisen out of these investigations." I again say that I think it would have been better if he had trusted to the credit which he had already acquired, instead of writing a letter to the *Lancet*; but it is for you to say that he, having been, as he says, misrepresented, and writing this letter to set himself right, whether that materially detracts from the credit which is due to him.

Then Dr. Rees follows, and he corroborates the evidence given by Dr. Taylor. Here, therefore, is Dr. Rees, whom no one can suppose to have an interest in the matter. I do not know what interest it can be supposed that Dr. Taylor had in the matter, for he was regularly employed in his profession; he knew nothing about Mr. Palmer until he was called on by Mr. Stevens to analyse the contents of the jar; he had no animosity against him, and no interest whatever in misrepresenting the matter.

Mr. SERJEANT SHEE—He said that the experiments with the two rabbits were made after the inquest.

Lord Campbell

LORD CAMPBELL—Certainly; it cannot matter whether they were made before or after if they are witnesses of truth. It is the case that there was the death of the animals by strychnia, and that after death no strychnia could be found in the animals; and, if the experiments had been made this morning, the effect would have been the same. Dr. Taylor has been questioned about the indiscreet letter which he wrote to the *Lancet* and some indiscreet conversation which he had with the editor of the *Illustrated Times*; but with regard to Dr. Rees that imputation does not exist, and he concurs with Dr. Taylor in the evidence that the rabbits were killed by strychnia, and that, although they did everything in their power, according to their skill and knowledge, to discover the strychnia, as they did with regard to the contents of the jar, yet no strychnia could be found. You will judge from the vomiting that took place at Shrewsbury, and afterwards at Stafford, whether antimony may have been administered to Cook at Shrewsbury or Stafford. Antimony may not produce death; but it is part of the transaction, and deserves your deliberate consideration.

The Court then adjourned.

Twelfth Day, Tuesday, 27th May, 1856.

The Court met at ten o'clock.

Lord Campbell

LORD CAMPBELL—Gentlemen of the jury, at the adjournment of the Court yesterday evening I had finished the task of laying before you all the evidence on the part of the prosecution; and certainly that case, if not answered, does present for your consideration a serious case against the prisoner at the bar. It appears that in the middle of November he was involved in pecuniary difficulties of the most formidable nature; he had engagements to perform that he was unable to perform without some most extraordinary expedients; he had to make payments for which he was unprepared; there were actions brought against both himself and his mother upon the forged acceptances; he had no credit in any quarter upon which money could be raised. It so happened that at that time Cook, the deceased, by the winning of the race on the 13th November, became the master of at least £1000, and there is evidence from which an inference may be drawn that the prisoner formed the design of appropriating that money to his own use, and that he is prepared to do whatever was necessary to accomplish that object. There is some evidence that he did appropriate that money to the payment of debts for which he alone was liable. There is evidence from which it may be inferred that he drew a cheque in the name of Cook, which was a forgery, upon which to obtain payment of part of the money which was due to Cook; and there is further evidence that he employed Herring to collect money on the Monday and to appropriate it to his own use. What effect would have been produced by the survival of Cook, under such circumstances, you are to consider. However, it appears that from Cook's death he contemplated the advantage of obtaining possession of the horse "Polestar," which had belonged to Cook; and you have evidence of his having fabricated a document which was to declare that certain bills of exchange with which it appears that Cook had no concern were negotiated for Cook's advantage, and that the prisoner at the bar had derived no benefit from them. Gentlemen, that was brought forward after Cook's death, and if Cook had survived that fraud must have been exposed, and might have been punished. Then, gentlemen, with respect to the joint liability of Cook and Palmer, which, it is said, would now be thrown entirely upon Palmer, that was rather a distant object; and if Palmer had got possession of all Cook's property by the means that he resorted to, he would not have been a sufferer by his death. Then, gentlemen, as to the important question whether Cook must be supposed to have died by natural disease or by poison. You have the evidence of Sir Benjamin Brodie and other most skilful and honourable men, who say that, in their opinion, he did not die from natural disease; they know no natural disease in the whole catalogue of diseases which attack the human frame that will account for those symptoms. Further, gentlemen, the witnesses go on to say that they believe that the symptoms that were exhibited by Cook were the symptoms of strychnia, that they were what would be expected from strychnia, and that, comparing those symptoms with natural tetanus, they do not correspond with it, but they do correspond with the symptoms brought on by a man being poisoned by the administration of strychnia. Then, gentlemen, with respect to the consideration that no strychnia was found in the body, that is for you to consider, and no doubt you will pay great attention to it; but there is no point of law according to which the poison must be found in the body of the deceased; and all that we know respecting the poison not being in the body of Cook is that in that part of the body that was analysed by Drs. Taylor and Rees they found no strychnia. But witnesses of great reputation have said, Dr. Christison among the number, that, under certain circumstances, where there has been poison by strychnia, they would not expect the strychnia should be detected; and you have the evidence of Dr. Taylor and Dr. Rees, who made the examination, that they having experimented upon animals killed by strychnia which they themselves administered, and by resorting to the same means that they had employed in examining the body of Cook, no strychnia could be found.

Then, gentlemen, with regard to the length of time that occurred between the alleged administration of the strychnia and the time that the symptoms appeared, the evidence seems to me to lead to this conclusion, that, where it is administered to animals with a view of making experiments and with a view of observing its operations as quickly as possible, it generally operates more rapidly than in the human frame when it is put in the shape of pills, and that will depend upon the manner in which those pills are compounded, and likewise on the state of the health and body of the person to whom they are to be administered, and whether there may or may not have been any previous tampering with the health of that person. Instances are referred to where, even in the human body, a greater space of time has elapsed than in this case between the administration of the poison and the symptoms which were exhibited.

Mr. SERJEANT SHEE—I think that is not so upon the evidence, my lord.

Lord Campbell

LORD CAMPBELL—There are instances referred to in which it has been detected; there have been instances referred to in the course of this trial in which there has been as long an interval.

Mr. SERJEANT SHEE—I believe that is a mistake.

LORD CAMPBELL—With regard to there being no blood in the heart, which seems to have been relied upon, it appears that the result is this, that if the death is produced by an obstruction of the respiratory organs, producing asphyxia, the blood is found in the heart; but if it be produced by a spasm upon the heart itself, the heart contracts, the blood is expelled, and no blood is found after death. Now, taking the evidence before us, there are two instances where that took place.

Then, gentlemen, we have to look to the evidence as it implicates the prisoner at the bar. You must consider the evidence to show that he must have tampered with the health of the deceased, by administering something to him in the brandy and water, in the broth, and in the other things which were administered to him at Rugeley. One part of the broth was taken by Elizabeth Mills, as she swears, and the consequence which followed, according to her evidence and the evidence of Lavinia Barnes, was that she was taken ill with a vomiting in the stomach as Cook the deceased had been.

Then, gentlemen, you have antimony found in the body of the deceased; antimony, which would show that tartar emetic, producing vomiting, had been administered, and it seems to be clearly proved that that substance was found in his body, from what source you are to say from the evidence before you.

Lord Campbell

Then, gentlemen, comes the more direct evidence that the prisoner at the bar, if you believe the witnesses, procured this very poison on the Monday and on the Tuesday—3 grains, I think, on the Monday, and 6 on the Tuesday. For what purpose was that obtained? The evidence of the witness who swears to the poison being obtained on the Monday is impeached, but no impeachment rests upon the evidence of the witness who swears to the poison being sold by him on the Tuesday to the prisoner at the bar. You have no account of that poison; what was the intention with which it was purchased, and what was the application of it, you are to infer. Then, gentlemen, it is impossible that you should not pay attention to the conduct of the prisoner at the bar, and there are some instances of his conduct which you will say whether they belong to what might be expected from an innocent or a guilty man. He was eager to have the body fastened down in the coffin. Then, with regard to the betting book, there is certainly evidence from which you may infer that he did get possession of the betting book, that he abstracted it and concealed it. Then, gentlemen, you must not omit his conduct in trying to bribe the postboy to overturn the carriage in which the jar was being conveyed, to be analysed in London, and from which evidence might be obtained of his guilt. Again, you find him tampering with the postmaster, and procuring from the postmaster the opening of a letter from Dr. Taylor, who had been examining the contents of the jar, to Mr. Gardner, the attorney employed upon the part of Mr. Stevens. And then, gentlemen, you have tampering with the coroner, and trying to induce him to procure a verdict from the coroner's jury which would amount to an acquittal. These are serious matters for your consideration, but you, and you alone, will say what inference is to be drawn from them. If not answered, they certainly present a serious case for your consideration. It is for you to say whether the answer is satisfactory. Either you may be of opinion that the case on the part of the prosecution is insufficient, or you may be of opinion that the answer to it is satisfactory.

Then, gentlemen, that answer consists of two parts—first, of the medical evidence, and, secondly, of the evidence of facts. With regard to the medical evidence, I must say that there were examined on the part of the prisoner a number of gentlemen of high honour and solid integrity and proved scientific knowledge, who came here only to speak the truth and assist in the administration of justice. You may be of opinion that others came whose object was to procure an acquittal of the prisoner. Gentlemen, it is material, in the due administration of justice, that a witness should not be turned into an advocate, any more than an advocate should be turned into a witness. It is for you to say whether some of those who were called on the part of the prisoner did not belong to the category which I described as witnesses becoming advocates.

Gentlemen, the first witness on the part of the prisoner was Mr. Thomas Nunneley. (The learned judge read the evidence of Mr. Nunneley and the documents therein referred to.) You will recollect what he says, and you will form your opinion as to the weight that is to be given to it. He certainly seemed to me to give his evidence in a manner not quite becoming a witness in a Court of justice, but you will give all attention to the facts to which he refers in the evidence he gave. He differs very materially in his general opinion from several of the witnesses who were examined on the part of the prosecution. He speaks of there being an extraordinary rigidity of the body after death, when there has been a death of this description, with other symptoms, and he attaches considerable importance to the heart being empty, but you will say what weight ought to be attached to his opinion.

Lord Campbell

Mr. William Herapath is then called. (The examination-in-chief of Mr. Herapath was read.) He seems to differ from Mr. Nunneley with respect to the rigidity produced by this poison. Now, gentlemen, Mr. Herapath is a very skilful chemist, and I have no doubt he spoke sincerely what he thought, and what was his opinion? That when there has been death by strychnia, strychnia ought to be discovered; but it seems he intimated an opinion on this very case of Cook that there might have been strychnia, and that Dr. Taylor did not use the proper means to detect it. Now, the only evidence that we have in this case that there was not strychnia is the analysis by Dr. Taylor and Dr. Rees that they did not discover it. As I before pointed out to you, in two other cases in which there certainly had been poisoning by strychnia the result was the same—they could not discover it.

Then the next witness is Mr. Rogers. Now, this is a gentleman whom there seems no reason to doubt; there seems no reason to doubt the facts that he stated, and that he does sincerely entertain the opinion that he expresses; and, according to his evidence, where there has been strychnia mixed with impure matter, it may be expected that it would be detected by skilful experimentalists, and by using the proper tests. Then Dr. Letheby is called; he is the medical officer of health to the city of London and of the London Hospital. I doubt not that Dr. Letheby speaks sincerely, and according to his experience and opinion, but he does say truly that cases vary very much, and that there may be cases which he calls "exceptional," alluding to the case of the lady at Romsey; and it may probably be the fair result that enough of this disease is not known to be aware of all its varieties, and that any peculiarity that may arise where there is strong probability of strychnia having been administered would not be anything like conclusive evidence to rebut that result.

Then Mr. Robert Gray is examined. Now, gentlemen, here you have a case of what is called idiopathic tetanus; but you are to say whether from this you can infer that the illness of Mr. Cook was idiopathic tetanus. The great weight of evidence seems to me to show that it was not idiopathic any more than traumatic tetanus; but that whatever form of disease it might be, it would not be idiopathic tetanus; and you will find that the symptoms vary most materially in their appearance from the case that is here detailed in the duration as well as the rest of the course of events.

The next witness that was called was Mr. Brown Ross. Now, gentlemen, I do not know for what purpose the case alluded to by Mr. Ross was brought before you, unless to lead to an inference that Mr. Cook's was a case of tetanus of the same sort with this which is here described, because this was tetanus; and I suppose it was intended that you are to infer that Mr. Cook's was of the same description; but whether you call it idiopathic or traumatic, it was a case of tetanus—was directly to be ascribed to wounds which were upon his body, and which are here described. No such wounds were upon the body of Mr. Cook; and other witnesses who were examined on the part of the defence say that this was not a case of tetanus at all; but then, even in this case that has been described, you see there were the symptoms so nearly approaching those of strychnia that strychnia was suspected, but there was no ground for it; and in the case described there was no ground for supposing strychnia could by possibility be the cause of death.

The next witness is a witness worthy of all praise for the sincerity which he exhibited. I mean Dr. Wrightson. Now, gentlemen, this witness, who, I have no doubt, is a most scientific and a very honourable man, speaks as a man of science, and, according to him, the poison would be found in the body; but he speaks with proper caution, and upon his evidence you ought to say whether, under particular circumstances, it might not be discoverable, or whether the person seeking for it might fail to employ the proper means for detecting it in the body.

Then comes Mr. Partridge, a most respectable gentleman, who says he has been many years in practice as a surgeon, and is professor of anatomy at King's College. Now, gentlemen, you have here the opinion of a very respectable witness as to the different topics that he touches upon; and the most important one is that he thinks that the symptoms that were exhibited did not correspond with what he should expect from strychnia; but he speaks from his own experience, and you have it from the other witnesses that the symptoms vary considerably in different cases.

The next witness is Mr. John Gay. Now, gentlemen, this was a case, you see, of tetanus arising from the toe being smashed; and it seems to me, although, of course, you will form your own opinion upon it, bears no analogy whatever to the case of Cook, with regard to whom no such cause could be assigned. Again, gentlemen, he says, what is very material, that, in the event of a given state of tetanus, it would be extremely difficult, if not impossible, without collateral evidence, to ascribe the tetanic disease to any cause in the absence of any evidence as to the cause. But you will form your own opinion upon it. Therefore you are to look to collateral evidence; and if the collateral evidence would impute the symptoms of tetanic convulsions to any particular cause, according to this witness that cause may be assigned. That I say with a view to get what is called the moral evidence with regard to the conduct of a particular person, and with regard to what he may have done or what he may have had in his possession.

Now comes Dr. M'Donald. You will observe that he gives an account of experiments he made for the prisoner, and you will see the lengths to which he goes in adopting a new form of disease of epilepsy with these complications. You are to say what weight you give to that evidence compared with the witnesses who have given evidence before you.

The next witness is Mr. John Bainbridge. The object of this witness's evidence seems to be to induce you to believe that this was a case of epilepsy, and from the symptoms you will say whether you can come to that conclusion.

The next witness is Mr. Edward Steady. The case referred to by this witness seems to be a case of traumatic tetanus; and you will say, if it were idiopathic, whether the course of it in the slightest degree resembles the symptoms of Cook, the deceased.

The next witness is Dr. Robinson. Now, gentlemen, you have this respectable physician, who gives an account from which you are called to infer that Cook's case was a case of epilepsy. He says he should only take it to be epilepsy in the absence of evidence of strychnia being administered. He says that all the symptoms described by Jones on the Tuesday night are consistent with strychnia; and, with regard to epilepsy, he says in no case where epilepsy had existed would it cause death without a loss of consciousness. Cook, you will remember, remained conscious to the last, and you will say whether, upon the evidence that is laid before you, there was or was not a bending of the body, which is characteristic of tetanus, and what the witnesses have described as being inconsistent with epilepsy.

The next witness is Dr. Richardson, who now brings in for the first time angina pectoris as a disease of which it may be presumed Cook died. Now, gentlemen, you have to attend to this case; the witness, who seems most highly respectable, says this case being detailed by him, the symptoms were consistent with strychnia, and that, if he had known as much of strychnia then as he does now, he would have made an analysis to see whether strychnia was in the body. The great question that I propounded for your consideration was whether Cook's symptoms were consistent with strychnia, and, if they were not, then the conclusion would be in favour of the prisoner; but if they were consistent with strychnia, then you are not upon that alone to find a verdict of guilty against him; but you are to consider the other evidence and see whether the death arose from strychnia or not. Dr. Wrightson is recalled, and he says that, in his opinion, when strychnia is entirely absorbed in the system it is diffused equally throughout the entire system. Dr. Wrightson is a philosopher, and, as a man of science, he speaks with caution, and you have heard his evidence. He says that if the minimum dose were taken to destroy life, and then a long interval elapsed between the taking of the poison and death, the more complete would be the absorption, and the less chance there would be of finding it in the stomach.

Mr. SERJEANT SHEE—I think he said he would expect to find it in the spleen, the liver, and the blood.

LORD CAMPBELL—Yes; "I should look for it elsewhere, in the spleen, the liver, and the blood."

Then comes Mr. Oliver Pemberton. The evidence of this witness only goes to show that, in his opinion, an examination of the body at that time was not of much value, and did not afford the means of coming to a satisfactory opinion, differing in opinion, therefore, from others that had been called.

His lordship then dealt with the witnesses as to facts, and pointed out that, according to the trains, Palmer could not have arrived in Rugeley on the Monday night before ten o'clock.

Now, gentlemen, comes a very material witness, who, if he were to be believed, would be very important, particularly upon one part of the case. I mean Jeremiah Smith—and you, having heard the whole of his evidence, the examination and cross-examination, are to say what faith or reliance you can place upon his testimony. Now, gentlemen, this would show, if true, that the genuine and very identical pills that Bamford had made, and in the state in which he had prepared them, were taken by Cook before Palmer arrived from London at Rugeley, or, at any rate, before he came to the Talbot Arms. It is for you to say whether you can place reliance upon such testimony. You saw how he conducted himself in the witness-box, and how he at last denied that the signature to the instrument which he purported to have attested, and which he received from the prisoner at the bar, was in his handwriting. He said it was like it, but it was not his handwriting. Then it appears that he did receive £5, and you are to say whether it was not clearly for attesting that very assignment. The counterfoil of the cheque for £5, from William Palmer the prisoner, is shown him; and with that piece of paper he goes to the bank and receives the £5. Can you believe a man who so disgraces himself in the witness-box? It is for you to say what faith you can place in a witness who, by his own admission, engaged in such fraudulent proceedings. We are now upon veracity, and you are to say whether you can believe a witness who at last acknowledges that he had been applied to and had been engaged in procuring an insurance on the life of Walter Palmer, who had been a bankrupt six years before, and who had no means of living except by the allowance of his friends and an allowance made to him by the prisoner at the bar.

Lord Campbell

Again, he acknowledges that he was engaged in the proposal to insure the life of Bates for £10,000. Bates being at that time superintending the stables of the prisoner at the bar, living in lodgings at 6s. 6d. a week, apparently having no property, and nothing depending upon his life, his life was to be insured for £10,000. Smith gets himself appointed agent to an insurance office, and, with a knowledge of these facts, he proposes the insurance to be accepted by the office which he represents; and can you believe such a witness who acknowledges himself to have been engaged in such fraudulent proceedings, and who, now being examined upon his oath, denies the handwriting of his own attestation to that document? Gentlemen, of his credit you are to judge. His evidence would be material as to what took place on the Monday night, because it would show that the pills that Cook took that night were taken as they had been prepared by Bamford, and before the prisoner at the bar had had any opportunity to substitute others for them in the pill box. Such is the case with regard to what took place on the Tuesday. If it stood there, and if it were believed, it would be evidence in favour of the prisoner at the bar; and you are to say whether you believe it, or, if you disbelieve it, what effect it has upon the other testimony that has been brought forward.

Gentlemen, the case is now in your hands; and, unless upon the part of the prosecution a clear conviction has been brought to your minds of the guilt of the prisoner, it is your duty to acquit him. You are not to proceed even upon a strong suspicion; there must be the strongest conviction in your minds that he was guilty of this offence; and if there be any reasonable doubt remaining in your mind, you will give him the benefit of that doubt; but if you come to a clear conviction that he was guilty, you will not be deterred from doing your duty by any considerations such as have been suggested to you. You will remember the oath that you have taken, and you will act accordingly. Gentlemen, I have performed my task; you have now to discharge yours, and may God direct you to a right finding.

Mr. SERJEANT SHEE—Your lordship stated to the jury that *the* question for them to consider was whether the evidence that has been brought forward is consistent with the death of Cook by strychnia. I submit to your lordship that that is not the question which ought to be submitted to the jury.

LORD CAMPBELL—Serjeant Shee, that is not *the* question that I have submitted to the jury; it is *a* question. I told them that unless they considered that the symptoms were consistent with death by strychnia they ought to acquit the prisoner.

Lord Campbell

Mr. SERJEANT SHEE—It is my duty, my lord, not to be deterred by any expression of displeasure at my stating it; I am accountable not only to your lordships, but I am accountable to a much higher tribunal; and I am bound to submit to you what occurs to me to be the proper question to be put to the jury in this case—it is your lordship's duty to overrule it if you think proper. I submit to your lordships that the question, whether the symptoms of Cook's disease were consistent with death by strychnia is a wrong question, unless it is followed by this, "and inconsistent with death by other and natural causes"—and that the question should be, whether the medical evidence establishes beyond all reasonable doubt the death of Cook by strychnia—it is my duty to submit that to your lordship.

LORD CAMPBELL—Gentlemen of the jury, I did not submit to you that the question upon which your verdict alone was to turn was whether the symptoms of Cook were consistent with death by strychnia, but I said that that was a most material question for you; and I desired you to consider that question with a view to guide your judgment as to whether he died from natural disease, or whether he did not die by poison, by strychnia administered by the prisoner. Then I went on to say that if you were of opinion that the symptoms were consistent with death from strychnia, you should go on to consider the other evidence given in the case, whether strychnia had been administered to him; and whether strychnia had been administered to him by the prisoner at the bar; and those are the questions that I again put to you. If you come to the conclusion that those symptoms were consistent with the strychnia, do you believe from the evidence that it was strychnia, and do you believe that that strychnia was administered by the prisoner at the bar? Do not find a verdict of guilty unless you believe that the strychnia was administered to the deceased by the prisoner at the bar. But if you believe that, it is your duty to God and man to find a verdict of guilty.

The jury retired, and, after an absence of an hour and eighteen minutes, returned a verdict of guilty.

The prisoner was asked what he had to say why the Court should not pass sentence of death upon him according to law, and he made no answer.

Lord Campbell

LORD CAMPBELL then said—William Palmer, after a long and impartial trial you have been convicted by a jury of your country of the crime of wilful murder. In that verdict my two learned brothers, who have so anxiously watched this trial, and myself entirely concur, and consider that verdict altogether satisfactory. The case is attended with such circumstances of aggravation that I do not dare to touch upon them. Whether it is the first and only offence of this sort which you have committed is certainly known only to God and your own conscience. It is seldom that such a familiarity with the means of death should be shown without long experience; but for this offence of which you have been found guilty your life is forfeited. You must prepare to die; and I trust that, as you can expect no mercy in this world, you will, by repentance of your crimes, seek to obtain mercy from Almighty God. The Act of Parliament under which you have been tried, and under which you have been brought to the bar of this Court at your own request, gives leave to the Court to direct that the sentence under such circumstances shall be executed either within the jurisdiction of the Central Criminal Court or in the county where the offence was committed. We think that, for the sake of example, the sentence ought to be executed in the county of Stafford. Now, I hope that this terrible example will deter others from committing such atrocious crimes, and that it will be seen that whatever art, or caution, or experience may accomplish, such an offence will be detected and punished. However destructive poisons may be, it is so ordained by Providence that there are means for the safety of His creatures for detecting and punishing those who administer them. I again implore you to repent and prepare for the awful change which awaits you. I will not seek to harrow up your feelings by any enumeration of the circumstances of this foul murder. I will content myself now with passing upon you the sentence of the law, which is, that you be taken hence to the gaol of Newgate, and thence removed to the gaol of the county of Stafford, the county in which the offence of which you are justly convicted was committed; and that you be taken thence to a place of execution, and be there hanged by the neck until you be dead; and that your body be afterwards buried within the precincts of the prison in which you shall be last confined after your conviction; and may the Lord have mercy upon your soul. Amen!

The prisoner was executed at eight o'clock on Saturday morning, 14th June, 1856, in front of Stafford gaol. He reiterated that he was "innocent of poisoning Cook by strychnia."

APPENDICES.

APPENDIX I.

LETTER FROM THOMAS PALMER, BROTHER OF WILLIAM PALMER, TO THE
LORD CHIEF-JUSTICE CAMPBELL.

The following extract from the Diary of Lord Chief-Justice Campbell will
serve as introduction to the following letter:—

June 28.

Since my last notice in this journal the great event has been the trial of
William Palmer at the Central Criminal Court for poisoning, which began on
Wednesday, May 14th, and did not finish till Tuesday, May 27th—the most
memorable judicial proceedings for the last fifty years, engaging the attention
not only of this country but of all Europe.

My labour and anxiety were fearful; but I have been rewarded by public
approbation. The Court sat eight hours a day. When I got home, renouncing
all other engagements, I employed myself till midnight in revising my notes
and considering the evidence. Luckily I had a Sunday to prepare for my
summing up, and to this I devoted fourteen continuous hours. The following
day, after reading in Court ten hours, I had only got through the proofs for
the prosecution. My anxiety was over on the last day, when the verdict of
guilty was pronounced and I had sentenced the prisoner to die, for I had no
doubt of his guilt, and I was conscious that by God's assistance I had done
my duty. Such was the expressed opinion of the public and of all the
respectable part of the Press. But a most ruffian-like attempt was made by
the friends of the prisoner to abuse me, and to obtain a pardon or reprieve
on the ground that the prisoner had not had a fair trial. Having unbounded
funds at their command, they corrupted some disreputable journals to admit
these diatribes against me. They published a most libellous pamphlet under
the title of "A Letter from the Rev. T. Palmer," the prisoner's brother, to
Lord Chief-Justice Campbell, in which the Chief-Justice was represented to
be worse than his predecessor Jeffreys, and it was asserted that there had
been nothing in England like the last trial since the "Bloody Assize."
However, the Home Secretary remained firm and the law took its course.

The Rev. T. Palmer has since disclaimed the pamphlet, and it is said to have
been written by a blackguard barrister. I bear him no enmity. He has done
me no harm; but for the sake of example he ought to be disbarred.

A LETTER TO THE LORD CHIEF-JUSTICE CAMPBELL.

After a struggle with internal emotions too dreadful to be described, amid the tears and lamentations of my family, the bereavement of a household knit together in bonds of strongest love and amity, and the smothered, not wholly-concealed indignation of relatives and friends, I address your lordship, not only as the man who has sealed my brother's fate and borne him to the foot of the scaffold, but as the judge who will have to render an account to your fellow-men, to posterity, and to God of your dealing towards a human being whose fate was, to a certain extent, placed in your hands, and on whose destiny you operated in a manner hitherto unknown, at least in our days. The law, with bitter irony, propounds it is an axiom dear to Englishmen that a magistrate invested with powers like your lordship is "counsel for the prisoner"; but every man who witnesses the late mockery at the Old Bailey, in which you played so prominent a part, confesses—to his own heart, at least, whatever he may own in public—that a more infamous delusion has never been solemnly enacted before a British audience since those days of shame when Jeffreys went forth upon the "bloody assize," and, in the name of Justice and the Law, consigned the young, the innocent, the helpless, and the stricken with years to the dungeon and the gallows, professing all the while to be actuated by a sense of duty to the Crown and to the people.

These may appear strong words, and this a heavy accusation, but I will demonstrate it to all who read this letter. What though I may not hope to move your lordship to justice, yet I may, at least, awaken within you a sense of that awful day which approaches you as certainly as it looms on my brother, and which, at your advanced age, cannot be far removed. I may awaken within you a feeling of compunction, or, at all events, of solemn reflection; for you, also, will have to stand before a Judge enthroned in majesty and power; before whom you will be, indeed, as nought; and when upon your brow appears the awful record of your administration of justice to the man whom you have condemned, in that hour also shall you remember this word from the brother of his affections. May it avail you before that terrific moment! May it serve to save yourself from yourself, and to warn you in time that it is the duty of a British judge to hear, not to condemn; to adjudicate, not to execute; to administer the law as the representative of the country, not to pervert it to his own purposes with the anxiety of a hangman.

My lord, in one week—in some short days from this—William Palmer, my brother, will stand before his God; he will have to answer for his life, and for the sins of his life; he will have to endure that fearful scrutiny into his past from which even the best of us may well shrink with terror. But there is one crime for which he will not have to answer, and that is the crime for which your lordship has convicted him. My brother, William Palmer, is no murderer. His whole life, his whole character, his whole bearing at and since the trial are quite convincing of the fact. From childhood upward no man was gentler of heart; his charity was inexhaustible; his kindliness to all who were in distress was well known. To him the wanderer resorted in his afflictions; by him the poor and houseless were fed and comforted. I write in the face of the public, with my character as a gentleman and a clergyman at stake, and I avow only facts that cannot be denied. His liberality was a proverb, his frank sincerity, his courage, his faithful loyalty to his friends, his temperance, his performance of the duties of religion, his social relations in the character of father, husband, and son won for him the love and confidence of all who approached him; and though it is true that in one fatal instance he violated the laws of his country, and subjected himself to a severe penalty for an infringement of its commercial code, yet this excepted, his was in all respects the very opposite of that cool, calculating, cowardly, crafty temper which is essential to the poisoner, and which we know cannot co-exist with these qualities which my brother possessed from his earliest years down even to the day when your lordship sent him to his death. My lord, beware, lest while you convict of murder you are not yourself a party to a murder! It is not the first time that the annals of our own jurisprudence have exhibited traces of blood; it is not the first time that judges have persuaded juries to convict to death on circumstantial evidence. The records of every country abound in remarkable cases of persons judicially destroyed for crimes of which they were entirely innocent. A mistaken resemblance to the actual perpetrator, the fact of having been seen near the spot where the crime was committed, an apparent motive of self-interest, a confusion of manner when he was accused, or some other suspicious circumstance has contributed to bring the odium of guilt and consequent punishment on the wrong party. At one time cases of frightful injustice were committed by condemning individuals for murder when it was not proved that a murder had been perpetrated. The now well-recognised principle in criminal law—violated, indeed, by your lordship in my brother's case—that no murder can be held as having been committed till the body of the deceased has been discovered, had, apparently, terminated this form of legal oppression until your lordship persuaded a jury to find a man guilty of blood where there was no actual positive proof that a homicide had at all been perpetrated, and when the chemical analysis had even demonstrated that it had not. Another, and perhaps one of the most common causes of prejudice in trials of this nature was the prevarication or the suspicious conduct of the party charged with the offence, and this, likewise, your lordship told the jury was proof of my brother's guiltiness. Finding himself, though innocent, placed in an awkward predicament, the accused sometimes invented a plausible story in his defence, and the deceit being discovered, he was at once presumed to be in every respect guilty. Sir Matthew Hale mentions a melancholy instance of this kind. An uncle, who had the bringing up of his niece, to whom he was heir-at-law, correcting her for some offence, she was heard to say, "Good uncle, do not kill me!" after which she could not be found. The uncle was committed on suspicion of having murdered her, and was admonished by the judge of the assize to find out the child by the next assizes. Being unable to discover his niece, he brought another child, dressed like her, and resembling her in person and years; but, on examination, the fraud was detected, and upon the presumption of guilt which those circumstances afforded, he was sentenced to be hanged, and the sentence was executed. The child afterwards reappeared, when of age, to claim her land. On being beaten by her uncle she had run away, and had been received by a stranger; a jury, worked upon by suspicion, and probably also by a judge who pandered then, as judges pander now, to public prejudice, had thus murdered an innocent man; and that great Chief-Justice has preserved the fact as a warning for all time to beware of judgment in cases of life and death. Yet your lordship, who has succeeded that noble luminary of the law, forgot this memorable case in the moment when you ought most to have remembered it; though I take upon myself to say the circumstantial evidence against my brother was not half as powerful as that against this gentleman whose fate has thus been commemorated in vain by your lordship's wise and Christian predecessor in the judgment seat. Yet do I believe that, as surely as the sun shines or that God lives in the heavens, there will come a day when my brother's innocence will be demonstrated before all men, and though your lordship may not live to see it, yet will his blood cry out from his prison grave, and his fate will blacken the memory of all who were parties to his death with immortal infamy. For it is at your door the public will lay his conviction—not at that of the jury who were worked upon to convict, and who would have been more than men if they had resisted your looks, your gestures, your actions, and your arguments. My lord, since this conviction of death has been recorded I have seen William Palmer. I have visited him in his condemned hold. I have beheld that darling brother, the playmate of my infancy, the companion of my youthful sports, in whom my heart's blood circulates, and with whom my love is entwined. And how did he present himself? And how did he bear our presence? I say, like Socrates in his cell; I say, like Sidney in the Tower; I say, like Calas before the wheel. He preserves a cheerful, an undaunted, an English heart and spirit, and I am proud of him even in his death doom. Your lordship has not crushed or trampled my brother's soul. He maintains his energy and his hope in justice, not indeed from men, for he was condemned long since, but in the course of events, in the discoveries of science, in the confession or conviction of those perjured witnesses against him; or, these all failing, in the God of truth. Though I never doubted his innocence, yet did I resolve to make all certain and positive before I hazarded this letter. I fell on my knees before him. I implored him by our past love and kindred, by our early recollections and hopes, by our common faith, by all the duties which he owed to man and God, to disburthen his conscience if he were guilty, and not to enter before the presence of his Creator with a falsehood upon his lips. I adjured him to say if he were guilty or not guilty. Oh, my lord! he did not wince; he did not change his noble composure; he spoke and looked all innocence. Calmly, earnestly, and solemnly he answered, and the seriousness of his words went into our hearts with the fullest persuasion of his perfect guiltlessness of blood; the most complete reliance on that dying tongue which never spoke falsely to one of us, but to whose language we listened ever with full assurance in its integrity and its faith. Under these circumstances, therefore, I make no apology for addressing your lordship. A great, a majestic duty is now imposed on you. If you shrink from executing it you are undone. There are but seven days between this and the irrevocable hour of death. All your repentance, all your shame will be unavailing if that dread sentence be rashly carried into effect. I ask you not to recommend a pardon for my brother—for that, I know, you will not do; but I ask you— for in you it lies—to obtain a respite for him till his guilt or innocence be demonstrated to the satisfaction of the world. Bear in mind that my brother's counsel offered fearlessly at the trial that an experiment should be made. Bear in mind that some of the most able chemical analysts in the world have declared upon their oaths that if strychnia were administered it can be found; that the Attorney-General himself, to a certain extent, repudiated Dr. Taylor, and supported himself by Mr. Herapath's supposition that strychnia was there, though Taylor could not find it; bear in mind that Taylor's theory of the absorption and decomposition of strychnia was never heard of until this trial; that it was hit upon by him to bolster up his credit, and that all the ablest of the chemists at the trial unanimously repudiated it as a heresy, unworthy of credit, and whose fallacy they had themselves proved by actual experiment; bear in mind, I say, all this, and remember with what a harsh and angry denial you refused to permit such an experiment, though upon it depended the blood of a man. I say deliberately that if these chemists have sworn the truth, and that there is no strychnia discernible in Cook's body, then will William Palmer be murdered as effectually under the semblance of English law as ever the most innocent was butchered under the worst forms of the Papal Inquisition; and that the most fearful responsibility of blood that ever rested upon human head will be upon those who refuse to concede the test which is now challenged. I ask that that experiment shall be performed, which will set at rest for ever the imputation of judicial murder that will sear your lordship's character with the present and with the future; an experiment which may probably clear your soul from the stain of blood that it must risk if you oppose this application. What is there unusual, what is there criminal, what is there illegal in only asking for a respite until it be proved—as it can be proved incontrovertibly—whether Cook died of strychnia or not? And if he did not die of strychnia, then is my brother's innocence made manifest, even to your satisfaction! While, if it is shown that he did so die, then is the voice of accusation silent for ever, and the much-vaunted majesty, the supposed impartiality and purity of English law vindicated in triumph before mankind. The precise mode in which this experiment might be made it is not for me to suggest. I have no objection that it shall be made in any way which may appear satisfactory to the Home Office, provided only that neither Dr. Taylor nor Dr. Rees is entrusted with its management. In this pair of worthies I have no confidence. The first pronounced my brother guilty of poisoning on grounds the most ridiculous that can be imagined, upon which even a Stafford Grand Jury did not think there was sufficient to warrant them in finding even a *prima facie* case for investigation at the assizes. He wrote letters to the newspapers branding the accused as a most desperate criminal; he largely assisted in getting up the prosecution, and was busily engaged all through the trial in writing notes and making suggestions to the Attorney-General and the other prosecuting counsel; he smiled perceptibly when the case was strong against my brother, and could not conceal his chagrin as it grew weak. As to Rees, he seems to endorse all that Taylor says, and I have no confidence whatever in him. A writer in the papers, who is unknown to me, makes a suggestion which you may bring if you choose before the Home Secretary; but it matters little by whom the experiment is made so that it is done by an honest man. "If it is proved," says the writer, "that Cook died from strychnia, there is no difficulty in connecting Palmer with the administration of it. But if that fact is not proved, then the other circumstances do not lead to the irresistible inference of his guilt." For the sake of all parties concerned in the case, for the sake of society at large, and, above all, for the sake of justice, let that point be set at rest; and let that be done in this manner—Mr. Herapath says he can detect strychnia wherever present. Then let there be a certain number of animals killed, some by strychnia and some by other means; let their interiors be taken out and put in jars, each separately and numbered, and verified with all the necessary formalities, Mr. Herapath being kept in the dark as to which was the poisoned jar and which was not; and if he then can distinguish between those which contained strychnia and those that did not, let the Home Secretary have the moral courage to step in and avert the disgraceful and horrible-to-contemplate possibility of having one day, in token of his acknowledged innocence, to wave a flag over the grave of William Palmer, to which he has been consigned upon insufficient evidence, despite of the revelations of science, and because (to use the words of Dr. Taylor), "society demands a victim."

My lord, I have been told by lawyers that all presumptive evidence of crime should be admitted cautiously, for the law holds that it is better that ten guilty persons escape than that one innocent suffer. And there is a famous case which so strongly illustrates this noble principle of the law that I may remind your lordship of it here. The mother and reputed father of a bastard child were observed to take it to the margin of the dock in Liverpool, and, after stripping it, to throw it into the dock. The body of the infant was not afterwards seen, but, as the tide of the sea flowed and reflowed into and out of the dock, the learned judge who tried the father and mother for the murder of their child, observed that it was possible the tide might have carried out the living infant, and the prisoners were acquitted. The case is mentioned by Garrow, one of the ablest and purest judges that ever adorned the bench; and it has been brought before me as illustrative of the wise and merciful caution which the judges of the past were used to exercise before they persuaded juries to condemn men who might possibly be innocent. How your lordship would have decided this trial had it taken place before you, and had the public Press, under the influence of insurance societies, hounded on the many to a cry for blood, I can easily anticipate; but that the great judge who ruled for mercy adjudicated according to the well-known principles of the Constitution is what I am assured by every man who has made the English law his study, and who is too pure to be influenced by a shout of "Crucify him! crucify him!" will admit without the slightest shadow of a doubt. Take, again, the ordinary case which I find mentioned in an anonymous letter in one of the morning papers, and which, I am informed, is so strongly illustrative of the caution exercised in all criminal cases where the judge is impartial, and where medical science must occasionally be fallible, that it needs no words of mine to add to its force. Its value is increased by this fact, that neither I nor any person connected with my family has the least knowledge of who the writer is, and, therefore, no considerations but those which do him honour can be supposed to operate on his mind.

"To establish," he says, "a perfect chain of circumstantial evidence, every circumstance in the case must be proved beyond all cavil. And the first and most important and absolutely indispensable circumstance in a case like that of Palmer's is the fact of a murder having been committed. That is the groundwork of the circumstantial fabric, without which the rest of the edifice topples over. It is a circumstance of which merely the conduct, however suspicious, antecedent or subsequent to its occurrence, of the alleged murderer furnishes no valid proof. To convict a man of poisoning, you should distinctly trace the death of the deceased to poison.

"Take a case in point. It is of frequent occurrence in this country that a woman is charged with the murder of her newly-born infant. She is unmarried; she is proved to have been suspected of pregnancy, and to have denied the fact; she is proved to have been recently delivered of a child; she has been seen going to a water-closet, and, after she has left, there are found, rammed down the pipe of that water-closet, the dissected members of an infant's body; a knife smeared with blood is discovered hidden away, and traced to the prisoner's possession; she has made no provision for the reception of the child, which, should it survive the moment of its birth, must prove an incubus upon its mother and a living witness to her shame. Here are circumstances of a damning nature. A strong motive, a cool premeditation, a mutilated body, and physical traces which cannot be mistaken. Mark the result. A surgeon is called at the trial, and states that he cannot positively swear that the child was born alive; that it may by possibility have been born dead; that there being no proof that the child was ever alive, he cannot be sure that it was killed by being cut in pieces. In that case there is no Professor Taylor, who, while the case was *pendente lite*, has written letters in a newspaper stating that 'society demands a victim,' and whose sworn testimony is to the effect that, inasmuch as 99 children in 100 are born alive, his solemn belief is that so was this child, and that he has therefore come to the conclusion that the cutting off of its head was the cause of death. There is no Chief Justice to tell the jury that they are to take all the circumstances surrounding the case into consideration, and that, although it was not proved beyond a doubt that death was the result of mortal agency, yet if they arrived at the conclusion that the prisoner had a strong motive for destroying the deceased, and had possession of an instrument by which to effect that purpose, there was a *prima facie* case made out which would lead them to the next question, namely, was the state of the body, or was it not, consistent with the fact of a violent death? There is no infuriated and Press-prejudiced populace regarding the prisoner as a great criminal, and thirsting after her blood. No! The judge says to the jury you cannot, according to the law of the land, whatever your suspicions in this case may be, find a verdict of guilty; there is no proof of a murder having been committed, and the prisoner must be acquitted on that charge. That may be a vicious law, but it is the law, and had no more right to be violated in the case of William Palmer than in that of any other individual. If it be, the whole proceedings of the trial are a mockery and a delusion—a disgraceful pandering to out-of-door prejudices and a lasting disgrace to this country."

This is the language of a man who writes as an unprejudiced observer, and, I am told, with a deep knowledge of the law. If it be, as he says, that this is the law in cases of this nature, with what face can my brother be executed when precisely the very reverse was done by your lordship in his case, and, when forgetting or despising all the precedents of mercy with which our jurisprudence abounds, you took only the sanguinary view of the evidence, and enforced everything against the prisoner by argument, by gesture, and by look.

That the law is wise in exercising this salutary caution I think may be proved even by the testimony of the actor who next, after your lordship, had most influence in the verdict against my brother—I mean Dr. Taylor. In that writer's work on "Poisons," page 139, I find the following statement:—"It often happens, in the hands of the ablest analyst, that the last steps of a process lead to a result very different from that which was anticipated at the commencement; and, therefore, a suspicion derived from a few incipient experiments is very likely to be overthrown by continuing the investigation. In the Boughton case Dr. Rattray gives an opinion, in the first instance, that the poison administered to the deceased was arsenic; but he subsequently attributed death to laurel-water! A case occurred within my knowledge where arsenic was pronounced to be present when sulphuric acid was really the poison. In another case, tried at the Kingston Assizes in 1832, the medical witness admitted that at the coroner's inquest he stated the poison to be arsenic, but by subsequent experiments he found that it was oxalic acid, and in a case which has but recently occurred the poison was at first stated to be oxalic acid, but on a more careful examination it was shown to be arsenic!" Whether or not all the unhappy persons in whose cases these chemical mistakes were thus made, and thus coolly avowed, suffered death is not stated, but, as I am told that one of them, Donellan, was certainly executed, and as it is even now a question deeply involved in doubt whether the person whom he is supposed to have poisoned was poisoned at all, and the most able medical authorities incline to the opinion that he was not, it is likely that the others also were as ruthlessly sacrificed to what is called "public opinion," and that they have been sent to their graves with the stigma of murder when they were, in fact, but victims to medical delusions, or toxicological mistakes, which are as coolly confessed by Taylor as if they were merely ordinary trifles, not affecting in any way the life and death of the wretches whose interests were at stake.

My lord, how comes it to pass that not one of these most important facts was mentioned by Taylor at the trial? that his henchman, Rees, who swore exactly as Taylor swore, did not give the jury the slightest information upon these questions of vital value to the prisoner? Why were they kept back from the knowledge of the jury? Why were they concealed from your lordship? It was proved at the trial that Dr. Harland sent Stevens his medical notes of the first post-mortem examination; that Stevens handed them over to Taylor, and that, up to the third day of the trial, Taylor withheld, even from the knowledge of the Attorney-General and the Crown solicitor, that he possessed these notes, which contained circumstances strongly favourable to the case of the prisoner. Was not his silence as to the medical facts just mentioned of a piece with his suppression of this material document? Your lordship made no comment to the jury upon this extraordinary conduct. You severely attacked Mr. Nunneley, you bitterly censured others of the witnesses for the defence, you weakened, by all the means within your power, the effect of their evidence when it told for the prisoner; but not one syllable of censure had you for Taylor, who kept the jury in ignorance of these facts, and the cases mentioned by him in his own book, though he was sworn in the language of the law to tell "the truth and the whole truth." The whole truth, indeed, he did not tell; otherwise these matters which I have now quoted would have come before the jurors, and, as I believe, with all-powerful influence.

If the wilful suppression of evidence by the prosecution had ended with Taylor the case would have been infamous enough; the Crown would have showed that it prosecuted for victory, not for truth, for I take it to be the unquestioned duty of a prosecutor, more especially when he is backed by the Crown authorities and the Home Office, not merely to squabble for a petty triumph on a prisoner charged with murder, or to attempt to higgle a jury out of an adverse verdict, but to present not a part but the whole case fairly before the public—the features favourable to a prisoner as well as those that are unfavourable, the weak portions of the accusations against him as well as those that are strong, so that the jury, who are (in theory) his judges, may see and know every circumstance, however minute, and, from an aggregate of the whole, come to a right conclusion as to the verdict which they are to pronounce. But this salutary rule was not followed by the Crown prosecutors in the present case; they wilfully deceived and misled the counsel for my brother, and by this trick, which I shall presently expose, they deprived the prisoner of two of the most material witnesses, who could prove his innocence, that it was possible for man to have. The first of these witnesses was a man named Henry Cockayne. Your lordship remembers the questions which Serjeant Shee put to that wretched Bates; and you recollect also, I doubt not, the artful way in which he answered those questions. It was of importance to my brother to show for what purpose he had purchased, and in what manner he had used, the strychnia, which he never denied, and does not now mean to deny, that he bought from Roberts on the Tuesday.

He had a number of valuable brood mares in a paddock, separated from the adjoining land only by a thin fence, over which the dogs were in the habit of leaping and hunting these animals (nine in all), so much so that even Bates was obliged to admit that one of them, the "Duchess of Kent," had slipped her foal; and it is a fact that "Goldfinder" had suffered from a like mishap, though Bates refused to acknowledge it. Indeed, Bates would scarcely admit anything, or give a direct reply to any of the questions put to him. Here is an example, taken from the verbatim report of the trial—"Can you give me any notion of their value?" "I do not pretend," answers Bates, "to tell the value of the stock myself." No one had asked him to do so, yet this stable-boy, brewer, farmer, or whatever else he chooses to call himself, who has been about horses all his life, could not give Serjeant Shee a notion of the value of these brood mares. "Do you know," pursued the serjeant, "that one of them sold for 800 guineas?" Now, Bates knew this as well as my brother himself, but mark his answer—"I have heard so." Again, he is asked—"Were any of them in foal shortly before or at the beginning of the month of November?" Bates, you will remember, was in the stables and paddocks every day, yet he answers this question, "I cannot say whether they were or not. I should suppose there were some in foal." A witness who answered in this way would probably have been rebuked by any fair judge, and ordered to answer the questions put to him; but your lordship, who was so dreadfully sarcastic on Mr. Nunneley and Dr. Macdonald, had no word of reproof for Bates. This man was again asked, "had any complaint been made about dogs going about the paddock?" Mark the artful way in which he evaded this interrogatory— "I think I once said to Harry, 'The turf seems a good deal cut up here; how is it?'" Your lordship sees Bates had not been asked what he had said to Harry (this was Cockayne), but he had been asked about repeated and well-known complaints made by my brother as to the way in which his mares were constantly hunted by the dogs in the neighbourhood; and you now see, though you would not at the trial, the evasive and equivocating way in which he replied. Serjeant Shee then proceeded—"What did you see on the turf that induced you to make that observation?—I saw it cut up, which I supposed to be with horses' feet, for they could not cut it up without they galloped. Did you attribute that to anything?—I attributed it to the mares galloping about. Had you any reason to think they had been run by dogs?—I never saw any dogs run them." This was no answer to the question, but your lordship said not a word, and this Bates, who was with Day in the paddock, who, to use the words of the Attorney-General, "was a hanger-on of Palmer's, working in his stables," could not tell, as he pretended, how it was that the mares were galloping about and cutting up the turf. The serjeant then proceeded—"Did Harry keep a gun there?—I have seen a gun there. (This again was not a direct answer, but an evasion.) Did he keep a gun, which belonged to his master, for any purpose?—I have seen a gun at the paddock. Did it belong to his master?—I cannot say. Did you ever see it used?—No. Was it in a condition to be used?—I never had it in my hands to examine it." In ordinary cases I am told that where a witness misconducts himself in this manner, the Crown immediately gives him up, and the judge informs the jury that no reliance is to be placed on his testimony. But, so far from abandoning him, the Attorney-General relied all through upon this man, and pressed against my brother the effect of the evidence which he gave. Now, your lordship was told at the trial, by Serjeant Shee, that the object for which the poison was purchased was to destroy these dogs. Bates was found to admit that a gun was kept in the stables, and though he cunningly kept back for what purpose the gun was used, yet was there another witness on the back of the indictment who had been examined before the coroner, and who was present in the Court, of whose evidence your lordship was well aware, for it was in the depositions, and this witness the Crown withheld from the jury.

Had Cockayne been called, as he ought to have been called, he would have proved that he kept a gun loaded in the stable, by order of my brother, to shoot the dogs that worried his brood mares; that he had also threatened to poison them, that the strychnia was purchased for that object, and that he had missed dogs since then which had been in the habit of prowling about the paddock and hunting the mares. That my brother left poisoned food about the place is a matter which can be proved only by himself, for these things are not always trusted to servants; and, as it is a positive medical fact that animals to which this poison has been given go away into secret, concealed, and quiet places, where they die undiscovered, and would be mortally attacked in so short a time that they could not get to their own homes. Is it not almost demonstrated that this has been the case here, and that my brother is thus made the victim of circumstances, harmless in themselves, but which, having occurred at this precise period, tell now with fearful weight upon his unfortunate case? The Crown may cry out, "Produce the dogs, and show us the strychnia in them." With how much more freedom may the condemned man say, "Produce the poison from Cook's body before you hang me to satisfy a medical theory invented for this trial and broached against me by a deadly foe!"

In the same way, the non-discovery of the money which Cook is said to have possessed at Shrewsbury was urged by your lordship as startling evidence against my brother, and you signified to the jury, by gestures, by looks, and shakes of the head, that my brother had fraudulently got possession of that money, and poisoned Cook in order to conceal the fact. But your lordship was well aware at the time, for it was in the depositions of Saunders, who was also in Court, and who had been examined before the coroner and the Grand Jury, that Cook had sent for Saunders on the Monday before his death, that he had paid him £10 (his account), and excused himself for not paying any more, by stating that he had given my brother all his money to take with him to London, to settle his affairs. Thus the disposal of the money was accounted for by Cook himself; and Saunders, whose testimony was thus highly favourable to my brother, ought to have been called to prove this fact. But, strange to say, Saunders, though in Court, was not called; he waited until the end of the case for the prosecution, and then was sent away by the Crown lawyers, who not only thus deprived the prisoner of the advantage of his testimony, had they called Saunders for the prosecution, but absolutely put it out of the power of the prisoner to call him for the defence by sending him away into the country at the last moment, when they had all along left the counsel for the defence under the idea that it was intended to examine Saunders as a witness on behalf of the prosecution. A more scandalous trick than this, I believe, was never committed, and I do not envy the feelings of the parties who perpetrated it.

It may be asked, why did not Mr. Smith, an able, indefatigable, and skilful lawyer, get Cockayne and Saunders put into the box as witnesses for the prisoner? My lord, the answer is already given. They were the witnesses for the Crown; they were kept in London, in the custody of the Crown, until after the case for the prosecution had terminated; they were then sent out of London, into a distant part of England not so easily accessible as was needed by the prisoner; and if we are to take your lordship's manifest and angry impatience at the ten minutes' delay in calling witnesses for the defence, which occurred on the morning of Saturday, the tenth day of the trial, as indicative of your feelings, we may be very certain that if you so chafed at that brief interval, repeatedly during those few minutes asking Serjeant Shee if he could not go on—if, I say, we are to consider that angry haste significant of anything, we may very well conclude that you would not have waited until Saunders and Cockayne were brought up from the centre of England, if, indeed, it was possible for the prisoner at all to discover their exact lodgings at the time. I have myself heard, on many occasions, in Courts of justice where judges themselves called witnesses whose names were in the indictment and order them to give their evidence for the Crown. But this was where the judges were not biassed against the accused—where they had no desire to become the objects of public praise or to prostitute their high places to the low desire of popularity acquired by pandering to a cry for blood. Why your lordship did not follow the well-known precedents of law in my brother's case is best known to yourself. Yet there are many of the public also who can form a pretty accurate guess as to your real motives. Let me revert, however, to the subject, from which this is a digression, and pursue the confession made by Dr. Taylor of the general inaccuracy of medical men when they are retained to carry out a theory by the prosecution. These, which I have quoted, are not the only instances in which mistakes have been made for want of proper caution. Taylor (p. 63) mentions the case of M. Pralet, where "several medical witnesses deposed that the deceased had died from prussic acid, administered to him by M. L'Heritier, the accused. Orfila was requested to examine the medical evidence, and found it extremely defective. The inferences drawn from the application of the medical tests were highly improper, and the results were extremely negative. Had it not been for the interference of Orfila, it is most probable that the accused would have been convicted, more from the strong medical opinions against him than from the medical facts of the case. The witnesses appear to have acted on the principle that the whole of their duty consisted in rendering the charge of poisoning probable, whereas we shall hereafter see that no person can be convicted of this crime on mere probability. The fact of poisoning must be made reasonably certain either by medical or moral evidence, or by both combined." He cites also (p. 110) a case reported by Anglada, in which there were circumstances of grave suspicion, though the party suspected was wholly innocent. "A lady, in perfect health, while supping with her husband and family, complained, after having taken two or three mouthfuls, of severe pain in the region of her heart. She fell back in her chair and died instantly. The parties not having lived on the best of terms, the husband was openly accused of having been accessory to the poisoning of his wife—a circumstance which was rendered still more probable in the opinion of his neighbours by the fact that the wife had lately made a holograph will in his favour. One of his servants, with whom he was said to live in adultery, was arrested, and a paper containing a white powder was found in her possession. The husband endeavoured to compromise the affair by offering to give up the will. Here, then, were strong moral presumptions of death from poisoning. Three surgeons (experts!) were appointed to examine the body. They opened the abdomen, and, observing some green spots in the stomach, produced (as it afterwards appeared, by imbibition from the gall bladder), pronounced an opinion that the organ was in a gangrenous state from the effects of some corrosive poison. Some doubt arising on the correctness of this view, four other surgeons were directed to re-examine the body. They found that the stomach had not even been opened, and that its mucous membrane, as well as that of the intestines, was perfectly healthy. It contained a small quantity of undigested food, which was free from any trace of poison. The deceased had died from natural causes. The white powder found in the possession of the servant was nothing more than white sugar!" Nor does he omit the case of Hunter (p. 144), whose trial at Liverpool Assizes somewhat resembles that of my poor brother, but who was fortunate enough to be tried by an honest judge and an impartial jury. "A woman was charged with having poisoned her husband by arsenic. The medical evidence rested chiefly on the symptoms and post-mortem appearances, for no arsenic was discovered in the body. The mucous membrane of the stomach and intestines was found throughout its whole extent exceedingly inflamed and softened. The medical witnesses for the prosecution referred (as they always do) this condition to the action of arsenic; those for the defence considered that it might be owing to idiopathic gastroenteritis, independently of the exhibition of any irritant. The circumstances of the case were very suspicious, but the prisoner was acquitted, not merely on account of the variance in the medical evidence, but from the absence of positive proof of poison, i.e., its detection by chemical analysis." This generally weighs much with a Court of law. Yet your lordship so contrived that it did not weigh one hair in my brother's case. The principles of law being thus clear, and the mistakes of medical science being also equally admitted, let me follow them up by a further quotation from the gentleman out of whose powerful letter I have already extracted a passage— "Is there clear, and distinct, and unimpeachable proof that beyond all reasonable doubt Mr. Cook died a violent death? Let us see how that question is answered. For the prosecution a number of medical men of eminence state that the symptoms in his case were such as they would expect to have resulted from the administration of strychnia, and were irreconcilable with death from any other cause. Upon the part of the prisoner a number of equally eminent medical men state that they can account for the death of the deceased without being compelled to resort to the hypothesis of strychnia, and that in many important particulars the symptoms were different from those which that poison invariably produces. Each set of witnesses, upon cross-examination, qualified their statements in some degree, but in the result such is the substance of their respective experience.

"Then comes Professor Taylor, who analysed the contents of the stomach, &c., and who states that he found no strychnia nor any poison which could account for the death of Mr. Cook. As Lord Campbell said with a sneer, 'Of course, upon this the whole defence rests.' It strikes me as being a very feasible defence indeed, but more of that presently. However, Dr. Taylor states that you must not draw the conclusion that because no strychnia was found, therefore none was administered, because he had known cases (though of very rare occurrence) where he had himself administered that drug to animals, and afterwards tested for and failed to discover it; and from the symptoms he is convinced that Mr. Cook must have died from strychnia. Dr. Rees is of a similar opinion. Now, the result of this evidence is to destroy the practical utility of analysis for strychnia altogether; for although if strychnia be detected, it is proof that it has been administered, yet if it be not detected, that is no proof that it has not been administered.

"Then let us look at the other side. Mr. Herepath, who is confessedly one of the greatest analytical chemists of the present day, states that if the minutest particle of strychnia were present in the body, he would guarantee to find it, and in that statement he is corroborated by a series of eminent toxicologists. It is suggested, in answer to this evidence, that Professor Taylor did not apply the proper tests. Surely, if he did not, it did not lie in the mouth of the prosecution to urge that argument. He was their witness; he was employed by them to make the analysis, and they trusted to his capacity to do so; and when he states that he found no strychnia, the fair and logical deduction is, not that he did not use the proper tests, but that there was no strychnia to be found. Notwithstanding this, Lord Campbell put it very strongly—and, as I conceive, very unjustifiably and illegally, to the jury—that Professor Taylor might not have used the proper tests, and that it was for them to consider whether, if the proper tests had been applied, strychnia might not have been discovered. But, however, Mr. Herepath, whose testimony is borne out by other chemical witnesses for the defence, states that he will guarantee to find strychnia in all cases where it is present, however infinitesimal the quantity; that he never found his tests to fail, and that the only conclusion he could draw from the fact of strychnia not being found is that none was administered. Upon the one hand, therefore, you have the positive opinions of fallible medical men, founded upon a second-hand knowledge of the symptoms, as to the impossibility of their resulting from any other cause than strychnia. Upon the other hand you have the equally positive opinions of medical men similarly situated as to the effect of those symptoms being reconcilable with natural causes. Cast into the scales the unerring inspirations of chemical science, add that the life of a fellow-creature is at stake, and which way lies the balance of evidence?"

My lord, what answer can you make to this argument? You will say, perhaps, that you have convinced yourself that my brother is guilty. This, indeed, may satisfy a man of weak or of no conscience; but how will it fall upon the great body of the enlightened British public, who have been wound up, it is true, to the most awful excitement against this unhappy man, but who will assuredly awaken from that excitement and demand in tones of thunder how it came to pass that you, who should have stood between the prisoner and prejudice, ministered to that prejudice, and were found to be his accuser rather than his judge!

And here, my lord, before I proceed further, let me exonerate you from all the blame of this sham trial. You had a brother judge by your side who shares with you all the responsibility of prejudice against my brother, who made no secret, but rather an indecent display of that prejudice in a manner which astonished the whole auditory, and who ought also to be recorded with you to all time coming as having participated in the laurels of blood with which you should be crowned—I allude to Mr. Baron Alderson. That learned functionary, who inaugurated the first day's proceedings by falling asleep and nearly tumbling over his desk during the Attorney-General's opening speech, amused himself during the progress of the trial by suggesting questions to Mr. James, the counsel for the prosecution, by lifting up his hands in apparent astonishment when anything favourable to the prisoner was elicited on cross-examination, by looking at the jury with every mark of incredulity and contempt when Serjeant Shee suggested any matter beneficial to my brother, and by joining with your lordship in overruling every legal objection which was raised by the counsel for the defence. Once also, when Serjeant Shee asked one of the witnesses, "Where are the pathionic glands?" Baron Alderson started up with every mark of anger and exclaimed, "Humbug!" And on another occasion, when your lordship, or Mr. Justice Cresswell, addressed the serjeant as "Brother Shee," Baron Alderson impatiently cried out, "Oh, bother Shee!" I can feel no surprise, therefore, when I find your lordship, while pronouncing sentence on my brother, declaring that Baron Alderson concurred with the finding of the jury, though, unless he concurred with you before the verdict was pronounced, he certainly did not do so in Court, as no communication passed between you and either of the judges after that fatal word. But of Mr. Justice Cresswell I feel bound to declare the feeling of my brother, of all my family, and, unanimously, as I am told, that of my brother's counsel, that his conduct was in accordance with all that we hear or know of the purity of the bench; that his demeanour was dignified, noble, impartial, and most honourable; and that, but for his interference, visible, as was remarked on many important occasions, your lordship would have admitted evidence illegally against my brother, or excluded testimony which his advisers hoped would operate favourably for him on the minds of his jury. Never shall the memory of his conduct be erased from our hearts; we all have felt, and we shall always continue to feel it; nor shall any sunset close on me for the remainder of my days that shall not witness my earnest prayer for him who did all that a judge should do to maintain the character of our country and its criminal jurisprudence; and who probably would have exerted himself still more strenuously but for the feeling that upon your lordship, as chief judge, the great responsibility of this case rested, and that he himself was but an appendage rather than a ministering officer at the trial.

My lord, the remarks which I have up to this time made may be considered preliminary to my investigations of your charge, but they seem to me of consequence to a right understanding of the language in which you thought it proper to address them, and to a due appreciation of the kind of way in which the guilt has been fastened upon my brother's shoulders. A writer in a daily paper says—"However horrible it may be that a systematic poisoner should escape the penalty of his crimes by an effort of legal chicanery, there is something even more repugnant to the principles of British law, and that is, that a man should be found guilty upon insufficient evidence; and there is something still more revolting, both to the constitution of the country and to human nature, namely, that a man should be hanged for a murder which there is no satisfactory proof had ever been committed."

Yet, my lord, there is something still more dreadful, and it is this, that the time-renowned prestige of British trial by jury should be abrogated, as abrogated it will be, if your lordship's precedent is to be followed by present or future judges. Did your lordship really leave any question to the jury upon which to exercise an impartial reason? Did you throw upon them the whole responsibility of the verdict, as by the theory of the law you ought to have done? Did you merely lay down the legal principles governing the case, or did you not step out of the way to comment (like an advocate) on the evidence? To get up this witness and to knock down that one, to praise those who supported Dr. Taylor's theory and to censure those who were independent of such nonsense? Did not your lordship convey, as clearly to the jury, by meaning looks, by thumping the desk with peculiar energy, by laying emphasis on certain parts of the evidence, and then pausing and gazing intently upon the jurymen, by shaking your head, as if your thoughts of my brother's guilt were too dreadful for utterance; by repeating over and over again those parts which told heaviest against him; by running on the evidence for the prisoner so that it was impossible for the jury to understand it; by charging against him, for a whole day and on the morning of the second, recapitulating with fearful emphasis and solemnity all your arguments of the preceding night, condensing them and summing them into one argumentative whole, from which it was almost impossible for the jury to draw any other conclusion than that you wished them to find a verdict of guilty? And when you had done all this you devoted the rest of the day— about two hours and a half—to the prisoner's evidence, having given upwards of eleven hours to the evidence for the prosecution. If you think this consistent with your duty and with trial by jury, I can only say you stand alone; for if any faith is to be placed in the public Press, in the tone of general conversation, in the loudly-expressed voice of all independent persons, you have struck a blow at trial by jury from which it never will recover, unless the great mass of the community now protest against such a course in language that cannot be mistaken. If persons are thus persuaded into giving verdicts by judges in high station there is an end to the liberties of Englishmen. Trial by jury becomes, in the language of Lord Denman, "a mockery, a delusion, and a snare," and the most glorious privilege which we have inherited from our ancestors degenerates into an engine of tyranny, cruelty, and falsehood, to entrap and destroy those who regard it as their dearest birthright. My lord, if there be no sympathy for my brother, let there be at least a feeling for our own rights when they are invaded, and let the public meditate in time that it is by little and little the grandest rights of states and empires are insidiously sapped until they perish.

I am not about to recapitulate the arguments of Serjeant Shee, which prove that this charge of murder is one of the most improbable in the annals of criminal jurisprudence. These arguments failed with the jury because they were not permitted to exercise a calm judgment upon them. But I may call attention to the gross fallacy on which the whole prosecution was founded— that of starting with the positive theory of a murder and then endeavouring by all means to fix that murder upon my brother.

It is, therefore, clear that in this case a great, and what would have proved in any other an insurmountable difficulty meets one at the threshold—that in order to obtain a conviction one must reverse the legal and customary order of proceeding. Instead of proving a murder first and discovering the murderer afterwards, you first prove the murderer and thence deduce a murder. That is the course which the necessities of the case compelled the Attorney-General to pursue, and it was your duty to have exploded that theory in your summing up. But you did no such thing. On the contrary, you went into all the antecedents of the prisoner, and put them to the jury as an element in the consideration of whether a murder had or had not been committed. And having thus prepared the minds of the jury by the antimony of motives, suspicious circumstances, &c., you then administer to them the strychnia of a murder. You descanted more especially upon the purchase of strychnia by the prisoner just before Cook's death as strong evidence that Cook was poisoned. That circumstance, coming after proof of Cook's death by strychnia, would reduce the case to one of almost geometrical accuracy; but by itself, in the absence of such proof—nay, in presence of scientific proof to the contrary—of what value is it? Besides, it is quite incompatible with the case for the prosecution. The prosecution suggests that my brother had a deliberate intention to murder Cook, and had for ten days been adopting preliminary measures to carry that intention into effect; that when the time for the completion of his infernal purpose approached (which was on the Sunday), he wrote for Mr. Jones, of Lutterworth, a surgeon, and a personal friend of the deceased, to come over and be present at his last moments, in order that his presence there might stave off suspicion. Now, if that were so, is it not reasonable to suppose that he would have had the poison ready to be administered, and not trust to the doctrine of chances to procure it at a village like Rugeley when wanted for immediate use? Surely the professional poisoner might naturally be expected to keep a good stock-in-trade? Nothing of the sort. On the Monday night (if the case for the prosecution is to be believed) he gets from Newton three grains of strychnia, which he gives almost immediately afterwards to Cook. Cook is attacked with strychnia-tetanus, but recovers, and is nearly quite well the next day. The prisoner, finding Cook not dead, gets six grains from Roberts on the Tuesday, which he also gives to Cook, and this time he succeeds in his purpose. Now, is not this—the blackest part of the case against my brother—very improbable? Would the poisoner of fourteen people do his work in such a clumsy fashion? But, then, the possession or destination of those six grains is not attempted to be accounted for. That certainly is a most inculpatory circumstance. But we must remember this, that until it was known that the prisoner had had this strychnia, it was never suspected that Cook died from strychnia. It was that circumstance which originated the train of ideas as to my brother's guilt; and when charged with murder he may naturally have thought that the strychnia, if found in his possession, would be evidence of his guilt, and so may have destroyed it; whereas, if he had preserved it, it would have been the strongest proof of his innocence. Then, if he did destroy it, he could give no proof of the fact, for, of course, it would be done without the privity of any one else. Now, if he had been in France he himself would have been subjected to a strict examination upon all the points of the case, and his own statement upon that point, whether for or against him, would have been in evidence. Moreover, how does this part of the case reconcile with the medical evidence? It is admitted on all hands that half a grain is sufficient to destroy life; but a grain, or two, or three, no man could survive that. Still, the inference unquestionably is that that quantity was administered on Monday night but did not kill, and the next day the dose was doubled! Nine grains in all! And of these nine grains of strychnia, which unquestionably were administered if Cook died from that poison, no trace whatever can be discovered in the body!

I will not further dwell upon this subject, but come to your lordship's conduct and charge, which are the more immediate objects of this letter.

The first thing which appeared to me unfair was the order which your lordship made that the medical witnesses for the Crown should be accommodated with seats in the most convenient part of the Court, while the greater number of witnesses for the defence were obliged to stand during the greater part of the trial—no slight mode of exhausting them mentally as well as physically. And so rigidly was this carried out that none of the medical witnesses for the defence were admitted into Court until all the witnesses for the prosecution had taken their seats, and fully preoccupied all the vacant space. This may appear a slight thing, but I know how greatly it affected some of the older medical witnesses for my brother, and how much it weakened them for the violent attacks which the Attorney-General made upon them. There are few men, however vigorous, who will not be worn out by standing for eight or nine days in the crowded atmosphere of such a Court as the Old Bailey.

The next thing which appeared to me unfair was your permitting the Attorney-General to open to the jury all the facts connected with Bates's insurance, and this you did after Serjeant Shee objected. It is true that evidence of this negotiation was afterwards excluded as being irrelevant, but why did you not exclude the statement which you must have known beforehand would prejudice the jury against my brother? The simple fact of that affair was that my brother wanted to raise money for Bates, whom he pitied; that this device was resorted to for that purpose, and I am told that not on the turf alone, but in commercial circles, it is a common thing to raise loans upon the deposit of insurance policies. Your lordship, however, allowed the jury to infer that my brother and Cook wanted to insure Bates's life in order that they might afterwards murder him!

It is a principle of the law that nothing which is said in the absence of a prisoner can be given in evidence against him. But you permitted a conversation between Cook and Fisher to be proved when my brother was not present, and when he could, consequently, have had no means of contradicting Cook's drunken folly about the "dosing." In this, I am told by a most accomplished member of the bar, you violated one of the leading rules of evidence—one adapted for the protection of all men, as it is obvious that if private slander be once permitted to be detailed before a jury, the most innocent man living may be hanged on statements made behind his back. In your charge to the jury you seemed conscious of the impropriety you had committed, and you did not read that portion of the evidence to them, but it had already produced a fatal influence on their minds. Yet you would have read it, as I could plainly see, only that Judge Cresswell interposed just as you came to it. What renders this more indefensible is that Serjeant Shee objected to it, but you overruled his objection. (See verbatim report of trial, p. 26.) And the Attorney-General himself refrained from stating it in his opening address, because he said it was not evidence (report, p. 9). Upon its manifest falsehood I need not say a word. It is incredible that Cook should say to Fisher my brother poisoned him, and yet afterwards go to Rugeley with him, dine with him, send for him every hour in the day, entrust him with all his moneys, make no mention of "dosing" to his oldest friend, Dr. Jones, and retain his affectionate faith in William to the last. Yet, not one word of these obvious reflections did you put before the jury to weaken the force of the illegal evidence you allowed to go before them. You only said that it was "mysterious," whereas, in truth, it was incredible; and you added that "Cook was under the influence of Palmer to a very great degree," as if he would have continued so after an attempt to kill him. It was very soon apparent that your lordship was resolved not only to admit illegal evidence, but also to allow the prosecuting counsel great liberties in their mode of examination. Serjeant Shee repeatedly called your attention to Mr. James putting "leading questions" to the witnesses, but you overruled him, until he told Mr. Smith that it was quite useless to object any further. I am told that every member of the bar in Court was of opinion that the questions were irregular in the leading shape in which they were put.

In his opening speech the Attorney-General made the following statement to the jury:—"The next morning, at an early hour, Palmer was with him, and from that time, during the whole of Saturday and Sunday, he was constantly in attendance on him. He ordered him some coffee. Coffee was brought up by the chambermaid, Elizabeth Mills. It was taken into the room, given to the prisoner, and she left. Palmer, having received the coffee, gave it to the man, who was in bed, and had, therefore, an opportunity of dealing with it" (report, p. 12). Elizabeth Mills was called to prove this statement. So far from proving that it was given to Palmer, she distinctly swore that she "placed it in Cook's hands," so that Palmer had no opportunity of tampering with it (report, p. 33). Yet your lordship, whose duty it was to see that none of these misstatements should be unobserved upon to the jury, did not point out this remarkable discrepancy, nor did you think it incumbent on you to set them right upon a point of such material import to my brother. You allowed them to believe that he had poisoned that coffee when the evidence negatived his dealing with it at all.

In commenting upon the evidence of this woman, Elizabeth Mills, you said that Serjeant Shee had made "a most foul charge against her and Stevens," representing that she had been bribed, but that you did "not see the smallest pretence for such a suggestion." I wonder that, after your three score and ten years in this wicked world, you could have been so exceedingly innocent and simple. You come from a country where the inhabitants are keen-sighted enough, yet you thrust yourself forward as the defender of Eliza Mills, a woman upon whose countenance her character was written, and whose whole demeanour flashed conviction to every mind of the sort of person she was. This woman was brought away from Rugeley by Stevens, she was lodged by him at Dolly's, where she saw him "always" in the sitting-room, that gentleman having called "merely to see how I liked London, and whether I was well in health, and all that, to see whether I liked the place," though she afterwards added that he called about "sometimes one thing, sometimes another," and "many more things which I cannot remember. I do not keep things in my head for weeks or months together. I do not pretend to keep in my head what the conversation was," yet "there were many more things talked about that I do not wish to mention. Perhaps my thoughts were occupied about something else." And when the same woman is asked to give some account of herself, and her visit to the man Dutton at Hitchingley, and asked to name "who are your friends?" she answers, "I have some friends there." "Who are they?" says Serjeant Shee, to which Mills answered, "Friends are friends, I suppose," and then she gave an account that she slept with the mother, and was "engaged to the son," though what she meant by this she did not venture to explain. Your lordship, however, "saw not the smallest pretence," &c.

Again, when the deposition of the same woman was read, in which there was no mention of the "twitchings and jerkings," and all those other horrors which she imparted into her narrative, and which she enforced by so much pantomimic action; and when in the deposition she proved that the "broth was very good," while in the evidence at the trial she swore that "it poisoned her," you coolly told the jury that it was "an important omission; but you will say whether that which is stated is not substantially the same as the evidence which she gave on oath when examined before you." Whereas you ought to have said that they were substantially opposite, the two statements being reconcilable by no manner of even Scotch chicanery. In fact, the manner in which you supported this woman was exactly opposite to that which judges usually do when persons of that description come before them; and I have heard of judges telling juries to place no reliance on witnesses whose conduct and demeanour were every way superior to that of Mills. I can conceive no greater blow to public trial than the support given by a judge to a witness like Mills, but "a fellow feeling makes us wondrous kind," and you adopted her with all the fervour of a champion of romance. When it was proposed to contradict this woman by Dr. Collier, who was in Court, Judge Alderson said, with unrestrained anger, "It is better Dr. Collier should be absent from the Court. If he is to be examined as to facts, he ought not to be here at all; he is here under the false pretence of being a doctor," forgetting that Taylor, Rees, and Monkton, who were also to be examined as to facts on behalf of the Crown, were then present, though not, of course, "under the false pretence of being doctors!" The jury very soon saw what the judges thought of the case. Mr. Gardner, the lawyer of Rugeley, was then called to prove that the coroner had not asked several questions of Mills, and that the jurymen had expostulated with him for not doing so. This illegal course you permitted, assigning the following strange reason for it:—"What was said there is part of the transaction of taking the evidence. It cannot be evidence against the prisoner, but it may explain the manner in which the depositions are taken." It requires no lawyer to tell me that "if it cannot be evidence against the prisoner, then it has no right to go upon your notes, or to be stated in the presence of the jury at all, whom it cannot fail to affect, although they are sworn to decide according to the evidence." Yet all this you permitted, allowing the Attorney-General to damage the character of the coroner in every way he could; and there is no knowing what you could not have got Gardner to say had not Judge Cresswell interposed and terminated the scene. He said "the depositions which had been put in did not show that any questions had been put by the jurymen. If they had contained such questions they would have shown the motive of the jury in putting them. But the Court was left totally in the dark as to whether questions had been put by the coroner or any other person. For anything that appeared to the contrary, the witnesses might have made a voluntary statement without any questions at all being put to them. No foundation was, therefore, laid for the Attorney-General's inquiries." Every one in Court saw how chagrined you were at this interposition of Judge Cresswell, but you were obliged to submit, as Alderson concurred with him. One word with reference to Ward, the coroner. He is a very able lawyer. The jury wanted to put questions as to various rumours about my brother William poisoning Lord George Bentinck, Bladen the brewer, and twenty other people; and as the coroner overruled all such folly, the sapient jurymen did expostulate with him, and this was Gardner's mare's nest!

The next witness examined was Mrs. Brooks, and though she gave evidence of the most valuable kind to the prisoner, yet not one syllable of it did you comment upon to the jury. The main evidence against my brother, connected with Shrewsbury, related to the sickness with which Cook was seized. If, therefore, other persons in various parts of the town were similarly affected, it could not fail to benefit William, for he could not be said to have poisoned or "dosed" all the others, especially as he was not at Shrewsbury at all when they were sick, but was at home at Rugeley. Serjeant Shee asked Mrs. Brooks (report, p. 54), "Do you know whether other racing men were taken ill on the Wednesday at Shrewsbury?—There were a great number; one of my company was dreadfully ill, and there was a wonder what could cause it. We made an observation. We thought the water might have been poisoned at Shrewsbury. We were all afflicted in some way by sickness—sick and purged." After twelve days the jury can be scarcely expected to have remembered this most important admission. It was your incumbent duty to have recalled their attention to it, for it was strongly in my brother's favour; but, if they recollected it at all, you took care that they should pay no attention to it, for, after reading to them all that she said in her direct examination, you remarked, "This ends the affair about Mr. Cook's illness at Shrewsbury, and, taken by itself, it really amounts to very little, but, you observe, it is connected with what follows when he returned to Rugeley" (report, p. 311). You then passed on, not saying a word about the incident just mentioned, and, associating in the minds of the jury with subsequent transactions at Rugeley that part of Mrs. Brooks' evidence which was brought forward for the prosecution, you kept back the most valuable portion of her testimony to my brother, and entirely ignored its existence in the case.

Dr. Jones, of Lutterworth, the friend of Cook, to whom my brother writes, gave evidence of the most valuable kind, showing Cook's broken constitution, his sores, his syphilis, his secondary symptoms, his unbounded confidence in William, and William's brotherly kindness to him, yet not one word of comment did you offer to the jury upon these matters. The only remark you made was one highly damaging to my brother, and was as follows:—"At first sight it would appear very much to be in his favour that he sends for a medical man, who is a friend of Cook's, and who took a lively interest in him, and wished him well. But, at the same time, there are circumstances in this case that may enable you to draw a different conclusion, but I will not suggest" (report, p. 312). No, you did not suggest in words, but, pausing here, you looked at the jury and shook your head at them for half a minute in the most mysterious manner, so that they must have been the dullest of all mankind if they had not perfectly well known what you meant. I have heard more than one person remark upon the Scotch subtlety of this mode of proceeding. Your lordship is a sort of biographer of the Chief Justices of England, though I am told that the unfortunate Dr. Giles, whom you had the pleasure of sentencing at Oxford to twelve months' imprisonment, is the real author of that production; and I suppose you hope to figure one day in the literary gallery with those whom you have commemorated. It would be impossible, perhaps, for a future historian who merely read your proceedings in my brother's trial, to form an accurate notion of your demeanour; but, with the light which this letter will throw upon the transaction, such an annalist—if ever you should be thought worthy of notice—will be able to inform future times how you managed to convince a jury without leaving any trace behind of the means by which you did it.

The next witness of any consequence was Newton; and here I should have thought your lordship's feelings as a man, if they had not entirely perished, would have exhibited some trace of natural passion. Newton, according to his own account, was an accessory to the murder, and the murderer after the fact; he knew the current gossip of Rugeley and Stafford, that Cook had been poisoned by my brother; he assisted at the post-mortem examinations for the purpose of detecting the poison which the murderer had used; he had an interview on the Sunday after Cook's death with William, in which this skilful poisoner (whose chemical knowledge of the minimum dose of strychnia which destroys life, and of the hitherto unknown fact that antimony neutralises the discovery of strychnia, places him a hundred years in advance of all the chemists of the age), asks the ignorant shopboy of the nature and the effects of strychnia! And when the learned Newton gives him information on the matter, the poisoner snaps his fingers in joy and exclaims, "That will do"; and after that he goes with him to the post-mortem examination; and after that Newton swears against him at the inquest; and after that he keeps the deadly secret buried in his bosom from November until the middle of the month of May, just one day before the trial! And after the trial he communicates the further fact to the Attorney-General that it was he who made up the deadly pills for my brother on the Monday night. With reference to the credibility of this monstrous witness you have not one word to say, though you did not hesitate to stigmatise Mr. Nunneley and Dr. M'Donald as persons on whom the jury could place no reliance; and in the course of their cross-examination you looked at them in a manner significant of total incredulity of their testimony. Observe the mode in which you support Newton. You say, "There is no contradiction of anything that he has said." Why did you not tell the jury that, as he fixed no time or place when any one but the prisoner himself, whose mouth was sealed, was by, it was impossible he could be contradicted? You go on (report, p. 313)—"Well, then, you are to consider what is the probability of his inventing this wicked and most abominable lie? He had no ill-will towards the prisoner at the bar." (Who told you that? Who proved it? What right had you to assume it? What right had you to tell it to the jury?) "He had nothing to gain by injuring him much less by saying anything to affect his life." (I ask again who told you all this, and on what pretence did you venture to say so to the jury?) "I see no motive that Mr. Newton could have for inventing a lie to take away the life of another person." (Are you omniscient, then, and do you profess to read that inscrutable mystery, the human heart, and have you not read in the annals of crime of innumerable murders and perjuries committed without apparent motive?) "No inducement could be held out to him by the Crown; he says himself that no inducement was held out to him, and that he at last disclosed it from a sense of justice." (As if a man who screened a murderer for six months could have any sense of justice.) "If you believe him, certainly the evidence is very strong against the prisoner at the bar." Not a word of caution is here given; not one Scotch hint of doubt in this witness. Your "canny" countrymen are not always so credulous; they are not at all times so easy of belief in persons of this description. Yet your milk of human kindness is so pure that you cannot for your life imagine the least reason why Newton should not be believed.

But it was on the evidence of Roberts that your lordship used observations which had the most powerful effect on the jury, and since then upon the public mind. I have already explained how it was that the prisoner, even if he were a guilty man, might have denied the purchase of the strychnia from Roberts, as he always denied its purchase from Newton, was deprived by artifice of the witness Cockayne, who could have thrown a new light upon this affair, and I have shown how Bates prevaricated with reference to the dogs and the brood mares. My brother being in this way at the mercy of Bates, and juggled out of Cockayne, in what possible way could he account for the disposal of the strychnia? Yet you, who knew all this a thousand times better than the jury, told them that "a very serious case is adduced, supposing you should come to the conclusion that the symptoms of Mr. Cook were consistent with that of poison. If you think the symptoms are accounted for by merely ordinary tetanus, of course the fact of strychnia being obtained by the prisoner at the bar is of very little weight; but, if you should come to the conclusion that the symptoms which Mr. Cook exhibited on the Monday night and Tuesday night are consistent with strychnia, then a fearful case is made out against him." The learned counsel did not favour us with the theory which he had formed in his own mind respecting that strychnia, and how he considered it to be consistent with the view that he suggested. There is no evidence of the intention with which it was purchased. There is no evidence how it was applied, and what became of it, or what was done with it (report, p. 313). What modern judge before yourself in a case of death ever ventured to tell a jury that "a fearful crime was made out against the prisoner"? Scraggs or Belknap might have done it; Jeffreys might not have blushed to use the words, but that they should now be used in the face of an open Court, and with a pantomimic gesture and grim stare at the jury such as you gave, are facts discreditable to any law. By what right, with what face, on what authority did you venture to tell the jury that his "learned counsel" was bound to prove his innocence or to account for his possession or disposal of the strychnia? I have always understood it to be the law that every man was presumed to be innocent until he was proved to be guilty; but you have reversed this majestic, merciful principle, and intimate that every man is guilty until his counsel proves him to be innocent. A more shameful perversion of the law than this, I am told by persons in authority, has never been witnessed. Well also did you know that Serjeant Shee was not entitled to put forward to the jury "the theory which he had formed in his own mind respecting the strychnia." Had he ventured to do so I have no doubt you would have interrupted him with unfeeling harshness, and repeated to him in even stronger language than you did that species of insult "that a witness had no more right to make himself an advocate than an advocate to make himself a witness." And then you glaringly tell the jury that there has been no "evidence of the intention," as if you did not well know that if such evidence were possible to be given it could only be given by my brother William himself (who, by law, could not speak); and that, even if he could speak and was about to mention his intention, you would have stopped him, and said that such evidence was illegal, facts, not intentions, being the only admissible evidence in a Court of law. Yet you gravely complain as if the thing might have been done, and the jury, who probably believed you, convicted my brother because he could not prove an impossibility.

My lord, if our present system of representation were anything but a mockery, and if the House of Commons were constituted as it was in the days of Pym, Vane, and Hampden, I verily believe you would be impeached for such a charge as this, for you stated to the jury that the prisoner was guilty because he did not do that which you absolutely knew he could not do, namely, prove his intention. But, under the present system of things, judges may do anything they please with impunity, and no one calls attention to it, because the wretches whom they hang or exile are friendless outcasts, deprived of all sympathy from the world, enemies often of society, which thus becomes their enemy; and the great body of the community not being acquainted with the law, and the only persons who are, namely, the bar, being a body of degraded, crawling, sneaking slaves and sycophants who do not venture to arraign a judge, because if they do they fear that attorneys will desert them; in this way the most frightful licentiousness of power is given to men like you, and they are as despotic as the Cadis in the remotest part of Turkey. In civil cases, indeed, there is a check upon them, because there the parties are rich, and there is an opportunity for a new trial, but in criminal cases there is no new trial, even in the most scandalous and infamous conduct of the judge; and the consequence is that a wicked man may commit almost any conceivable crime upon the bench, and gratify his love of blood to the utmost without restraint or fear, than which I can conceive no more shocking infamy to exist.

Next, as to the evidence of Mr. Stevens, you made it a rule all through violently to censure Serjeant Shee whenever he said anything against the witnesses for the Crown, but not one syllable did you say against the Attorney-General for his attack on the medical witnesses for my brother. Thus you say here (report, p. 313)—"The learned counsel in the discharge of his duty did, as he was perfectly justified in doing, make very violent attacks upon the character and conduct of Mr. Stevens. It rests with you to say whether that attack was well founded." But had you not said that he was justified in doing so, and did not this imply that Stevens deserved it? And if it "rested with the jury," what right had you to add, "I own I can see nothing in Mr. Stevens in the slightest degree calling for it"? Thus you first say Serjeant Shee was "justified," then you say it "rests with the jury," and then, lest they may jointly agree with the serjeant, you volunteer your own opinion, that Serjeant Shee was not justified. Conduct like this requires no comment, but if my brother is hanged upon such a charge, who is guilty of his blood?

The next witness was Mary Keeling. She gave important evidence as to the condition of the body. Mills and one or two other of the witnesses had endeavoured to show that the body was "bent like a bow," to use the imaginative language of that man Taylor, and this was pressed in to support your view of the case that "the death was consistent with strychnia." Now, Mary Keeling proved the exact reverse of this, but you did not either take it in your notes or read it to the jury. Serjeant Shee was obliged to interrupt you. I copy from the report, p. 313—

"Mr. Serjeant Shee—I am not quite sure whether your lordship read that the witness said that the body was lying straight on the back on the bed?

"Lord Campbell—I have read all that I have taken down. Is it in the cross-examination?

"Mr. Serjeant Shee—No, in the examination in chief. 'How was the body lying?—On the back, straight down on the bed.'

"Mr. James—Where do you read that from?

"Mr. Serjeant Shee—It is in two reports; one in the *Times* and one from the shorthand writer's notes.

"Lord Campbell—Bamford says it was lying straight on the bed.

"Mr. Serjeant Shee—I did not allude to Bamford's examination. This witness says so too."

And there the matter ended, and though it was admitted that it had been said, and though it corroborated Dr. Bamford and Dr. Jones, and entirely refuted the "opisthotonos" theory of Taylor and Mills, and thus got rid of one of the most remarkable symptoms "consistent with poisoning by strychnia," yet not one word of comment did you offer upon it; but, as you said, it was not upon your notes—where it ought to have been—you left the jury unadvised upon this essential contradiction, which, taken with the evidence of the two medical men, entirely demolished Mills and her congenial companion Taylor, and took out of the mouth of Sir Benjamin Brodie and the other medical witnesses one of those vital symptoms on which they founded their diagnosis of the causes of death. For, if there was no opisthotonos, or bent bow-like shape, then Cook did not die of strychnia; and this being proved not to have been so by these three witnesses, or, at all events, left in deep doubt, my brother was entitled to the benefit of that doubt, and should have been acquitted.

The same wish of omission was manifest in your notes when you read out the evidence of Devonshire to the jury; you forgot to tell the jury that Cook's left lung was diseased, which was important, as his death arose from natural causes. Serjeant Shee was again obliged to interfere (report, p. 314)—

"Mr. Serjeant Shee—I think the witness said there were traces of emphysema in the left lung?

"Mr. Baron Alderson—Yes."

But not one word of comment did you make.

Myatt, the postboy, whose testimony was wholly incredible, you bolstered up with this remark, "Now, there seems no reason to doubt the evidence of this poor boy." As if you could fathom the secret motives of man.

Upon the letter which my brother addressed to the coroner you say—"This letter is a most improper letter, addressed by the prisoner to Mr. Ward, the coroner, who is, of course, a judge. It so happens that I myself am the chief coroner of England, but all the coroners are judges as much as I am, and ought, with equal integrity and indifference, to administer the law of the country." This self praise, my lord, is of that species which is said to stink. It would have been better if you had not eulogised your conduct upon this trial, but allowed others to do so. You did the same thing when you were sentencing my brother, for you prefaced your "hanging speech" by these words—"William Palmer, after a fair and impartial trial," &c., &c. You then go on, and suggest to the jury that my brother was guilty because he wrote that letter. "You will say whether this is consistent with innocence; it is clear tampering with the judge." Yet the conduct of the gentleman mentioned by Sir Matthew Hale, or the French gentleman who offered to surrender his wife's will, was just as suspicious, though the first was hanged innocently, and the last, fortunately for himself, not tried by you.

When Cheshire was cross-examined by Serjeant Shee he asked him, "Did he not say I knew they would not, for I am as innocent as a baby?" You immediately interrupted, in a most angry tone, saying, "He has already said that," whereas in truth he had not done so, but the phrase was likely to have an influence on the jury.

Again, when Herring was examined, and Mr. Welsby proposed to give some evidence from the pages of the lost betting book, about whose disappearance one of the greatest points was made against William, Serjeant Shee said, "We cannot have the contents."

"Lord Campbell—The last account we have got is that it was in Mr. Palmer's possession.

"Mr. Serjeant Shee—I do not think there is any proof of its ever having been in Mr. Palmer's possession.

"Mr. Attorney-General—We show that it was in the dead man's room on the Tuesday night before his death, and Mr. Palmer is afterwards seen looking about; we have no one else, my lord, that we can resort to." ... (This was utterly false, for the last person who saw it, or swore she saw it, was Mills, and that was on Monday night.)

"Lord Campbell—I do not think we can receive this evidence" (report, p. 41).

Thus you were about to admit the contents of that book on the plea that my brother possessed it, a plea entirely untrue, and not only not supported, but even negatived by the evidence. My lord, if you do these things in matters of life and death, who among us is safe?

When Bates was called, it was proposed to give in evidence the facts of the insurance, and you permitted a discussion to arise which put the jury in possession of all the facts. You then said, "On the Attorney-General's opening I doubted whether this would be relevant and proper evidence to be received at this trial" (yet you permitted him to open it!), "and upon consideration my brothers agree with me it is too remote to be admissible." But all the evil had then been done, the jury having been prejudiced by the statement and discussion. And not one word did you say to them in your charge about disabusing their minds of the false impression which it might have made.

When you commented on the medical evidence you told the jury that my brother had an opportunity of substituting for Bamford's pills others made by himself. What right had you to do that? Was it not leading their minds to an inference that he did so, and that the substituted pills contained poison? (report, p. 315).

You introduced Sir Benjamin Brodie with great praises; in fact, you praised all the medical witnesses for the Crown, and confined your applause to only one of those for the prisoner, who slightly coincided with Taylor's notions. You said of Sir Benjamin—"You will take into consideration the solemn opinion of this distinguished medical man, that he never knew a case in which the symptoms that he heard described arose from any disease. He has seen and known the various diseases that afflict the human frame in all their multiplicity, and he knows of no natural disease such as will answer the symptoms which he heard described in the case of Cook; and if it did not arise from natural disease, then the inference is that it arose from other causes" (report, p. 316). Now, Sir Benjamin formed his opinion upon two inconsistent statements made by Mills and Dr. Jones. If what Mills swore was all true, then, perhaps, Sir Benjamin Brodie would have been justified in saying that no disease that he had seen accorded with that description; but if what Mills swore was all false, and it was entirely inconsistent with what Dr. Jones proved, then also it would not be consistent with natural disease, or with anything in Nature, and yet my brother be innocent of this crime. If Mills invented a number of symptoms which no medical man had ever seen, and it is what an ignorant chambermaid who was disposed to perjure herself might be supposed to do, then what Sir Benjamin Brodie proved would have been correct, and he could not assign to any natural disease that which was, in truth, but a fictitious narrative; but it would not necessarily follow from that that Cook died of poison, as you told the jury it would, but it would as logically follow that the whole of the symptoms not being in accordance with any known disease were invented by an unskilful person, and unskilfully put together for the occasion. I think you saw in its full force the effect of this, for it will be seen by the report that you prevented Serjeant Shee from discovering on which of these two witnesses Sir Benjamin relied in premising his opinion.

"Considering how rarely tetanus is witnessed at all, would you think that the description of a chambermaid, and of a provincial medical man who had only seen one case of tetanus, could be relied upon by you to state what description of disease the disease observed was?—I must say I thought the description very clearly given." (How could it be given clearly if it accorded with no known disease? Besides, the answer is an evasion of the question.)

"Mr. Serjeant Shee—On which of the two would you rely, supposing they differed—the chambermaid or the medical man?

"Lord Campbell—That is hardly a proper question" (report, p. 120).

In my judgment no question could be more proper, for if Sir Benjamin relied on Mills, then the jury would have known why he pronounced so strong an opinion, and if they disliked her, the opinion would go for nothing; but if Sir Benjamin relied on Dr. Jones, then the symptoms described by him were accordant with many known diseases, and Sir Benjamin Brodie must have said so. This ruling therefore hanged my brother!

But let me hasten to a close. I am so heartbroken, so wearied out with fatigue, and pain, and grief; I am so utterly disgusted by these enumerations that I feel I cannot go on. From the first to the last my brother had no chance. You introduced him to the jury as a forger in the following words:—"There has been evidence which certainly implicates the prisoner in transactions of a very discreditable nature. It appears that he had forged a great many bills of exchange, and that he had entered into transactions not of a reputable nature." If all this was irrelevant why did you introduce it? In the same tone was your allusion to the "student's book," which even the Crown abandoned. "This book has been laid before you in evidence, and certainly I think I need hardly beg of you to pay no regard to it, because it was a book that Palmer had when he was a surgeon, and at a time when I have no doubt he would have shrunk with horror at any such crime as that with which he is charged here to-day. There is, in the title page of the book, 'Strychnia kills by causing tetanic fixing of the respiratory muscles,' and in another part there is a description of what nux vomica is, and how strychnia is produced from it, with these words—'Strychnia kills by causing tetanic fixing of the respiratory muscles.' Again I say that I think this being found in his possession ought not to weigh at all against the prisoner at the bar" (report, p. 315). If it ought not to weigh against him, why, in Heaven's name, did you so solemnly drag it in? Why did you read and re-read it? Would it not have been fairer to put it aside altogether than to impress it on the minds of the jury, and then tell them it ought not to weigh at all? Is it possible to believe you were sincere? Is it possible the jury could have drawn any other conclusion from your dwelling on it than that you wished them to regard it as proof of guilt?

With what regret I have written this letter I need not say. My own avocations are mercy, peace, and charity, but there is a time when duty compels a man to lay aside his garb of peacefulness, and to assume the weapon of the world. I feel I should have been a traitor to the truth, to my family, yea, even to the country, if I had feared, from any selfish motives, to abate one word that I have here written. Against yourself personally I feel no anger; but, indeed, I am sorry for you, and I tremble. My lord, you are in a fearful condition. If your mind is so tainted that you decide all other cases as you decided this, you will have a most dreadful account to render to a most just God. Before Him how contemptible is human nature in its pride, and robes, and silken vanity, and self-worship; before Him what a wretched insect is the judge who makes others tremble, and flings about his sentences of death, and dabbles in blood as if it were water. You are now exulting in your station, but in a few short weeks, or months (for you can scarcely hope for years) you will be no more; nothing but a noisome corpse from which all will flee—loathsome and abominable, dust and ashes, a shadow and a name. You will be shut up in a box, and put away into the earth, to form food for worms and to deal with abomination; and all your state, and all your bowing, sycophantic train will fear to look upon you, and will fly to others, and you will have left nothing but perishable mercy and a vain name, and your life will have been like smoke. But there is within you a part that liveth, and will have to answer for the past, and to render up an account of the things done in the body, before a Lord and Judge who makes the heavens tremble and before whom the mountains are but as grains of dust. Answer me, and say how will you face that fearful tribunal if you leave one stone unturned in the present case to discover the whole truth, or if you oppose the application that will be made for a respite until science has made clear either guilt or innocence! All human testimony is fallible; most dangerous it is to destroy life upon a train of circumstances depending on the veracity of such persons as Mills, and Taylor, and Wyatt, and Newton. But the conclusions of science are certain, and this fact, the first chemists of the day aver, can be made as clear as light, that if strychnia were administered to Cook in his lifetime, it is now in his body, and can be detected by means that are infallible. If, then, it is undoubted that my brother poisoned Cook, what objection can there be to exhume the body, and convince the whole world of the fact? but if it be not certain, what a frightful crime are we then plunging into, to hang a man about whose guilt there still remains a tremendous body of doubt? or what reparation shall you make to his orphan boy, to his mother and sister, who love and have faith in him, if a few short weeks shall demonstrate, as in the rapid advance of science they may do, that William Palmer has been murdered on a scientific theory invented for the purpose of blood, and scouted by men of the greatest eminence in chemical analysis? Even while these pages pass through the press I read in the papers a letter which utterly destroys Taylor's new hypothesis, and annihilates for ever the foundations on which he rested. It is published also in a morning journal, the *Times*, which cries aloud for my brother's blood and fixes his guilt, not upon the fact proved at the trial, for the editors of that able paper knew that these facts are but as cobwebs, but upon what he is supposed to have done when he was taken to Stafford prison, upon his threat, if he used the threat, to destroy his life. Weak and miserable must be the case for the prosecution when their advocates are compelled to resort to this flimsy *ad captandum* argument for the vulgar. Who is there so hardy as to be able to answer for himself that, under similar accusations, he would not resort to suicide, or who but the most uncharitable would regard that suicide as proof conclusive of the guilt of poisoning? He was overwhelmed with debts which he had no means of paying, he had violated the civil law, and had forged his mother's name to the extent of thousands; he was accused of fourteen or fifteen hideous and dreadful murders. He was prostrated in mind and body by sickness, by weakness, by anxiety, by a thousand conflicting passions of grief, despair, remorse, and indignation at the fearful torrents of calumny against him; and because the human mind gave way under this awful load of calamities, and he declared that he would willingly die—who is the man that can fairly say he is therefore guilty of a murder? The editor of the *Times* has indeed said so; and many influential persons will, perhaps, blame him, but I, for one, consider that his conduct, though censurable, was natural, and what might have been expected, and I draw no such conclusion from the circumstances as the *Times* has done. But however this may be, it is not to the *Times*, but to you and the Home Secretary I look, and in your hands is the life of William Palmer. I have not flattered you in aught, but I have spoken as I felt. I ask you not to respite him for my sake, for the sake of his family, nor even for public justice and humanity. These appeals would probably be lost on you. But I, as a minister of the Gospel, ask you to respite him for your own sake—for you will have the guilt of his blood and the infamy of his death if he is wrongly executed; and if his innocence should be hereafter demonstrated, his memory will cling upon your soul; it will be like a mountain of lead upon your heart; it will stifle your cries to God, and drag you down with that darkness of hell which is prepared for those who violate the commandment, "Thou shalt not kill."

THOMAS PALMER.

APPENDIX II.

SHORT ACCOUNT OF THE JUDGES AND COUNSEL ENGAGED IN THE CASE.

JOHN CAMPBELL, Baron Campbell, Lord Chief Justice of the Queen's Bench. Lord Campbell had been Lord Chief Justice six years when he presided at the trial. He was seventy-seven years of age. Three years after he resigned the Chief Justiceship, and became Lord Chancellor at eighty, a greater age than any of his predecessors on the Woolsack had reached on being appointed. He held his office for two years longer, and died at eighty-two, an age which none of his successors reached while holding it. On the day of his death, in 1861, he had sat in Court and attended a Cabinet Council. Lord Campbell's life as Chancellor and politician, and as the writer of the celebrated lives of the Lord Chancellors and the Chief Justices, forms too considerable a part of general history and literature to be detailed here. As a lawyer and judge his name stands high. His contemporaries never denied his abilities; but they considered his personal character and ambitions were selfish and by no means magnanimous. He is said by Sir John Macdonnell in the Dictionary of National Biography to have shown on the bench somewhat too openly an unworthy love of applause; and a tradition still lingers amongst lawyers of an ostentatious kind of politeness assumed by him when he intended anything deadly. The Usher of the Court at the Palmer trial is credited with saying that he knew the Chief meant to hang Palmer; he was so polite in requesting him to be seated. The tone of the letter we print from Palmer's brother expresses much of a prevalent feeling against Campbell. But, in Sir John Macdonnell's words, whatever difference of opinion there may be as to the spirit in which he served his country, there is none as to the value of the services themselves.

MR. BARON ALDERSON. Sir Edward Hall Alderson was in 1856 a Baron of the Court of Exchequer, where he was transferred in 1834, his original appointment as judge having been in 1830 to the Court of Common Pleas. He was born in 1787, so that he was now sixty-nine years of age. He was of Norfolk, and his father was Recorder of Yarmouth, Norwich, and Ipswich. His career at Cambridge was remarkable. In the year 1809, when he took his degree, he was Senior Wrangler and first Smith's prizeman, besides being first Chancellor's medallist, which was the highest honour then for classics. From 1817 to 1822 he was joint editor of the well-known Barnewall and Alderson's Reports of those years in the Court of King's Bench; and whilst so reporting he was, unlike reporters of these days, rapidly acquiring a practice, though he never took silk. He made no particular mark on the bench during his twenty-seven years of occupancy, and he died in 1857, the year after the trial. It is rather curious, in view of the attack made on him for prejudice in the letter to Lord Campbell, that he should have been known as a humane judge, with a desire to restrict capital punishment.

MR. JUSTICE CRESSWELL. Sir Cresswell Cresswell was the junior judge on the bench. His age was sixty-two, and he had been on the bench in the Court of Common Pleas since 1842, where he had established a reputation as a learned and strong judge. At the bar he had a large practice, and his legal name, apart from his judicial career, would have lived as one of the editors of the Barnewall and Cresswell's Reports in the King's Bench from 1822 to 1830. But his most abiding fame rests on his having been the first appointed judge of the new Probate and Divorce Court which was established in 1858. He became for the new principles and practice of divorce what Mansfield had been for commercial law—their creator and expounder. He sat in this Court, achieving a distinction which falls to the lot of few judges, until 1863. In July of this year he was knocked down in Constitution Hill by runaway horses belonging to Lord Aveland, which had been frightened by the breakdown of the carriage, and he died from the shock. On being made judge of the Probate and Divorce Court he was offered a peerage, but declined it, probably, as he was a bachelor, being sufficiently content with the ancestral name of Cresswell of Cresswell, near Morpeth. Though as a judge he was considered overbearing, it is noticeable that he did not intervene very much in the trial; the letter to Lord Campbell makes a point of contrasting his opinions on admission of evidence, and in other respects, as being in favour of the prisoner, while those of Lord Campbell and Mr. Baron Alderson were asserted to show bias and even strong and unfair prejudice.

SIR ALEXANDER JAMES EDMUND COCKBURN was appointed Solicitor-General in July, 1850, and early next year, in succession to Sir John Romilly, was made Attorney-General. He had up to the former year been obtaining considerable reputation as an advocate, had been appointed Q.C. in 1841, and especially had attracted attention by his defence of M'Naughten, who shot Mr. Drummond, Sir Robert Peel's secretary. He obtained his acquittal on the ground of insanity; a defence less credible and easy in 1843 than it subsequently became. But he first obtained real public distinction, and proved his qualifications to be of the highest class, in 1850 by speeches in Parliament,

Mr. Baron Alderson.

which led immediately to his appointment as Solicitor and Attorney-General as above mentioned. In the Don Pacifico debate Lord Palmerston had made the great speech of his life; and the law had been prepared for him by Cockburn. On the fourth night of the debate Mr. Cockburn replied to a long speech made by Mr. Gladstone against Palmerston's policy. At the end of his reply, according to a description by Sir Robert Peel, "one half of the Treasury benches were left empty, while honourable members ran one after another, tumbling over each other in their haste to shake hands with the honourable and learned member." He remained Attorney-General in Palmerston's Government until November, 1856; and thus it fell to him to conduct the Palmer prosecution. It is worth mentioning that Cockburn's reply at the end of the case was made without a single note. Palmer had therefore against him the greatest figure at the bar, and one of the most accomplished orators of his generation. It was in November, 1856, that Cockburn gave up his enormous income, and his Parliamentary position, to become Chief Justice of the Common Pleas; and the rest of his distinguished career, until his death in 1880, was spent in that office, or in that of Lord Chief Justice of England, which under the Judicature Acts superseded the two ancient Chief Justiceships. Sir Alexander Cockburn was of an ancient Scottish family; he was several times offered a peerage, but declined; he was never married, and his baronetcy expired with him.

JOHN EDWIN JAMES was forty-four years of age in 1856. "With the appearance of a prize fighter," he failed when he went on the stage as a young man and played "George Barnwell." His father, being a solicitor and an officer of the city of London it was natural for him to turn to the bar, and he was called at the Inner Temple in 1836, when he was twenty-four. By 1856 he was a noted advocate, had been made a Queen's Counsel, was Recorder of Brighton, and had a professional income of £7000 a year. He was member of Parliament for Marylebone in 1859; but in 1861 his retirement was announced. He was overwhelmed with pecuniary difficulties, and owed £100,000. An inquiry by his Inn in 1861 showed that he had in 1857 and 1860 inveigled a young man, a son of Lord Yarborough, into debts of £35,000; had obtained, three years before the trial, £20,000 from a solicitor by false misrepresentations; and in a case in which he was acting for the plaintiff had borrowed £1250 from defendant, promising to let him off easily in cross-examination. He was disbarred; went to America in 1861; was admitted to the bar there and practised; but in 1865 was playing at the Winter Garden Theatre, New York. He returned to England in 1873, and failed in persuading the judges to reconsider his case. He had married in 1861, but his wife divorced him in 1863. After his failure to return to the bar he was articled as a solicitor, but was not admitted; and he even offered himself again as candidate for Marylebone. He practised as an expert in American and English law, but sank into very poor circumstances, and a subscription was being made for him when he died in 1882.

SIR WILLIAM HENRY BODKIN. Three years after the trial Mr. Bodkin was appointed assistant judge of the Middlesex Sessions, and in 1867 was knighted. He held his office until a few weeks of his death, in 1874, at the age of eighty-three. At the time of the trial he was sixty-five, and was the most distinguished of the practitioners in specialised criminal business. In 1832 he had been appointed Recorder of Dover, after being only six years at the bar. He acquired a large practice on the Home Circuit and at the Middlesex, Westminster, and Kentish Sessions; he was counsel to the Treasury at the Central Criminal Court in 1856, and was *ex officio* of the counsel for the Crown in prosecutions in that Court. He retained this appointment until he was made a judge. As an expert on the practice of the poor law and secretary of the Mendicity Society he took great interest in poor law questions. In 1841 he had been returned to Parliament as a Conservative member for Rochester, but lost his seat at the election in 1847 for having supported Sir Robert Peel's Corn Law Bill. While he sat in Parliament he brought forward and passed an important measure of reform as to the chargeability of irremovable poor, which has become a permanent feature of our poor law system. Sir William held several distinguished and important offices. He was President of the Society of Arts, a Deputy-Lieutenant of Middlesex, and chairman of the Metropolitan Assessment Sessions. By his marriage in 1812 to Sarah Sophia, daughter of Peter Raymond Poland of Winchester Hall, Highgate, he became connected with the family of the distinguished lawyer, Sir Harry Bodkin Poland, whose own professional career has followed so closely that of his uncle. Sir Harry Bodkin Poland succeeded him in his Recordership of Dover and his office at the Central Criminal Court. This family and legal connection alike suggested the dedication of this book to Sir Harry Bodkin Poland. None of those who actually took part in the trial are now living.

WILLIAM NEWLAND WELSBY had been called to the bar in 1826, was made Recorder of Chester in 1841, and eventually became the leader on the North Wales Circuit. When Sir John Jervis, who became Lord Chief Justice of the Common Pleas, was made Attorney-General in 1846, Welsby was appointed by him junior counsel to the Treasury; in other words, junior counsel with the Attorney-General in all his legal duties, thence known in English legal professional slang as the Attorney-General's "devil," a very important and lucrative post, which generally leads to a judgeship. It was probably his experience of criminal law in this office, and his general reputation for knowledge of criminal law, founded on his editing numerous law books as well as on his practice at the bar, that led to his being associated with the Attorney-General at the trial. He had enormous industry, and besides editing a large number of legal books was an editor of one of the most celebrated series of Reports, the seventeen volumes of "Meeson and Welsby," the product of their reports for years in the Court of Exchequer in the earlier part of Welsby's career. He died eight years after the trial, at sixty-one, without having reached the bench, broken down, it was believed, by his excessive labours.

SIR JOHN WALTER HUDDLESTON (Mr. Baron Huddleston). A year after the trial Mr. Huddleston was made a Q.C. From 1865 to 1875 he was Judge-

Advocate of the Fleet. In the latter year he became a judge of the Common Pleas, and was afterwards transferred to the Court of Exchequer; hence the name of Mr. Baron Huddleston, by which in later years he continued to be known, even after the reconstitution of the Courts by the Judicature Acts, when all the judges took the title of Justices of the High Court. Huddleston was a remarkable man. His father was a captain in the merchant service. He was educated at Trinity College, Dublin, but did not take a degree, and he became usher in an English school. He was called by Gray's Inn in 1839, when he was twenty-four years of age, so that he was forty-one at the time of the trial. He was member of Parliament for Canterbury from 1865 to 1868, and for Norwich in 1874 and until he was made a judge. He was a great advocate, but not so great a judge. His reputation increased rather on the social than the legal side. He had married in 1872 Lady Diana De Vere Beauclerk, daughter of the ninth Duke of St. Albans, and he was accounted to be ambitious most of all of social distinction. He was fitted for this, if not by family connections, by his brilliance as a conversationalist, and his gifts as a man of the world and his associations with the theatre and the turf. His accomplishments included an extensive knowledge of French literature and a facility of speaking in French which few Englishmen have. He thus represented gracefully the English bar at the funeral in 1868 of Berryer, the great French advocate, over whose grave he made a speech in French. He died in 1890, aged seventy-five.

SIR WILLIAM SHEE. The leading counsel for Palmer, Mr. Serjeant Shee, was in his fifty-second year; seven years afterwards he was appointed a judge of the Queen's Bench, the first Roman Catholic judge since the Reformation. He was Irish, but educated at a French school in Somers Town, London, subsequently at St. Cuthbert's College, near Durham, where his cousin, afterwards famous as Cardinal Wiseman, was, and then at Edinburgh University. A student of Lincoln's Inn when nineteen, he had become a serjeant at law by 1840, and was one of the leading counsel in London and on the Home Circuit. In 1852 he became member of Parliament for Kilkenny, and represented it for five years. He had been prominent as an advocate for Catholic Emancipation very early in his career, and in Parliament he was a zealous promoter of measures connected with Irish land tenancy, and dealing with the Church endowments, measures precursory of later land legislation and the Disestablishment of the Irish Church. He lost his seat for Kilkenny in 1857, and he never sat in Parliament afterwards. In 1860, three years before he was made a judge, he refused the Chief Justiceship of Madras. Four years after his appointment, in 1868, he died of apoplexy at the age of sixty-three. It is noticeable that though Serjeant Shee had been in most of the great trials he had never defended in a murder trial until he defended Palmer. We have referred to his declaration of belief in Palmer's innocence; and this was not the only point on which his speech was criticised at the time. The leading legal Journal characterised it in terms which will most likely be agreed with by the present-day reader, even more decisively than by the reader of half a century ago, when the taste was more for florid speaking than it is now. "The defence of Mr. Serjeant Shee was clever, ingenious, and eloquent, but wanting in judgment and taste. The peroration was a striking instance of this defect, for the allusion to the family of the prisoner, and to his supposed affection for his wife, grated sorely, and almost ludicrously, on the sense of propriety in the face of the undisguised fact, known to all his audience, that he was accused of murdering his wife, that he slept with his maid servant on the very night she died, and that he had confessed himself guilty of forgery upon his mother. Equally injudicious was the philippic against the insurance offices. In worse taste still was his solemn assertion to the jury that he was convinced by the evidence of the prisoner's innocence."

SIR WILLIAM ROBERT GROVE. Palmer's second counsel, Mr. Grove, Q.C., was in one respect the most distinguished of all the persons who took part in the trial. At the time he had a European reputation, but this was due to his career as a scientific investigator, and not as a lawyer. Without mentioning more, it is sufficient to say that he had published in 1846 the great book, "The Correlation of Physical Forces," which placed him in the front rank of European science. The book was translated into French in the year of the trial. He had been called to the bar in 1835, and was in 1856 forty-five; but he had ill-health, and he turned to science rather than to practice. He was at his call a member of the Royal Institution, and in 1844 he had become its vice-president. By 1853 his health had improved, and he was then a Q.C., having a practice chiefly in patent and scientific cases; but he had also become a leader on his Circuit. It was probably his scientific eminence that led to his brief in the Palmer case. Grove was appointed a judge in 1871, retired in 1887, and died in 1896 at eighty-five. He did not gain any special distinction as a judge nor add to his scientific reputation after he left the bench, though he published several scientific studies.

EDWARD VAUGHAN HYDE KENEALY was the junior counsel for Palmer, and was thirty-seven years old. He was a graduate of Trinity College, Dublin, in 1840, the year of his call to the Irish bar. In 1847 he was called to the English bar by Gray's Inn, and by 1850 he was a Doctor of Laws of Trinity College, Dublin. He had published poems as translations from many Eastern and European languages, and especially in 1850 a poem which has been described as marked by genius, "Goethe, a new Pantomime." Between the year of the trial and 1868 he had risen rapidly, and in the latter year he was made a Queen's Counsel and a Bencher of his Inn. He was the leading counsel for the prosecution in the great Overend and Gurney case of 1869; and in 1873 came the most extraordinary period of his career, when he became chief counsel for the Tichborne claimant. His conduct of that person's defence on the prosecution for perjury, and his editing of the wild paper called *The Englishman*, and his scurrilous attacks on the Chief Justice and others, led to his expulsion from the Circuit, the deprival of his legal distinctions, and finally to his disbarring. He was elected in 1875 as member for Stoke, solely as the champion of the Tichborne claimant. He sat until 1880, but was defeated then at the General Election, and in that year he died. He was an accomplished and successful advocate, and a scholar of unusual learning, but his gifts seemed of that order of genius which is allied to madness. In 1860 he published a translation of a Celtic poem, and in 1864 a volume of "Poems"; in 1878, "Prayers and Meditations," "An Introduction to the Apocalypse," and "Fo, the Third Messenger of God."

JOHN GRAY. Mr. Gray was born at Aberdeen in 1807, and educated at Gordon's Hospital. First a solicitor in London, he was called to the bar in 1838. After attaining the rank of Queen's Counsel in 1863, seven years after the Palmer trial, he was appointed solicitor to the Treasury in 1870. It was while holding this office, in 1873, that he conducted the prosecution of Arthur Orton; so that his career and Dr. Kenealy's touched in two points. He was the author of a number of valuable contemporary legal text books. He died in 1875, owing, it was said, to his labours in preparing and directing the Orton prosecution.

———

Letter from William Palmer to his wife.
(Reproduced from the original in the possession of
Dr. Kurt Loewenfeld, Bramhall, Cheshire.)

Went to London to pay Rent —	7	00	—	—
Ret'd home by Fly from Stafford			
Sat up with Cook all night			

Attending on Cook all day

dined at the Yard —

up with Cook all night

xx+x Cook died at 10 O'Clock this morning

Jere & W'm Saunders dined

Sent Bright a 3 mos Bill

S'. Cecilia

Paid Spilsbury for Hay for W'm Saunders	32	19	9
Paid Spilsbury for my Hay	13	2	6
Paid Busnett for Spirits	13	13	

Cook's friend & Jones came & I dined with them at Masters'

Went to Lichfield for London & return'd home at ½ p 7 —

Mr Stevens came at ½ p 7

Paid Harriman	18	.
— Henry	14	.
— Michael	12	.
— Charles	8	.

At Church Hamilton preached — dined (ho)

- 327 -